BALTIMORE IN THE NATION, 1789–1861

Baltimore in the Nation,

1789–1861

BY GARY LAWSON BROWNE

The University of North Carolina Press

Chapel Hill

© 1980 The University of North Carolina Press

All rights reserved

Manufactured in the United States of America

ISBN 0-8078-1397-4

Library of Congress Catalog Card Number 79-13180

Library of Congress Cataloging in Publication Data

Browne, Gary Lawson, 1939–

Baltimore in the Nation, 1789–1861.

Bibliography: p.

Includes index.

1. Baltimore—Economic conditions.   2. Baltimore—
Social conditions.   3. Baltimore—History.   I. Title.

HC108.B2B76   1980   309.1′752′603   79-13180

ISBN 0-8078-1397-4

For my parents who pointed the way,

Forrest who showed me how,

and Valerie who followed her own

CONTENTS

Preface *xi*

PROLOGUE
The Promise of Baltimore *3*

**Part One
Foundations, 1789–1815**

Introduction to Part One *17*

CHAPTER I
The Business Revolution *19*

CHAPTER II
Emergence of the City *34*

CHAPTER III
Industrialization and the Crisis of War *51*

**Part Two
Transitions, 1815–1843**

Introduction to Part Two *69*

CHAPTER IV
Economic Crisis and New Directions, 1815–1831 *70*

CHAPTER V
Fragmentation of the Old Order *90*

CHAPTER VI
The Commercial Revolution, 1831–1843 *114*

Contents

CHAPTER VII
The Passing of the Old Order *139*

Part Three
The New Order, 1843–1861

Introduction to Part Three *161*

CHAPTER VIII
Industrialization and Triumphant Commercialism *162*

CHAPTER IX
An Industrial Society *177*

CHAPTER X
A Municipal Polity *196*

EPILOGUE
In Retrospect *216*

Notes *239*

Bibliography *295*

Index *339*

MAPS AND TABLES

MAPS

1. Baltimore in 1792 6

2. Baltimore in 1822 *108*

3. Baltimore in 1836 *150*

4. Baltimore in 1853 *188*

TABLES

1. Occupations of Members of the First Branch
of the Baltimore City Council, 1797–1815
44

2. Occupations of Members of the Second Branch
of the Baltimore City Council, 1797–1815
45

3. White Male Occupations in Baltimore,
1799 and 1810
60

4. Yearly Changes of Circulation and Deposits
in Baltimore Banks, 1817–1830 (by percentage)
73

5. Decennial Changes in Household Social Structure, 1790–1830
99

6. Banking in Baltimore, 1829–1841
(except 1831 and 1832)
128

PREFACE

It is curious that professional historians, and especially urban specialists, have neglected Baltimore's development. Not one monograph addresses the history of this Chesapeake city; yet Baltimore played an important and distinctive role in America's past. The city seemingly grew overnight to rival Philadelphia and New York by the 1790s, and Baltimoreans expected to become the commercial center of the New Republic. Even at the time of the Civil War, Baltimore was the third largest American city, a major exporter of wheat and flour, an important supplier of industrial goods to the South, and a leading importer of South American goods. It was also the largest city in the slave South and contained the largest free black population among the cities of that region. Half Northern and half Southern, the city embraced a variety of potential contradictions: commerce, industry, slavery; Germans, Irish, Know-Nothings; African Methodists, Baptists, Roman Catholics; entrepreneurs, privateers, engineers— all contributed to Baltimore's development in intriguing ways.

Not everyone has ignored Baltimore, of course. Local historians such as Francis Beirne, Thomas Griffith, Clayton Colman Hall, George Howard, Hamilton Owens, Thomas Scharf, Annie Sioussat, and Maria Stockett have looked at the city's antebellum experience in a variety of ways. They recorded much information and edited or wrote popular and traditional narratives, and we have learned a great deal from them. But none provides a broad-based, integrated picture of the city's development over time, or one informed by the riches of the social sciences other than history. The few attempts at such an interdisciplinary approach have appeared since World War II and deal merely with one part or another of the city's history.

Having these considerations in mind, I chose to survey the transformation of Baltimore's social economy from the Revolution to the Civil War, paying particular attention to the processes of modernization and industrial revolution. Historians have addressed such themes at the state level in connection with the roles of governments (Peter Coleman, Oscar and Mary Handlin, Louis Hartz, Milton Heath, and James Primm, for example), and Sam Bass Warner, Jr. has touched upon them in his Philadelphia study, but the more pertinent work has been done by anthropologists, economists, geographers, and sociologists. I am thinking here of the work of Calvin Goldscheider, Bert Hoselitz, Jane Jacobs, Wilbert Moore, Allan Pred, Neil Smelser, Wilbur Thompson, and David Ward, in addition to Stephen Thernstrom. Their insights are sprinkled throughout my text and notes.

My purpose in this study is to examine Baltimore's experience from a broader and more integrated perspective of urban economic development than is found in the literature on that subject in general, and on Baltimore in particular. I deliberately focused upon the interaction of economic, political, and social developments from an economic and business point of view, because Baltimore became a modern industrial and business community during this period. Occasionally, this has forced me to explain what happened in Baltimore through references to wider national and even international developments; but I wish no misunderstanding on this point. Though much of what happened in Baltimore also occurred elsewhere in America, Baltimore's experience was not a microcosm of the nation's. Nor did what happened in Baltimore mirror what occurred in other seaports. Moreover, it was never my intention to offer a complete history of the city; consequently, my discussion lacks several features usually found in urban biographies. For example, the reader will find neither an analysis of Baltimore's entire class structure nor an extended discussion of the evolution of political parties. Such deficiencies, together with my approach and interpretations, may provoke rebuttal; if so, I hope that we may all learn something in the process.

Many people have helped me over the course of this project. It began as my doctoral dissertation at Wayne State University where Professors Grady McWhiney, Peter Coleman, Richard Miles, Goldwin Smith, and the late Alfred Kelly provided various forms of encouragement. Grants and fellowships from Wayne, the Lincoln Education Foundation, and the Institute for Humane Studies enabled me to research the topic in widely scattered historical repositories over the years, and particularly at the Maryland Historical Society. At the society, Nancy Boles, P. W. Filby, Mary K. Meyer, and Esther Rich were especially helpful. The revision of the dissertation into this book involved much new work, and I have benefited from the suggestions of several of my colleagues at the University of Maryland, Baltimore County, particularly Joseph L. Arnold, and from the anonymous readers for this press. But I owe most of my professional debt to my mentor, Forrest McDonald. His encouragement, patient reading, suggestions, and dedication to scholarship have served as a model for me to pass on to my students. I am proud and honored that we have become friends. Only one other person played a greater role in the fashioning of this work—Valerie Gerrard Browne, my former wife. Because this book was as much her effort as it was mine, she deserves to share in whatever credit it may bring. Of course, I alone am responsible for the statements that it contains.

Catonsville, Maryland   Gary Lawson Browne
21 September 1979

Baltimore in the Nation,
1789–1861

PROLOGUE
The Promise of Baltimore

The rise of Baltimore from 1750 to 1790 was a spectacular process. From a village of twenty-five houses and two hundred people in 1752, the community grew into the ninth largest town in British North America by 1776 and surged on to become the fourth largest city in the new American nation in 1790. Most American ports were growing during this period, to be sure, but not nearly so rapidly. New England towns grew at the slowest rate: the younger ports of Newburyport, Salem, and Providence roughly doubled in population, but Boston and Newport, the principal older entrepôts, increased very little. To the south and west, the growth rate was much greater, Philadelphia and Norfolk quadrupling and New York and Charleston tripling in population. And yet, in 1790 only Philadelphia, New York, and Boston exceeded Baltimore in population, and ten years later Baltimore would surpass Boston to become the third largest city in the new United States.[1]

The crowds who flowed into Baltimore were mainly of British descent and of nonconforming Protestant faith—that is, they were English, Presbyterians, Baptists, and Methodists. Few were Roman Catholics or non-British except for German Lutherans, who constituted about 6 percent of the city's population in 1790. Most of these immigrants found their way to Baltimore after first landing in Philadelphia, and then following one of the several streams of migration south and west from America's largest city.

Physical location and the economic patterns that it encouraged directed Baltimore's early growth. Situated at the mouth of the Patapsco River on the northwest shore of the Chesapeake Bay, 190 miles or four day's sail from the mouth of the bay, Baltimore enjoyed the best of two geographic worlds. Largely sheltered from the open sea and fed by scores of rivers, the Chesapeake Bay presented Baltimore with a sizeable and varied market in an essentially enclosed area. Across the bay alone, Baltimore commanded a potentially larger trading area than that of any other American seaport. Also, the town reached into the hinterland via the Patapsco and several other rivers that flowed from the north and west into the bay both in and above the community. As people settled the northern and western part of Maryland and south-central Pennsylvania,

Baltimore became the market outlet for their produce and the supplier of their needs.

Though the bay and hinterland trade provided the potential for Baltimore's growth, the community's connection with the West Indies trade actuated its spectacular rise. By the middle of the eighteenth century, European demand had stimulated the plantation and slave-labor system of the islands to specialize in such high-priced and easily marketed crops as sugar, cocoa, tobacco, rice, and coffee; and as a result, the islanders looked elsewhere for supplies of food and other commodities not abundant in the islands. Because the nearest British colonies were those in North America, and eighteenth-century vessels could navigate up and down that coast with ease, the colonies from New York and south came to supply the West Indies with corn, wheat, pork, beef, lumber, and iron and, in turn, to carry away West Indies commodities for sale in Great Britain or in the North American coasting trade. Baltimore's rapid growth resulted from its capitalizing upon this expanding market.[2]

Beginning with the exportation of wheat in the late 1740s, Baltimore's contact with the islands transformed both the village and its relationship with its hinterland. Roads were built into the back country, especially to tap the rich wheat lands of the Monocacy River Valley where Frederick, Maryland, was located; and by the 1770s a network of roads and streams connected Baltimore with most of northern Maryland around the head of the Chesapeake Bay and parts of southern Pennsylvania as well. Meanwhile, a small-scale but burgeoning iron industry developed in the vicinity. And as Baltimore's export economy grew in conjunction with the town's hinterland, more people flocked into both areas.[3]

But there were both physical and social impediments to the continued growth of the community. The physical impediment was that larger ships of the deeper drafts demanded by overseas trade could not be accommodated in Baltimore's basin. The basin was located between two points of land. Fell's Point to the east and Whetstone Point to the south, which jutted out into the bay toward one another, blocked the wind between them and impeded the maneuverability of the larger ships. Moreover, the basin was too shallow for the largest ships, those over three hundred tons. Until technology and steam power solved these problems in the nineteenth century, local merchants were forced to resort to cumbersome techniques. They built wharves out into the basin; larger ships were either anchored out in the bay and loaded and unloaded by smaller craft called lighters, or else they landed at Fell's Point, about a mile east of town and separated from it by Jones's Falls. Thus Baltimore grew as two villages—Fell's Point and the commercial dock area at the head of the basin—until technology forged them into one harbor in the early nineteenth century.

The social impediment was more complex. The early pattern of immigration and economic development set Baltimore and its hinterland off sharply from the older, more established parts of Maryland. Southern Maryland and the Eastern Shore were dominated by a landed gentry, primarily of Anglicans and Roman Catholics, who were part of the Chesapeake society that had developed in the seventeenth and early eighteenth centuries on the basis of tobacco planting and slave labor. The different ethnoreligious composition of Baltimore and northwestern Maryland, together with the emphasis there upon the production of wheat and iron, stimulated the development of a social economy that was strikingly different from that of the tobacco-plantation area. Moreover, Baltimore's rapid rise, coming at a time when the tobacco business was in the doldrums, excited the jealousy of the tobacco planters—and the planters had the political power in the colony. Thus Annapolis, the seat of the colonial, and later the state, legislature, was made the only port of entry in Maryland prior to the American Revolution, and for long afterward the authority of the state was otherwise exerted to restrain the city of Baltimore. Indeed, this antagonism between the city and the state, and the state's ultimate constitutional power over the municipality, would deter Baltimore from developing its full commercial and industrial potential throughout the antebellum period.[4]

For all that, Annapolis simply was not a match for Baltimore, and for several reasons. One was that the West Indies trade in general and the wheat trade in particular were extremely profitable in times of war—and the Atlantic world was at war with scant interruption from 1739 to 1763 and again from 1775 to 1783, and would be yet again from 1792 to 1815. Also, the profitability of tobacco normally declined in wartime and, in the particular context in question, was reduced by an overall decline in prices in years of peace. Many planters in southern Maryland and on the Eastern Shore therefore began shifting away from tobacco into wheat. Moreover, the magnitude of Baltimore's growth in conjunction with these long periods of war created a society inured to abrupt change and transient opportunities. The very dynamics of the institutions, values, and social relationships that Baltimore developed in response to these conditions were geared to dealing with adversity and change. The hostility of Annapolis simply represented one more adversity to the Baltimoreans. And finally, the qualities of Baltimore's growth, its social determinants, responded to developments beyond the control of the rival city; Annapolis could no more exert an effective check upon

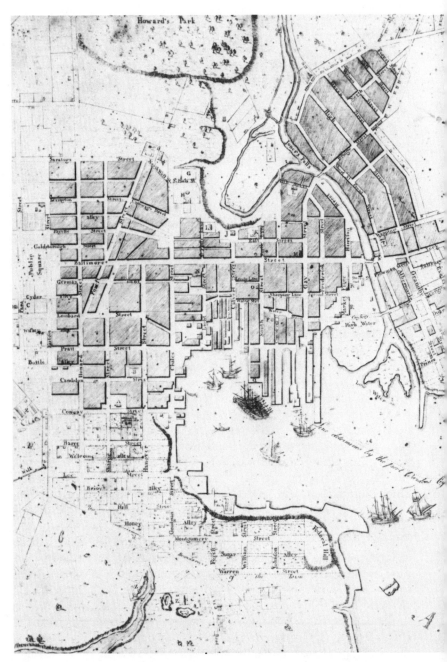

Baltimore in 1792 (courtesy of the Maryland Historical Society)

these responses than it could upon the larger trends and processes. Baltimore grew in spite of Annapolis, and in different directions.[5]

Outwardly, Baltimore society resembled most other and older west European seaports. The village community that matured into Baltimore society was adaptive from the beginning, of course, but new people were assimilated into it through familiar and traditional behavioral patterns. Cultural conservatism, rather than economic opportunity, welded disparate social elements into the social framework common among larger seaports. This framework projected a preindustrial mercantile community that was sedentary, deferential, aristocratic, and with social relationships fixed in a hierarchical order with the merchants at its top. Society was private in the sense that it included only the unspecialized elite. Indeed, many inhabitants of the city lived out their lives virtually without any economic, political, or social status or identity. Moreover, given the mercantile basis of the community, all its members shared a common interest, and thus political differences were based upon division of opinion rather than upon conflicts of interest. Newcomers, especially if they came from other seaports, had little trouble understanding how Baltimore society was constituted and how to find a place in it.[6]

But this social framework was by no means static, for the evolution of its different components through wartime conditions and economic crises were dynamic processes themselves, and distinguished the character of the community from other seaports. The commercial aristocracy, for example, got its start in the late 1750s by capitalizing upon changing needs and opportunities and most especially by operating on their own accounts as buyers and sellers in the grain trade. Gradually accumulating and reinvesting profits, they had by 1790 assumed a service function, acting as commission merchants and factors, and thereby acquired both the wealth and status to join the rural aristocracy on terms of equality. However, because the foundation of their social and economic power was paper money, something still new in the mid-eighteenth century, they were intimately involved in the most important trend of the time: the development of the British money economy. More than any other group in Baltimore, the merchants were affected, first, by the financial fluctuations during the Seven Years' War and, second, by the financial disturbances that accompanied the attempt of the British ministries to reorganize colonial finances following the war. In their responses to these disturbances, the merchants strengthened their position and power within the community and, incidentally, led the community into the American Revolution.[7]

When the European wars for empire started in earnest during the Seven Years' War from 1756 to 1763, Baltimore's merchants found their new

West Indies markets disrupted, prices rising, European goods growing scarcer, and trade becoming highly risky; but they also found unprecedented profits. Conducting trade by customary book credit became of little use, for no one knew whom to trust during the war, and money or an acceptable substitute became of crucial importance. In these circumstances the merchants took advantage of the opportunities the war offered by increasing their trading via bills of exchange—notes issued against future delivery of a commodity to a correspondent merchant in another port. As trade expanded during the wartime boom, the merchants expanded this "money" supply by issuing increasing amounts of bills of exchange, and the bills would circulate as long as traders believed in the solvency of the particular merchants who issued them.

The weakness in this institutionalized system of private paper money became apparent only when the war ended and the mercantile economy contracted. As the flow of trade slowed, the merchants needed more time to ship their goods, collect their profits, and then pay off their accumulated notes—or else to ship goods directly for their redemption. On top of this was added a new British policy, designed to reorganize imperial finances and raise revenues. Although only the Stamp Act and the Townshend Duties directly affected the financial operations of the merchants, the impact of the new British policy was far broader: it politicized the merchants by making them realize that their economic responses, such as nonimportation agreements, were political objections to changes in traditional or constitutional behavioral patterns. In turn, this politicization extended and intensified the merchants' leadership role within Baltimore, for the merchants, being new men themselves, argued for the conservation of Baltimore's way of life as it had been before the new British policy—which is to say, for conservation of the wartime expansion and prosperity of the 1750s.[8]

The economic prosperity brought on by the War for American Independence increased opportunities and thereby added to the complexities of society even more than during the Seven Years' War. Once again higher prices, the scarcity of European goods, and the risks of trade drove profits upward. Moreover, several specific developments operated to Baltimore's advantage during the Revolution. Until 1780 the British appeared in the Chesapeake Bay only intermittently and for short periods, and they did not patrol the West Indies very carefully. Thus, running the blockade was fairly easy for Baltimoreans, and it was natural to carry on their traditional trade there. Then, when the British began to move into the bay in force in the fall of 1780, many Baltimore shippers began operations as quasi-privateers; that is, their ships, carrying letters of marque, were armed and performed as privateers, but they were also merchantmen carrying cargoes as well, chiefly to the West Indies. Seizing opportunities out of adversity, these merchants did not abandon trade for privateering in 1780 and 1781, but added to it the lucrative possibility of capturing prize goods. Baltimore also became a focal point of the French war effort after France entered the war in February of 1778. The town's connections in the West Indies were kept open, its merchants fed the French army and fleet, and Baltimore became the central trading depot in the American war effort by 1779. This new role as a trade depot was the most important development that accounted for the town's prosperity during the war. Agricultural products that had long been marketed through Philadelphia now flowed into Baltimore. Moreover, as Baltimore's market economy grew, government contractors looked to the city to supply the Maryland militia and the Continental army with food, clothing, and military supplies. And even after the British withdrew from Philadelphia to New York in 1778, Baltimore continued to serve as an important seaport supplier of the American effort because of its open connection with the West Indies, where the French fleet was.[9]

These wartime developments revolutionized Baltimore society. The town grew by about two thousand people during the war, an increase of almost one-third in eight years. But where pre-Revolution newcomers were assimilated into the society along traditional mercantile patterns, newcomers during the Revolution were assimilated through the social specialization that resulted from both the altered condition and the new opportunities that were created by the war. For example, two entirely new groups appeared, manufacturers and merchant-millers, who, together with the merchants, signaled the growing sophistication and maturity of Baltimore society.

Though of some immediate social significance, the development of manufacturing had far greater potential implications, for it created a minority interest which was divergent from that of the primary mercantile pursuits. Some of the manufacturing establishments, such as shipyards, tanneries, and flour, saw, and textile mills, were fairly large operations. Others were relatively small shops, consisting of journeymen and apprentices working under master craftsmen, which made linen and woolen goods, paper, and nails. Still others, the even smaller shops of artisans, made boots and shoes, saddlery, pottery, various carpentered products, and a host of other items. No matter their size or whether engaged in handicrafts or the processing of agricultural commodities and livestock, these manufacturers were established as an important alternative way of life to trade in Baltimore by 1783, and they were quite able to articulate the needs of their interest.

The rise of one new form of manufacturing, that of flour milling in and around the town, did have large and immediate social significance. Though Baltimore's special wartime circumstances made the sudden emergence of this industry possible, the roots of its development lay in the disruption of Philadelphia's trade by the British and the fact that several Quaker flour millers fled from Pennsylvania to Baltimore. These refugees were really merchant-millers because they milled flour for the export trade and the war effort rather than for local market consumption. This entailed a large milling establishment, the arrangement of foreign sales, and sometimes owning or chartering ships. In other words, these merchant-millers were men of capital, influence, and business acumen, who were welcome additions to Baltimore both because of the business they brought and because of the expanded opportunities their presence created. They fit easily into Baltimore's commercial aristocracy.[10]

Not all social segments benefited from the opportunities presented by the Revolution, however; in fact, different opportunities operated against certain established social relationships. For example, the excitement, adventure, and potential wealth to be gained by privateering induced many apprentices to run away from their masters; citizens who enlisted in the state militia were substantially exempted from paying their debts; and recruiting officers were allowed to enlist servants and apprentices by paying their masters for their remaining time of service. Such means enabled many males to escape their places, which weakened the guild structure and credit system of the society. Though the individuals undoubtedly thought of their change as opportunistic, such changes in the social aggregate contributed to the increasing complexity of society by breaking down existing social forms while simultaneously strengthening the leadership of the commercial aristocracy.

In several respects and in varying degrees, then, the American Revolution was a catalyst in Baltimore's development. During the Revolution, Baltimore surpassed Annapolis to become the leading port on the Chesapeake Bay, and the pattern of its trade was set for the next two generations: flour, cereals, corn, iron, and lumber were shipped to the West Indies, to Mediterranean Europe, and to the other Atlantic seaports in the new American nation; tobacco was shipped to continental Europe, chiefly France and Holland; and the town became a reexport center on the Chesapeake for European goods. Baltimore also developed a diversified economy during the war as a result of the proliferation of manufacturing, particularly in flour milling and such related activities as the manufacture of wooden staves and barrels and of iron hoops and nails.[11]

Social specialization and a matured society accompanied these economic developments: Baltimore was no longer merely an overgrown village. New social groups representing different interests appeared and supplemented the primary mercantile pursuits of the commerical aristocracy. Though the war promoted a certain amount of social mobility that, together with the new social interests, seemingly tore the fabric of society, the Revolution was such a time of disparate opportunity and fortune building that a cluster of families emerged at the end of the war as the unchallenged leaders of Baltimore's aristocracy. This mixture of merchants and the landed gentry would dominate the community for the following two generations. The new flour millers were the Ellicotts, Hollingsworths, and Tysons; the landed gentry were the Carrolls, Dorseys, Howards, Keys, Lloyds, Ridgelys, and Tilghmans; and the merchants included the Buchanans, Calhouns, Cursons, Gilmors, Hoffmans, McHenrys, Pattersons, Pringles, Smiths, Spears, Steretts, Stewarts, Taylors, and Wilsons.

Baltimore thus looked forward to a promising future when the British recognized the nation's independence in 1783. Though no longer serving as a central trade depot after the liberation of Philadelphia and the restoration of that city's trade, Baltimore maintained its trade patterns with the West Indies as well as with the newly opened French markets. The stream of people into Baltimore, though large during the Revolution, was even greater afterward, from 1783 to 1790, when the population increased over 68 percent. But an old problem reappeared to mar the prosperity and the hopes of the Baltimoreans: a postwar adjustment of the paper money that had been issued during the war. Peacetime brought a large-scale contraction, during which the merchants suffered a temporary money squeeze while they redeemed their outstanding bills of exchange, just as they had done following the Seven Years' War. They might have weathered this period, and indeed their trade was thriving, but for the stupidity of the Maryland legislature in its winter session of 1784–85. For inexplicable reasons, the legislature passed at that time a law calling for the redemption of all the state's outstanding paper currency within five years and making the annual interest on that currency payable only in specie. As a result, Baltimoreans of most classes suffered a severe money crisis because, as paper money disappeared from circulation, there was simply not enough specie to serve as an adequate monetary vehicle. Interest rates soared for a time to 25 and 30 percent, and prices and real estate values plummeted.[12]

In this context, a soft-money political faction came temporarily to dominate Baltimore politics and almost to gain political control of the state. The faction was headed by the brilliant Annapolis lawyer-merchant Samuel Chase, in alliance with the political "boss" of Baltimore County, Charles Ridgely, and his connections in Baltimore town, John Dorsey and the Sterett brothers, John, Joseph, and Samuel. Together, they gained control of the lower branch of the state legislature, the House of Delegates; but their soft-money plans were thwarted by the archconservative, planter-dominated state Senate. Moreover, any likelihood that Baltimore would continue to be a power base for the Chase faction was destroyed when Chase opted to oppose the new United States Constitution of 1787.[13]

The Constitution promised the establishment of a new order that Baltimoreans found irresistible. Its dynamic leaders, aggressive men in a new society, looked forward to breaking the fetters of localism and particularism in trade and to overcoming the political weakness of their town in Maryland as well as in relation to the other large American cities. Their viewpoint is readily understood. Here was their community, already grown to be the fourth largest urban area in America and still rapidly expanding, and yet the town was unincorporated and enjoyed virtually no degree of municipal autonomy. To Baltimore's leadership, the new constitutional order, vesting a national Congress with power over state commercial procedures, seemed to offer fulfillment of the promise of the Revolution by spurring Baltimore's already rapid growth. Perhaps it might even enable Baltimore to gain political power consistent with its economic and social power.

On that note of promise, our story begins.

PART ONE

Foundations, 1789–1815

Introduction to Part One

The formal characteristics of Baltimore society first appeared in the period between the organization of the new federal government under the Constitution and the War of 1812. They marked the maturation of the community's growth in the sense that social and economic processes were formalized and institutionalized. In addition, Baltimore acquired the legal status of a city, a new group of men gained control of the municipal administration and used it for their own purposes, and a new technology was adapted to various processing, production, and transportation methods. Though such changes were responses to Baltimore's particular circumstances at the time, nevertheless they constituted the foundations for the society's later development.

The importance of these changes lay in their defining the nature of Baltimore society. Indeed, because these were economic, political, and social processes that established the forms and norms of human behavior, they could be said, in the language of structural anthropology, to have established the structure of society. A business revolution, for example, established techniques for a variety of public activities, not merely those of business enterprise; the emergence of the city established a political style and created a political economy whose function was more to regulate the marketplace than to provide social services; and a new technology, socialized by wartime necessity, changed the market orientation of producers and merchants as well as their methods of production.

Such developments produced problems, both immediate and long term. In the short run, the very act of defining the society reduced its flexibility. Institutionalizing procedures and vesting them with legal powers cast all activities, particularly those of business, into molds that required individual conformity to the new institutional standards. Moreover, structuring activities to meet conditions of prosperity could be socially disastrous when conditions changed. For example, a panic and financial breakdown in 1798–99, the first of a series of such panics in Baltimore's history, grew out of the financial structure that had been created to aid Baltimore's merchants in the international markets. Yet institutionalists saw neither this nor subsequent panics from that perspective; instead, they elaborated a theory which, given time and experience, would itself become formalized in the theory of business cycles. And this self-rationalization also became an inherent part of the new social structure.

The long-term problem relates to the fact that these developments were products of a particular historical milieu. They expressed the assumptions and values of those opportunists and optimists living in the most rapidly growing urban area in late eighteenth-century America, and they were responses to the conditions peculiar to Baltimore in that age. And yet, these culture-bound creations of time and place would continue to shape Baltimore's development long after the conditions and men that had created them were gone. What their historical origins illustrate is their original purpose and how they functioned in a particular setting. That is the subject of Part One of this book. Later, in Parts Two and Three, we shall consider what happened to this social structure under the impact of new circumstances and different people.

CHAPTER I

The Business Revolution

In the two decades following the ratification of the Constitution, Baltimore experienced an invisible revolution, a business revolution that institutionalized and depersonalized its previously flexible and intensely personal eighteenth-century society. So profound were the changes that Baltimore would never again be the same, and yet so subtle were they that Baltimoreans not only failed to perceive how they had happened but failed until long afterward to realize that they had happened at all.

The business revolution created new social instrumentalities which maximized the economic opportunities that arose from independence, population growth, and the awesome commercial expansion attending the wars of the French Revolution. Given what Baltimore had already become when those wars began, the community was impelled to seek to profit from them. In many ways it was admirably equipped to do so, but new opportunities arose faster than Baltimoreans could take advantage of them within the framework of their existing institutions, and so they created new ones. These new institutions, in turn, took on a life of their own. They became a vital part of the social order and increasingly defined Baltimoreans' relationship to their social and economic environment.

Most Baltimoreans were not conscious of the social implications of what was happening. The changes were adopted largely as ad hoc solutions to certain immediate problems that confronted the society, and it was difficult to imagine them as anything other than temporary conveniences. One of the components of the business revolution, for example, was group or associational activities, which were intended, and for a considerable time actually functioned, as mere supplements and complements to individual activities, not as replacements of them. Another reason contemporaries were unaware of what was happening was that the techniques of the business revolution were, or rather seemed to be, basically conservative. The new institutions, being operated at first by men steeped in the eighteenth-century social values of a personal and private society, were inevitably run in accordance with those values. For that reason, and also because both pursued private profit in conjunction with the public good, associational activities did not seem much different from individual activities. Finally, the business revolution was invisible to contemporaries because it conformed to cultural mores, did not sharply break with the past, and contributed to the very expansion and economic growth that conditioned its appearance.

The Business Revolution

There were two components of the business revolution. One, as indicated, was the replacement of individual activities that were formalized or institutionalized. The replacement was not an event or conscious decision but a gradual and cumulative process. Nevertheless, in the long run the business revolution superimposed associational activities upon the individual basis of Baltimore's eighteenth-century social economy and thereby provided new social forms which necessitated a transition to an impersonal kind of society. Had the instigators of the movement foreseen the consequences they doubtless would never have had any part of it. In joining together for particular group ventures they could scarcely have known that they were altering the web of relationships among individuals and their community; but the result was that such group activities would increasingly come to play greater roles in Baltimore than individual activities. The process was even more insidious, because as these group activities gained greater social prominence, they also became more necessary and valuable to Baltimoreans. In due course, they became normative.[1]

Such activities began in the form of joint-stock companies, used for private entrepreneurial purposes as well as to provide public services for the municipality. Other informal group activities, such as libraries, trading companies, and craft and ethnic societies, also functioned for both private and public purposes. But whether institutionalized or continuing to depend upon volunteer help, these group activities operated against the more intensely individual aspects of eighteenth-century Baltimore society economically, politically, and socially. For example, between 1787 and 1815, ten insurance companies (five of them for marine risks), seven turnpike road companies, two bridge companies, and a water company were created to provide various services in the city. In addition, three manufacturing companies were created. Only one company, a fire insurance company chartered in 1787, had existed in Baltimore before 1790, but the rapid adoption of formalized associational activity after 1790 suggests how readily this new form met the circumstances of Baltimore's growth. Or, to view this from a slightly different perspective, the new group activities reflected specialization and diversification that resulted from the expansion of Baltimore's economy during the 1790s and early 1800s.[2]

The second component of the business revolution, the monetization of credit, was probably even more important than the first. Beginning in the seventeenth century and continuing through the eighteenth, monetizing credit had gradually created a money system based upon anticipated wealth rather than on wealth itself. Two general trends resulted. On one hand, social relationships were altered profoundly but subtly as the subjectivity of the debtor's personality supplanted the objectivity of actual wealth. Gradually, the granting of credit was ritualized as both creditors and potential debtors depended increasingly upon a set of rules: the potential debtor must be honest, industrious, and thrifty, and lead a moral life in general. On the other hand, monetizing credit necessitated certain changes in the relationship of men to one another. Relationships became more formal and legal as they were filtered through the new ritual of credit. Together with associational activities, this monetization of credit provided the social forms necessary to the later industrial revolution.[3]

Indeed, the financial revolution of the 1790s and early 1800s was crucial to both the business and the industrial revolutions. To say that the business and industrial revolutions were functions of capital, a common observation among economic historians, is misleading in regard to Baltimore's experience. In comparison with Boston, New York, or Philadelphia, commercial profits in the form of specie, and therefore capital, had always been smaller in Baltimore than in these other towns. Capital in the form of specie was simply a state of wealth having the highest degree of liquidity. Being the newest of these seaports, Baltimore had neither the time to accumulate such wealth nor the volume of trade to do so immediately. What Baltimore or any other rapidly expanding social economy in the late eighteenth century needed was immediate capital; and since capital accumulation was impractical, Baltimoreans had to use another kind of capital—the promise of wealth or capital as monetized debt.[4]

Capital as monetized debt fit Baltimore's expanding and prosperous social economy so well that the city's mercantile leadership quickly institutionalized monetized debt in the form of banking capital to enable it to circulate throughout the community. A financial revolution thus appeared in Baltimore during the 1790s in the form of paper money premised upon the expectation of future wealth. This type of money further stimulated Baltimore's trade, facilitated the expansion of its social economy, and gave people the means to participate in the new form of associational activities. An even more important impact of this new money system was that it became the arbiter of social differences. That is, this new system was incorporated into the community's eighteenth-century elitist social order, which it perpetuated because only the aristocracy had credit or wealth in the first place; but the money system gradually undermined this social order by changing the nature of Baltimore's elite from a cultural to a monetary basis. Such a change was inevitable precisely because money was the vehicle of expansion and prosperity and served as the means that made the new institutional activities possible.

Before the appearance of the first bank in Baltimore in 1790, monetized credit was circulated in two forms of "mercantile credit." The most risky form was the promissory notes of merchants. These were usually simple, unsecured notes given by one merchant to another from whom goods were purchased. The other form of monetized credit was the bill of exchange. This form was less risky and more widely circulated than the promissory notes, because it was based upon the exchange of goods. A Baltimore merchant who exported goods to a merchant in another seaport, for example, might draw up a bill of exchange for an amount of money that was less than the value of the exported goods. This bill was a demand upon the merchant to whom the goods were consigned, instructing him to pay over the face amount of the bill to a designated third party either on sight, when the merchant who had received the goods also received the bill, or so many days after he received the bill. Unless the Baltimore merchant who originally drew up the bill and exported the goods needed the money in the seaport where he sent the goods—to pay his own debts or to purchase goods—he would sell this bill to another merchant in Baltimore who did need money in the other seaport. These bills of exchange thus operated as checks drawn upon merchants' accounts with merchants in other seaports. They circulated as money in Baltimore because they were transferable from the original maker of the bill, and they filled a definite need in an expanding export economy such as Baltimore's. In both forms of monetized credit, the promissory note and the bill of exchange, "mercantile credit" was an individual and highly personalized form of credit that was limited to men who were known to the mercantile community.[5]

Banks in eighteenth-century Baltimore grew out of the mercantile idea of monetized credit by using evidences of debt as money; and these banks combined the two notions of money as wealth and money as anticipated wealth. Banks were innovations because they extrapolated the idea of mercantile credit from the individual to the group and introduced certain modifications in the credit system that allowed for its expansion. Banks were associations of people who now performed an activity as a group that individuals alone previously had done; and this group activity made the relationship between creditor and debtor less personal. Also, banks satisfied the conditions created by Baltimore's expanding social economy in a peculiar way. A bank was a reification of an activity; and though it was artificial in the eighteenth century, it was a legal fiction, for this artificial reality was empowered by the Maryland legislature to function in a certain way and for a certain social purpose.[6]

But, whereas these two forms of monetized credit were generated by the Baltimoreans themselves, the town's merchants also enjoyed access to, and were perhaps more dependent upon, outside, and especially European, sources of mercantile credit. These sources were filtered into Baltimore through the wealthiest, most extensive, and best-known merchants of the community, who also acted as agents for European merchant bankers. The most important agencies during the 1790s were Robert Gilmor and Adrian Valck for Wilhelm and Jan Willinks of Amsterdam; and Robert and John Oliver for Baring Brothers and John Kirwan and Sons of London, and for Hope and Company of Amsterdam. These agents asked other merchants to consign their goods to these foreign bankers or to their mercantile agencies in foreign ports. Custom did not allow the agents a commission from the bankers for such services, but what they received was far more valuable both for themselves and for the community of Baltimore. First, their own accounts were handled more attentively by the European bankers and advice was given them for more profitable employments of money. This opened a larger world of financial capitalism to Baltimore's first rank of merchants and cemented their leadership in the community. Second, the agents received commissions from the other services involved in moving the shipments. Third, the agents also received commissions and interest from handling the bills of exchange passing between the Baltimore shipping merchant and the foreign banker. Fourth, the agents received interest on credits advanced to the shipping merchants, which credits sometimes amounted to the usual two-thirds amount of goods consigned overseas. Fifth, the agents themselves became known in Europe as the banker's trusted agents in Baltimore; and this frequently led them to act as investment bankers for Europeans who wished to invest capital in America, where interest rates were higher than in Europe. Sixth, as the duties of banker and commission trader gradually became more important to the agent than trading goods on his own account, he himself found it easier and more familiar to loan money to Baltimore merchants. Of course, these activities enhanced the position of the Baltimore agent; but in larger perspective, the primary importance of the agents' activities in the mercantile credit structure was to enlarge Baltimore's world through credit, capital, and ideas.[7]

Although this general mercantile credit structure played a primary and antecedent role to banks in financing Baltimore's economy, it was merely one limited means of financing trade. Many people needed credit who had no contact with foreign merchant bankers, or even with Gilmor, Valck, or the Olivers. The majority of these people were traders in a smaller way who simply wished short-term loans, while others wished credit for long-term activities, such as purchasing real estate, building houses, and engaging in manufacturing. During the 1780s, several Baltimoreans had thought that a bank, modeled after the Bank of North America in Philadelphia, would answer these social needs; but the scarcity of cash apparently prevented such a bank from being capitalized until 1790, when the Bank of Maryland was chartered by the state legislature with a capital of $300,000.

The Bank of Maryland began its operations in 1791 with sixty-nine stockholders, all of whom were members of Baltimore's mercantile elite or landed gentry and eighteen of whom were in the names of business partnerships. Thus, a group of prominent merchants in Baltimore pooled their capital, obtained a charter from the state of Maryland, gained additional capital by selling subscriptions for shares of stock in the bank, and then sat as directors of the bank. This bank went on to monetize credit in the sense that it made loans of credit in the form of bank notes or paper money. The usual form of such loans was called a discount: the amount of bank credit in the bank's notes after the interest had been deducted from the loan in advance. The amount and kind of collateral security required by the bank depended upon the standing of the debtor in the community. In most cases he gave none; in others he gave an endorser.[8]

The introduction of banking in Baltimore was subsequently quite successful, because monetized credit answered the needs of this capital-poor but rapidly growing community. Four banks were opened in Baltimore from 1790 through 1807; and though they were capitalized at a total of $5,500,000, only 74 percent, or $5,066,725, of the capital was actually paid in. In fact, the Bank of Maryland, the very first bank, was the only one to have its capital completely paid in. Apparently the other three banks were able to operate just as well even without having their authorized capital paid in—further illustrating how credit filled the needs of Baltimoreans.

But the economic success of this financial revolution bred social conflict between two groups of people. One group was composed of people who desired long-term, usually nonbusiness loans that were called "accommodations," but who could not receive them because banking practices extended from the mercantile credit structure whereby loans were on a short-term, temporary basis. This group was not especially power-ful, for Baltimore was such a new and rapidly expanding town that the demand for credit came overwhelmingly from the mercantile groups in the community. The other group that opposed the practices of these early banks was much more powerful and, in the long run, much more suc-cessful, because they came from within the trading community. Com-posed of merchants who wanted to expand bank credit facilities even fur-ther, this group couched its demands in the form of objections to the monopolization of mercantile bank credit by a few men. In reality their position was justified. By the late 1790s and early 1800s, two things about Baltimore's banks had become clear. First, the directors themselves were absorbing much of the discounts of the banks, not as short-term, mercantile loans, but as long-term, "accommodation" loans. Second, the banks began to reflect the occupational specialization of their directors. In short, Baltimore's banking credit structure was becoming as much dominated by a few men as was Baltimore's access to foreign mercan-tile credit.[9]

The crucial fact about this conflict was that it affirmed the desirability of banking and thereby paved the way for the success of the financial revolution. The antibank people proposed to reform the banking system, not to abolish it; indeed, they were the real carriers of the financial revolution because they wanted more, not less, bank credit. They wished to extend its social benefits, to break through the elitist domination of bank credit, and to make money too. The conflict thus affirmed the prac-tical value of bank credit to the community at large.

Patterns of Trade

Although the new money system and institutional activities were founda-tions for a later industrial revolution, it was the expansion of Baltimore's social economy that made the business revolution itself both necessary and possible in the first place. Generally speaking, Baltimore's rapid growth before and during the Revolutionary War continued during the 1780s, accelerated during the 1790s, and decelerated during the early 1800s. The city's maritime economy reflected this pattern. From 1783 through 1793, Baltimore's export trade followed essentially three pat-terns: Maryland tobacco was shipped to France, Holland, and certain Hanseatic towns; foodstuffs, lumber, and naval supplies went to the Danish, Dutch, French, Spanish, and Swedish West Indies; and food-stuffs went to Mediterranean Europe. But between 1793 and 1812, the British, then the French, and then the British again captured Baltimore ships, cargoes, and men. Throughout this period, however, Baltimore's conflict with the British was more serious than with the French. Essentially, two reasons accounted for this. One was Britain's domination of the Atlantic sea lanes, especially after the British defeated the French navy in 1798 and again in 1805; and the other was the peculiar trade pattern in which Baltimore had been involved since 1778, wherein trade with the French and Spanish West Indies was pivotal. The British were unwilling to allow the Baltimoreans to continue shipping between the French and Spanish West Indies and France and Spain except upon British terms. Those Baltimore merchants who wished to avoid war and yet engage in the highly profitable wartime trade accepted the British terms that were laid down in Jay's Treaty in 1795; and those merchants who were willing to risk war for any of a number of reasons roundly condemned Jay's Treaty.[10]

Although Jay's Treaty provided a framework for Anglo-American trade relations from 1795 to 1805, it solved few of the Baltimoreans' problems and, in fact, created others. For example, the treaty did not prevent British ships from seizing Baltimore ships on the high seas; and these seizures continued, albeit sporadically, until 1815. The terms of the treaty that opened the British West Indies trade to American vessels of seventy tons or less operated more in favor of British than Baltimore shippers during the periods of peace. Similarly, the provision placing British trade with the United States on a most-favored-nation basis operated in favor of British shippers. The same was true of the British admission of Baltimore ships into the British East Indies on a nondiscriminatory basis: Baltimoreans prospered whenever the war was going on, but during the intervals of peace British shippers returned to the trade and monopolized it. Baltimore shippers thus prospered in the trade between British ports only during wartime when British courts allowed them to carry goods between an enemy port and a neutral one.

Despite the continuing seizure of Baltimore ships by the British, who were looking for deserters from the British navy as well as for contraband goods, France was convinced that the Baltimoreans were pawns of the British, and responded accordingly. To the French, the Baltimoreans were entirely too willing to forsake the Franco-American Alliance of 1778 in favor of economic consideration from Great Britain. Moreover, the French were at war with Great Britain and expected their American allies to aid them instead of claiming neutrality. Consequently, French ships devoured Baltimore shipping on the high seas as voraciously as the British did until the Treaty of Morfontaine in September of 1800 replaced the Franco-American Alliance.[11]

Both because and in spite of the British and French captures, neutral trade was far too lucrative for Baltimore shippers to abandon it. In the normal course of events, Maryland produce was exported to both Europe and the West Indies. In the West Indies it was exchanged for coffee, sugars, and other island products, which were returned to Baltimore if they were from the French and Spanish colonies; if they were from the Danish, Dutch, or Swedish islands they were usually carried directly to Europe. If it went to Baltimore, this West Indies produce was subsequently reexported to Europe along with Maryland produce. Until the Chesapeake and Leopard Affair in 1807, Baltimore's prosperity in this reexport trade varied with the vicissitudes of the European wars.[12]

For America in general, the reexport trade was most prosperous for the seaports and the shipping interests. But this prosperity was not uniform because America's shipping interests were as diverse as the number of seaports in the United States; and this diversity, in turn, depended upon the individual characteristics of each seaport. A port's patterns of trade, its distance from Europe and the West Indies, the products of its hinterland, the adequacy of its harbor facilities and capital, and its local political support all conditioned its growth relative to other American seaports between 1793 and 1807. Moreover, such considerations also conditioned the response of each seaport to the political decisions of the new national government.

From the viewpoint of successive administrations of America's new national government during these years, American neutrality remained a question of nationality. The differences between Federalists and Republicans were mainly differences in policy that were altered by changing international circumstances. The Federalists' settlement with the British in 1795, for example, lasted until 1805, when British policies toward American neutrality changed.

The wars of the French Revolution were particularly prosperous for Baltimore, because they created vastly expanded opportunities for profit from previously existing patterns of trade between Europe, and European colonial possessions in the West Indies, and the North American continent—a trade pattern that had served as the basis of Baltimore's rise since the 1740s. Benefiting from their geographical accessibility to carry American foodstuffs to the West Indies and West Indies products to the nations at war, America in general and Baltimore in particular found an identity of interests in this wartime trade. But apart from geography, Baltimoreans had been trading with the West Indies for two generations and had developed a particular sailing craft for that trade. The trade was carried in schooner-rigged vessels that were modified over time along the lines of what was called the Virginia Pilot Boat, built low in the water with a very sheer rake. Although these relatively small vessels carried sizable cargoes, they were the fastest-sailing vessels afloat and were the forerunners of the later clipper ships, which were often simply enlargements. Thus geographic position, sailing technology, and long-established mercantile connections served as the bases for Baltimore's prosperous development vis-à-vis the West Indies trade with Europe.[13]

After the outbreak of the wars in 1793 and President Washington's proclamation of American neutrality in April, Baltimore merchants were confronted by frequent captures of their ships by both the British and the French. "*John Bull* has been as troublesome to our Commerce as *French fraternity*," lamented the Quaker merchant-millers Samuel and Thomas Hollingsworth in 1799; "one party Captures & the other recaptures, and thus the Spoils of American enterprise & industry are Divided amongst the villains of Europe." But such captures scarcely deterred Baltimore's merchants from the trade. The value of exports from the city increased from $1,782,861 in 1792 to $2,092,660 in 1793, to $3,456,421 in 1794, and to $4,421,924 in 1795. By the end of the decade, the annual value of Baltimore's exports had risen above $10 million—half of what the entire country's had been in 1790. The profits generated by trade on such a scale were worth all the risks it entailed.[14]

Usually, fast-sailing schooners and brigs made the West Indies leg of Baltimore's double-V trade with Europe (it was mainly not a triangular but a V-shaped trade, at one angle to the West Indies and back, at another to Europe and back). They carried six hundred or seven hundred barrels of flour or sixty or seventy hogsheads of tobacco to the islands, where these goods were exchanged for cotton, coffee, cocoa, sugars, rice, and indigo, which were returned to Baltimore. Freight rates were usually three or four dollars per barrel, or about thirty dollars per hogshead. But prices of everything, from the commodities carried to seamen's wages and freight rates, varied with market and war conditions; consequently, profits varied enormously. Once they were in Baltimore, the West Indies goods were usually transferred from small, fast-sailing vessels to larger and slower craft—brigs and ships usually over two hundred tons—for the trip to Europe.[15]

With respect to the European leg of Baltimore's double-V trade, however, Maryland no longer furnished any commodities (save occasional grain and flour shipments) for the English markets. After 1793, Baltimore was no longer a regular market for Virginia and Maryland tobacco, which had been the mainstay of the Chesapeake Bay trade to England for the previous 150 years. Tobacco's declining value in English markets, culminating in the general collapse of the English commodity market in 1797, coupled with the simultaneously increasing demand for flour created by the wars, stimulated a transition from tobacco to wheat production in the area around Baltimore and especially on the Eastern Shore in 1798–99. By 1803 or 1804 the state warehousing system of tobacco inspections had become so unprofitable that it was abandoned to private individuals who were allowed to perpetuate the system at their option, provided they conformed to the state inspection laws.[16]

Thus Baltimore's connection with the European leg of the trade pattern was unlike that of most other American seaports: Baltimoreans did not usually trade with England. The few direct shipments to England were made by Baltimore merchants who consigned the goods to their connections there either for particular reasons or simply to make up a freight for ships already bound for England. In either case, Baltimore withdrew from the English trade during the 1790s and increased its connections with the more lucrative West Indies and continental European trade pattern—a shift that would have disastrous results after 1815, when industrialization made such English connections crucial to the growth of American seaports.

Institutional Responses

Though the business revolution enabled Baltimoreans to exploit the great opportunities of the 1790s and early 1800s, it also made society less flexible in responding to change. Institutionalizing activities and monetizing credit circumscribed individual and social behavior by establishing new norms and conditions. The process locked Baltimoreans into particular and exclusive forms of behavior, and taught them a pattern of responding to opportunities that would govern their behavior in the future. Even more importantly, the business revolution created institutions that were geared for prosperous conditions and were themselves opportunities. Consequently, they took on a greater importance than that of the individuals who organized and participated in them, and preservation of them became more important than the preservation of individuals when prosperity turned into adversity. What happened in the panic of 1798–99, the first of many financial panics in Baltimore's subsequent history, is a case in point.

Baltimore's war-based commercial boom was sharply and severely, though temporarily, interrupted in 1798. The causes of the recession were many and varied and the recession affected American ports differently according to their different trade patterns. Baltimore's specific problems unfolded as follows. Holland, Germany, and France were the principal markets for Maryland tobacco, and the first two for West Indies produce reexported from Baltimore. Spain, Portugal, and the West

Indies continued to be the more important markets for Baltimore flour. Because of Baltimore's close affiliation with merchants in Bremen, Hamburg, and Holland, the city suffered more than any other American seaport from a depression that hit those European markets in 1798–99. Indeed, this depression was far more detrimental to Baltimore's export trade than was the undeclared naval war with France from 1798 to 1800.[17]

The general West European depression began in the English markets in 1797 when, in the wake of the mutinies at Spitshead and the Noire, commodity prices sharply declined, many English merchants failed, and the Bank of England suspended specie payments. The depression then spread to Bremen, Hamburg, and the Dutch ports, whose merchants used English merchant bankers to finance their trade in American and West Indies produce. Merchants in these continental ports began failing in 1798 because their English credits were restricted and prices of American and West Indies produce had sharply declined in their own markets. Consequently, they could not pay the bills of exchange that had been drawn on them in America for produce shipped to them. These bills were therefore protested for nonpayment in the continental ports and then returned to the American merchants who drew them.

Many of these protested bills originated in Baltimore. Like all American merchants, those in Baltimore paid cash for their produce but sold their imported goods on time. When shipping to Europe, they customarily sent American and West Indies produce to the foreign market on an advance of two-thirds of its value. The consignee remitted the advance when the produce arrived in his port. If, however, the Baltimore merchant preferred a letter of credit (to the amount of two-thirds advance), he would forward the invoice, bill of lading, and evidence of insurance to a merchant banker, usually in London or Amsterdam, instead of sending the documents along with the produce to the consignee. This alternative gave the American merchant funds in Europe for whatever purpose he wished.[18]

But the depression in the continental ports in 1798 prevented the European buyers from accepting (that is, paying) these bills when they fell due. By the fall of 1799, so many of these unpaid bills were returned to Baltimore's merchants that the collections of several of them did not cover their own payments, and many prominent mercantile houses failed during December of 1799 and January of 1800. The worst of these failures was over by March 1800, but the effects of the panic lingered on in Baltimore because of a temporary peace between France and Great Britain. Only when war was renewed in 1803 was there sufficient stimulus to revive Baltimore's trade at the levels of 1793–98.[19]

The depression of 1798–1803 was the first financial panic to be experienced within the framework of the business revolution, and the repercussions were considerable. It quickly became manifest that the interests of Baltimore's elite "society," or at least the portion of it involved in banking, were not at all identical with the interests of the community as a whole. The directors of the two city banks, acting in accordance with the banks' needs, contracted their credit facilities at the very time when the community needed credit most; then it was revealed that the directors had benefited more than the public by using the bank's credit as their own. But instead of reacting against banking, the mercantile community gradually became convinced that three banks (the two local institutions and the local branch of the Bank of the United States) were simply not sufficient for the needs of the community in such a crisis. This new awareness resulted largely from actions by the branch of the Bank of the United States, which did more to restore faith in bank credit than the contractions of the Bank of Maryland and the Bank of Baltimore did to injure it. In January 1800, at the time of the worst failures in Baltimore, President Archibald Campbell of the Baltimore branch of the Bank of the United States brought together the banks, the insurance companies, and the individuals who were not affected by the failure to form an "Association of Relief." Under the direction of a board of managers, this association lent sixty-day notes (renewable at the option of the debtors) against collateral in the form of produce and stocks that were deposited by the associations' members. To facilitate this operation the Baltimore branch of the Bank of the United States agreed to discount an additional twenty-five thousand dollars per week over and above its normal loans. President Campbell also prevailed upon the Bank of Baltimore to discount twenty-five thousand dollars weekly and upon the Bank of Maryland to discount fifteen thousand dollars. These actions demonstrated to Baltimoreans that bank credit, in the form of public institutions, had more social possibilities than did private mercantile credit.[20]

The community's response was to create two additional banks between 1804 and 1807; and, though the motivations behind them were various, all were premised upon the assumption that bank credit was a positive social good. The Union Bank of Maryland, like the Merchants' Bank of New York, the Philadelphia Bank, and the Potomac Bank of Virginia, was a Republican-party creation in 1804. The purpose of the Union Bank was to compete with, if not outrival, the Federalist-dominated Bank of Baltimore, whose directors, it was alleged, acted as if the bank's capital was their own. The Republicans were so eager to prove the superior social value of their bank that they put it into operation before it was chartered by the state; and by the time it was given legal status, the bank held as its paid-in capital many notes from banks in Baltimore and the District of Columbia. Apart from politics, however, the Republican bank introduced an important change in banking that filled a social demand: the Union Bank held large amounts of long-term accommodation paper, which the other banks had shunned in favor of short-term business paper.[21]

To summarize, the appearance of banking in Baltimore answered the needs of the community for a medium of exchange in the form of paper money, and it stimulated the expansion of the social economy by increasing the amount of credit available. But it also institutionalized the availability of credit. Banks were not merchants. They were legal creations, fictious devices that specialized in one mercantile activity, the extension of credit, to the exclusion of all other activities; and so they promoted specialization in Baltimore's social economy. Furthermore, these banks depersonalized credit in a way that credit from a merchant did not. Bank notes loosened the relationship between debtor and creditor by giving the debtor more freedom and thus making this relationship more public, less personal and private; and as the relationship became more public, what had been customary, individual, and private would have to be standardized and given the force of law.

In the final analysis, then, the business revolution was historically necessary, because it solved the problems Baltimore faced in a particular historical context and proved socially cohesive into the bargain. For example, the rapid growth of Baltimore's population diversified and specialized the social economy, and associational activities helped to mitigate potentially divisive effects by identifying and coordinating the activities of several people into one activity. Joint-stock companies brought together people with widely diverse backgrounds, linking them in a common interest. Perhaps most importantly, they did so in ways that were advantageous for all concerned—by minimizing risks in relation to potential profits, providing monetary profit for the individuals concerned, and offering social profit for the community as a whole. Finally, by minimizing the individual's capital investment, such group activities broadened individual participation in them and in the community they served, thus contributing to the democratization of eighteenth-century Baltimore society.

For similar reasons, the business revolution was a necessary first stage of the industrial revolution, the broader social revolution that was to come. In a formal sense, the old elitist society continued to prevail, but many new men entered into it, both newcomers to Baltimore and locals who were rising through the social and economic ranks. For others potentially like them, and for the community at large, which had never experienced such group institutions before, it was necessary to make information about associational activities public knowledge. Where an individual entrepreneur would never publicize his mode of operations, the charters of these new group institutions were published in the newspapers. Such procedures democratized society and stamped the business revolution as a process of standardization and uniformity. This was how the business revolution prepared Baltimore's eighteenth-century society for industrial revolution.

CHAPTER II

Emergence of the City

The emergence of the city as a corporate being occurred simultaneously with and partly in consequence of the business revolution. Commercial prosperity, an expanding population, and social and economic diversification necessitated political adjustments, and especially some change in Baltimore's legal or constitutional status. The turning point came in 1796, when Baltimore was incorporated as a city by the state legislature and given certain home-rule powers. The Baltimoreans enjoyed a measure of self-government for the first time, and though the city had not gained political autonomy from the state, and never would, it now had the nuclear powers of government and taxation to shape its own development. Thus did Baltimore, previously just a social economy, become a political economy as well.

The changed status of the city also saw the rise of new social groups to positions of power in the community. Their appearance was intimately linked to the new status of the city, and they became the chief carriers of its new political culture, a culture whose main emphasis linked civic pride with nationalism. The groups that mainly benefited from the incorporation of Baltimore were the "mechanics"—skilled master craftsmen—and the tradesmen who played crucial roles in the urban process. Fixed in place by their everyday operations, and being employers whose livelihood depended upon their provision of services to the community, both the master craftsmen and the tradesmen had a vested interest in the new municipal institutions. Together with certain allies they found among the merchants, they played primary roles in the municipal administration and constituted a new middle class who opposed the more conservative merchants and their landed-gentry family connections. However, by arguing the rhetoric of American Republicanism when rising to power, they perforce popularized a rhetoric that their supporters below them, the propertyless and the unskilled, could use. Consequently, this new middle class had to learn to use their democratic rhetoric as a two-edged sword: to maintain themselves in power against the conservative merchants above them, and to deflect the aspirants from below who would democratize the social order to a greater degree than they wanted. The political roles of these new men characterized Baltimore's municipal administration as a "burgher government"[1] for nearly two generations after 1796.

Baltimore's new legal status, together with its new middle-class leadership, sharply distinguished town from country, ended the rural domination of the town, and created an urban political economy. Municipal inspection laws, taxes, and marketing licenses were forms of urban control over agricultural prices and production, and the construction and maintenance of streets and roads facilitated the transportation of agricultural products. All of these things better regulated the market place and stabilized commercial transactions, but in doing so they institutionalized the relationship between country producer and city merchant. In turn, this institutionalization further reduced the flexibility of Baltimore's society. For example, these municipal regulations fixed cost structures and sometimes froze prices at levels quite independent from actual market conditions. Baltimore's merchants, not the country sellers, bore the initial brunt of such disparities in prices, because they dealt directly in the money economy, where the country sellers had a barter relationship with the city merchants. Thus, the city merchants sometimes found themselves locked into a price structure created by the political economy of Baltimore that was not immediately adjustable to fluctuations in the supply-demand conditions of the marketplace.

The institutionalization of various urban processes incorporated certain private and personal characteristics of Baltimore society that antedated the business revolution and the emergence of the city. Before the new institutions emerged, custom and tradition had characterized urban life, and institutions having the force of law played a minor role compared to private and informal relations premised upon trust and morality. Since the new institutions were built upon many of these customs and traditions, ideas and values, they provided cultural continuity, preserving and carrying remnants of eighteenth-century Baltimore society into nineteenth-century settings, and thereby confounding the life of the institutions with that of the society.[2]

One element of Baltimore's private society was its exclusionism: contemporaries did not think of their society as being a whole greater than the sum of individuals in it, nor did they consider the sum of individuals in Baltimore to be their society; rather, the society was the status elite. This elitism was evident in tangible forms (only adult, white, free, male property owners could exercise decision-making authority, for example, or hold positions of power or leadership) as well as in less tangible ones —such as that Baltimore society was deferential and that status, or position in the social hierarchy, had not traditionally been simply a function of wealth. Gentility, for instance, had been a recognized set of personal qualities (not necessarily connected with wealth), which entitled one to a place in the elite. This particular characteristic was rapidly changing, however: the tremendous prosperity of the 1790s and early 1800s, together with the new institutional modes of behavior and values, were bringing ideas of gentility into a closer identification with wealth. The new middle class was mainly responsible for changing this definition, because the new definition was its only way into the gentry.

Another element also illustrates how this status society functioned: the family, not the individual, was its most important social unit. Families played the fundamental roles in various economic, political, and social activities, and they were the basis of the household censuses—commonly but mistakenly called population censuses today—that were compiled decennially by the new federal government. However, the accelerating role of associational activities and the monetization of credit began undermining the importance of families. As institutionalization of social processes dissolved the society's exclusive character by allowing new men to rise in status, and democratized society further by publicizing its processes, family controls also tended to give way to depersonalized institutional controls.

A third element of the private society was its most visible component: public services were performed by private persons and groups. Although the city had an implicit right of eminent domain, such municipal services as fire protection, water facilities, and new street construction were provided by private individuals and companies. They reflected the Baltimoreans' belief that private profit and public service were synonymous. This form of such services also illustrated how the Baltimoreans conceptualized urban life in terms of their historically older values of privatism. However anomalous the term *private city* may sound to twentieth-century Americans accustomed to thinking of cities as being public entities by definition, Baltimore functioned as a private city throughout the early years of the Republic.[3]

Baltimore society was thus resistant to change brought by the new legal status of the community, much as it was to the forces of the business revolution. However, municipalization contributed to undermining the old order as surely as the business revolution did, and in similar ways. Without past institutional experience, Baltimore's leaders had to be adaptive and pragmatic in establishing their institutions of city government, and just as they looked elsewhere for models of economic institutions, so they also copied their political institutions from others. In both cases, adjustments were made in the institutions after they were implemented to better fit Baltimore realities. Indeed, Baltimore continued to be a society in the making as long as the conditions that supported such a process remained essentially the same. When the conditions disappeared, the institutions in large measure became the realities.

From Town to City

Baltimore became a city by state law in December 1796. This law specified that the town was to be the "City of Baltimore" and that its inhabitants constituted "a body politic and corporate" to be known as the "Mayor and City Council of Baltimore." The powers expressly delegated to Baltimore gave the new city control over the general areas of health, police, bridge construction, the harbor, the establishment of new streets, lanes and alleys, fire protection, and the regulation and standardization of trade, "and to pass all ordinances necessary to give effect and operation to all the powers vested in the corporation of the city of Baltimore." The financing of these powers came from the city's right to establish fees, fines, penalties, forfeitures, and a property tax that would not exceed two dollars for each one hundred pounds assessed in any given year.[4]

However, the representatives of Maryland's landed gentry in the state legislature, from Annapolis and from Baltimore county, did not intend for Baltimore to be an autonomous polity. For example, the new city was not granted its own court system but had to continue using the Baltimore County Court for resolving its urban problems. Though cumbersome and occasionally impracticable, this system allowed the landed gentry in the county to continue exercising some powers over the new city until Baltimore's renewed growth immediately after the War of 1812 induced the creation of a municipal court system. Thus, now and in the future, Maryland's landed gentry—the rural, the Roman Catholic and Episcopalian squirarchy on the Eastern Shore and in the southern part of the Western Shore including Baltimore County—showed its animosity and fear of the city through the state legislature. Specifically, the planters would circumscribe Baltimore's potential political power along two lines: one was to alter periodically the charter arrangements that defined the municipality, and the other was to restrict the city's representation in the state legislature to two respresentatives. Annapolis, the state capital, and each county also sent two representatives to the state legislature; and by so restricting Baltimore's representation in spite of its large and growing population, rural Maryland interests were able to control the state legislature and to intervene in city affairs. This would remain the pattern throughout the antebellum period.

The governmental structure that was drawn up for Baltimore thus represented both a culmination in the relationship between the town and the state legislature and a victory for the legislature. The Baltimoreans had begun their drive for political power and status consistent with their obviously growing social and economic power by supporting the movement for a new federal government during the 1780s. Undoubtedly, their nationalist motives were genuine, for the U.S. Constitution promised to resolve the commercial problems that all American seaports confronted; but by so combining civic pride with nationalism, they also hoped to gain in political power and status by becoming the center of Maryland's nationalist interest. The nationalism of the Baltimoreans was excessive at best and desperate at least: they supported the ratification of the Constitution much too zealously; they sought to be the site for the capital of the new national government; and they tried to exert their influence across the state by dominating the statewide congressional elections of 1790. Such noisy nationalism achieved some partial success, the chartering of their town as a city with limited power of home rule being the most conspicuous example. But in the process they alienated rural Federalists (their only potential allies in the state), who now identified with the state legislature in state politics. As a result, the city's constitutional subordination to the state was made explicit in the charter itself.[5]

The rural gentry's distrust of the city was also reflected in the cumbersome form of municipal administration that the new charter provided. Power was split between the mayor and the bicameral City Council, in conscious imitation of the new U.S. Constitution. Town commissioners were appointed by the state legislature to supervise the division of the city into eight wards. The First Branch of the City Council consisted of two members selected annually from each ward; members were required to be twenty-one years of age, residents of their wards, and residents in the city for three years, and to have property worth at least one thousand dollars. Requirements for voting for members of the First Branch were the same as for electing delegates to the General Assembly of Maryland. The annual elections of members of the First Branch were the closest legal form to direct, participatory democracy in Baltimore.[6]

The Second Branch of the City Council was to function as a more deliberative body, and qualifications for membership were therefore more strict than those for the First Branch. Members of the Second Branch were chosen by a miniature electoral college, each elector from each ward; they did not represent wards but the city at large; and they were to number no more than eight, regardless of population increases or ward changes. Each member was to be over twenty-five years of age, a citizen of the United States, a resident of Baltimore for four years prior to his election, and to have property valued at a minimum of two thousand dollars. The term of office was two years. Voting for members of both the First and Second Branches of the City Council was by viva voce.

Just as the two branches of the City Council were strikingly similar in structure and functions to the two branches of the new federal Congress, so the office of mayor resembled that of the president of the United States. In fact, the elaborate scheme for electing the mayor was much the same for electing the president; and both systems reflected the eighteenth-century distrust of executive power. Elected every other year, the mayor was to be a man of known integrity, experience, and sound judgment. He was also to be over twenty-five years of age, a resident of Baltimore prior to his election, a citizen of the United States for at least ten years, and possessed of property worth at least two thousand dollars.

The procedure for electing the mayor resembled that for electing the president in another respect as well: both aimed at avoiding party or factional politics. At designated polling stations within their respective wards, qualified voters elected by ballot two persons from each ward to serve as electors of the mayor. These electors were to meet the same qualifications as the members of the First Branch of the City Council. They were to serve as judges of their own elections, returns, and qualifications; and no elector could be a member of either branch of the City Council or hold any office of the municipality. All electors were required to take an oath that they would elect a mayor without favor, partiality, or prejudice.

Although the mayor could convene the City Council as often as needed, the council customarily convened itself in February of each year. Three-fourths of the members constituted a quorum, and they could, and sometimes did, compel the attendance of absentees. They appointed their own presidents, settled their own rules, were judges of their own elections, and could expel a member if three-fourths concurred, though not twice for the same cause. True, the mayor could veto decisions of the City Council, but three-fourths of the council could override the veto. Moreover, all city officers were appointed by the mayor from a list of nominees furnished to him by the Second Branch. Thus, Maryland's planter-dominated state legislature expressed what Americans wished: to subordinate executive to representative political power as much as possible.

In one important respect this scheme of municipal organization was readily adjusted to changing realities. The sea of new people flooding into the community was steadily accommodated by the democratization of electoral procedures. Thus, in 1805 all voting in Baltimore was changed from viva voce to ballot; and in 1808 the Second Branch of the City Council was opened to popular election instead of by electors, its members merely required to live in and represent each of the eight wards. Also in 1808, property qualifications for both branches of the City Council were greatly reduced—from one thousand to three hundred dollars for the First Branch and from two thousand to five hundred dollars for the Second Branch. These were, however, merely institutional adjustments to new demographic conditions within Baltimore, and they did not alter such fundamental facts as Baltimore's subordinate municipal authority within Maryland.

The City's Leadership

The men responsible for Baltimore's new legal status, and who moved into control of the municipal administration and shaped its policies, were part of the leadership who had supported the federal Constitution in 1788–89. Almost immediately, however, this group then divided over the events of the early 1790s. Most of them, mainly merchants and lawyers, remained loyal to the Federalist policies of the national administrations. But because these policies frequently departed from Baltimore realities, and sometimes even went against the community's interest, these people were occasionally forced to defend the national against the local interest. In so doing, they weakened their local leadership positions. Though this process was gradual and cumulative, and highly individualistic, in the course of time it created opportunities at the local level for others to fill.

These "others" consisted of a few highly influential merchants who continued their Federalist orientation, but who, unlike those in the first group, never abandoned their identification of Baltimore with nationalism. More accurately, they continued to believe that national policies should reflect local interests. Their point of view was not localism *versus* nationalism, but localism *and* nationalism; they believed that what was good for Baltimore was good for the nation, and that things should also work the other way around.

Because this second group exercised leadership as municipal officeholders, they were well known to those men who were prominent in the everyday life of the community—such as master craftsmen and tradesmen. The latter were property owners and employers, though their political role was that of voters rather than officeholders. These two groups of localists thus complemented each other, the one providing traditional officeholding leadership and the other having social and economic power, although their political power remained supportive in the traditional way. However, when the alliance between the two groups occurred in 1796, political-leadership opportunities were opened to the latter group for the first time.

The occasion for the alliance was the incorporation and chartering of the town as a city, together with the almost simultaneous break in the previously solid political ranks of the merchants. The connection between the two events was the "Smith faction"—the faction that dominated the smaller group of officeholders, continued to identify the national interest with Baltimore's, and did not always feel obliged to support the national interest when it departed from its civic moorings.

The nucleus of this faction was the Smith family, one of the twenty-five or so families that made up Baltimore's economic, political, and social oligarchy. Together with three other of Baltimore's oligarchal families— the Buchanans, Purviances, and Spears—the Smiths had been part of the Scotch-Irish, Presbyterian immigration from northern Ireland during the 1720s which settled Donegal and Lancaster counties in Pennsylvania. These four families, together with other Scotch-Irish families (who were Quakers and Baptists besides Presbyterians) such as the Calhouns, Hollingsworths, McKims, and Steretts, were subsequently part of the movement from southeastern Pennsylvania to Baltimore during the 1760s and 1770s, drawn by Baltimore's expanding wheat trade. Together, these families had formed the nucleus of Baltimore's support for the American cause during the Revolution.[7]

Samuel Smith's father, John, had prospered as a merchant in Baltimore and then served in the Maryland Senate during the 1780s. Samuel was trained as a merchant, served as an officer in the Maryland militia during the Revolution, and entered into a mercantile partnership with his younger brother John during the 1780s. Their younger brother, Robert, graduated from Princeton in 1778, studied law for five years with Robert Goldsborough, and came to be regarded during the 1790s as one of Maryland's more brilliant younger attorneys. In politics the brothers and their father were overshadowed by the father's younger brother, William Smith. William had played a prominent role during the Revolution. He served on the Committee of Correspondence and Observation, was a delegate to the Continental Congress, served as a member of Baltimore's Committee of Safety, and then retired to mercantile pursuits during the 1780s. One of his daughters married Otho Holland Williams, customs collector in Baltimore and former aide-de-camp to General Washington during the Revolutionary War (as did another Baltimore merchant and physician, James Mc-

Henry), and a younger daughter married her first cousin, Robert Smith. The Smiths, Williamses, and McHenrys, together with their wider family connections, were part of the core of Baltimore merchants who led their community's overwhelming support of the federal Constitution in the 1787–88 elections.[8]

The emerging importance of Baltimore and the demonstrated nationalism of its leadership virtually insured that many among them would play roles in the new federal government. Otho Williams was appointed collector of customs (where he preferred to remain) for the port; James McHenry served as secretary of war in the cabinets of Presidents Washington and Adams from 1796 to 1800; and John Eager Howard, the largest landowner in Baltimore city, served in the U.S. Senate from 1796 to 1803. But unlike the others, the Smiths continued to involve themselves in local as well as national politics: William served as Baltimore's representative in the first Congress of the United States under the new Constitution from 1789 to 1791, and Samuel, who served as one of Baltimore's two representatives to the Maryland House of Delegates in 1790–91, was then elected to the federal Congress, where he began a forty-year career. Robert began his political career in 1796 when he was elected one of Baltimore's two representatives to the House of Delegates. Moreover, unlike McHenry and Howard, the Smiths rooted their political power in Baltimore realities. The growing wealth from their shipping firms financed their political campaigns, and during the summers of election years, Samuel used his rank as brigadier general in the Maryland militia to travel the circuit of militia musters, haranguing the voters who were so conveniently gathered together. Perhaps most importantly, Samuel, John, and Robert were brothers-in-law to seven other prominent merchants in Baltimore: Otho Williams, John Donnell, John Hollins, William Patterson, William L. Forman, and John and Joseph Spear. Together with William Smith and his friends, these ten men and their shipping connections constituted this openly acknowledged "Smith faction." They led the fight for the incorporation and chartering of Baltimore as a city in 1796; they broke with the McHenry-Howard wing of the Federalist party when this wing tried to eliminate Samuel from the party in 1798; they allied themselves with the tradesmen and "mechanics"—master craftsmen—in the new Republican party and reelected Samuel Smith to Congress in 1798, thereby introducing middle-class politics into Baltimore; and they were chiefly responsible for setting the tone of Baltimore's society and for establishing the city's national reputation during the late 1790s and early 1800s.[9]

An analysis of officeholders in the municipal administration from its

creation in 1797 through the War of 1812 demonstrates three characteristics about the personnel of Baltimore's emerging political economy:
first, that the Republicans eventually came to dominate the administration over time; second, that these Republicans were merchants, tradesmen (storekeepers of various kinds), and "mechanics," middlemen in the
commercial process who understood how marketing dominated production; and third, that they were also political middlemen who used democratic rhetoric to gain support for their own goals, but who then reduced
rather than abolished the property qualifications and residence requirements for voting and for holding office. They understood the difference
between power and ideology.

Actually, Republicans began to play important roles in Baltimore's
administration from its inception in 1797. The first mayor, seven of the
first sixteen members of the First Branch of the City Council, and one of
the first eight members of the Second Branch were Republicans. In addition, eight of the nineteen justices of the peace, one of the three judges of
the Orphan's Court, two of the three commissioners for watching and
lighting the city, one of the five commissioners for the health of the city,
and two of the four commissioners for maintaining the harbor were Republicans. In the eighteen years from 1797 to 1815, Republicans occupied
the mayor's office for all but four, and they held a majority in the First
Branch of the City Council every year beginning in 1798. Their domination of the Second Branch came more slowly: they established a balance
in 1803 and a majority in 1805, and thereafter controlled that branch.[10]

Though Baltimore's prosperity and the democratic rhetoric of the Republicans were mainly responsible for their success, the institutional
arrangements of the city government also contributed to it. Not only did
the operations of the municipal administration invite, they virtually demanded a comparison with those of the federal, rather than the state,
government. Newcomers into political office looked to the federal government as a model for administrative procedures as well as for explana-
tions and justifications of them. After 1800, when the federal government
was located just thirty-five miles to the southwest, and Republicans dominated that government too, Baltimore Republicanism was strengthened
even further.

The socioeconomic makeup of the municipal administration was fairly
uniform. As befitted the defenders of wealth and property, they were
owners of real and personal property: the mean value of wealth held by
the ninety-one members of the First Branch was $6,017.82 and the mean
number of slaves of the First Branch was .89; for the thirty-five members
of the Second Branch, the figures are $9,202.14 and 2.31. The first mayor

TABLE I
Occupations of Members of the First Branch
of the Baltimore City Council, 1797–1815

Occupation	Number	Percentage of Total
Merchants	21	31.81
Professionals	13	19.70
Gentlemen	11	16.67
Storekeepers	11	16.67
Manufacturers	10	15.15
Totals	66	100.00

SOURCES: Scharf, *History of Baltimore*, pp. 187–90; Mullin, comp., *Baltimore Directory, for 1799*; Fry, comp., *Baltimore Directory for 1810*; Jackson, comp., *Baltimore Directory . . . 1819*.

(James Calhoun, Republican, 1797–1804) was a merchant who owned $12,600 worth of real estate and 11 slaves in 1798; the second (Thorowgood Smith, Federalist, 1804–8) was president of the Maryland Insurance Company and owned $11,000 worth of real estate and three slaves; and the third (Edward Johnson, Republican, 1808–16) was a physician, who also owned the largest brewery in town, and had real estate valued at $10,160 but did not own slaves.

Seats on the City Council were occupied mainly by commercial middlemen. Sixty-six of the ninety-one members of the First Branch are identified by occupation in Table 1. Of the members of the Second Branch, twenty-eight of the thirty-five are identified in Table 2.

There were two important developments within this static picture of the entire period from 1799 to 1810. For one thing, there was much shifting of occupational designation through time. More than half the members of the First Branch changed their occupations over the eleven-year period, while less than one-third in the Second Branch did. In both cases, the most common shift was from "storekeeper" or "manufacturer" to "merchant" or "gentleman," though a minor trend, especially in the more institutionally democratic First Branch, was toward specialization. The other development involved ward characteristics. In the shipbuilding and manufacturing wards, for example, legal people—attorneys, justices of the peace, judges, and court clerks—represented the wards when they

TABLE 2
*Occupations of Members of the Second Branch
of the Baltimore City Council, 1797–1815*

Occupation	Number	Percentage of Total
Merchants	13	46.42
Professionals	5	17.86
Gentlemen	4	14.29
Manufacturers	4	14.29
Storekeepers	2	7.14
Totals	28	100.00

SOURCES: Scharf, *History of Baltimore*, pp. 192–93; Mullin, comp., *Baltimore Directory, for 1799*; Fry, comp., *Baltimore Directory for 1810*; Jackson, comp., *Baltimore Directory . . . 1819*.

were first organized. But by 1810, such wards were represented by block and pump makers and ship joiners. In the business wards, in contrast, the shift was from a profession of storekeeping to "merchant" or "gentleman." These occupational shifts in conformity with one's ward identification occurred mainly in the First Branch.

Baltimore's middle class did not merely acquire political power when the city was incorporated, they used their new power to promote their own stability and continuity of power. In spite of the democratic rhetoric of the Republican majority of officeholders, the facts of their tenure in office illustrate their concern with a low rate of turnover in the administration. In the First Branch the turnover rate was barely one-third among all officeholders from 1797 to 1815, and the mean number of years in office was 5.28. Almost one-half of these ninety-five office holders were in office for 3 or more years: two were in office for 9 years, one for 8, two for 7, ten for 6, eight for 5, thirteen for 4, and six for 3. In comparison, officeholding in the Second Branch was much more democratic. Here the turnover rate was almost one-half and the mean number of years in office was 1.94 or about one regular 2-year term. With its higher property qualifications and longer residency requirement, the exclusiveness of the Second Branch apparently encouraged an aristocratic democracy, and, by the same token, the party identification and longevity of officeholding in the First Branch—the most democratic branch of government in the society at large—was apparently used to control decision makers and decision making.

The City as Market Place

Actually, the identification of the municipal leaders with these political ideas and values was not as important to the development of Baltimore as was their conception of the city as a marketplace. Because of this latter belief, two immediate and interrelated problems had to be confronted: one was to raise revenues to fund the cost of government, and the other was to design the structure of the revenue system in such a way as to promote stability and regularity in the marketplace. From its very beginning, then, Baltimore's leaders consciously pursued and practiced "political economy" within the municipality.

In part, Baltimore's revenue-producing structure was shaped by the city's constitutional subordination to the state. The city's charter, for example, prohibited Baltimore from taxing personal and real estate at a rate of more than fifteen shillings Maryland currency (equal to two dollars in 1797 and seventy-five cents in 1818 when this limitation was raised) per one hundred pounds sterling (about five hundred dollars) of assessed value. Because of the limited revenue that this tax brought in, the municipality had to rely upon a variety of other taxes rather than upon the direct tax. Consequently, and naturally, given the prosperity of the community, the city taxed trade, the life of the city, instead of relying upon property assessments made at a given point in time. For the most part, these were duties on consumer goods and on trade, taxes on transportation vehicles, levies on auction sales, and various license fees.[11]

Not only were these the mushrooming seaport's most lucrative sources of revenue, they were also more efficiently and far less expensively collected than were taxes upon personal and real estate. This fact was reflected in the method of farming out the collection of municipal taxes. A city collector was appointed by the City Council to receive tax monies due the city. The collector bonded himself to the city for his collection of municipal taxes, and his remuneration was a commission on the tax monies received. On direct, personal, and real-estate taxes, he received from 6 to 8 percent of all monies received; on other taxes which he was responsible for collecting, he received from 5 to 8 percent. On taxes in the form of licenses and duties which were paid by traders, he received 5 percent. This was far less than the expense of collecting direct property taxes.[12]

The importance of this taxation policy was that it made property

ownership attractive (which, in turn, reinforced the stake-in-society political assumption of Baltimore's middle-class leaders) and passed on costs
to consumers. Such a commercialman's policy, coming as it did on top of
enormously expanded demand markets, furthered the inflationary price
spiral engendered by short supplies during wartime conditions. But more
importantly, it became an instutitional part of Baltimore's political economy and wedded the city's revenue structure to the peculiar condition of
prosperity.

Municipal taxation of trade implied municipal regulation of trade, of
course, and that sometimes led to conflict with the state. To be sure, in
some cases—the city's regulation of markets, for example—Baltimore's
authority went unchallenged by the state. For each of the city's three
markets the mayor appointed a salaried clerk, who was responsible for
renting the market spaces and collecting the money. When he rented each
space, he issued a certificate that stated the rental conditions to the market trader. The trader took this certificate to the mayor for his approval
and then exchanged it for the annual license. All market traders were
subject to this process.[13]

But the city was far less successful in trying to regulate the goods stored
on the city's three public wharves. A harbor master collected a storage
duty, which ranged in rate from half a cent to twenty cents per package,
depending upon the type of commodity. In 1813, a city ordinance discriminated among Baltimore's merchants by exempting owners of property fronting upon the public wharves from paying any wharfage charges
upon goods received or delivered. The next year, responding to pleas by
Baltimore merchants who did not own frontage property, the Maryland
legislature prohibited Baltimore from taxing any goods on the municipality's public wharves. Having no recourse, the city rescinded its ordinance establishing the duties on goods on public wharves and substituted duties on the tonnage of ships landing at the public wharves to
restore the revenues. If this contradicted the U.S. Constitution, no one
protested, and these duties remained in force throughout the antebellum
period.[14]

All of these institutional conditions had a bearing on the kinds of
municipal services that Baltimore offered its residents from 1793 to
1816. The most important determinants, of course, remained the values
of the personal society. In a society where private profit and public service were one, it could be expected that public services would be privately owned, and so they were. But Baltimore's institutional circumstances,
and especially the reliance upon trade for revenues and the concomitant
fluctuation of revenues with the state of trade, reinforced this social pre-
dilection. They made it both advantageous and necessary to turn the per-

formance of municipal services over to private individuals and groups. The voluntary activities of firemen, policemen, and administrators of the poor relief, together with the services of commercial companies in furnishing the city with water and gas, fulfilled vital functions that were too expensive for the corporation of Baltimore to assume from 1796 to 1816, given its revenue structure and the fluctuating income that flowed from it. Moreover, the operations of the private water company were far more socially efficient than they would become later, after it was municipalized, for its costs were borne directly by its consumers and no others, and especially not the community as a whole.

In a variety of other ways, too, the operations of Baltimore's municipal services interacted with the structure of government to reflect and strengthen the personal and private society. For example, the repairing and paving of what we consider the public streets and roadways constituted the largest single expenditure in the city's budget from 1797 through 1813 but was scarcely a function of the municipality. True, a board of city commissioners was vested with all powers over repairing and paving streets, lanes, and alleys; and their only limitation was that a majority of the inhabitants living along one of the public ways must consent to having it paved. But the commissioners did no more than select the particular streets, lanes, or alleys to be repaired or paved, contract to have the work done, and assess those whose property adjoined the improved thoroughfare. The initiative for such activities usually came from the private sector, the property owners.[15]

Other municipal services, such as fire prevention and the supply of water and gas to the city, were carried out in essentially the same way, as more or less a partnership between the private society and the municipality. Privately organized fire companies served the city until the 1850s, providing the manpower and equipment while the city furnished the water and some financial aid. The municipality did control a portion of the city's water supply, and several ordinances provided for the maintenance of old wells and pumps as well as for the building of new ones. Here again, the service was socially efficient because a pump tax was levied only upon the property that was serviced. This did not produce a sufficient supply of water for the community as a whole, however, and in 1805 the Baltimore Water Company was incorporated to increase the supply of water in the city through private enterprise. At its own expense, and with the aid of contributions, this company brought water into the city and built a public reservoir. To this purpose, they were given the free use of Baltimore's streets as well as municipal protection for their property. In much the same fashion, the city contracted with the Baltimore Gas Light Company in 1816 to light the city's street lamps with gas instead of oil, provided that no greater municipal expenditure would be made by the change.[16]

Not all municipal services developed so smoothly. Prior to 1818, for example, there was no municipal agency for the relief of the poor. In 1805, Maryland law transferred the administration of the almshouse to Baltimore County; and poor relief in the city depended upon private charity until 1818, though in emergency situations specially appointed groups were designated by city ordinances to aid the poor. Relief of the indigent sick was of more municipal concern, however. The general hospital that private philanthropy had founded in 1794 was purchased by Baltimore's Committee on Health in 1798 and was funded by municipal and state appropriations. In 1808 the administration of this hospital was placed in the hands of a private group, though the city continued to pay for its public patients and exercised supervisory powers through a board of five "visitors."[17]

Public-health facilities and maintenance of the harbor (for the two were closely related and would long continue to be) were the only two municipal services over which the city exercised fairly strong control. In fact, Baltimore's control over its public-health facilities stemmed directly from its 1796 charter, which empowered the corporation to pass any ordinance "necessary to preserve the health of the city; prevent and remove nuisances; to prevent the introduction of contagious diseases within the city and within three miles of the same." A board of commissioners of health, created in 1797, steadily expanded in number and authority until 1809, when it was merged with the city commissioners in a new, joint board entitled the City Commissioners and Commissioners of Health. This new board continued in existence until 1820, when it was superseded by a municipal board of health.[18]

Baltimore's charter also empowered the city to build public wharves and maintain them, and to deepen and otherwise extend its harbor facilities. Accordingly, a city ordinance of 1797 created the office of harbor master and empowered him to appoint his own deputies, with the approval of the mayor. This office was enlarged in 1809 to include two harbor masters, and in 1813 the precharter institution of port warden was revived with three persons serving as port wardens and with the two harbor masters placed under their direction. These men and their deputies were responsible for the general maintenance of the public wharves, docks, and the harbor; they also inspected shipping, collected wharfage and tonnage duties, and were responsible for the continuing improvement of Baltimore's harbor facilities.[19]

By the time of the War of 1812, Baltimore had thus developed a complex of urban institutions that organized community life in various ways.

Some of these institutions met community-wide needs, and others concerned administrative procedures, but most regulated economic activities. Fundamentally, then, town government complemented the social and economic fabric that defined Baltimore, and to define Baltimore simply as a political entity without its social and economic roots would distort reality and misrepresent its political character. The test of municipal leadership was the pursuance of the community interest, and when the two diverged the leadership was changed. Until the return of peace in 1815, circumstances favored the commitment to localism and a one-party system in municipal politics.

That the leadership did change, bringing men into power who were more intimately involved in the life of the community, indicates the importance of Baltimore's new legal status within the state. The new institutions that established, legitimatized, and regularized community life distinguished the character of Baltimore within the larger society of Maryland. Not only was urban, commercial Baltimore a very different society from that of rural and agricultural Maryland, it was also constitutionally subordinate to the state. At best, Baltimore was a semi-autonomous society within this larger society; and, in the long run, the development of the city would be circumscribed by Maryland in much the same fashion as the development of the state was by the federal government—through politics.

CHAPTER III

Industrialization and the Crisis of War

Independence and prosperity had created the business revolution and the new legal status of the city as two of the three foundations that governed Baltimore's later development. The third foundation—industrialization—resulted from another dimension of Baltimore's experience, the rise of a flourishing manufacturing interest during the city's progressive involvement in the European wars, beginning in 1807. Industrialization, patriotism, privateering, profits, the breakdown of the guild system, and the militarization of society: all were interrelated and contributed to forming nineteenth-century social norms, as much as the business revolution and the emergence of the city did. However, the appearance of industrialization cannot be separated from these other elements, because the wartime conditions surrounding its appearance played a more formative role in the social changes than industrialization by itself did.

The wartime crisis from 1807 to 1815 was crucial to the appearance of industrialization, as it married civic concern with national patriotism and intensified Baltimore's identification with the nation. But while Baltimore's identification with the American nationality reached its apogee during the War of 1812, the concern with security and the different kinds of opportunities that the crisis of war presented obscured important social changes. Patriotism now joined with profit to sanction social and technological innovations; indeed, they became the reason for the very existence of innovation. Thus, the conditions of war, like the conditions of prosperity before them, encouraged and legitimatized the social changes that transformed Baltimore society.

Though the wartime background of industrialization distinguished its origins from the other two foundations, all three were interwoven in the broader historical context. Both the business revolution and the emergence of the city, but especially the business revolution, were necessary preludes to industrial revolution. The two former events introduced new ways of making monetary profits and created a number of formal, legal, institutionalized, and ritualized relationships among people. These developments had to have begun before men could take advantage of the application of steam power to various productive, processing, and transportation methods, all of which amounted to a completely new technology, unlike anything seen before. The new conditions made it possible for businessmen to perceive (as earlier generations could not) that the new technology offered substantial savings per unit of production or processing. Moreover, the business revolution provided a means of supplying the large initial investment that was involved in utilizing the new technology, namely monetized credit, and the legal status of the city enabled businessmen to regularize their marketplace at home.

Industrialization alone did not produce industrial revolution. To be sure, industrialization had considerable social impact in its own right. For example, in the factory enclaves built around the city before 1807, manufacturers had traditionally employed poor women and children assigned to them by the orphan's court, and this social pattern continued after the application of steam power to production. This did not conflict with either slave labor or the white guild labor system. But as the flow of peacetime trade slowed to a trickle, unemployment, especially among sailors, rose and offered an alternative labor force for manufacturers. The latter built more factories, some of them in town. In this way industrialization helped to break down the eighteenth-century guild system. But the chief importance of industrialization before the War of 1812 remained its potential rather than its reality; eventually, it would turn Baltimore's social economy away from its eighteenth-century agricultural and trading basis toward a nineteenth-century industrial or self-generating productive basis.

Industrialization in Baltimore, as in other American ports, was greatly stimulated by the stagnation of maritime trade that began with President Jefferson's Embargo Proclamation of December 1807. Within a month after the embargo began, prices of most imported goods, especially dry goods, had risen and the maritime business was in the doldrums. By March the depression had deepened: vessels were laid up and the crews discharged, flour mills were idled and millers let go. Baltimore's commerce continued to be virtually paralyzed for the remainder of the year and until the spring of 1809, when it briefly revived.[1]

Stagnation soon set in again, however, and from the late summer of 1809 to June of 1812, when the United States declared war against Great Britain, Baltimore's foreign trade was fitful at best. The uncertainties of trade—arising from the intractability of the British in continuing to stop American ships on the high seas and the confiscations, captures, and burnings of American ships by the French—led the majority of Baltimore's merchants to curtail their businesses. The more prescient among them wound up their affairs and got out of trade altogether. As early as the fall of 1809, for example, Robert and John Oliver stopped buying, settled their accounts as best they could, and merely continued to sell their inventoried goods.[2]

Trade did revive somewhat in the late fall and winter of 1811 to 1812, however, after the possibility of war against Great Britain became a probability. Then, the risks and uncertainties on the high seas could be calculated against the potential profits of the cargoes should they reach a Baltimore at war. And so a late flurry of trade in the winter and spring of 1812 occurred as Baltimore's merchants sought this last advantage before the war.

The problems confronting Baltimore merchants during this period were compounded by a financial crisis, which stemmed from two sources. One was financial panic in Great Britain among merchants in the American trade that began in late July of 1810, when the embargo and its sequel, the Nonintercourse Act, caught up with these merchants and forced them to stop payments. In most cases, the merchants had purchased American commodities at the lowest price they had seen in years. However, American trade restrictions continued and prices went even lower. These merchants were now caught with high-priced perishable commodities which would sell for a loss. In a few other cases, merchants had contracted for the delivery of American commodities in Europe, but because of the continuing trade restrictions, American merchants could not forward them. The British merchants were caught in the middle and had to dun their American suppliers for either the commodities or else the money that the British merchants had already advanced. Needless to say, this financial crisis occurred mainly among the speculators in the American trade.

The panic among the British merchants in the American trade further depressed prices of American produce in England, and Baltimore merchants who had been sending commodities to Great Britain via Spanish, Portuguese, and Dutch ports no longer did so. Consequently, the exchange rate of English sterling bills sank lower and lower, and exchange was often unsalable. Baltimore merchants were hurt by the British panic in several ways: some were under contract to deliver commodities to British merchants at prices that were higher than they were now; some had purchased exchange at a previously higher price and could now calculate how much they had lost; and some simply found themselves unable to send commodities to a market where they were unsalable. Many Baltimore merchants failed as a result of this British contraction.

Other failures soon followed during the winter of 1810–11 as a result of another source of Baltimore's financial problems, the closing of the

Bank of the United States (BUS). The BUS branch in Baltimore began curtailing its discounts in December 1810, after Congress met and rumors were circulated that the charter of the bank would not be renewed. As events proved, the BUS pursued a sound policy: by curtailing discounts and demanding payment from its debtors, the bank covered its liabilities when it ceased business six months later. But the other banks in the city curtailed their discounts as well, and a widespread credit crisis ensued.[3]

Thus financial problems as well as practically dormant export trade plagued Baltimore's merchants, meaning that adversity characterized Baltimore's social economy on the eve of the War of 1812. The reexport trade after 1793 had been crucial to the city's accelerated expansion, because it changed the mercantile base from one of merely importing consumer goods and exporting raw materials to one in which the quantity of goods moved was far larger than could be accounted for by local consumption. This had spurred specialization in the mercantile economy by introducing middlemen and activities coincident with the greater movement of commodities. This process, together with the expansion of manufacturing and its shift from foreign to domestic markets, had created a potential for changing the very nature of the community. Banks, insurance companies, and manufacturing facilities all contributed to economic growth; but at the same time they threatened to undermine the very existence of eighteenth-century society.

The response of the city's leaders to the commercial stagnation after 1807 was as logical and in character as their response to the new conditions of 1793 had been, and it was even more destructive to the established order. The most important response was a turn to industrialization. In context, import substitution was the logical answer to their situation: it satisfied the need for finished and semifinished European (and especially British) goods that were becoming scarce; it satisfied the need of Baltimore's merchants to employ their capitals in a profitable way; and it satisfied the demand of the community at large for employment in order to maintain the level of development that Baltimore's social economy had reached in 1807. The city's population was large, its social economy was a sophisticated network of specialized interests and occupations and, in spite of the huge influx of immigrants, it had a fairly high literacy rate and a fairly low mortality rate. This cultural development had accompanied the accelerated growth of Baltimore from 1793 to 1807, a growth that was now threatened by the British; and this is why the crisis in Baltimore from 1807 to 1812 was such a deep and culturally divisive one.[4]

Industrialization

The war crisis of 1807 stimulated the utilization of the new technology based upon application of steam power to productive, processing, and transportation methods. This new technology signaled a major shift in Baltimore's social economy because merchants (being the only group who could afford to do so) embraced it, introduced it into factory situations, focused upon textile manufacturing, and produced exclusively for the home market. Each of these developments was new and potentially revolutionary for Baltimore society.

Between the Embargo Proclamation and the outbreak of the War of 1812, three large textile factories were built and a company was formed to market their products in and around Baltimore. The Union Manufacturing Company, incorporated in 1808 with a capitalization of one million dollars, was the largest factory undertaking; its twenty thousand shares at $50.00 each were owned by over three hundred investors. The second largest was the Washington Cotton Manufacturing Company, chartered in 1809 and capitalized at $100,000 in shares of $50 each, and the third was the Powhatan Cotton Mills, owned and built by Nathan Levering in 1810. In addition, the Athenian Society of Baltimore was formed in 1810 and incorporated in 1811 for marketing the new domestic textiles. Modeled after the Domestic Society of Philadelphia, this company built a warehouse where American-made textiles were received and sold on commission. In a few cases, advances were given to small household manufacturers. The society thus encouraged new manufacturers as well as provided marketing aid. An indication of the success of Baltimore's new textile manufacturers is suggested by the huge increase in sales by the Athenian Society: from $17,608 in 1809 to $80,893 in 1812.[5]

Baltimore's traditional manufacturers also adapted the new technology to their own concerns. First were flour millers who fell into one of two categories of generalist-manufacturers. Generalists either lived outside of the city in a patriarchal factory village that included a grist mill, a saw mill, a store, a blacksmith's shop, a slaughterhouse, a smoke and salting house, and perhaps a textile mill and distillery; or they were merchant-millers, the type who lived in town. Merchant-millers sometimes owned the farms on which the wheat was grown and rented out the land to tenant farmers. But they more commonly bought wheat from farmers, ground it into flour, loaded it aboard their own ships, and marketed it themselves. These merchant-millers constituted one of the most dynamic groups in Baltimore; and in 1813 they became the first to introduce steam power into the city when Charles Gwinn applied steam power to flour milling. Quite significantly, steam-powered flour milling occurred in mills built directly on the wharves, where the freshly ground flour could be more conveniently loaded aboard ships and thereby reduce transportation costs.[6]

The generalist-manufacturers were members of the local elite, as were the other large-scale manufacturers in the paternalist tradition—the owners of the iron forges and textile factories. Many of these people (such as the Comegyes, Ellicotts, Hollingsworths, Lormans, Ridgelys, McKims, and Tysons) demanded and received access to bank credit; and they served as directors on the boards of the Bank of Maryland, the Bank of Baltimore, and the Union Bank.

However, the men behind the chartering of the Mechanics' Bank in 1806 were a different kind of manufacturing group. They were manufacturers in the sense of being master craftsmen. Most of them were members of the Baltimore Mechanical Society, an association of master craftsmen in various trades—tanners, tailors, shoemakers, harness and saddle makers, cabinet makers, and the like—and they controlled their own guild associations. Many of them served on the boards of directors of their two banks, the Mechanics' and the Franklin, chartered in 1810. These master craftsmen lived in town, owned shops where they employed apprentices and journeymen, and produced consumer goods for local market consumption.[7]

The differences between these two groups of manufacturers were as large in eighteenth-century Baltimore as they would later be in the nineteenth century. The flour millers were exporters and were connected with the elite through credit and capital. To be sure, they were not usually connected by marriage, for most of them were Quakers from southeastern Pennsylvania who tended to marry within their own religion until the great schism of the 1820s. Nevertheless, they were large-scale entrepreneurs, men of wealth, education, and foreign connections; and this gave them a status virtually equal to the Scotch-Irish, Presbyterian shipping merchants and the English, Episcopalian, and Roman Catholic landed gentry. The master craftsmen, on the other hand, enjoyed no such status. They did not engage in foreign trade; and because they produced consumer goods for the local market economy, their opportunities were much more restricted than were those of the flour millers, and their horizons more limited.

Yet what was socially important about industrialization was not the shift from shipping into manufacturing or its ready adoption by traditional manufacturers: it was the shift in marketing orientation among Baltimore's merchant-manufacturers. Many of the city's merchant-landed gentry had been interested in flour, iron, and powder manufacturing

long before 1807; but such manufacturing was subsidiary though necessary to their more fundamental concern, the trading of commodities.
When the approach of war after 1807 caused many of these merchant-
manufacturers to shift from flour to textile manufacturing, however, they
also shifted their market orientation from foreign to domestic consumers. Previously all manufacturers, whether merchant-manufacturers or
master craftsmen, had shared an interest in the domestic market, but the
former had been mainly concerned with foreign markets and the master
craftsmen with the domestic market only. Now the two groups shared an
interest in the domestic economy.

There was another shift as well. Between 1790 and 1807 the two types
of manufacturing were distinguished by differences in production methods. How goods were produced, handicraft or factory, and the geographical and social differences between them, these were crucial to the social
economy of eighteenth-century Baltimore. Before steam-powered production altered the scale of life, manufacturing conformed to sources
and supply of water power; and nature circumscribed the human community before the industrial revolution far more than it did afterward.

Even after the introduction of steam power changed these relationships, merchant-manufacturers continued to think of themselves as more
merchant than manufacturer and continued to hold themselves aloof
from Baltimore's tradesmen-manufacturers. But the new techniques of
production and their new mutual interest in the domestic economy served
as the basis for a distinct social group that would appear during the
1820s, the manufacturers proper. In these ways, industrialization contributed to the creation of a class society and shaped the direction of
the industrial revolution.

The manufacturing census for 1810 shows twenty-four different types
of industries in Baltimore city in that year and values their manufactured
products at $1,890,300. In rank order of importance according to their
value (no other characteristic is recorded), the six most important types
of industries accounted for 51 percent of the total value of Baltimore's
manufactured goods. Four of these six types were handicraft industries,
indicating that factory production was the least valuable form of manufacturing. None of the twenty-four industries that are listed should really
be classified as a factory-production industry; they vary more in relation
to the degree of skill involved in each process than they do by the level
of rationalized and mechanized production they had reached.[8]

The most interesting characteristic of manufacturing revealed by the
1810 census is its spatial structure. All of the higher-valued handicraft industries were located inside the corporate limits of the city. These
were shop industries; small shops, producing for current and local needs,

in which craftsmen such as saddlers, tanners, woodworkers, shoemakers, and tailors plied their skills. These shops usually consisted of the owner —a master workman—a few journeymen and apprentices, and sometimes also indentured servants, white and black. Very few slaves were employed in the shop industries. On the whole, these industries were small, fairly independent, and family-oriented. They relied upon nonslave labor and were organized along the traditional lines of master-journeyman-apprentice, in accordance with the eighteenth-century social form of industrial production in Baltimore.

The outline of manufacturing in Baltimore suggested by the 1810 census is elaborated by an analysis of the occupations listed in the city directory for 1810. All told, 4,576 white males are listed in this directory, of whom 4,248 can be identified as having one or another of 272 different occupations. An analysis of these occupations reveals the following rank order based upon the number of white males in each category: 1,504 were craftsmen or other skilled workers, 1,084 were engaged in trade, 730 were unskilled or semiskilled, 296 were engaged in manufacturing, 273 were professional men or white-collar workers, 148 were sailors, 144 were "gentlemen," and 99 were connected with housing—innkeeping, tavern keeping, and the like.[9]

The 296 white men who listed themselves as being some type of manufacturer or "maker" spread themselves over 51 different occupations. The diversity of household manufacturing is suggested by the fact that 22 of the occupations have merely one member, 7 have two members, 6 have three members, 2 have four members, 2 have five members, 2 have seven members, 1 has eight members, 2 have ten members, 2 have twelve members, 2 have fourteen members, 1 has nineteen members, 1 has thirty-two members, and 1 has thirty-eight members. However, more than half of the 296 men were concentrated in 8 occupations: boot and shoemakers, 38; brickmakers, 32; block and pump makers, 19; hat manufacturers, 14; soap and candle manufacturers, 14; sugar refiners, 12; brush and comb manufacturers, 12; and tobacco manufacturers or glass manufacturers, 10. Thus in terms of occupational employment, manufacturing was concentrated in a mere handful of household industries.

Black men were not manufacturers in 1810. Of the eighty-five black men whose occupations were listed in the city directory, only one, a brickmaker, could be classified in the manufacturing category. The other eighty-four were found in twenty-nine occupations: twenty-two in nine skilled occupations, forty-four in unskilled occupations, four were tradesmen, seven were sailors, six were shopkeepers, and one was a preacher. The fact that better than half of the black men were in unskilled occupations points out their status in the community relative to white labor. Twenty of the eighty-five black men were laborers.

A more meaningful insight into the impact of industrialization in Baltimore society in the early years of the nineteenth century can be gained by comparing the analysis of the 1810 occupations with a similar analysis of occupations found in the 1799 city directory. Such a comparison, presented in Table 3, reveals a few of the directions in which industrialization was heading. One obvious difference among the occupation changes is the decline of maritime pursuits in relation to the rise of manufacturing and the maritime depression. Another difference is the increase in number of "gentlemen" (the elite) over the decade. Still another difference is the decline of people who were connected with one form or another of rented housing—boarding houses, hotels, and inns. Presumably, more people were living in single-family dwellings or else fewer people considered the management of rental property an occupation.[10]

But the most interesting feature of this comparison of occupation groupings is the fact that skilled workers, retail traders, food services, and the professional and white-collar occupations maintained their positions in society relative to one another. Though domestic manufacturing occupations went from the tenth to the fifth position, the immediate impact of industrialization upon Baltimore's society was neither revolutionary nor profound. The most noticeable change occurred within the professional and white-collar occupations. From 1799 to 1810, the number of attorneys increased from sixteen to forty-three, a 168 percent increase; the number of physicians increased from thirty-five to fifty-six, a 60 percent increase; the number of clergymen increased from six to twenty-two, a 266 percent increase; and the number of teachers increased from twenty-four to thirty-one, a 29 percent increase. The largest increase resulting from the business revolution was the transformation of four "bookkeepers" in 1799 to thirty-eight "accountants" in 1810, an increase of 850 percent.

Outside the city, by contrast, the social structure of manufacturing was very different. Almost all factories, as opposed to shops, that existed *as* factory systems were in enclaves outside the city limits. As such, they were expressions of paternal capitalism, the characteristic form of eighteenth-century capitalism. Their merchant and planter owners operated them much as large plantations were operated. In many cases, most of the unskilled labor was performed by slaves, indentured servants, women, and children, supplemented by free labor employed on a yearly basis. Living accommodations were usually provided along with enough land for a garden. Such facilities combined several manufacturing operations

TABLE 3
White Male Occupations in Baltimore, 1799 and 1810

1799		
Occupation	Number	Percent
Construction and craftsmen	735	32.00
Retail trade	331	14.41
Food services	297	12.93
Overseas trade	265	11.54
Sailors	164	7.14
Housing (inns, taverns)	121	5.27
Ship construction	96	4.18
White collar	76	3.31
Unskilled	68	2.96
Domestic manufacturing	62	2.70
Professional	61	2.66
Wholesale trade	13	.57
Elite	8	.35
Totals	2297	100.02

SOURCE: Mullin, comp., *Baltimore Directory, for 1799*; Fry, comp., *Baltimore Directory for 1810*.

(for example, flour and saw mills existed beside the textile factory) in order to take advantage of the single source of power, the stream. In this way, the manufacturing enclaves resembled company towns having barrackslike housing, a school, a provisions store, and sometimes a physician.

The Society at War

No one paid much attention to these realities as the threat of war became the War of 1812. The war thinned Baltimore's social fabric in a variety

1810		
Occupation	Number	Percent
Construction and craftsmen	1288	30.32
Food services	641	15.09
Retail trade	562	13.23
Overseas trade	483	11.37
Domestic manufacturing	296	6.97
Ship construction	216	5.08
Sailors	148	3.48
White collar	145	3.41
Elite	144	3.39
Professional	128	3.01
Housing	99	2.33
Unskilled	59	1.39
Wholesale trade	39	.92
	4248	99.99

of ways: the opportunities of privateering and the requisite military service weakened the guild system, the increase of steam-powered factory production helped to break down the remains of the eighteenth-century deference society, and the war crisis itself detracted from the eighteenth-century emphasis upon social orders and its identification of individuals with groups, especially the family, which had been the basic social unit of production in the eighteenth century.[11]

The War of 1812 thus precipitated the transformation of Baltimore's society, because wartime events—emergency militia duty, the lucrative opportunities of privateering, and the application of steam power to industrial production—broke down the formal organization of eighteenth-century society. Mobilization against imminent British invasion shattered the old hierarchic and static social forms, and eroded social deference. All helped to destroy the guild system and pave the way for the emergence of an urban, mass society of wage earners.

Drafting men for militia duty, and enforcing the duty laws, severely upset Baltimore's social order. All able-bodied white male citizens eighteen years of age and older were members of the militia, regardless of social and economic distinctions among them. Before the war, enforcement of the militia laws was somewhat lax, and certain private-interest groups were generally able to circumvent the militia musters in one way or another. But during the wartime emergency, everyone from apprentices to merchants attended the militia musters—either voluntarily or under compulsion. And when they did attend, Baltimore's normal social life was virtually paralyzed.

A legal case that illustrates this upsetting of the traditional order was *Wells and Pocock* v. *Kennedy*, argued in the Baltimore County Court in August of 1813. David Wells and John Pocock were apprentices between eighteen and twenty-one years of age who did not appear at a militia muster on Monday, August 9, 1813. The captain of the company in which they were enrolled, John Kennedy, sent a detachment of men who forced Wells and Pocock to attend the muster. The masters of the apprentices applied to the county court to have their apprentices released on petitions of habeas corpus. Judge Theodorick Bland delivered his decision on August 16, and denied the petitions on the following grounds: (1) that the militia law did not excuse any white male citizens eighteen years of age and over who were apprentices; (2) that when the militia was called out, militia men were subject to the articles of war; and (3) that state law superseded the master's right to apprentices because the master's right stemmed from state law. After this decision the militia musters of 1813 and 1814 not only suspended Baltimore's normal social life, they accelerated the decline of the eighteenth-century guild system.[12]

This decision was merely one way in which wartime conditions dislocated Baltimore's social order. Another concerned the lucrative opportunities for privateering that the war afforded. Privateering, the capturing of enemy shipping by privately outfitted vessels sailing with the sanction of government, was a legal form of warfare until the 1820s when its abuses in connection with the Spanish-American rebellions made it synonymous with piracy. Baltimore was famous, and infamous, for its privateers. About 126 privately armed vessels were fitted out in Baltimore during the War of 1812, and they captured 556 British prizes. This was almost one third of the total of British prizes (1,634) taken by all American vessels, both naval and private, and almost half of the British prizes taken by all privately armed American vessels (1,380). The value of Baltimore's British prizes has been estimated at $16 million.[13]

Potentially, everyone made money in privateering. By United States law, prizes belonged to their captors, and a bounty of twenty dollars was paid by the federal government for men captured alive aboard an enemy ship of equal or greater size than the American privateer. This bounty was soon increased to one hundred dollars. The division of the sale prices of prizes between the owners of the vessel, its officers, and its crew varied from one privateer to another; but customarily, half of the profits from the sale of the prize goods went to the owners of the privateer, the other half to the officers and crew. Of this latter half, a privateer captain usually received twenty shares, his mates ten to fifteen shares, and ordinary seamen one share. For the sailor, privateering offered an opportunity to gain several months' pay in one voyage.[14]

But privateering was also lucrative in another way. These privately armed vessels continued to carry cargoes whose prices in foreign markets offered very high profits. And for the ordinary seaman, prize goods were not the only means of increasing one's income. Because of the danger involved in such cruises, seamen also received higher wages than they received during peacetime, ranging up to thirty dollars a month. This greatly increased the owner's expenses, because such privately armed vessels commonly carried crews ranging from a hundred to two hundred men, not all of whom were seamen. It was thus imperative that the vessel capture enemy shipping to pay its way.

The high wages of privateering, the opportunity of a share in British prizes, the promise of adventure, and the fact that one did not have to be an experienced seaman—all helped to destroy the formal guild structure as much as militia duty did during the war. Baltimore's newspapers carried many advertisements of master craftsmen warning the public of their runaway apprentices and especially cautioning sea captains not to ship such apprentices. Most of such advertisements were by Baltimore masters, though some came from Philadelphia and as far away as Bridgetown, New Jersey. Not only were apprentices running away, but apprentices and journeymen were in short supply. The Baltimore papers contained almost as many advertisements asking for laboring help as they did warning about runaway apprentices. And this shortage of labor also helped to precipitate the industrial revolution in Baltimore.[15]

The rising demand for labor stemmed from the profound change that the war triggered in Baltimore's manufacturing facilities. The war stimulated technological innovations far more than the commercial depression of 1807–12 did, and the social importance of these innovations was their introduction of manufacturing into the town from the countryside. Steam power freed manufacturers from the geographic necessity of locating plants at sources of water power. This movement departed from the paternal capitalism of the manufacturing enclaves outside the town and the high investment cost of the new steam technology forced manufacturers to specialize. The new steam-powered mills in town became separate and independent operations.[16]

Most of the men responsible for this technological change did not fit the economic historians' stereotype of unemployed shippers looking to invest their surplus capital. Almost all of them had long been connected with manufacturing in one way or another. Some, such as the McKims, had been interested in textile manufacturing as early as 1789 and had led the expansion of textile manufacturing following the Embargo of 1807. Others, such as Charles Gwinn, were merchant-millers, the social group that originated in Baltimore during the 1790s when foreign demand for flour eroded the demand for tobacco and wheat. Thus, men who had experience, capital, credit, and connections initiated the technological change, and thus contributed to the obscurity of its revolutionary social implications.

How these changes and their social implications were generally disregarded is best evidenced by what happened in Baltimore after news of peace reached the city on February 13, 1815. A sea of immigrants from many sections of the country, but mainly from the Northern cities and New England, flooded the city, and most of them thought Baltimore's prewar prosperity would pick up where it had left off. For the remainder of 1815 and into 1816, the revival of trade and the demand for skilled and unskilled labor of all types indicated Baltimore's future prosperity. Indeed, during these two years Baltimore boomed as did no other city in America except New York. New buildings went up, new, wide, and regular streets were laid out, and the city expanded in all directions. But the prosperity was commercial, not industrial.[17]

Commercial prosperity was not the only attraction of Baltimore for immigrants, however, for the city symbolized the heroic patriotism and the triumph of American Republicanism in the Second War for American Independence, just ended. Baltimore's Republicans had long and consistently advocated war against Great Britain or France or both as a matter of principle, not of expediency. They understood that Baltimore was a maritime community and that free trade was imperative to its continued existence. Baltimoreans had vociferously supported the war against the British because patriotism and their self-interest were one and the same. In turn, this was the reason (or so Americans believed) that the British attacked Baltimore after burning Washington in August of 1814; and when the Federalist-dominated Maryland legislature refused to vote financial aid to Republican Baltimore, Baltimoreans defended themselves. They authorized a municipal-bond issue of five hundred thousand dollars, borrowed eighty thousand dollars from the banks in the city, and allowed the banks to ship their specie out of the city into the interior and to circulate paper currency in denominations of one-, two-, and three-dollar bills. Everyone in Baltimore shared in the defense of his community, and the wonder was that Baltimore was the only American community which successfully resisted British bombardment. Out of the bombing and battles of September 12 and 13, 1814, "The Star-Spangled Banner" emerged to symbolize the community's, and eventually the nation's, Republican triumph; and for generations to come, September 12 was Baltimore's Fourth of July.

Baltimore's experience during the Second War for American Independence fittingly climaxed its longer development since the mid-eighteenth century, and it was ready to resume its progress in the nation. However, its growth into a mature, semiautonomous society had created a complex of cultural foundations that were responses to and products of the peculiar conditions of wartime prosperity. Though these conditions disappeared after 1815, the foundations continued to define and shape Baltimore's development. That they did so suggests how a society creates and preserves its own unities independent of changing circumstances.

PART TWO
Transitions, 1815–1843

Introduction to Part Two

It was not long after the war that Baltimore's meteoric growth and prosperity came to an abrupt end, replaced by a long, frustrating, and painful experience during the 1820s and 1830s. Probably no community in America emerged from the war with such high expectations, and then found itself enmeshed in new circumstances that denied their fulfillment. Almost perversely, the efforts of the Baltimoreans to overcome the new realities continued to direct their social economy and polity into new and unforeseen channels.

Yet, in reacting to these changes, Baltimoreans fashioned their political and social forms and standards into a new framework that created a new cultural plateau. Indeed, this period, especially the first ten years of it was a watershed in Baltimore's history. New men with different ideas, values, and ways of doing things came into power during the generation following the war, and created what would become the nineteenth-century sociopolitical framework for articulating community processes. True, this framework did not suddenly and fully redefine the life of the community—later generations would flesh it out—but the objective basis of such things as free public schooling, political democracy and its ideology, and a host of public-service organizations came into being. That they were statistically insignificant should not obscure their importance, for participants rarely anticipate the long-range impact of contemporary changes.

The new framework evolved as a process of cultural conservatism. Though they responded to their new situation both creatively and resourcefully, especially through their new industrial technology, Baltimoreans used the prewar institutions and cultural processes that had worked so well, and to which the new technology was now subordinated. Instead of abandoning the cultural structure they had created during more prosperous times, they now applied it in modified forms to their new realities. Baltimore's transformation thus originated with two social groups: those who tried to preserve a former way of life, and those who responded directly to the prevailing conditions. Somewhat ironically, the latter group initiated the changes but the former succeeded in implementing them; in the process, the emerging sharp divisions and cultural contradictions revealed the necessities and uses of institutions to the community as never before.

CHAPTER IV

Economic Crisis and New Directions, 1815–1831

Baltimore's circumstances changed dramatically during the generation that followed the War of 1812. The prosperity from the wars of the French Revolution suddenly vanished, reducing the city's economic capacity and forcing changes in its life style. Baltimore's maritime trade plummeted as West European nations restored their prerevolutionary mercantile systems; business activity and prices declined; and the community experienced several financial panics amidst the long depression. In particular, the events surrounding the panic of 1819 symbolized the end of one age and the beginning of another; never again would Baltimoreans know the world as it had been during the wars of the French Revolution.

Searching desperately for ways to restore their prosperity, the city's commercial leaders boldly changed economic directions. Reasoning that a greater diversity of exports would restore their overseas trade, they expanded their export base by tapping the surrounding countryside through internal improvements. Unfortunately, they understood neither the complexity of their situation nor what internal improvements, especially steam-powered transportation, would do to their social economy; thus all their efforts accomplished was to hasten the breakdown of the old order. As events proved, nothing they did, or even could have done, restored their prosperity.

The New Business Conditions

Three general problems confronted the maritime economy of the United States when peace arrived in 1815: the exclusion of American shipping from the British colonial trade, a devastating competition in the general carrying trade by European competitors now at peace, and the glutting of American markets with European manufactured goods that had been inventoried during the war. These problems persisted in varying degrees throughout the period from 1815 to 1831, and the solutions that were proposed tended to compound rather than solve them. The British colonial trade, for example, was opened, then closed, then opened, then closed again in a series of negotiated but temporary settlements. The American government tried dealing with European shipping competition through a series of commercial reciprocity agreements. But while they aided the movement of American produce, they were actually prejudicial to American shipping interests and helped to further the decline of the American carrying trade. Finally, a series of tariffs and alterations in the international marketing structure eventually halved the amount of European manufactured goods dumped in American markets, but at the cost of provoking a severe ideological split within the community.[1]

In Baltimore, these adverse general conditions were aggravated by others, that were peculiar to the city, or nearly so. Of these, the most important was Baltimore's virtual dependence on its ties to the West Indies trade, which were closer than those of any other major seaport; and that trade, though vacillating from year to year, never fully recovered after the war. Three other postwar developments were immediately felt in the other Atlantic seaports but not so intensely as in Baltimore: the breakdowns of the national marketing system and the international marketing structure, and the infection of the banking system with corruption and mismanagement.[2]

The collapse of the marketing system within the United States stemmed from a fluky cash-flow crisis. When news of the war's end reached Baltimore in February 1815, Westerners in Baltimore's hinterland were caught with an expanded currency system and high commodity prices. One month later, they were confronted by lowered commodity prices and a declining acceptance of their currency in the Eastern seaport where their purchases were made. In October 1815, all Baltimore banks refused to accept what they termed "foreign paper," the notes of the country banks. Nevertheless, Baltimore's merchants who traded with the West continued to accept country bank paper from their country merchant customers. But after three years of accepting nonnegotiable country bank paper, the merchants were also forced to act in unison and to refuse acceptance of this currency.[3]

By early 1819, then, Baltimore merchants were refusing to sell to country merchants until the country merchants paid their debts. But payment was impossible, for country merchants found their Western bank notes unacceptable and Baltimore merchants were unwilling to accept Western produce because of its rapidly declining market price. Baltimore's merchants, in turn, were holding large quantities of Western paper, which the Baltimore banks would not accept, and had no way of receiving from their Western debtors income sufficient to pay their own debts.

The breakdown of the international marketing structure occurred independently of the collapse of the domestic relationship between country buyer and seaport seller, though the two developments interacted. Beginning with the spring trade in 1816, British and German manufacturers and merchants sent progressively heavier consignments of unordered goods, especially textiles and earthenware, to Baltimore importers. The importers paid the customary nine months' credit on the goods they did not return to their suppliers, but by 1818 they were returning many more of the unordered goods than they were accepting. Faced with lowering prices in an oversupplied market, Baltimore's importers extended their credits to their country merchant buyers beyond the customary twelve months to eighteen and even twenty-four months. By the fall of 1818, unless the importer was extremely prudent in his sales—in effect, making none—he found himself caught in the liquidity crisis of having to pay his suppliers, but without collections receivable for several months. To the importer, the depression of 1819 was due to the disequilibrium of the financial system. Forced to sell his goods to country merchants whose bank notes were almost worthless, he reverted to a credit system. Having no specie, the country buyer could pay only in Western commodities; but their value diminished from 1816 to 1819. So the country buyer agreed to pay for his goods at a future date, hoping for a rise in the value of Western commodities, but helplessly watching their prices diminish. Credits to the country buyer became longer as increased volumes of commodities were needed to cover losses due to their declining prices. The country buyer was helpless, as was his seaboard supplier, the Baltimore importer. Both were victims of the cash-flow problem.[4]

Compounding both marketing problems was the banking system—or the lack of one. From 1815 to 1819 the Baltimore banks were in a wretched condition. They could not aid the importer by giving him temporary loans to cover his payments until his collections were made, because their officers were involved in other matters. In 1815 nine banks with a paid-in capital totaling $6,503,685 were operating in the city. Their specie holdings cannot be ascertained, but from contemporaries' comments, Baltimore apparently had very little in comparison with Philadelphia and New York. The specie that was received in Baltimore from 1815 to 1819 came largely from the South American trade, and most of it was drained off by New York and Philadelphia banks drafting upon Baltimore's banks. From New York and Philadelphia, the specie went into the East Indies trade and to Great Britain to pay for the importations inundating American seaports.[5]

In theory and practice, Baltimore's bankers generally followed Philadelphia's bankers. Theoretically, bankers aided the merchants by creating bank credits through accommodations and discounts. Since banking was primarily a function of the credit system rather than the monetary sys-

TABLE 4
Yearly Changes of Circulation
and Deposits in Baltimore Banks,
1817–1830 (by percentage)

Year	Circulation Increase (Decrease)	Deposits Increase (Decrease)	Total Circulation Increase (Decrease)	Percentage of Circulation to Total Circulation Plus Deposits	Percentage of Deposits to Total Circulation Plus Deposits
1817				56	44
1818	(36)	(20)	(29)	51	49
1819	(5)	(26)	(15)	57	43
1820	(26)	(2)	(16)	50	50
1821	(17)	13	(2)	42	58
1822	19	11	14	44	56
1823	(15)	(18)	(17)	45	55
1824	8	14	11	44	56
1825	38	10	15	52	48
1826	(1)	(3)	4	50	50
1827	(11)	7	(2)	45	55
1828	(6)	6	1	42	58
1829	12	(5)	2	47	53
1830	(9)	(17)	(13)	49	51

SOURCE: Bryan, *History of State Banking in Maryland*, p. 137.

tem, the issuing of bank notes frequently had little to do with monetary policies. From 1817 to 1821, as Table 4 illustrates, the Baltimore banks apparently lost specie, lost deposits, curtailed credit, and reduced the number of outstanding bank notes as loans were paid off and not renewed. To Baltimore's general mercantile community this meant both less credit and less money.

Next to the creation of the second Bank of the United States, the resumption of specie payments was the major banking issue in the immediate postwar years. Prior to the opening of the national bank early in 1817, Baltimore bankers did not favor resumption, or even modified resumption such as proposed by Secretary of the Treasury Alexander James Dallas in July 1816. The bankers argued that the general scarcity of specie in Baltimore and the constant demand for it from Philadelphia and New York were reasons why resumption was impractical at that time. Nevertheless, the resumption of specie payments on February 20, 1817, forced by the beginning operations of the national bank, really imposed no strain upon Baltimore banks until July 1817, when demands for specie from them were intensified by the national bank. Baltimore banks were then forced to restrict drastically their credit facilities by reducing their discounts and accommodation paper. In August 1817, the banks uniformly refused to discount the paper of the auctioneers in the city (who were doing the heaviest importing business); and in the following month, the Baltimore branch of the national bank stopped issuing drafts to Eastern banks (especially those in New York) who were drafting specie from Baltimore. This situation worsened until the spring of 1819, when the gross abuses within the national-bank branch in Baltimore became known and precipitated a general collapse in May 1819.[6]

The abuses and frauds of the officers and several directors of the national-bank branch in Baltimore were rumored, investigated, and somewhat substantiated from February through May 1819. More than any other single factor, the financial collapse, on May 20, 21, and 22, of the "Club" of speculators who were officers of the branch triggered the depression of 1819 in Baltimore. News of banking and mercantile failures elsewhere in the nation did not reach Baltimore until June 21, when the Baltimoreans learned that their problem was part of a more general one.[7]

The activities of this "Club" of speculators had begun with the initial organization of the national bank in 1816 and early 1817; its purpose, aside from speculations in the bank's stock, was to dominate the institution. The members of the "Club" were some of the most active, influential, and wealthy merchants of Baltimore; and they were connected with the Smith faction. James A. Buchanan, partner and first cousin of Samuel Smith in one of the largest mercantile firms in the United States, Smith and Buchanan, probably directed the "Club's" operations. Nationally known to merchants and politicians, he had been nominated by John Jacob Astor for the presidency of the national bank; and after William Jones was appointed president, Buchanan occasionally wrote to Jones with suggestions about bank policies. Given his national connections and his standing in the community, it was only natural that Buchanan became president of the national-bank branch in Baltimore.[8]

The cashier of the branch was James William McCulloh of *McCulloch v. Maryland* fame (which decision was given by Chief Justice Marshall in

March 1819). Born in Philadelphia and educated in George Williams's countinghouse, he was twenty-seven-years old in 1819. His later career as banker, lawyer, speaker of the House of Delegates in the Maryland legislature, land speculator in association with Duff Green, and first comptroller in the United States Treasury Department testifies at least to his energy and precocity. He, too, wrote President Jones letters suggesting national-bank policies, usually in a manner redolent of Buchanan's letters. A clique of Massachusetts brothers and their Rhode Island cousin were also members of the "Club"; George, Amos A., and Cumberland Dugan Williams, together with their cousin Nathaniel Williams, participated in the stock speculations from the very beginning, as did two other merchants, Lemuel Taylor and Dennis A. Smith (no relation to Samuel). Not limiting themselves to financing their stock purchases by using the very stock as collateral security, the "Club" members soon used their credit at the bank without any collateral security. From these practices, financial irregularity became fraud as the "Club" began using bank credit and money as their own to finance their private, individual mercantile operations. The accounts of the branch were increasingly confused by this blending of private with public enterprise; and during 1818 bank-stock prices began declining in relation to the developing depression and because of public rumors about the speculators.

In addition to this financial pressure, the change in management and policies under the new president of the Bank of the United States, Langdon Cheves, who replaced William Jones in January 1819, brought new pressure to bear against the "Club." Cheves's more prudent policies affected Baltimore in February as the parent bank demanded specie from the branch and, in turn, the branch had to demand specie from the other banks in Baltimore. Of course, this produced a crisis among the banks, because the public was also demanding specie by presenting their bank notes for redemption in specie.

On February 24, the Maryland legislature tried to improve conditions by prohibiting bank officers from trading in notes of Maryland banks for less than their denominational value, and prohibiting banks from redeeming for specie those notes presented by money brokers. But these laws neither prevented the continued drain of specie nor the contraction of deposits and credit among the Baltimore banks. Failures among merchants began in March, increased in April, and peaked in May. In this last month the City Bank failed and the Union Bank of Maryland almost failed, because their cashiers, James Sterett and Ralph Higginbotham, respectively, were using their bank's funds to speculate in the stock of the national bank for their own accounts. The actual money loss of these three banks was estimated at $806,548. There is no way of knowing the exact amount of specie lost, if any really was, and there is no way of ascertaining the exact credit losses (debts outstanding) to the banks. In any event, the panic of 1819 in Baltimore had begun.[9]

By July about one hundred of Baltimore's most prominent merchants had failed, including Samuel Smith, Baltimore's most famous Republican, and many of his connections. These failures and the rumors of the fraudulent and immoral conduct of the merchants, especially those connected with the branch Bank of the United States, the City Bank, and the Union Bank of Maryland, blackened Baltimore's national reputation for years to come. "No city perhaps rose faster than this and it is to be hoped none did or ever will go down faster than it has done," wrote one of Baltimore's surviving merchants to his partner, who was visiting Boston in June 1819. But the classic expression of outraged morality came from a Bostonian, John Quincy Adams, long an enemy of Samuel Smith:

> The moral, political, and commercial character of this city of Baltimore has for twenty-five years been formed, controlled, and modified almost entirely by this house of Smith and Buchanan, their connections and dependents. It may be added that there is not a city in the Union which has had so much apparent prosperity, or within which there has been such complication of profligacy.

Baltimore's reputation in the nation was never the same after the crisis in mid-1819, which marked a turning point in the city's history. The eighteenth century was over. The grand style of Baltimore's eighteenth-century merchant aristocracy came to an end, and the very promise of Baltimore seemed to founder. For Baltimoreans, the world to come would be very different from the one they had known.[10]

As a first step, now that it was too late, several changes were made in business institutions and practices. Given high priority was an overhaul of bankruptcy procedures. Under existing state laws, enacted in 1805 and 1806, Baltimore applicants for bankruptcy were required to have resided in Maryland for two years and to have the prior assent of two-thirds of their creditors. They were to appear before the Baltimore County Court with a list of their property; the court publicized the application and set a court date when creditors and the debtor were to appear; on that date a trustee for the debtor's property was appointed. The court retained, however, the right to limit the time for creditors to appear and to examine their claims. By 1816, bankruptcy applicants were so numerous that they filled the docket of the county court, and procedures had become more complicated because of the unsettled postwar conditions. A state law of that year alleviated those conditions by providing for the appointment of three commissioners for Baltimore County who were responsible for the procedures, but who reported their findings to the clerk of the county court. After the panic of 1819, the commissioners handled increasing numbers of bankruptcy cases, and they found their powers progressively enlarged by state laws from 1819 through 1822.[11]

Changes in banking procedures were also forthcoming, and these involved major social readjustments. The banking failures of 1819 had been more than mere failures in the financial mechanism of the community. In the context of a personal social economy they were breaches of faith and trust and, as such, they tore at Baltimore's very social fabric. Specifically, the malpractices at the City Bank, the Union Bank, and the branch Bank of the United States had been possible because their officers had been trusted to operate the banks independently of their boards of directors. After May 1819, bank officers were entrusted only with responsibility for the routine affairs of their offices; all policy decisions were made by directors or committees of directors appointed to fulfill particular functions.

Another and more important alteration in banking procedures changed the credit, and therefore the social, system. Prior to the war new credit and extensions of old were granted by the addition of endorsers (cosigners) to the debtor's note. During 1819 this policy was gradually abandoned, and the debtor was required to pledge collateral (that is, some form of property) instead of adding endorsers to his loan application. This was a fundamental alteration of the nature of credit, epitomizing the way the panic of 1819 affected the social basis of financial relationships. The failures of 1819 were moral failures of men; and in a society of disintegrating landmarks of trust, where failures had become so widespread that creditors did not know whom to trust, the substitution of property for men as collateral for loans seemed justified. But the long-run implications of this change of credit policy were vast, and not the least of the implications was to bring banking itself into disrepute. Property was, of course, a central value of society at large; but as the panic of 1819 slid into the depression of the twenties, the banks found themselves holding an increasing amount of property. Understandably, this focused public attacks against them, and especially against the second Bank of the United States, which initiated the change for this reason and another to be mentioned.[12]

Even more important changes in American society in general and in Baltimore in particular arose from new functions introduced by the second Bank of the United States in 1819. In fact, these new functions circumscribed Baltimore's position in the nation during the 1820s and 1830s, and helped to define certain historical trends, which then continued throughout the remainder of the antebellum period.

The second Bank of the United States, under the administration of Langdon Cheves and especially Nicholas Biddle, served as the vehicle for the first pervasive monetization of credit in American society during the 1820; in this role the bank acted as a democratizing influence in American society. When discussing the initial organization and operations of the bank from 1817 to about 1823, historians have usually focused upon the economic problems of the bank in conjunction with the depression and have disregarded the more fundamental social effects of the bank's operations. These effects completely altered the national marketing structure, especially the traditional relations between country and city merchants. Establishing branch banks in Western communities standardized domestic exchange markets and provided a nationally accepted currency for the country merchants to use on their buying trips to the seaports. For example, the country merchant now exchanged his country bank notes for Bank of the United States notes, at par value, in one of the Western branches and brought the Bank of the United States notes with him to the Atlantic seaboard, using them to purchase his goods. He now was freed from the older credit system that had restricted him in his purchases to those who would sell to him (that is, advance him credit) by taking the chance of accepting country bank notes at a large discount. Now, with the Bank of the United States in operation, even if the country merchant did not begin with cash but with credit, he could use the credit of the Bank of the United States on his buying trips and thus extract himself from dependency for credit upon the seaport merchants.[13]

The operations of the Bank of the United States thus changed the nature of the seaport markets. Under the old credit system, the country merchant had faced a sellers' market in the seaports, which dictated the kinds of goods, their prices, and the credit facilities available. The new system democratized the seaport markets by effecting a shift to a buyers' market and money system. The country merchant was now more free to purchase to his best advantage. He was no longer restricted to a particular seller; no longer required to take older, out-of-date, or unfashionable goods; and, most importantly for Baltimore, he was no longer restricted to a particular selling market. Money made the country merchant mobile. If goods were cheaper, newer, more abundant, and in greater variety in New York or Philadelphia because of their direct and cheaper connection with Liverpool, then the country merchant was more likely to purchase in those markets (providing that what he saved on price offset his greater transportation costs) than in Baltimore. This monetization of the American national marketing structure coincided with developments in the international marketing structure, with internal improvements, and with the long downward trend of the maritime economy during the 1820s to bend the dispersed, localized market economies in the direction of a national, even international, market economy.[14]

Accompanying this transformation was the substitution of a price system for lines of credit. With the country merchants bringing money, dictating the kinds of goods they wanted and what prices they would pay, and suggesting what credit period they wanted, pricing rather than credit became central to the new national marketing structure. The lowest price, not the longest credit, came to be the major consideration among the selling merchants. And what of Baltimore's importers whose prices were necessarily higher than those in New York or Philadelphia? By the mid-1820s it was perfectly clear that Baltimore had to use its closer proximity to the West to offset its greater distance from Europe than either of these two cities. For this reason, Baltimore's entrepreneurs launched one of the most daring and imaginative projects of the day: an effort to connect Baltimore with the upper Ohio-Mississippi Valley by a railroad.[15]

Several other important changes occurred simultaneously. The most important was the change within the international marketing structure. Until 1819, this structure itself had actually contributed as much to the oversupply of British goods in Baltimore as the finance of marketing had. British manufacturers and merchants usually shipped goods on consignment without orders from Baltimore's merchants. Unless the merchants returned the goods, which they increasingly did as business conditions worsened, they glutted an already oversupplied market. The British manufacturers and merchants simply misunderstood the conditions of Baltimore's selling market. They thought Baltimore's merchants still sold "by the advance," that is, by a percentage markup, which could be reduced to make the goods a more attractive purchase to the country merchants. For this reason, the British suppliers priced the cost of their goods at an inflated value that included all of their costs as well as profit. As a result, Baltimore's merchants were forced to pay higher import duties, because the cost of the goods, to them, was high. Even more importantly, from 1815 to 1820, Baltimore's merchants were finding the country merchants less interested in the price of the goods than in the length of credits offered. Of course, the country merchants were interested in the lowest price at which they could buy; but these prices varied according to the length of credit granted; and credit, more than price, was the main concern of the country merchant before the second Bank of the United States changed the national marketing structure. Faced with the shift after 1820 from a credit and a sellers' to a money and buyers' market, Baltimore's merchants argued that their British suppliers should invoice their goods at their lowest cost and not record the expected percentage profit. This would reduce the customs duties Baltimore's merchants would have to pay, would allow them to sell on a "lowest-price" basis, and would allow them to better regulate credit terms. In short, the Baltimore merchants would be in better control of their market. Gradually, this type of international marketing structure did evolve during the 1820s, for it conformed much better to the new cash method of business relations in Baltimore's selling markets.[16]

The effect of the new cash method of enterprise on businessmen depended upon general business conditions and upon each businessman's position in the marketplace. In general, the postwar period witnessed both a maritime depression and a long deflation, when investments in land, whether for speculation or for agricultural production, were very unpromising. Throughout the 1820s, agricultural prices maintained relatively low levels, because the foreign demand for flour and wheat dwindled with the return of peace to Europe. Consequently, trade and the profits from trade declined. Credit contracted. For example, whereas nine banks had been chartered in Baltimore during its prosperous "Golden Age" from 1790 to 1813, not one was created during the entire generation from 1813 to 1834. Such a financial contraction, coupled with the changing structure of the markets, necessitated still further changes in the rules for conducting business activity.

Many merchants adapted to the new conditions with varying degrees of success: the Brunes, John Donnell, the Gilmors, the Hoffmans, the Olivers, the Pattersons, and the Wilsons. But in the group who failed in 1819 were many of the men who had helped to build Baltimore—Hugh Boyle, James A. Buchanan, James Calhoun, John D'Arcy, Christopher Deshon, Henry Didier, George Grundy, John Hollins, Joseph Karrick, Aaron and John Levering, Michael McBlair, Leonard Matthews, Thomas Moreau, Thomas Sheppard, Samuel Smith, Lemuel Taylor, and the Williamses, to name the more prominent ones. Shippers, privateers, and their suppliers, these men were daring, imaginative, and speculative. After 1819 most of them continued to engage in trade on a smaller scale, a few moved to other cities or even to other countries, and several went into a new, rather speculative venture, but one which after 1820 seemed increasingly profitable: textile manufacturing. In this way, the panic of 1819 and subsequent depression stimulated several traders (Buchanan, Calhoun, Hollins, Levering, Matthews, McBlair, and the

Williamses from the above group, for example) to invest their capitals and energies in manufacturing.[17]

Most merchants remained in trade, however, and their ability to adapt to their changing economic conditions was amazing. After the initial impact of the postwar contraction, the slowly worsening conditions struck the merchants selectively, depending upon their individual functions and proximity to the marketplace. In the movement of commodities from a buyers' to a seller's market, for instance, importers and shippers shared an ability to shield themselves from depressed market conditions: the importer by conducting a commission business instead of operating on his own account, and the shipper by shipping for freight instead of on his own account. Among both groups, of course, those who were irregular or marginal traders were most vulnerable during shrinkages of the volume of trade and were the first to suspend operations when conditions worsened. Those who sacrificed large profits for regularity and frequency in the markets usually endured the sudden contractions.

Manufacturers and exporters, in the nature of things, were less flexible than importers and shippers. That is to say, because they were involved in producing goods for sale or buying them for resale, they were inescapably bound to the market. Thus, whereas importers and shippers could abstract themselves from the market during depressed times, manufacturers and exporters had little choice but to curtail production or stop buying. The differences and antagonisms between these two pairs of groups were gradually clarified during the 1820s, as their respective interests clashed over the tariff issues.

Finance also determined the impact of the depression upon businessmen. Businessmen who profited from the depression were those who thought in terms of financial operations rather than the simple flow in volume of commodities. Some businessmen were learning, for example, that high buying prices in one market and low selling prices in another could be offset by any one or a combination of several items. The granting of longer credits was the most obvious and most resorted to by the majority of the merchants, but fluctuating exchange rates were also used to reduce costs. However, the operations of the second Bank of the United States stabilized domestic exchange markets and, to a certain extent, foreign-exchange rates.[18]

Indeed, the operations of the second Bank of the United States had an ironic effect upon Baltimore. True, the bank was an important feature of the paternal nationalism that characterized the 1820s and its operations benefited the nation as a whole, but it simultaneously hurt the city. The bank's operations prevented the noninnovative among Baltimore's old guard from adjusting their financial relationships to their markets. And worse yet, these operations upset conventional wisdom regarding such things as inventory accumulation, marketing costs, and even pricing—in short, general business strategy. No wonder they came to hate it.

Metropolitanism Begins: From Overseas to Overland

Eventually, Baltimore's old guard would strike out against the institutions of paternal nationalism, but the city's new circumstances drew their immediate attention to more tangible problems. And here the results were mixed. Baltimore was farther from Europe than the other leading seaports; consequently, goods arrived later and freight rates and prices were higher than in the other cities. Baltimore's development of overseas markets, especially in the West Indies during the midst of war, had overridden this disadvantage in the past; but now, in peacetime, these foreign markets vanished, and country buyers abandoned Baltimore for the lower-priced New York and Philadelphia markets. As a result, Baltimore's maritime economy stagnated between 1821 and 1828. In five of those eight years the balance of trade ran against the city, and, for the period as a whole, the excess value of imports over exports amounted to almost one and a half million dollars. Financial failures occurred every year. Baltimore's share of all United States exports fluctuated, remaining about the same or declining a little. Also, the city's share of all imports into the United States remained about the same, and its share of all American registered tonnage (foreign trade) declined almost in proportion to its declining share of the value of American exports. Baltimore's importers could not afford to speculate under such conditions, but were forced to decrease or even to eliminate their marginally profitable trade across the Atlantic. Thus the depression of the twenties affected Baltimore more adversely than it affected Philadelphia or New York, and did so in two ways. On the macrolevel, the general deflation operated to stagnate Baltimore's economy relative to the other seaport economies. On the microlevel, the depression resulted in lowered prices, inactive trade, and curtailed capital and credit, all of which impeded the expansion and proliferation of Baltimore's economy into the interior.[19]

Nevertheless the Baltimoreans *believed* that they could solve their problem through metropolitanism. They hoped that the extension of the city into the countryside through internal improvements would increase Baltimore's export base in general, and might develop an export for Liverpool, the center of world industrialization, in particular. New York and Philadelphia had already established regular packet-line connections with Liverpool, but Baltimore was ill-equipped to follow their lead. The Baltimoreans had largely abandoned the English trade during the 1790s, and because Liverpool had never been much of a market for Chesapeake produce, their trade with that port was irregular and small. Accordingly, given the deflated conditions of the 1820s, they had little choice but to pin their hopes upon expanding their market contacts with the interior.

Indeed, it made the most sense economically, for Baltimore lay 150 miles closer to the trans-Allegheny West than Philadelphia and 200 miles closer than New York. Potentially, Baltimore's advantageous location for the interior trade would overcome its disadvantageous location in the transatlantic trade. Unfortunately, however, metropolitanism remained conditioned by geography and had not yet become merely a function of technology. In addition, both a shortage of capital and the animosity of the state legislature plagued the Baltimoreans. But geography was the chief impediment, for Baltimore faced the formidable task of bridging an elevation of 2,754 feet across the Alleghenies, while New York's Erie Canal was to overcome a mere 578 feet and Philadelphia's greater capital and resources eventually allowed that community to overcome an elevation of more than 3,000 feet. In the 1820s, when internal improvements meant roads, canals, and unsophisticated railroads, Baltimore was clearly at a disadvantage and was not able to exploit its closer proximity to Western markets.[20]

In these circumstances, Baltimore concentrated upon expanding its market economy on a more limited scale. Four turnpikes had been built in 1796, 1806, 1812, and 1818 to connect Baltimore with Washington, D.C., about forty miles to the southwest; a canal connecting the two cities was begun in 1818; and the Baltimore & Washington Railroad was chartered in 1829. But Baltimoreans directed their major efforts to linking their city with two more important, agriculturally valuable sections: the Susquehanna Valley area in Pennsylvania, almost due north of Baltimore, and the rich wheat land area of western Maryland.[21]

Baltimore's connection with the Susquehanna River Valley was an easy route, since the mouth of the river was a mere forty miles northeast of Baltimore at the head of the Chesapeake Bay. Beginning in New York and meandering almost due south through Pennsylvania, the Susquehanna flows through a varied terrain and some of the richest farmland in Pennsylvania. The river's importance was that Pennsylvania goods were carried into Maryland on it—which gave Maryland the benefits of Pennsylvania produce, though the political relations of Pennsylvania and Maryland were marred. It was natural that Baltimore tried to become the terminus of the Susquehanna River trade by canals in 1783 and 1826, by turnpikes in 1798, 1805, 1814, and 1816, and by railroad when the Baltimore & Susquehanna Railroad was chartered in 1828. In this process, communities along these routes, such as Havre de Grace, Port Deposit, Conowingo, and Castleton, became dependent upon the Susquehanna trade and thereby economic satellites of Baltimore.[22]

Equally important to Baltimore, and in the long run even more so, was the trade of western Maryland. Tapping the rich wheat lands of Carroll, Frederick, and Washington counties became increasingly important as those areas were settled by immigrants passing westward through Baltimore, by Pennsylvanians descending the rivers into Maryland, and by others from the South who followed the Potomac River northward. Unlike that of the Susquehanna River area in Pennsylvania, the western-Maryland trade was more amenable to Baltimore influence through the state legislature. In addition to the National Road, a total of seven other turnpikes were built from Baltimore into western Maryland in 1798, 1805, 1814, and 1816; and in 1828 the Baltimore & Westminster Railroad was chartered. Here, too, the towns that sprang up as collection and transshipment centers for agricultural produce destined for the seaboard—Frederick, Libertytown, Reisterstown, and Westminster—came into the greater marketing orbit of their seaport terminus, Baltimore.[23]

The most dramatic effort to reach into the Western interior, and the one on which Baltimoreans pinned most of their hopes, was the Baltimore & Ohio Railroad. Like several other efforts, it grew out of the crisis in Baltimore's social economy precipitated by New York's prospects in connection with its Erie Canal. So many merchants closed their shops and moved to New York that Baltimore's newspapers remarked about a prevailing "gone-to-New-York" spirit among its businessmen; and every Baltimorean looked to the railroad to rescue their community's stagnant economy. Chartered as a private corporation by state law in 1827, and financed largely by private subscriptions (though the municipality also subscribed), the Baltimore & Ohio Railroad reflected the entrepreneurial spirit of Baltimoreans in the midst of adversity. Progress was slow and expensive, however, and burdened with social and political problems. The road reached the Potomac River, almost due west of Baltimore, where construction stopped in 1832 because of five circumstances: its limited capital resources, the unsophisticated technology confronting a formidable geographic terrain, the animosity of the state legislature, the withdrawal of federal government aid, and opposition by the backers of the Chesapeake and Ohio Canal. This ended the first phase of the road, its phase as the effort of the Baltimoreans in their private capacities to tap the Western markets.[24]

These new transportation arteries expanded Baltimore's economy not only in scale but also in quality. By the late 1820s, both western Maryland and the Susquehanna Valley were becoming as important for minerals as for their agricultural produce. Bituminous coal and iron ore had long been mined in both areas, but Baltimore's demand for these two products substantially increased during the 1820s. The application of steam power to manufacturing and transportation in and around Baltimore spurred the local demand for coal and iron, of course, but industrialization in other areas, especially around Philadelphia, New York, and Norfolk, increased the demand for this coal and iron ore even more. As a result, Baltimore became a transshipment center for these minerals as well as for the agricultural produce of western Maryland and the Susquehanna Valley. By 1830 Baltimoreans had formed three mining and three steamboat companies to facilitate this new and growing trade.[25]

By the end of the twenties, the central importance of industrialization to metropolitanism was clear, and commercial men now recognized that steam power was necessary to expand their markets. In Baltimore, at least, this insured the successful adaptation of the new technology to the new peacetime conditions, because the commercial interest did not uniformly oppose industrialization. Moreover, as this link was forged during the decade, commercial men came to realize how the application of steam power to processing and producing facilities could aid their "transportation revolution." And therein lay the most potent reason for the success of industrialization, for once they were committed to the principle of steam power, opposition to its specific applications could never really succeed.

But the successful linkage of industrialization to metropolitanism was, from the commercial men's point of view, a victorious battle in a lost war. That is, in comparison with New York or Philadelphia, the expansion of Baltimore into the interior was relatively small and failed to achieve its purpose of expanding Baltimore's foreign trade and establishing a connection with Liverpool. In addition to its other disadvantages in competition with New York and Philadelphia, Baltimore was plagued by the inability to compete with them in reexporting cotton to Liverpool, which was one trade that remained lucrative throughout the period. Profits in that trade were a function of shipping costs and exchange rates, rather than of simple price differentials between the American and English markets, and Baltimore's extra distance from Europe and relatively limited capital were too much to overcome. Consequently, Liverpool— the single most important source of capital, credit, information, new ideas, and trade for American seaports in the antebellum period—was less accessible to Baltimore than to New York and Philadelphia. Moreover, by missing out on this Liverpool connection, Baltimore lacked the crucial source of imports with which to expand its export base; and without a competitively expanding export base, Baltimore could not hope to even maintain its place in the race for metropolitan leadership against New York and Philadelphia.[26]

Manufacturing and a Home Market

The application of steam power to processing and producing facilities had neither the significance nor the success that it had with transportation facilities. Baltimore did not become an industrial economy during the 1820s, partly because industrializing production was of less importance than industrializing commerce, and partly because the depression prevented steam-powered manufacturing from expanding beyond its foundations established during the War of 1812. Not until 1829, when Charles Crook, Jr., began operating the Baltimore City Cotton Factory with about two hundred employees, did industrial manufacturing make much of a social impact upon Baltimore. Throughout the twenties, then, the wide array of consumer goods continued to be produced in the small shops of handicraft producers much as they had been in the eighteenth century.

Nevertheless, industrialization introduced qualitative changes in Baltimore's economy. The most apparent, because it was so different, was the founding of Baltimore's first technological "base" for the emerging new metals industry. By the early 1830s, two chemical factories, three copper factories, two iron-rolling mills, and three steam-engine establishments were in operation. Though virtually nothing is known about the inventors, Baltimoreans did patent several industrial innovations between 1815 and 1830, a number of which served as the basis for these new firms. George and Evan J. Ellicott, for example, patented processes for rolling bar iron and for making iron plates and sheets; William Howard for a locomotive engine; Elisha Bigelow, William Church, and Junia Curtis for steam engines; John Barker, Anthony Hermange, and Royal Yeaman for different types of steam boilers; and Henry B. Chew, E. V. Freeman, and Isaac Tyson for processing different kinds of ores using different chemicals. From the beginning of Baltimore's new metals industry, technological innovation spurred business enterprise.[27]

Another more oblique, qualitative change was the rise of an urban cottage weaving industry. Actually, this development occurred because of rural-urban differences in the textile industry in and around Baltimore. Almost all the big textile operations were located in the countryside around the town; the only in-town exception was the Baltimore Steam Works Factory, built by Robert and Alexander McKim in 1814, which employed seven men, twelve women, and fifty girls from eight to thirteen years of age in 1820. All manufacturers, whether spinners or weavers and whether industrialized or not, generally benefited from the protective tariffs of 1816, 1824, and 1828, but their inferior technology as well as the demand for better quality woven goods created the cottage industry within Baltimore. Specifically, eight master weavers came to Baltimore during the 1820s and began calling themselves "domestic manufacturers," "manufacturers of domestic goods," and "cotton manufacturers," and employed individual journeymen and women to weave yarn into cloth. Some of the masters paid their weavers cash wages, but the common arrangement was to pay them partly in cash and partly in credit from the master's general-merchandise store. The new importance of this cottage industry can be gauged from the fact that the number of weavers, who had included only 1 in 1799 and 11 in 1810, suddenly ballooned from 17 in 1819 to 101 in 1829.[28]

Such economic diversification undoubtedly provided much of the sustenance for the city's continued population growth during the otherwise depressed 1820s. Indeed, the population increase of 17,882—from 62,738 in 1820 to 80,620 in 1830, an increase that was, itself, larger than most American cities at the time—wrought perhaps the most significant economic change of all, for so complex and specialized did Baltimore's social economy become that the city became an economy itself: a domestic economy of consumer goods and services furnished to an ever-expanding population.

Producers played the important role in this change and fashioned a "home-market" ideology for it. Essentially, Baltimore's small-shop, handicraft producers of such things as furniture, leather goods, and various articles of clothing—master craftsmen employing two to ten journeymen and apprentices—aped the style and accepted the arguments of the large-scale and industrialized manufacturers in favor of protective tariffs. Growing in numbers and diversity of specialities throughout the twenties, the small-scale, handicraft shop continued as Baltimore's basic unit of production, but now it was called a "manufactory" and the master styled himself a "manufacturer." The masters also associated with the large-scale manufacturers in such associations as the American Society for the Promotion of National Industry (founded in 1819) and the Maryland Association for the Encouragement of American Manufacturing and Domestic Economy (also founded in 1819), which publicized the notion of domestic economy and its protectionist ideology among all types of producers, a notion that pervades the manufacturing census of 1820. Most manufacturers—whether industrialized or handicraft, employers of hundreds or just two—used this census to lay their individual problems at the feet of cheap foreign competition and to claim that only the national government could alleviate their plight by increasing tariff protection. The master craftsmen turned "manufacturer" thus sharply identified his interest in the domestic economy and distinguished it from that of commercial men.[29]

At the same time that Baltimore's eighteenth-century master craftsmen began to think of themselves as nineteenth-century manufacturers, a huge foreign immigration expanded the kinds and qualities of consumer goods and services. Occupational diversity proliferated as more than ten thousand immigrants landed in Baltimore during the twenties and, undoubtedly, many others came after first landing elsewhere, especially in Philadelphia. Indeed, the influx was so great that it strained the private resources of the various immigrant-aid societies. By the late 1820s, all the societies—St. Andrew's for the Scots, the Hibernian and Friends of Ireland Societies, St. George's for the English, the German Society, and St. David's for the Welsh—experienced the same financial difficulties, the common problem being that these societies were more fraternal and informal than efficient. Naturally, they appealed to the public at large for financial help. When the immigrant-aid societies professed that their function was to serve the community and the public rather than to retain their private, ethnic exclusiveness, foreign immigration became an integral part of the culture at large.[30]

On the whole, the development of industrialization after the war followed the vicissitudes of the maritime economy. When peace did not restore shipping prosperity but, on the contrary, continued the commercial crisis without the benefit of wartime markets and privateering, manufacturing was bound to assume a more important if not respectable role in Baltimore's social economy. At first, the return of peace raised false hopes among shippers and paralyzed manufacturing by the headlong rush into trade. But once Baltimore's commercial men understood that the return of West European mercantilism meant commercial deflation for their city, they turned to the industrial expansion of their American markets as a means of rescuing their commercial economy. The increasing stream of cheap foreign labor together with the general economic contraction continued to stimulate this transition.

The application of steam power to production was a necessary but merely subsidiary development to this burgeoning industrial revolution. Production remained largely in its eighteenth-century, handicraft form, although now the master craftsmen were "manufacturers." Moreover, the continued growth of Baltimore's population, especially the steady increase of foreign immigration, amidst the commercial depression focused attention upon Baltimoreans' consumer needs. As this happened, the city began to function as an economy itself. But when the commercial depression barely lifted, and Baltimore's expansion into the interior through internal improvements failed to attract the expected imports, the ingredients were present to widen the city's manufacturing base to the point where Baltimore became the supplier of such goods to the countryside. Though this role was not assumed until the next generation, it was being formed during the 1820s.

CHAPTER V

Fragmentation of the Old Order

While reacting to their economic crisis and adjusting to the new postwar realities, the Baltimoreans wrought social and political changes that pointed toward later nineteenth-century democratic forms. In essence, the sociopolitical changes created a more open and democratic society through the fragmentation and pluralization of the old social order. The breakup of the old order took two principal forms. One was specialization. As a whole, society was specialized into multiple elite groups as economic activities were divorced from political and social activities, and each group pursued activities that became relatively autonomous and socially isolated from the others. Among the lower orders, society was also specialized by the new legal status, and the consequent social and political importance, of a day-laboring, wage-earning working class that existed outside of the traditional guild system. For society as a whole, specialization tended toward democratization, because none of the new groups could dominate society the way the old mercantile aristocracy had; and for much the same reason the effect of specialization was to create a laissez faire society.

The other way that Baltimore society became fragmented was through the institutionalization of social processes. Institutionalization, like specialization, had originated in the boom of the 1790s and early 1800s as a means whereby the old one-class (or undifferentiated) society could take advantage of war-born economic opportunities. Both contributed to the emergence of something entirely unforeseen, a formalized pattern of response to changes and opportunities that created a more or less rigid social "structure"; and both, as well as the fact of a structured society, took on lives of their own. In the 1820s institutional activities emerged as the "normal" way to do business. What was more, they came to be applied increasingly to other, noneconomic kinds of private and public activities. The city acquired greater autonomy from the state, dramatically shifted its taxation policies, and assumed responsibility for new and different public services. Thus, as institutions—public, formal, and legal expressions, some of which represented parts of society and others society as a whole—proliferated and played greater roles in the life of the community, they superseded private activities and interests and came increasingly to be identified *as the life of the community.* Moreover, because the institutional process was rooted in the immediate past, it was familiar and constituted, ironically, the culturally conservative element in the social and political transformation.

The New Business Elite

The crisis of the war, followed by the brief but intense postwar prosperity, initiated the transformation of Baltimore society. The war disrupted the social structure of peacetime pursuits, provided new opportunities, and broke down the guild system in a variety of ways. Peace attracted a huge migration of people to Baltimore who expected to share in the return of its prewar prosperity. In June 1815, Hezekiah Niles estimated that eight hundred people were settling in Baltimore each month. This huge influx was important because the newcomers came largely from the North and consisted mainly of nonslaveholders, and because its timing continued the breakdown of eighteenth-century society along the lines that had become visible for the first time during the war.[1]

The huge number of immigrants introduced a variety of developments into the community. The cost of living increased, of course, as rents and food prices doubled; construction of all types, boomed, especially housing; and the municipality found itself having to enlarge such basic social services as water and sanitation facilities, to extend streets into the countryside, and to provide additional police and judicial facilities. In their private capacities, the Baltimoreans responded to these changes with enormous creativity. In 1816 the leading merchants organized themselves into an association and began construction of the Exchange, a large building at the center of the city where the public offices of the city would be housed and where the leading merchants would congregate for two hours or so during the middle of each business day. Another group organized themselves into the Baltimore Gas Light Company in 1816 and contracted with the city to establish the first big-city street-lighting system in America. Other people as well—contractors, grocers, and tradesmen of various kinds—benefited from the increased demand for their goods and services.[2]

But then came the panic of 1819 and subsequent depression, which altered business and social relationships by reorienting both the social structure and its values to its new environment. This development specialized society in various ways. In a broad way, the business leadership became differentiated from the political leadership; in a more specific way, a new group of business leaders replaced the older group and stamped business enterprise with new values and methods; and in another specific way, the group of wage earners outside the guild structure acquired status as "workingmen" with specific economic, social, and eventually political interests. Though all three developments occurred simultaneously and marked the dissolution of eighteenth-century society, the latter two had greater significance than the first in stamping the new social order as a "business society."

The emergence of the new business elite had the greatest immediate impact. Revelations about the immoral business conduct of the traditional merchants who failed during the course of the panic provided the new businessmen with their point of departure: they insisted that correct moral behavior be enforced by law and not remain merely a part of custom and tradition. To the new leaders the experience during the panic proved that business relations could no longer remain private matters dependent upon the good will of men; they must become standardized, carry the force of law, and be made available to everyone. Accordingly, the new leaders led the movement to institutionalize and legalize economic relationships, a process that froze certain aspects of customary business enterprise, created new ones, and stamped all of them with their own notions of business morality.[3]

Though later enshrined in legend and institutions, their business morality was highly personal in the beginning. There was little difference, for example, between their private and public lives. They were extremely cautious and were as close and calculating with money in their personal lives as they were in business. Indeed, dollars and cents were a form of moral accountancy to them. Such an outlook led them to specialize and to concentrate their capitals in selected activities. "One business properly conducted is the surest & safest way to make money," warned Alexander Brown to his son William in 1819, and both of their extraordinarily successful business careers testified to the efficacy of specialization. Alexander and others like him shunned speculation, concentrated their capital in safe, virtually riskless ventures, and came to dominate Baltimore's economic life by the end of the decade.[4]

By contrast, the older and now discredited merchants had embodied the ideals of the eighteenth-century merchant: grand in manner, general in operations, and mercantile in orientation. They considered business an activity dealing with the movement of commodities, and they thought of each transaction as an "adventure"—risky, daring, and highly profitable. In a world of almost constant war, where insurance was more rare than common and where long credits were not usual, this kind of merchant relied upon great price differentials between markets to offset the relatively cheap costs of water transportation. But the return of peace in

1815 altered what had been usual, fundamental, even indispensable conditions for this merchant. Peace restored the cyclical market seasons of spring and fall and reduced the uncertainties of trade that war had wrought. To the extent that peace narrowed price differentials between markets, it aligned business enterprises more closely with social and environmental factors than abnormal wartime conditions had allowed. Many eighteenth-century merchants were out of place in this postwar world: they felt hedged in by the new conditions of trade, and they looked for those conditions which they better understood and in which they could operate more comfortably. They found them in the South American trade, in privateering and, to a lesser extent, in voyages to the Far East. But even most of these opportunities came to an end by 1830.[5]

How the business values of the new men became one of their historical contributions can be found in the contrasting attitudes between the new men and the older leadership toward the reinvestment of capital. Shortage of capital was one of Baltimore's greatest weaknesses throughout the antebellum period. In a maritime economy, capital is a derivative of trade; but in the Southern seaport economies from Baltimore to New Orleans, merchants had commonly diverted portions of their capital accumulated from trade into land, for speculation and for agricultural production as well as for status. By not usually concentrating their profits in trade, such merchants did not economically specialize or socially isolate themselves from the agricultural society that surrounded them. Together, both groups formed a compatible "rural gentry" before Baltimore, but not the countryside, was caught up in the developing public society that separated and emphasized antagonisms between them. Moreover, by diverting a portion of their profits from trade into land, Baltimore's eighteenth-century businessmen directed the returns from their profitable maritime economy in such a way as to exert an extensive rather than an intensive multiplier effect upon their city's social economy. This helped to preserve landed-gentry values in their commercial community.

The new men, by contrast, reinvested their profits from trade in trade, thus concentrating rather than diversifying their capital, and intensifying the multiplier effect of the maritime economy. This also perpetuated their dominance or monopoly of the business institutions connected with commercial activities. Concentration demanded stability, and stability led to dominance and control. The insight and the historical contribution of the new leaders was that business specialization and concentration under free-market conditions was just as profitable and only slightly less monopolistic than the tradition of legally chartered monopolies which they opposed. Given their perception and style of business activity, they were carriers of many ideas associated with economic laissez faire.[6]

Other contributions that they made related even more directly to their emphasis upon laissez faire business enterprise. One was their insistence upon money rather than credit as the medium of business relations. Their general distrust of credit was understandable: abuse of credit had been a causal factor in the panic of 1819. Also, their insistence upon cash or very short credit transactions enabled them to respond better to the price revolution and to Baltimore's position in the new money economy of the 1820s. Moreover, placing business relationships upon the footing of money enabled them to judge others by their personal notions of moral accountancy.[7]

But perhaps their greatest innovation was their application of the new steam-power technology to the expansion of commerce, which thereby infused industrialism with commercial values. Concerned about Baltimore's declining maritime economy and the loss of foreign markets, they argued for, and led, the expansion of their city's domestic economy via industrialization. Their leadership in forming the Baltimore & Ohio Railroad Company in 1827 was the most dramatic example of this, but they also served as corporate directors in nearly every other application of steam power to land and water transportation. And because they led the early expansion of Baltimore into the countryside, their business values and practices shaped the conduct of many of these enterprises throughout the antebellum period.[8]

Rentiers and Workingmen

In spite of their wealth and tremendous business influence, however, the new leaders were never quite members of the more prestigious social elite. Indeed, millionaires like Jacob Albert and Alexander Brown, and near-millionaires like William Lorman, were thought to be rather eccentric for their consuming interest in business affairs. By the late 1820s, the social elite came to regard the new leaders as "busy men," in a class by themselves and a rung above manufacturers on the social ladder. By the same token, the new leaders did not identify with the social elite by aping their ways. From their point of view, the social elite were somewhat parasitic because they were nonproductive; even worse, the social elite seemed to be akin to the older and discredited merchant elite.

Ironically, the methods of the new business elite made the emergence of the new social elite possible. Essentially, the social elite became *rentiers*; and though a few *rentiers* had existed as a status elite before the war, it was the regular and enormous issues of public-debt financing necessitated by the war, followed by the deficit financing of internal improvements by both the private and public sectors of the economy during the commercial deflation of the 1820s, that enabled the social elite to establish themselves as *rentiers* on a stable and permanent scale. To a lesser extent, the attraction of ground rents amid an increasing population and a declining maritime trade—further enhanced by a Maryland law that made tenants in possession of property responsible for two-thirds of its property taxes—sustained the new social elite. The appearance of these alternatives to actively employing money in agriculture, manufacturing, or trade constituted the means of this social specialization, for such investments, paying steady dividends of 5 percent or better, required little supervision and were far less risky than employing capital actively.[9]

The new social elite was identified with the older merchant elite in several ways. For one thing, many of the members of the social elite were cautious merchants who had retired from business during or after the War of 1812 (among the more prominent were the Brunes, Calhouns, Donnells, Gilmors, Hoffmans, Hollinses, Olivers, and Pattersons). They contributed much of the capital of the social elite. Moreover, some of the social elite were those who had failed or stopped payment during the panic of 1819 (the Buchanan, Higginbotham, McBlair, Samuel Smith, Sterett, and Williams families, for example). Also, the sons and daughters of these families intermarried with those of the landed-gentry families (the Carrolls, Dorseys, Howards, Keys, McHenrys, Ridgelys, Steuarts, and Williamses of Frederick County) who maintained Baltimore residences. The social elite thus blended eighteenth-century mercantile traditions with landed-gentry values.

The appearance of this status elite, and its bifurcation from the new business leaders or functional elite, was one of the most important social developments in antebellum Baltimore. The blending of the commercialism of financial capitalism with landed-gentry values produced the social group who became the arbiters of Baltimore's cultural values down to the Civil War. Remembering the glories of Baltimore's "Golden Age," the expansive years before 1815, this *rentier* class furnished social leadership and established a certain tone for the society; a sense of noblesse oblige, politics as avocation rather than vocation, a preference for land and natural production and a distaste for trade and manufacturing, a concern with family and breeding, and a commitment to amateurism and an aversion to professionalism. All revolved around landed-gentry ideals. Only a few Baltimoreans actually personified these *rentier* ideals, of course: Charles Ridgely Carroll, Roswell Lyman Colt, Robert Morgan Gibbes, Robert Gilmor, Jr., Charles Carroll Harper, Benjamin Chew and Charles Howard, James Howard McHenry, the four sons of William

Patterson, John Donnell Smith, John Spear Smith, and George Hume Steuart. Perhaps the most famous, John Pendleton Kennedy, would not achieve the ideal until the 1830s. Financial investments, managed either by themselves or by someone else, enabled them to concentrate upon a leisured and reflective existence, or one socially and politically service-able, depending upon their individual inclinations. Highly mobile and well educated, they initiated much of Baltimore's social and political life. In this way, many of Baltimore's dominant social ideals continued beyond their preindustrial roots.[10]

This creation of multiple elites was merely one way in which Balti-more's new realities specialized its society, however; another affected those individuals and groups most concerned with a daily existence. War-time had greatly increased the numbers of day-laboring wage earners outside the guild system of handicraft production. These workers were both skilled and unskilled; they worked for a daily wage only, without board or room; they lived apart from the place of their work; and they were much more dependent upon weather, seasons, and economic con-ditions for their sustenance than were guild workers. They were quite literally "free labor;" free to change employers or employment, free not to work at all, and free to starve. Although this class of labor was not large during the twenties, it expanded steadily as traditional guild con-trols and indentured servitude waned.

Though "workingmen" appeared as the lower-class counterpart of "busy men" during the 1820s, the change in the status of Baltimore's laboring classes was also accompanied by a change in the way many Baltimoreans thought about working people. The working classes repre-sented moral capitalism: the class was life's testing ground, and through-out the antebellum period its income barely rose above a subsistence lev-el. Individuals were expected to rise from it onto a higher economic plateau, not by dint of superior business acumen, but by their superior moral worth. Morality bred a worldly success born of frugality, modera-tion, temperance, and common sense. Socially, the class was anonymous because individual mobility was regarded as one of its essential charac-teristics. Politically, the class could have no interest; its members had only their individual self-interest: to rise and join the middle class. Eco-nomically, the class was regarded as productive only. It was not thought of as a mass, consumers' market, though more and more individuals found employment by providing consumer goods and services as Balti-more's population continued to grow in spite of the commercial depres-sion.[11]

There was just enough truth to these ideas to make such beliefs pos-sible; but they did not mirror reality. Indeed, the status of the workingmen changed precisely because economic, political, and social recognition were extended to them. In 1818, the first of several savings banks was created as a special depository for workingmen, to encourage their industry, thrift, and regularity; in 1826, a workingman was deliberately chosen for the first time to run for the mayoralty in order to attract workingmen's votes; and free public education, begun in Baltimore in 1829, was said to be in the particular interest of the workingmen. In the long run, such recognition created a new class interest, but in the short run other factors directed the changes into the reciprocal developments of political democratization and social specialization.[12]

Several factors prevented the changing status of the workingmen from becoming anything more than political recognition at the time. One was the life style of the workingmen themselves, which was a function of their wages, hours, and conditions of employment. Another was the impact of immigration upon labor and the decline of slaveholding. And a third was the tremendous growth of the free black population outside of the traditional white household structure. They were amenable to neither guild, nor white household, nor slave controls. The last two factors, immigration and free blacks, were part of the more general transformation of the household structure of labor to manufactory production, a transformation that seemed a social crisis to many Baltimoreans.[13]

Generally speaking, the new free labor in the city was not as well off as the women and children in the paternalistic enclaves outside the city. Working the same hours as the enclave workers, when weather permitted (usually a sixteen-hour day in winter and a fourteen-hour day in summer, six days a week), Baltimore's workers earned higher wages, but these were sometimes store wages used to purchase high-priced goods in the employers' stores, and the workers had to fend for themselves socially and economically. When they did not work—no matter the reason— their expenses continued, erasing savings and grinding them into debt. Few among the laboring classes rose above the subsistence level into the middle class, because the activities of almost all day laborers were seasonal to some extent. Construction of all kinds, for example, depended upon clement weather; and production depended upon demand until the 1840s, when technological advances changed marketing processes and awakened manufacturers to the possibilities of bypassing the merchants who controlled the demand markets and, indeed, of creating their own demand markets. During the 1820s, Baltimore's day-laboring classes found work and income usually from March through October, and unemployment and near starvation from November through February. During these winter months, the unemployed were generally thrown upon private and public charity for firewood, food, and clothing.[14]

Day laborers were distinguished from one another by occupation. Generally speaking, skilled tradesmen received better wages than unskilled tradesmen and factory workers, and were organized into craft societies. Although sailors' wages were declining (which, with the decline in freight rates, reflected the general decline of the maritime economy), shipyard-workers' wages increased briefly in 1825 in the expectation that Baltimore's port was to be designated a navy yard. The following wages of tradesmen in the shipyards were comparable to wages for men in the same trade in the community at large. Carpenters earned from $1.25 to $2.00 per day; blacksmiths from $1.25 to $1.50; caulkers, coopers, and sailmakers, $1.25; and joiners, riggers, and sawyers from $1.37½ to $1.50. Unskilled laborers earned $1.00 per day. But because work was seasonal, these wages cannot be extrapolated to a yearly basis. The unskilled laborer, for example, probably never earned much above $200.00 per year.[15]

A variety of factors made the life of the urban laborer difficult during the 1820s. Certainly, the irregularity of employment during the commercial depression, and the long working hours when there was employment, made his work life tenuous. In addition, the declining shipbuilding industry, together with the competition for jobs engendered by the steady increase of population, contributed to changes in the patterns and location of employment. Moreover, the general trend of master craftsmen to call themselves "manufacturers" and to turn their apprentices and journeymen into day-laboring wage earners undermined the security that had been inherent in traditional relationships. Finally, there was the economic threat of the foreign immigrants, many of whom willingly worked for wages lower than the prevailing rates.

Apart from such economics, urban white labor was also threatened, for the first time, by the changing position of free blacks in the community. Slaves, indentured servants, and free blacks living in white households were all forms of the common eighteenth-century paternalistic structure of labor. The fragmentation of the old order changed them into the modern form of free, day-laboring wage earners, but touched each group in different ways. Just as the persistence of a large, alternative and continuing supply of cheap immigrant labor eroded the pattern of slave-holding, so its persistence also altered the structural position of free blacks in the society. Foreign immigration into the port grew from 646 in 1820–21, to 1,960 in 1829–30, averaged 1,055 throughout the decade, (and grew even more during the 1830s) and contributed to the transition of free blacks into autonomous households separate from white ones. Such separation and independence from white household controls made free blacks into free-labor competitors of whites more directly than ever

TABLE 5
Decennial Changes in Household
Social Structure 1790–1830

	1790	1800	1810	1820	1830
Number of households in sample	1,725	2,357	2,153	976	4,571
Number of white slaveholders	389	665	528	270	798
White slaveholders as percentage of total households	22.55	28.21	24.52	27.66	17.46
Number of free black households	23	183	220	103	687
Free black households as percentage of total households	1.33	7.76	10.22	10.55	15.03

SOURCE: See note 16.

before. Table 5 illustrates these trends among white and black house-holders by revealing the incidence of slaveholding and free black house-holds from 1790 to 1830.[16]

The most glaring trend evident in these figures is the accelerating growth rate of free black households. Free black households were sepa-rate and independent from white households and therefore not under the direct control of the white heads of households. This breaking away of free blacks from the traditional white household controls, and not the simple increase of free blacks, accompanied the shift of Baltimore's anti-slavery movement away from abolitionism to colonization by the end of the decade.

There was another dimension to this changing structural position of free blacks. Unlike slaves, the total number of whom decreased nearly 20 percent, the number of free blacks increased nearly 50 percent during the twenties. In fact, the 1820s was the only antebellum decade in which free blacks increased relative to Baltimore's total population. After 1830 the relative position of free blacks in Baltimore, and even more so in the case of slaves, steadily declined until the city was nearly 90 percent white in 1860. Given their increasing numbers during the twenties, the disintegration of white household controls over them, and their entry into the class of day-laboring wage earners, free blacks became direct economic competitors of their white counterparts, both natives and immigrants. But because they lacked the political rights of the whites, they could be legally as well as culturally discriminated against—and they were. Beginning in 1825, the Baltimore Orphans' Court was empowered to indenture any free Negro or mulatto child in its care, without providing for its education. After that year, free blacks who were living without visible means of support were required to give security for their good behavior or leave the state, or be committed to prison, and the Baltimore Orphans' Court was authorized to indenture the children of such free blacks. Also beginning in 1826, free blacks who served prison terms were banished from the state upon their release or pardon, and if they remained in Maryland after sixty days from their release, they were liable to be sold into slavery for the time of their original sentence.[17]

This development of new social controls over the weakest political group seriously affected the abolitionist movement. After all, freed slaves became free blacks. Since the late eighteenth century, abolitionism had existed in Baltimore in the form of a local unit of the Maryland Society for Promoting the Abolition of Slavery. Its members were mainly Quakers, who were opposed to slavery in principle, though many of them owned slaves. During the middle and late 1820s, the leaders of Baltimore abolitionism were Benjamin Lundy, editor and publisher of the only anti-slavery newspaper in the United States at the time, the *Genius of Universal Emancipation*; his coeditor and printer, in 1829 and 1830, William Lloyd Garrison; and Daniel Raymond, lawyer and political economist, whose views were similar to those of the Careys of Philadelphia. Before the 1820s, abolitionists commonly argued in the traditional Quaker framework of the personal immorality of owning slaves, but during that decade they, and especially Lundy, secularized the argument and linked it with colonization of the free blacks overseas. The new argument made sense to those who were concerned about the changing status of the free blacks; but it also posed a dilemma. The constitutional status of slavery legitimized social controls over slaves; free blacks, however, occupied no such subordinate position in the organic view of society, and there were certain problems with establishing their subordinate status. Indeed, an entire body of statutory law would have to be developed to establish social controls over them. More importantly, there was no precedent in Maryland for subordinating free blacks to a status similar to that of slaves.

Most worrisome was the state's jurisdiction over the process. Not only was the matter out of Baltimore's control, but the politics of advancing legislation through the state government frequently had little to do with its content. At the state level, Baltimore had already encountered opposition from an array of interests that included planters on the Eastern Shore and the southern part of the Western Shore, the City of Annapolis and the counties who desired to preserve their own semiautonomous status through opposition to the city. Unless the society undertook the colonization of its free black citizens overseas wholly and, in many cases, forcefully, the easier solution was to affirm slavery and continue to legislate social controls over the free blacks in piecemeal fashion. The easier way is how it happened.

Specifically, abolitionism and colonization failed in Baltimore during the late 1820s. In 1826 candidates campaigning against abolitionism and colonization defeated Daniel Raymond in his bid for election to the First Branch of the City Council. Charles Carroll Harper's arguments against abolitionism and colonization are particularly revealing, because he apparently stated the opinion of the community: that social controls over slaves were established and that Baltimore's black citizens did not wish to emigrate overseas, which was true in the majority of cases. The community then moved against the abolitionist leaders. In 1830 Garrison's editorial attack upon slave traders in the *Genius of Universal Emancipation* provoked a libel suit that resulted in his conviction. Unable or unwilling to pay his fine, Garrison spent three months in the Baltimore City Jail. Subscriptions to the *Genius* fell off so drastically that it was published monthly instead of weekly, and in the fall of 1830 Garrison remained in Boston, where he had gone to solicit financial support. Lundy moved his operations to Washington, and Raymond concentrated on his writings and eventually moved from the city. Abolitionism was no longer a viable point of view in Baltimore after 1830. Here, again, cultural conservatism surfaced, for the commitment to slavery was made easier by the fact that slavery was visibly declining.[18]

The Changing Private and Public Orders

Baltimore's society absorbed these divisive changes by continuing to institutionalize relationships. Initiated during the business revolution, such institutionalization gradually altered the eighteenth-century human scale of life by abstracting such activities from their social roots in individuals and families. After 1815, the economically functional family, the social unit of production, became increasingly dysfunctional and was replaced by institutions as complexity eroded the essential simplicity of eighteenth-century life. In part, this change is reflected in the statistics of incorporations: 82 corporations were formed for Baltimore activities in the thirty-two years from 1783 through 1815, whereas 131 were formed during the short span of the fourteen years from 1816 through 1829.[19]

But there were many other forms of institutionalization as well. Some, such as more formalized bankruptcy procedures, the transformation of the immigrant-aid societies, the creation of the Savings Bank of Baltimore, and the appearance of free public schools, have already been mentioned; others included new fraternal organizations like the Odd Fellows, new places of learning such as the Apprentice's Library or the Maryland Institute for the Promotion of the Mechanic Arts, and new organizations that addressed the condition of the free-laboring wage earners such as the Female Penitent's Refuge, the Indigent Sick Society, and the Oblate Sisters of Providence, who were expressly concerned with the plight of the free blacks.[20]

But perhaps the one area of community life that was most affected by institutionalization procedures, apart from business enterprise itself, was religion. Where twenty churches had been established gradually in Baltimore from the colonial period through 1815, sixteen new congregations suddenly appeared between 1816 and 1830. All were Protestant; six were Methodist, three were Baptist, three were Presbyterian, and the Episcopalians, Lutherans, Friends, and Unitarians established one each. The Unitarian and Independent Methodist churches were the only new denominations founded. Two of the new congregations, the Episcopalian and one of the Methodists, were black. In addition to these new congregations, thirteen Bible, missionary, and tract societies appeared during the 1820s, organizational forms that had not existed previously. By 1830, religion, if defined institutionally, played a greater role in the life of the community than ever before.[21]

Though all of these institutional changes occurred in the private relationships among Baltimoreans, they were accompanied by even more important changes in the city's public sector, its municipal government. Indeed, the political changes after the war constituted a giant step in the evolution of Baltimore's public society. The tradition of elitism continued, of course, but political life became more organized than it had ever been, more specialized and differentiated from the community's social and economic life, and new political leaders emerged by the end of the decade. Generally speaking, Baltimore's continuing growth underpinned these developments, but such specific and unique events of the twenties as the devastating effects of the panic of 1819 and the new, overland direction of the city's economy were more important in fragmenting the political power of the old elite and giving rise to new political groups. Confronted by new realities and bids for power by new groups, the old elite naturally fell back upon a previously successful means of maintaining their power: they combined a democratic ideology with the institutionalization of political relationships. However, the successful and creative innovations of these cultural conservatives proved temporary in the long run, for the party institutions and the power that they wielded would be increasingly turned against the elite and their private controls over the city by the very political forces they were designed to contain.

Essentially, Baltimore's public sector expanded in scope and degree in response to actual as well as perceived realities, and the expansion followed the general rhythm of its economy. That is, government functions were enlarged during the heady years immediately following the war when everyone believed Baltimore would resume its remarkable prewar growth, and then, following the panic and commercial depression in the later twenties, the municipality became directly involved in the push toward its overland economy.

Political interests and rivalries also helped to shape these changes. In general, the prewar split within the Republican party continued throughout the postwar period. Retaining its prestige as Baltimore's patriotic leadership during the war, the Smith faction dominated the city during the mayoral administrations of George Stiles and Edward Johnson from 1816 to 1820. But many of its leaders became discredited by their involvement in the panic, and a rival faction led by John Montgomery was elected in 1820. For the following six years, the two factional leaders, Johnson and Montgomery, seesawed back and forth in power until 1826, when the Smith faction joined a new movement among Baltimore's property-owning middle class, led by housing contractor Jacob Small. In that year, the Smith faction supported Small's election, after which they created the Jacksonian party in 1827, and then fell out with Small. But from 1828 until 1832, Small's property-owning, middle-class constituency successfully drew support from Montgomery's faction, used the Irish Catholic and ethnic German vote against the Presbyterian, Quaker, and Scotch-Irish components of the Smith faction, and consistently opposed attempts by the Smithites to introduce their Jacksonian-party style into municipal politics. They failed in the long run, however, because the Smith faction gradually eroded the support of Small and William Steuart, his successor and another builder, through several means: by shifting their appeal away from ethnoreligious criteria toward the economic ones of "workingmen"; by insisting upon a uniformity between the voter's position on presidential and municipal politics—thereby introducing the Jacksonian-party machine into local elections; and by making fidelity to party the test of support as well as patronage. Though Small successfully withstood this attack and was reelected in 1828 and again in 1830, the Smith-faction-cum-Jacksonians elected Jesse Hunt in 1832 in what is known as Baltimore's first party race for the mayoralty. What happened here was remarkably similar to what the Smith faction did in 1798 and what the Chase-Ridgely faction had done during the 1780s. But now this political style became a part of the city's new party institutions, and the vertical integration of municipal with national politics via the "second American party system" bound Baltimore to the larger events in the nation as irretrievably as its metropolitan expansion did.[22]

The most well known of Baltimore's important postwar changes in the public sector continued an eighteenth-century tradition when, in 1816, several entrepreneurs formed the Gaslight Company of Baltimore and received authorization from the City Council to provide street lighting for the city. Incorporated in the following year and licensed to manufacture hydrogen gas, it was the first company in America to manufacture gas for street, business, and residential lighting; however, its work proceded very slowly, and Baltimore did not have a complete network of street lights for another two generations.[23]

Other immediate changes were direct responses to the enormous influx of people into the city, and both the Stiles and Johnson administrations enlarged the scope of municipal services. The number of superintendents of streets and pumps—those officials in charge of maintaining the streets, public wells, and water pumps—was doubled from two to four. Several new volunteer fire companies were formed, receiving city water and financial aid. And in 1820, the health and sanitation of the city was vested in a new, centralized institution, the Board of Health, following the yellow-fever epidemic of the previous year. Consisting of three commissioners and a physician appointed by the mayor, this board was responsible for the general sanitation of the city, the superintendence of street cleaning, and the enforcement of municipal sanitary regulations. This board helped to establish Baltimore's reputation for innovations in public health and medicine. Besides, a healthy city promoted trade.[24]

This same population growth also stimulated other kinds of municipal adjustments. Stiles's administration specialized the city's police into a night watch and day police, and increased the number of officers. A distinct municipal criminal court, the Baltimore City Court, was also instituted in 1817, and a special tax was authorized for its support. Civil cases in the city continued, however, under the jurisdiction of the county court, and the maintenance of the new city court was shared by both the city and county. Another adjustment of Baltimore's judicial system occurred in 1819 when the "Justices of the Peace of the State of Maryland in and for the City of Baltimore" were created. Two justices from each ward were appointed annually by the state governor, and these justices had powers of assignment of indentured servitude among their other ones.[25]

Stiles's administration also instituted a major change in the administration of poor relief. The city's first municipal poor-relief board, called the Managers of the Poor, was created in 1818. Composed of one person from each ward appointed annually by the mayor, this board was given power to commit the indigent sick and crippled to the county almshouse. Trustees of the almshouse were to keep separate expense accounts of the inmates from the city. Later, in 1822, Mayor Montgomery assigned the maintenance of the almshouse to a newly created institution, the Trustees for the Poor of Baltimore City and County, which was made up of seven persons, four from the city appointed by the state governor. The institution continued to function this way until 1854.[26]

Two other important changes that occurred during the immediate postwar years grew out of state legislative action. One involved the expansion of the city's boundaries in 1817 by annexing adjacent areas, called the "precincts," in Baltimore County, and was a bitterly fought political battle. Neither the city nor the precincts wanted annexation; but both were Republican and the remainder of the county Federalist, and the latter wanted annexation in hopes of making all four of its delegates to the state legislature Federalists. The city, limited to two delegates no matter its size, fought the annexation bill in the Federalist-dominated legislature, ultimately losing on a straight party vote. True, the town grew in area and population as a result of the annexation, but it was now more underrepresented in the Maryland General Assembly than ever before.[27]

The other change resembled a quid pro quo for this annexation. In 1818 the Federalist legislature enlarged Baltimore's municipal powers from its 1796 charter and established many of the forms that directed the city's subsequent development. The city was divided into twelve wards instead of eight, and provisions were outlined for increasing the number of wards to a maximum of twenty as the population increased. But the more important provisions of this law related to the greater financial freedom that Baltimore received. No limitations were placed upon the city's taxing power, and the city was authorized to lay and collect direct taxes on personal and real estate "to such amount as shall be thought necessary for the public or city purposes." Though Baltimore's debt from the war amounted to merely one hundred thousand dollars, the state authorized the city to issue stock or borrow money up to the amount of a million dollars for its needs. Finally, the legislature made explicit the right of eminent domain to be exercised in effecting municipal improvements. All of these features allowed Republican Baltimore a greater measure of autonomy than the city had ever known.[28]

However, the panic of 1819 and the long depression in Baltimore's maritime economy altered the conditions and character of its municipal administration. Samuel Smith and many of his connections were virtually, if not actually, bankrupted, and John Montgomery overwhelmed Mayor Johnson's bid for reelection in 1820. Like many Baltimoreans, Montgomery was part of the Scotch-Irish, Presbyterian emigration from Pennsylvania into Maryland around the head of the Chesapeake Bay. However, Montgomery settled in Harford County and did not come to Baltimore until 1811, after he had already served five years in the Maryland House of Delegates during the 1790s, as the state's attorney from 1793 to 1796, and nearly three terms as a Republican in the federal House of Representatives from 1807 to 1811. Even after establishing his residence in Baltimore, Montgomery spent most of his time in Annapolis, where he served as attorney general of Maryland from 1811 to 1818, and as Baltimore's representative to the House of Delegates in 1819. Thus, Montgomery was new to Baltimore literally and politically; he was not an intimate of the Smith faction; his political ties were statewide; and, though a Republican, he evidently served as a bridge to the Federalists who dominated state politics.

Such characteristics were important for Baltimore, because Montgomery inaugurated the city's most significant administrative changes of the 1820s: its shift away from taxes on trade to taxes on property as its chief source of revenue, and deficit spending as an integral part of municipal policy. Not only did this transition fit the qualitative shift within the city's economy that paired a declining maritime trade with a rising productive and sedentary domestic market, but it also fit the sociopolitical direction of postwar Baltimore. This latter direction democratized the sociopolitical order in singular fashion: beginning in 1818 occupants of a property were liable for its taxes, and the suffrage requirement was changed from "property holding" to "tax paying." In this way, the number of voters was expanded without abandoning the traditional stake-in-society definition of the electorate.[30]

Montgomery's policies, particularly those relating to taxation, produced two immediate results by the end of his first term: the municipal bureaucracy expanded and the mayor became involved in a patronage dispute with the Smith-faction members of the City Council. The number of appointed municipal employees increased from 96 in 1820 to 120 in 1822; and the mayor's refusal to appoint certain recommendees of the council, his firing of others, and his appointments of those whom he, but not the council members, liked, fed the feud between them. During the mayoral campaign of 1822, Montgomery was accused of being obstinate, vain, and dogmatic, a king and an aristocrat who lived in a palace and wished to extend his domains; he was alleged to have lost his statewide connections and the respect of the state, and to be very unpopular within the Democratic party. But the most serious charge was that he was a money spender at a time when Baltimoreans should "husband the pecuniary interests of our city." In the end, Edward Johnson narrowly defeated Montgomery by forty-eight votes.[31]

The ward pattern of voting in this and the subsequent elections between Montgomery and the Smith faction in 1820, 1824, and 1826 (and, for that matter, between Small and the Smith faction in 1828 and 1830) was strikingly continuous. Except for 1820, when the business failures and subsequent depression influenced Montgomery's victory to a greater degree than usual, his support came steadily from ward four, where the state penitentiary was and where the first textile factories and cottage weaving industry would be located by the end of the decade, and from wards eight through twelve, which formed a semicircle beginning at Whetstone Point to the south and extending westward around the city to its northern boundaries. These areas, particulary in the west and northwest, were rapidly growing in connection with the overland economy. Conversely, Johnson and the Smith faction drew their main support from the traditional centers of Baltimore's maritime economy: the business wards five and six immediately north of the basin, and the shipping wards one through three that lay east of Jones's Falls, and which included Fell's Point.[32]

The locations of the voting support of the two factions underlay what then happened in municipal politics. Oriented to the export notions of the shipping interest, Johnson's administration opted for the easiest and cheapest solution for overcoming the maritime depression. A series of town meetings in 1823 and 1824 resulted in the decision to emphasize Baltimore's contact with the Susquehanna River trade via canals rather than with its overland and Western Markets. This would mean slower growth for the northwestern, western and southwestern areas of the city. In addition, Johnson's administration financed the project by raising existing taxes levied on property and creating new ones. And existing tax rates increased dramatically: the direct tax was increased 25 percent, from two to two and a half dollars per one hundred dollars assessed valuation; the city-court tax, 50 percent, from thirty to forty-five cents; the poor tax 33 percent, from forty-five to sixty cents; and a new highway and bridge tax of thirty-five cents was created. However, municipal services were not enlarged in any significant way nor were new ones

Baltimore in 1822 (courtesy of the Maryland Historical Society)

created. Worse yet, these increases alone nearly equaled a week's wages for a workingman whose home was valued at five hundred dollars, and they occurred at a time when unemployment was more usual than not.[33]

The increase in taxes and northeast direction of the proposed growth of the city provoked strong opposition to both. Montgomery's faction favored a western canal linking Baltimore with the proposed Chesapeake and Ohio Canal, the latter project being financed by the state government and supported particularly by the counties lying along the Potomac River. But another movement appeared simultaneously whose strength, while citywide, was heaviest in the very northwestern, western, and southwestern wards that also supported Montgomery. This latter movement was composed of property-owning master craftsmen, journeymen, and tradesmen who bore the brunt of the property-tax increases in the midst of the depression. They also feared the impact of the city's link with the Susquehanna trade upon them. They were led by Jacob Small, a carpenter and house builder, who opposed both Johnson and Montgomery in the 1824 mayoral election. Though Small's movement attracted 13 percent of the citywide vote, and he even carried the ninth ward in the southwest, Montgomery's superior organization enabled his faction to both defeat the incumbent and overcome Small's challenge. For Johnson's faction the lesson was clear: if they had carried Small's votes they would have won the election; moreover, they would have gained support in precisely those wards in which they were weakest. Eventually, this happened, for what Montgomery's administration did in 1825 and 1826 hastened the coalition of its opponents.[34]

Administratively speaking, Montgomery's mayoral term from 1825 to 1827 constituted a turning point in Baltimore's municipal development. He institutionalized deficit spending through a new agency, the city Commissioners of Finance, further expanded the municipal bureaucracy but decentralized decision making, codified the city's ordinances, regulations and the inspection laws in more pervasive ways than they had been, and he introduced a new professionalism in city government. In short, Baltimore first began to function as a nineteenth-century city as a result of Montgomery's reforms. However, the change has been obscured by other, more dramatic developments external to the city that were seized upon by the coalition of his Johnson and Small opponents and projected as the real issues when they defeated him in the 1826 election.

For one thing, the completion of the Erie Canal in 1825 had a devastating psychological impact upon the city's businessmen. Many moved to New York in the conviction that most of the trans-Allegheny trade would go to that city; and those who remained knew that Baltimore could no longer rely merely upon the Susquehanna trade but would have to push westward. Also, the London-generated financial panic in 1825 affected New York and Philadelphia much more severely than Baltimore because of the latter's lag behind those cities in their contact with the British markets, and those business leaders who remained in Baltimore saw this as their opportunity to forge ahead of their metropolitan rivals. Unfortunately, Montgomery's statewide contacts were of little use under these new conditions because the counties along the Potomac River opposed the state's aiding Baltimore's westward expansion, which would compete with their own river traffic. Isolated within the state, Montgomery could only streamline his administration of the city and resort to deficit spending to help finance costs as well as Baltimore's metropolitan expansion.[35]

Though Montgomery's opponents represented various political crosscurrents, they concentrated in the alliance between the Smith faction and Jacob Small's followers, and Small overwhelmed Montgomery in the mayoral election of 1826. During the campaign, Montgomery was explicitly charged with having taken credit for actions that Senator Smith really deserved, with an overweening ambition and pride that alienated people and that had disrupted the community for several years, with opposition to Roman Catholics, and with favoring the suffrage for free black males. He was also condemned via invidious comparisons with Small. In one such comparison, a public meeting of Small's friends described their candidate in this fashion:

> That this meeting sincerely believed that the selection of a sound, honest, practical, industrious and persevering mechanic, would be highly beneficial to the general interest of the city, particularly in the judicious disbursements of its funds with the strictest economy, embracing the necessary objects of improvements and repairs, where practical knowledge is of vital importance.[36]

Not only did this "practical" candidate win 64 percent of the total vote, but he swept every ward except the fourth which had always been the mainstay of Montgomery's power.[37]

Mayor Small was hardly settled in his new office when an event occurred that was tangential to the city's administration in origin but would have increasing significance in municipal politics. This was the creation of the Jacksonian political party in Baltimore during the spring of 1827. Basically, the party was created by the Smith faction in reference to national rather than local issues and was aimed at the presidential elections in 1828. Because of this national orientation, and because the party's constituency, apart from the Smithites, was a mixture of professionals, (mainly lawyers) who were new to the city, the younger generation of Baltimore's landed gentry who expected to follow in their families' traditions of political leadership, and many middle-class tradesmen and shopkeepers who were new in politics, the party's cohesion was not strong enough to defeat Mayor Small in the municipal elections of 1828 and 1830. Indeed, a few prominent Jacksonians such as merchant Hugh McElderry, ropewalk owner James Biays, and militia major Edward Spedden argued consistently against the intrusion of the party into local politics. Nevertheless, several circumstances combined to gradually erode this resistance, and the Jacksonians eventually elected their own Jesse Hunt as mayor in 1832.[38]

One set of circumstances that led to the Jacksonians' success followed from a change made in the city's revenue structure in 1827. The change worked for the city's greater autonomy from the state in the long run, because the Maryland legislature gave Baltimore complete authority over assessing and collecting its property taxes. In return, the state assumed the auction sales tax that was collected in the city. However, the factional split between Small and the Jacksonians, especially during the mayoral and presidential elections in 1828, prevented Small's administration from appointing new tax assessors and collectors until 1829. And even then, existing assessments and rates of taxation were not changed because of the growing hostility on the part of the city's largest property holders, a hostility that fully manifested itself in January 1831, when eighty-five of the city's wealthiest property owners petitioned the Maryland legislature to limit what they called Baltimore's "frightening power of taxation." The legislature complied in March, and Small resigned within the month and was hired by the Baltimore & Ohio Railroad Company. Though very few of these property owners can be identified as Jacksonians, their non-support of William Steuart, Small's successor, contributed to the success of the Jacksonians in the following year.[39]

Small's problems with the property owners were inseparable from a second set of circumstances that began in 1828. In that year, the city began its long-term program of helping to finance the Baltimore & Ohio Railroad Company via deficit spending. But the project proved enormously more expensive than was originally thought, and after authorizing an initial stock issue of $500,000.00, Small's administration issued additional 5 percent stock in such amounts as the company needed. By 1831, he faced the predicament that Baltimore was reaching its $1 million limitation of municipal indebtedness, which Maryland law had established in 1818, and that the city's interest payments on this debt had grown from $19,895.63 in 1827, his first year in office, to $24,723.74 by 1831, all of which had to be met from current revenues. Moreover, the future looked even bleaker, for though Baltimore might succeed in having its debt limitation raised, the city's mounting deficit was increasing faster than was the growth rate of its revenues. Clearly, Baltimore's overland expansion in the future was going to depend upon state aid or raising city revenues, or some combination of both.[40]

Such problems would not be resolved until after the return of prosperity made it possible, at least in the minds of the Baltimoreans. By then, in the mid-thirties, the Jacksonians were in power in the city, in the state and in the nation, and they gained the credit for it. In much the same way, several other developments of the twenties were resolved during the thirties. Indeed, the 1820s was a pivotal decade because it was the last one before both industrialization and the second two-party system began to seriously undercut local and regional differences, thereby rendering Baltimore less autonomous in the nation.

Clearly, Baltimore began to change during the twenties in directions that its future would take. The specialization of its social economy made the community more sedentary at the very time that opportunities were opened in connection with an expanding domestic demand for goods and services. One fed the other. Also, the city's involvement in the expansion of its overland economy, that innocently grew out of the rhetoric of municipal responsibility for commercial well-being as well as the needs of the time, necessitated thinking about the city as a domestic economy. Furthermore, contemporaries began to see how the political process could be used to change private habits and relationships. Baltimoreans were not yet ready for this last development—indeed, they either rejected or barely supported what would later be called "social reforms"—but they did accept modifications of the others, though in the traditional manner of eighteenth-century privatism. This was important in its own right, however, for the municipal government itself thereby became more complex, more specialized, and more responsible for a greater variety of social services. "Society" and "public" were slowly becoming synonymous as elitism was giving way to democracy, but it remained for the Jacksonians to break through old forms and norms and to take the giant step toward nineteenth-century ones.

CHAPTER VI
The Commercial Revolution,
1831–1843

An astonishing thing happened in Baltimore during the 1830s: all the historical forces that had been at work for more than a generation suddenly cohered. The processes of democratic change—the specialization and isolation of social groups, the transformation of labor, the institutionalization of human relationships, the emergence of manufacturing as an alternative to agriculture and trade, and the other fundamental social changes historically associated with the development and utilization of steam power—broke through the forces of resistance that held the changes in check. Suddenly and swiftly, Baltimore changed its very appearance as well as its cultural ways. And though the momentum of the changes was too great to check, their course was channeled into Baltimore's more inclusive set of cultural values, and the result was to cast the democratic changes into their subsequent nineteenth-century ideology of laissez faire capitalism.

The nature of this passing of the old order and its various ramifications will be described in a later chapter. First it is necessary to consider the changed economic environment which, while by no means "causing" the reaction, made it possible. Baltimore's commercial economy had been caught in an international storm that raged from 1807 to 1819; it had foundered in the panic of 1819, and had appeared to be sinking throughout the long depression of the 1820s. But then, in 1831, came an abrupt change. For the next six years Baltimoreans went through an inflationary boom that was not fully attended by prosperity but seemed to be; and for six years after that they enjoyed relative prosperity in a context of general deflation and depression. These aberrant economic circumstances enveloped the powerful sociopolitical movement of the passing of the old order.

Baltimore's Position amid the New Realities

The profitable restoration of the traditional order was the springboard for the "commercial reaction," but economic and political conditions during the 1830s were far more complex than traditionalists thought they were.

The new developments of the period were many and varied, and the most important was one over which neither Baltimoreans nor any other Americans had control, a new commercial relationship with Great Britain. This new relationship resulted from a process that had been evolving for years and ended in a transition from dispersed, localized eighteenth-century seaport economies into an international economy dominated by Great Britain. The appearance of this international market economy was an integral part of the same process that was creating an American national economy; and, for Baltimore, it was equally important in its social and economic effects.

Baltimore's position in this scheme of things hinged mainly on the community's position in relation to Liverpool, the center of nineteenth-century industrialism. By the early 1830s Liverpool was the center of what was emerging as a world economy in which European (and chiefly British) markets dominated the market economies throughout the world. Not only were the financial aspects of the worldwide flow of commodities to and from Liverpool regulated in Liverpool, but Liverpool market indicators—prices, interest and insurance rates, and the like—frequently determined the indicators in other worldwide markets. Nevertheless, two factors conditioned the degree of influence that Liverpool exerted over foreign markets: geography and political considerations.

Among American ports, New York had the best connections with Liverpool, far better than Baltimore had. Historically, New York had accelerated its trade with Liverpool during the 1790s, the very time when Baltimore was abandoning its English connections. New York was physically closer to Liverpool than Baltimore by two or three sailing days. Also, New York had tapped the vast domestic American markets in the West since 1825, while Baltimore had not. Moreover, New York had the advantage of being about two degrees of latitude further north than Baltimore, which meant that New York's marketing season was earlier and shorter than Baltimore's. Almost naturally, Baltimore's relationship to Liverpool gravitated through New York. Goods and ideas were passed from Liverpool to New York; and after a trial in New York's market they were sent on to Baltimore and other Southern markets. By the early 1830s many of Baltimore's wholesale merchants had learned that it was more economical to go to New York for Liverpool's goods than it was to go to Liverpool, and they accepted this as a fact of life.[1]

In addition to the pull of Liverpool, there was another reason that Americans became increasingly oriented toward Britain during the thirties—namely, that British investment capital began to flow on a large scale to the United States just when the federal government was abandoning its direct support of internal improvements. After American currency was fixed upon a legal specie basis by the Coinage Act of 1834 and many states and municipalities (including Maryland and Baltimore) began assuming legal responsibility for financing internal improvements by issuing bonded debt, British investors felt safe in purchasing the securities of railroads, roads, canals, and even the stocks of the state of Maryland and the municipal corporation of Baltimore. Baltimore's domestic economy was thus drawn into closer dependency upon Great Britain's through finance at the same time that the American national market economy was brought into greater alignment with that of the British. One of the implications was that fluctuations in this new international economy would have a more direct and immediate effect upon Baltimore's market than ever before.[2]

This international market economy is the proper general context for understanding the economic upheavals of first inflation and then deflation that hit Baltimore in the 1830s. The inflation of the early thirties resulted from various causes: the reopening of the British West Indies trade; the accumulation of Mexican silver in the United States because of the contracted China trade; the influx of British capital as one substitute for federal government aid in financing internal improvements and the consequent American adoption, for practical purposes, of the gold standard in 1834; the tariff of 1833, which was the commercialmen's reaction to the manufacturers' demand for protection and which continued allowing duties to be paid on credit terms instead of paid immediately in specie; the removal of the federal government deposits from the second Bank of the United States into designated "pet" banks; and the boom in southwestern land sales coupled with the rise of cotton prices in England. Deflation began in 1836 when British capital, the most essential ingredient in this inflationary boom, was drastically curtailed.

Baltimore was not affected in the subsequent deflation as much as New York, Philadelphia, or New Orleans were, because Baltimore was not involved in the international market economy to the degree that those seaports were. Even during the inflationary boom, Baltimore's foreign trade had continued to decline; the city had never participated in the cotton trade to any large extent; and it was still without a direct and easy access to the domestic markets in the West.

The general pattern of Baltimore's mercantile economy during these years may be summarized briefly. Overall, Baltimore's balance of trade was in its favor for only four of the fifteen years from 1829 through 1843, and its total trade deficit during those years was more than sixteen million dollars. More specifically, total tonnage engaged in foreign trade increased only slightly; tonnage of entrances and clearances (the actual shipping activity of Baltimore's foreign trade) also increased only slightly; shipbuilding declined sharply; and the value of the city's imports and exports declined somewhat. But the general downward trend bottomed out in 1837, and the depression of 1837 to 1843 marked the beginning of a ten-year upswing in Baltimore's commerce. The increased tonnage after 1836, plus the fact that the number of ships engaged in foreign trade increased almost uniformly from 1834 through 1841, illustrates how shipping activity increased as it became more profitable during the early years of the depression. In fact, Baltimore's share of the nation's total foreign trade in 1837, 1840, and 1841 was equal to its share during the best years of the 1820s. Its share of imports declined very little during the depression years from that of the early 1830s, and its share of the nation's exports actually increased.[3]

What Baltimoreans Thought and Did

These were the objective conditions; but there were equally important and quite different subjective conditions, and it was subjective conditions that stimulated Baltimore's leaders to do what they did. Baltimoreans entirely failed to understand inflation. Since prices were generally rising until 1837, they assumed that times were good and even booming; and they could only have been confused when they wondered how prosperity and bankruptcy were occurring simultaneously.

Of the various causes of the inflation, Baltimoreans were fully aware of only three, and this limited awareness governed their conduct. One was President Jackson's veto of the bill to recharter the second Bank of the United States in 1832; of Jackson's banking policies and Baltimore's response to them more will be said presently. A second was the reopening of the British West Indies trade to American shipping in October of 1830, which turned out to have greater psychological effect than economic value to Baltimore. Living with the memory of past glories, Baltimoreans assumed that the reopening of the trade would restore their community's relative position in the nation. It did seem to give a boost to trade, for the volume of shipping to and from the West Indies increased considerably: the number of ships arriving from the West Indies increased from 98 in 1830 to 154 in 1832, decreased again from 1833 through 1835, and then rose to new highs from 1836 to 1839.[4]

The third cause of inflation that Baltimoreans were aware of, but also misinterpreted, was the provision in the tariff of 1832 allowing importers to pay their duties on a three-year credit basis instead of in cash. Such credits enabled importers to raise the prices of their goods and to increase sales by selling on equally long term credits. However, the profits from the increased prices and the interest rate difference between the importers' purchases and sales was inflationary and spurred a sense of mercantile opportunity which, together with the actually increasing West Indies trade, created a psychology of prosperity that was not justified by reality. Facts to the contrary notwithstanding, Baltimoreans believed that prosperity had at last returned after the depression of the 1820s and acted on that belief by overvaluing production and services. As a result, 1833 and 1834 witnessed a mixture of inflation and contraction as merchants, business institutions, and even banks failed, yet prices and real estate values rose.[5]

Easier credit, rising prices, and increased real estate values continued throughout 1835 and 1836, but without the failures of 1833 and 1834. For this reason, when financial crisis came in 1837, many believed it to be merely a tightening-up, a time when the inflationary spiral had caught up with those who had overtraded or overextended themselves. In turn, this caused many businessmen to miscalculate in 1838 and extend their operations, thinking they could either capture a larger share of the market or also take advantage of the lowered prices, which they assumed would soon rise. But a second contraction followed in 1839, one that was perforce far worse than that of 1837.[6]

Several circumstances explain Baltimore's uneven growth and overall, limited prosperity in the midst of the supposed Jacksonian boom of 1829 to 1837. First was the depression of 1829 and early 1830, which resulted from the tariff of 1828 and the retaliatory legislation passed by the British against American shipping. Manufactured by politicians for partisan purposes, the tariff gave unwanted protections to Baltimore's textile manufacturers. American-made textiles had, in fact, already reached the saturation point in the American market. The new tariff simply stimulated both production and competition. Prices quickly fell below the cost of production, and several manufacturers around Baltimore curtailed and even halted production. Meanwhile the British ministry, which had begun its economic warfare with the American tariff system in 1816, retaliated against the 1828 tariff: first in 1828 by lowering the duty paid by British ships carrying cotton from a British colony; and then, in 1830, by opening the British West Indies colonies to American ships on an equal footing with British ships. To American shipping merchants these British measures were clearly aimed at enlarging the British share of the cotton-carrying trade, and therefore of the transatlantic trade.[7]

A second circumstance that accounted for Baltimore's comparative stagnation in the early 1830s was the crucial political situation in Great Britain from 1830 to 1832. When William IV ascended the British throne in June 1830, Europe was already convulsed in revolution, and many feared the disorders would spread to Great Britain. British trade to the continent drastically declined in 1830 and continued depressed in 1831 because of the political disorders as well as the appearance of cholera epidemics in most of the continental seaports. In addition, the China trade was virtually closed. This lucrative market continued to be disrupted by the reorganization of the Hong (the Chinese merchants who were licensed by the emperor to trade with Westerners), which had begun in 1829 and was being exploited by anti-Western groups at the Chinese court, who opposed "foreign devils" in general and British ones in particular. In this context of international turmoil, the Bank of England overreacted by contracting its outstanding money supply from 19 million pounds sterling to 17 million pounds sterling within one year. The contraction resulted in a lowering of prices for securities and commodities, a decline in the demand for all American commodities and especially cotton, a severe credit contraction, and several bankruptcies among merchants. The situation steadily worsened until it finally reached crisis proportions in the late winter of 1832, just when it reached Baltimore.[8]

In the summer and fall of 1831, when British merchants and manufacturers found their credit restricted, English prices falling, and worldwide markets generally contracting, they sent more goods at lower prices to New York. Several Baltimore wholesalers, thinking to take advantage of what they regarded as a temporary decline in prices, purchased large supplies of these goods. But almost immediately the general contraction in Great Britain spread to the United States, and as prices continued to fall the Baltimore wholesalers were stuck with goods they had bought at prices which, in a matter of only eight months, had become exorbitant. Unable to acquire loans from the banks with which to pay their own debts, seven of Baltimore's leading importers and wholesalers were forced to suspend payments in February of 1832, and other Baltimore merchants began talking about the bad times of 1818 and 1819. Tight money—which is to say reduced credit facilities—and generally contracted market conditions resulted from these failures and continued throughout the spring and summer of 1832. This was the very time when the controversy over rechartering the second Bank of the United States absorbed the attention of many in the business community.[9]

At this point the policies of the Bank of the United States entered the equation and provided the third reason for Baltimore's inability to share in the vaunted Jacksonian boom of the 1830s. The Bank of the United States was confronted with two adverse situations: the worsening international economic picture and a group of politicians both hostile to and ignorant about the bank and its operations. These politicians (mainly President Jackson, Amos Kendall, and Roger Brooke Taney) insisted upon interpreting the business decisions of the bank as political actions and refused to discuss the recharter rationally—or, perhaps more properly, nonpolitically. Either they did not understand the operations of the bank, the American economy, and the emergent international economy, or else they deliberately cloaked their knowledge in prejudice and facile argument. But the main reason for the impasse in discussion was that the decision to recharter was ultimately a political rather than an economic decision, and it was made by politicians who were more concerned with the political than with the economic effects of their decision. If Jackson, Kendall, and Taney had been less ignorant about general business conditions and how business operations were conducted, the bank's recharter might still have been denied, but its demise would almost certainly have been attended with less acrimony and financial stringency, in Baltimore and elsewhere.[10]

The Jacksonians' principal charge, that the "contraction policies of the Bank of the United States" had adverse effects, needs clarification. This charge assumed that the bank was autonomous in its environment and capable of actually controlling economic conditions. But no institution controlled economic conditions, and in this respect the BUS was no different from any other institution, including the federal government. Institutions merely responded to environmental change by establishing procedures which tried to regularize and stabilize environmental processes and developments. In short, institutions merely brought order to a set of conditions. What needs explanation are the conditions, the economic environment, that confronted the BUS; by understanding the conditions we can explain the actions of institutions as the decisions of men based upon their beliefs and perceptions about their reality. The Jacksonian charge was both naive and, in a certain sense, false; but the worst thing about it was that it reflected the point of view not of institutional leaders but of those upon whom institutional decisions fell. And this was precisely why the charge was politically successful. *

From the viewpoint of those upon whom institutional decisions fell, the Jacksonians were entirely correct: there is no doubt that the BUS pursued a policy of "contraction" (meaning that it curtailed credit and reduced the supply of money) beginning in the early fall of 1831. What the Jacksonians neglected to mention was that this contraction was in re-

* This also illustrates the wider dimension of "Jacksonian Democracy" in its rhetorical inversion of values. The conservatism of the Jacksonians can be seen in their concern with short-term, almost presentist social effect. They did not project a long-range, coherent ideology; instead, they responsed to the new conditions in piecemeal fashion; and because their response was eclectic and fragmented, so also were the effects of their response.

sponse to the contraction of British market conditions and a preparation to pay holders of federal government redemption stock on January 1, 1832. The BUS continued its contraction policy during the spring and summer of 1832 because of the continued international market pressures, which were now also aggravated by cholera epidemics in American seaports, and because Jackson's administration announced in March that more federal government bonds would be partially redeemed on July 1, 1832. This meant that the contraction would continue during the months of April, May, and June—the spring marketing season in Baltimore. Since credit facilities were already taut, however, and in view of the failures in February and a controversy that was raging among Baltimore banks about paying interest on deposits, the Baltimore branch of the BUS refused to follow the parent board's order to proceed with further contraction. William McIlvaine, cashier of the Philadelphia bank, wrote to John White, cashier of the Baltimore branch, on April 21, 1832, praising White for reducing his branch's loans by $240,000 from March 12 to April 9, but scolding him for increasing his discounts to merchants and chiding him in this manner: "We desire to apprize you of the wish of the administration of the Bank gently but steadily to restrain its general business, with a view to be the better prepared for meeting those heavy reimbursements of public debt which will doubtless be required by the government, in the course of the present year." But White replied in no uncertain terms on May 5: "From the unanimity of sentiment amongst the Directors, it is very evident that the progress of curtailment here will depend entirely upon the wants of the Community—the Board appear to be resolved not to press upon Traders, & to consider it unpracticable to turn over any portion of their fair demands upon us to the Local Banks." And then White softened his remarks in this manner: "Notwithstanding the repugnance evinced to curtail, I feel satisfied that Board will find pleasure in seeing our line of Discounts decline if it can be accomplished without inconvenience to our customers or to the City."[11]

It should not be assumed that either Nicholas Biddle, president of the Bank of the United States, or Louis McLane, then secretary of the treasury, was insensitive to the needs of the mercantile community. They understood that postponing the redemption of the federal government bonds until fall, when the cholera epidemics would be over and trade would approach normality, would allow the bank to maximize its credit facilities as far as conditions permitted during the trying spring and summer months. Thus, sometime in June it was decided to postpone the redemption of the bonds from July 1 to October 1, 1832. But unfortunately, this decision actually served to prolong the tight money conditions in Baltimore, for the cholera epidemic virtually suspended trade during the late summer and early fall. This left the Bank of the United States still having to redeem the bonds on October 1. The single month of October was the only time when the bank could help the mercantile community. But by then the fall marketing season was too far advanced for the more stabilized credit system to be of much benefit. Moreover, the approaching presidential election absorbed the time, energy, and even loans of the Bank of the United States.

Jackson's reelection in November mortified many and surprised several of the bank's supporters. The Jacksonians, for their part, regarded it as the popular vindication of their antibank tactics, and were encouraged to continue their political attacks upon the bank. Consequently, in his annual message to Congress in December of 1832, Jackson questioned the safety of the United States Treasury funds in the bank. The implication of his remark, that the funds might be withdrawn, posed a serious problem for the bank. It appeared that the bank had no choice but to curtail credits in order to build up reserves to meet the possible transfer of federal government funds. In response, credit facilities in Baltimore tightened during the winter of 1832–33, loosened slightly but briefly for the spring trade in 1833, and then severely contracted in the late fall after a portion of the federal government's deposits were transferred from the Bank of the United States to the Union Bank of Maryland in Baltimore. This contraction worsened over the winter of 1833–34 and culminated in a financial panic during the spring of 1834.

Two aspects of this 1834 panic in Baltimore require explanation. First, the panic was really only indirectly related to the successive contractions by the Bank of the United States in the fall, winter, and spring of 1833–34. The panic involved the failures of the Bank of Maryland, the United States Insurance Company, and the Maryland Savings Institution, none of which were directly connected with the Bank of the United States. Actually, the origins of the panic lay in the mismanagement and even fraudulent management and overextended condition of the Bank of Maryland. The paper expansion of this bank without adequate specie reserves was accomplished by its introduction of a banking novelty in Baltimore during the winter of 1831–32: paying interest on deposits. By paying such interest, the bank attracted deposits from many Baltimoreans who were not traders but who had small capitals, funds too small to invest in public securities. For this reason this bank had little to do with the general economic situation of antebellum banking in Baltimore, the financing of trade, because its social base was different. For the same reason the social implications of the failure of the bank were far greater than the economic implications. The middle-class affiliation of the Bank of Maryland gave the financial crisis of 1834 a much wider social significance than such crises usually had in antebellum Baltimore. Alex Brown and Sons, the most prominent mercantile firm in Baltimore, described this social basis of the panic to their agent in New Orleans, Benjamin Story, who was also president of the state's Bank of Louisiana, in May 1834:

> Here there has been a great deal of distress by the failure of the Bank of Maryland, United States Ins. Co. & Saving Institution say to the amount of about three millions, a great part of which falls on the middling & lower classes of the people who were induced for the sake of saving a little interest to place their little all in these institutions which has been loaned out to designing men on little or no security & now those who are able can pay their debts to them at 50 cents in the dollar—we had no confidence in any of these institutions & are not invested for one dollar.[12]

The second aspect of Baltimore's 1834 panic was that the prospective demise of the BUS encouraged the financial speculations of those controlling the Bank of Maryland. In fact, the bank's president, Evan Poultney, enjoyed regular access to the latest news about Jackson's war against the BUS from Thomas Ellicott, president of the Union Bank of Maryland (one of Jackson's future "pet" banks), who was a personal friend of Roger Brooke Taney, Jackson's attorney general. Eventually, Taney was appointed secretary of the treasury for the express purpose of transferring the federal government's funds from the BUS to certain state banks. Evan Poultney's relationship with Thomas Ellicott long antedated 1834: Ellicott's son, William Miller Ellicott, was married to Sarah Poultney, Evan's sister; Poultney was a private banker whose firm, Evan Poultney and Company, was formed in 1829 with Ellicott's financial aid; Poultney had acquired his controlling interest in the Bank of Maryland in 1831 by loans from Ellicott's bank, the Union Bank; in July 1832, after Jackson's inner circle had already decided to definitely oppose recharter of the BUS as their principal political issue, the firm of Evan Poultney and Company was reorganized as Poultney, Ellicott and Company, and William Miller Ellicott became a partner; and in that summer the Bank of Maryland and Poultney, Ellicott and Company began their expansion.

Their first objective was to increase the note circulation of the Bank of Maryland, especially between Baltimore and the West and probably to the extent that the BUS contracted its circulation. Since he needed additional specie in order to increase his note circulation, Poultney decided to attract specie by paying interest on deposits. To attract depositors the Bank of Maryland offered to pay 5 percent interest on deposits payable thirty days after demand, and 3 percent on current deposits. Evan Poultney and Company, and later Poultney, Ellicott and Company, paid the same interest.

Their next objective was to give greater circulation to the Bank of Maryland's notes. To effect this purpose, a chain of agencies was established in Little Rock, Louisville, New Orleans, Cincinnati, and Elkton, Maryland. An attempt to establish an agency in New York did not succeed. Through these agencies, the speculators expected to circulate about two million dollars, which was almost seven times the capital of the Bank of Maryland. Coordinating the agencies was Evan Poultney and Company, and later Poultney, Ellicott and Company.

This was the basic outline of what Poultney was trying to do. He was joined by others who extended the bank's influence in Baltimore by becoming members of the boards of directors of existing business institutions, creating satellite business firms, and speculating in securities. In 1833, however, the speculators overreached themselves. During the winter of 1832–33, when Taney spearheaded the movement within Jackson's inner circle for the removal of the federal government's deposits from the BUS, he frequently sought the advice of his banker and friend, Thomas Ellicott. In turn, Ellicott took advantage of every opportunity to impress Jackson's administration with his abilities as a banker. At the time, when many state bankers were hesitant about supporting the removal of the deposits in the following spring, Ellicott vigorously defended the expediency, morality, and political correctness of such a move in letters and conversations with Taney, Jackson, and other state bankers. As the summer of 1833 approached, it became evident to Poultney and the other speculators at the Bank of Maryland that Ellicott's Union Bank of Maryland would be designated the depository for federal government funds in Baltimore. In June one of the speculators quietly began purchasing Union Bank stock for the group, thinking it would rise in market value once the bank was designated a depository. Thomas Ellicott apparently agreed with the premise of the speculation, for the Union Bank financed the operation. On September 26, Secretary of the Treasury Taney announced the removal of deposits, and the Union Bank of Maryland was the only Baltimorean bank specified to receive a portion of them. But the bank's stock never rose above what the speculators paid for it.

At this point, the expanding Bank of Maryland began to contract. Not able to sell their Union Bank stock for a profit, the speculators disbanded; and the overextended position of the Bank of Maryland began to be perilous. As money and credit tightened because of the BUS contraction in the fall and winter of 1833–34, the Western agencies of the Bank of Maryland were unable to continue their exchange business. The circulation of Bank of Maryland notes fell off accordingly, and the agencies gradually ceased operations. None returned any money to the bank in Baltimore. With no income, an increasing public reluctance to accept its notes, and an absurdly insufficient supply of specie to redeem its outstanding bank notes (its ratio of circulated bank notes to specie was more than fifty to one), the Bank of Maryland closed its doors on March 22, 1834. This failure, and Poultney's known intimacy with Thomas Ellicott, precipitated a run upon Ellicott's Jacksonian "pet," the Union Bank, on March 23 and 24. The arrival of Secretary Taney, coupled with the fact that the Union Bank had a large supply of specie, prevented the run from continuing or seriously spreading to the other Baltimore banks. Nevertheless the stoppage of the Bank of Maryland precipitated a cash crisis in the community at large, and other failures followed during April and May.

In terms of Baltimore's macroeconomy, however, this panic was brief and scarcely touched the regular business community. Apart from its direct economic consequences, about the only effect of the panic was that more Baltimoreans became interested in banks and banking than ever before because of the social bases of the institutions which failed. The scheme of the Bank of Maryland was what the nineteenth-century called a "puff." Only expansion, increasing the bank's circulation, kept the scheme solvent. Once expansion stopped, contraction would begin immediately, because once people began presenting the bank's notes and demanding specie, the bank could not continue to operate. The bank needed a constant cash flow; it needed exchange. Unfortunately for the speculators who ran the Bank of Maryland, the BUS contraction in the fall and winter of 1833–34 depressed all such business operations. To this extent, the Jacksonians' charge that the BUS contraction was harmful was well founded, though it neglected the even larger international context in which the BUS played but a pawn's role.

The False Prosperity of the Mid-1830s

Just as Baltimore's tangential position to Philadelphia and New York in relation to the British economy helps to explain Baltimore's panic of 1834, so this relationship also helps to explain what happened to Baltimore from 1834 through 1836. The long mercantile depression that began soon after the War of 1812 reached its nadir during these years: the total tonnage engaged in foreign trade further declined; the number of ships engaged in foreign trade was lower than at any other time before 1861; the balance of trade ran heavily against Baltimore, and its total for these four years alone represented about 60 percent of Baltimore's

total trade deficit for the entire period from 1829 through 1843; and finally, Baltimore's share of the total foreign trade of the United States was
lower from 1834 through 1836 than it ever was from 1821 until the 1850s.
Baltimore's mercantile economy seemingly bottomed out before the depression—which began in 1837—wrought its long-range effects.[13]

And yet, despite the severity of mercantile conditions between 1834 and
1836, a general optimism, or more properly a euphoria, pervaded the
business community and governed business decisions. There were several
causes for this optimism, all of which were more physical and visible
than the world that future historians would see. First, the British economy gradually recovered from the 1830–32 crisis during the years from
1833 to 1836. This recovery increased the demand for, and thus the
prices of, American commodities. British consumption of American cotton alone rose 31 percent, while cotton prices at New Orleans rose 52
percent and at New York rose 34 percent.[14]

Even more important than this recovery of Britain's market was a new
aspect of its economy: the export of specie to the United States for capital
investments. This second cause of Baltimore's euphoria occurred at a
crucial juncture in its history. It coincided with the federal government's
abandonment of eighteenth-century mercantilism; and British capital
made the American transition to laissez faire capitalism smoother by
facilitating private and public enterprise at the state level in an atmosphere of prosperity. In the general historical context, the Jacksonian
insistence upon "hard" money (specie-based money) aligned the United
States financially with Great Britain in 1834; and this paved the way for
the investment of British capital in America. In that year the Jacksonians
(especially encouraged by those from the gold-producing states of Georgia and North Carolina) raised the ratio of silver to gold in American
currency from fifteen for one to sixteen for one. Jackson, Benton, and
Taney said that they expected this devaluation of silver (whose abun-
dance stemmed from the discovery of Mexican silver mines in the 1820s)
and upgrading of gold* to result in gold coins replacing bank notes. In-

*Upgrading in the sense that its market value increased. In point of fact, this
second Coinage Act of June 28, 1834, devalued the American dollar. Under the
terms of the Mint Act of April 2, 1792, the American dollar contained 24.75
grains of gold; under the 1834 act the dollar contained 23.22 grains of gold.
Ostensibly, the intention of the Jacksonians was to devalue the American gold
dollar in order to replace bank notes on the basis of the thought-to-be huge gold
supplies. I say "ostensibly" because it is difficult to believe that some Jacksonians,
such as Philadelphia financier Reuben Whitney, did not understand how such a
national devaluation was an international revaluation upward and would result
in gold importations.

stead, the result was that bank notes continued to be printed and to circulate; and the importation of gold did rise enormously. Initially, the British were alarmed by the act, because they correctly surmised it would lead to gold being exported to America from Great Britian instead of silver, which was now worth less in relation to gold. But the long-range effect of the Coinage Act of 1834 was to provide the United States and Great Britain with a common financial standard and to draw their economies into closer alignment.[15]

This common financial standard led Americans to encourage and even demand payments from their debtors in gold, for British capitalists used the terms of the Coinage Act as the vehicle for their investments in America. The new specie standard thus became crucial to America's link with British capital markets and had to be maintained whatever the cost to individual American merchants, which is why Americans were anxious to maintain specie payments after the onset of the 1837 crisis. From the American point of view, adopting the gold standard had the effect of suddenly opening long-closed British capital markets to American entrepreneurial activities. Accordingly, Americans tried, after 1834, to maximize their business contact with that market. American securities of all kinds—of banks, of various types of internal improvement companies, and of various levels of government—found their way into English capital markets.[16]

Another reason for Baltimore's optimism and sense of prosperity from 1834 to 1836 was an almost direct response to the flow of British investment capital and the expansion of Baltimore banking facilities: the revival of internal improvements. The infusion of new sources of capital and credit saved Baltimore's internal-improvement schemes; it replaced the traditional reliance upon lotteries—indeed, driving them into disrepute —and eliminated the political controversy over the issue of federal government assistance to internal improvements. After Jackson's administration had declared its unwillingness to aid internal improvements in the Maysville Road veto message in 1830, many projects (such as the Baltimore & Ohio Railroad and the Chesapeake and Ohio Canal companies) virtually suspended their operations. By developing gold in the attempt to establish it as the common currency, the Coinage Act of 1834 encouraged British investments in American internal improvements, providing the investments were guaranteed by the legal entities, the states in this case, in which the internal improvements were being made. For example, Maryland lent its liability to the Baltimore & Ohio Railroad, the Chesapeake and Ohio Canal, and the Potomac Canal companies from 1834 to 1836 by issuing bonds totaling $9 million and authorizing the companies to sell them in the British capital markets. All this was done in the belief

TABLE 6
Banking in Baltimore, 1829–1841
(except 1831 and 1832)

Year	Specie	Circulation	Ratio c Circulati to Spec
1829	$ 788,762.43	$1,820,890.01	2.31
1830	752,903.00	1,102,147.00	1.46
1833	544,000.00	1,321,000.00	2.43
1834	406,436.97	805,129.33	1.98
1835	704,754.55	1,202,857.50	1.71
1836	692,911.20	1,755,300.69	2.53
1837	555,832.51	1,594,603.38	2.87
1838	835,971.96	1,977,235.65	2.37
1839	776,755.45	2,018,159.76	2.60
1840	833,152.98	1,938,906.00	2.33
1841	1,231,563.76	1,781,996.38	1.45

SOURCE: Figures for 1834 through 1839 are averages of mon
figures; all other years represent figures calculated in Decembe
January from the Annual Bank Reports to the Maryland leg
ture, Maryland Public Documents.
* Not available.

that these internal improvements were community projects in which all
citizens shared an interest; and in this sense, the opening of British capital
markets to American enterprise greatly stimulated that local pride which
constituted a cultural reformation in Baltimore in the early 1830s.[17]

Another major cause of Baltimore's inflation and accompanying euphoria was a proliferation of banking capital and credit, which was encouraged by the prospective demise of the BUS. In response to that
expectation, six new banks began operations in Baltimore. One (the Merchants Bank, which bought the specie of the BUS branch) was created by
the Maryland legislature during the session of 1834–35; the other five
were created during the session of 1835–36 (the Chesapeake, the Citizens, the Farmers and Planters, the Hamilton, and the Western). The
total capital of these banks, by the time the last one began operations in
January 1838 was $3,948,403. Table 6 illustrates the yearly changes in
specie, circulation, deposits, and discounts during the inflationary years

Deposits	Ratio of Circulation Plus Deposits to Specie	Discounts
$2,087,671.26	4.96	$ 7,774,602.88
1,473,866.00	3.42	6,188,771.00
1,985,000.00	6.08	n.a.*
1,532,222.97	5.73	6,252,023.49
2,330,943.24	5.01	7,070,430.04
2,163,363.20	5.56	10,105,796.57
2,550,367.66	7.46	11,360,545.15
2,744,830.99	5.65	12,095,925.08
2,518,806.94	5.84	12,338,346.27
2,801,587.11	5.69	11,497,389.56
2,572,831.34	3.54	8,795,213.57

from 1834 to 1837. During the most inflationary period, from the fall of 1836 to the spring of 1837, three of these banks (the Citizens, the Farmers and Planters, and the Western) began operations and introduced an additional capital of $1,505,431 into Baltimore's mercantile community. This had the effect of facilitating the expansion of trade at the very moment when the downward shift in the British economy was warning against it.[18]

Taken together, the recovery of the British economy, the export of British capital to America, the revival of internal improvements, and the expansion of domestic banking produced an inflationary boom in Baltimore during the mid-1830s. Yet, the fundamental result of these inputs of capital and credit was neither industrial expansion nor a revival of the mercantile economy; Baltimore's economy continued to decline during the 1830s even as it had in the 1820s. In almost all respects the inflationary boom was socially unproductive—for example, it resulted in wage earners' being confronted by declining real wages. What was more, it created the disparity between financial and economic reality that was the necessary condition for the depression of 1837 to 1843.

Panics and Deflation

The imbalance between financial and economic reality was partially corrected by the recession in 1837. This severe financial contraction originated with the Bank of England's decision in 1836 to raise its discount rates in an attempt to slow the dangerous decline of the stock of gold in England. The desired effect was achieved but at the cost of mercantile failures and suspension of specie payments throughout the United States in 1837. By the winter of 1837–38, however, trade and markets were settled on a lowered but more stable footing, which provided for a partial recovery in 1838. This revival, after being buoyed by the resumption of specie payments in August of 1838, continued through the summer of 1839, when a second panic resulted from another contraction of English financial markets and a bumper cotton crop. A second suspension of specie payments ensued in October of 1839, but this one was not followed by a period of recovery. Instead, most market indicators steadily and slowly contracted; and the succeeding four years marked a period of severe deflation in which the export of British capital to America ceased, the American financial system was prostrated, and importations of goods were greatly reduced.[19]

Thus, what has been traditionally regarded as a depression from 1837 to 1843 was in reality a period of deflation occurring in two waves. The first wave was the severe contraction of 1837, which resulted from the Bank of England's raising of interest rates in 1836; the second depressed general market conditions until 1843. This second wave had two causes. One was the suspension of British capital investments in America after several states (Maryland among them) defaulted in payment of interest on their debts, and two states, Michigan and Mississippi, repudiated their debts entirely. These debts had been taken on to pay for the construction of internal improvements that were not yet completed and therefore were not producing revenue (the single exception was the Baltimore & Ohio Railroad, which was able to continue amortizing its debt from its revenues). But to the British investor it looked very much as though the Americans had simply used British capital for their own purposes and were not willing to acknowledge legitimate British claims when the transportation facilities were nearing completion. A second cause of the 1839 crisis was the prostration of American finance following upon the withdrawal of British capital and credit from the general depression of trade. American banks were caught in the American commitment to the specie standard, which had linked America with British finance since 1834 and provided a transatlantic bridge for British capital investments to America. In spite of declining trade activity, it was fundamentally important for American banks to adhere to the international specie standard if the hope of future British capital investment was to remain alive.

Specie payments were such a controversial subject during these years because different men having different relationships to the British economy had correspondingly different views. Consider, for example, three groups: New York bankers, Baltimore bankers, and Maryland politicians. New York bankers had the most immediate and direct interest in maintaining specie payments, because their seaport had more direct and immediate contact with British capital markets than did any other American seaport. Baltimore bankers, on the other hand, were connected only second-handedly with British capital markets, either through New York or through such private bankers as Alex Brown and Sons, and they were accordingly less interested in maintaining specie payments, especially because such payments imposed financial hardships upon the local merchants. Furthermore, Baltimore bankers did not participate in the international financial community to the extent that New York bankers did. For these reasons, Baltimore bankers were more responsive to the needs of Baltimore merchants than New York bankers were to those of New York merchants.

In contrast with both groups of bankers were Maryland politicians who, irrespective of party, looked at the situation in terms of Maryland as a community and a political unity that owed money to British creditors and was dependent upon British capital for further development. Apart from the moral implications of paying one's debts, to the politicians the situation was one of simple economic expediency. But what they misunderstood or else discounted was the effect that maintenance of specie payments would have upon the mercantile community. If Baltimore banks were to make specie payments, they would have to contract currency and credit and thus place the merchants in an extremely awkward financial position. For this reason, when the Maryland legislature required all Maryland chartered banks to begin making specie payments in May of 1842, the result was about as disastrous as the situation in May of 1819. In other words, the price for maintaining Maryland's connection with British capital markets (a long-range decision) was high: immediate and severe mercantile failures.

Generally speaking, what happened in Baltimore from 1837 to 1843 was a severe deflation within a commercial economy. As in previous instances, the city's domestic economy and connections with other American markets expanded while those with foreign markets declined. For example, the depression in foreign trade was more than offset by the expansion of Baltimore's coastal trade. Indeed, in 1838, 1840, and 1841, the city's documented tonnage in the coastal trade surpassed that in its foreign trade probably for the only time between 1829 and 1860. After 1843 Baltimore's foreign trade revived and accounted for about 60 percent of the community's documented tonnage.[20]

Because the depression occurred in the sense that deflation caused bankruptcies and unemployment, it followed the pattern that had been created by the monetization of credit and had become apparent for the first time during the crisis of 1799. This and the subsequent crises of 1819, 1834, and 1837, for example, began as failures of the financial mechanism, then spread into the general credit system and thereby affected the wider community. But the panic of 1837 was as brief as, and less serious than, the panic of 1834. It did not become depression. Specie, bank-note circulation, deposits, and discounts all rose through 1838. But then, in October 1839, came another and worse panic that did turn into depression. People withdrew their bank deposits and demanded specie for their bank notes. To prevent the run on the banks from worsening, and to protect the business community, the banks increased their note circulation slightly and their discounts even more. But because the causes of the panic were national and international in scope, Baltimore's banks could do nothing more than temporarily alleviate its local effects, which generally worsened until 1843.

Nevertheless, the banks' efforts to aid the community bespoke their sense of social obligation and at the same time demonstrated their vital importance to the community. Indeed, the Baltimoreans learned from 1839 to 1843 just how crucial their banking institutions had become to them. Contemporaries worried about the solvency of banks; "preserving the banks" and "maintaining the currency" became rallying cries during these years; and as Baltimoreans accepted the logic of these arguments, which the historical development of banking virtually dictated, they accepted what these institutions did in their society after 1839. The continuing contraction of the money supply forced individuals to apply for credit from the banks; and the banks grew more selective in granting accommodations. The deflation thus strengthened the banking system by acting in a discriminatory way within the community.

In society at large, the contraction of money and credit aided the wealthier segments of the community at the expense of the less wealthy. Known and proven businessmen were accommodated; factory wage earners were not. The reason for this was that the structure of the banking system had developed in conformity with Baltimore's social structure. Banks were still occupationally specialized during the 1830s, their directors usually representing a common occupational interest. Among the new banks chartered in 1835, for example, the Western Bank was dominated by importers involved in the Western trade, and the Merchants' Bank was dominated by importers who sold to jobbers. Moreover, bank directors were the first recipients of their bank's credit; after them came their relatives, friends, and acquaintances and other people whom the directors and the rest of the community knew. Besides, factory workers who earned about six dollars per week had little occasion to enter a bank, since bank notes were not issued in denominations of less than five dollars. The banks created especially for wage earners were the savings institutions, which were places of deposit rather than banks of issue. Though products of monetization of credit, these kinds of banks originated more directly with the paternalistic concern over the breakdown of traditional social controls following the War of 1812 and, consequently, they functioned for moral rather than financial purposes. After May of 1837, such institutions found their function anachronistic. The contraction of money hurt the wage earners, the least wealthy and least articulate group in society, more than any other group; and it forced them to use up what little capital they had managed to accumulate and to plunge further into debt.[21]

Though the actions of the banks hurt individual Baltimoreans, they operated for the good of all. The suspension of specie payments, for example, was not always involuntary and did not always result in economic chaos. The suspension of October 1839 was not really necessary, for the banks' specie level was not endangered by their note circulation and deposit levels. Baltimore bankers merely followed the suspension by Philadelphia and New York bankers, because a general suspension by the nation's urban, financial centers reduced imbalances in domestic (and this had implications for international) exchange rates. In reducing imbalances in exchange rates, Baltimore's banks further aided merchants and manufacturers by facilitating their national and international exchange operations. This was the one instance of how the suspension of specie payments and the shifts toward a credit system actually aided Baltimore's economy at the time.

In the long run, however, this was a disastrous policy to follow, for the single most important relationship of the businessman to the marketplace was his cash flow. The failures in Baltimore in May of 1837 and in October 1839 stemmed from the classic cash-flow problem of creditors demanding payment from merchants who, for any of a number of reasons, were not receiving their collections in time to meet their payments.

On these two occasions the term *panic* is a proper description of what happened. But after 1839, all market conditions—a contracting credit system, lowering prices, and declining business activity—turned downward in a long, low, grinding process. Failures occurred sporadically but culminated in 1842, one of the worst years in antebellum Baltimore's financial history.[22]

The severity of the panic of 1842 was due to the peculiar circumstances surrounding the resumption of specie payments in the spring of that year. During its session from December 1841 to March 1842, the Maryland legislature passed two monetry laws: one prohibited the issuance of paper intended to circulate as money by any organization or individual not chartered as a bank under Maryland law, and the other required all Maryland chartered banks to resume specie payments on May 1, 1842, or forfeit their charters. The timing of these laws was incredible. Since 1839, the banks had been increasing their specie reserves, reducing their bank notes in circulation, and curtailing their discounts. To fill the demand for a circulating medium, especially for fractional currency under the five-dollar denomination that the banks were limited to, the Baltimore & Ohio Railroad had issued certificates that were passing as legal tender. As the time to resume specie payments drew closer, the banks had no recourse but a sharp contraction of their bank-note circulation and discounts. This caused a wave of failures among Baltimore's merchants and discounted Baltimore & Ohio certificates. As a result of these laws, the certificates were soon selling at a 50 percent discount. This extended the financial crisis to all social segments in Baltimore, not merely the business classes, and the panic in 1842 was similar to that in 1834.[23]

Manufacturing: Handmaiden of Commerce

Baltimore's problems from 1837 to 1843 were primarily commercial and financial, and they ended, temporarily, the optimistic resurgence of those forces during the early 1830s. In contrast, manufacturers, both industrial and handicraft, were relatively unscathed by the panics and depression. This was largely due to the reaction against manufacturers that had crystallized during the late 1820s and then hardened throughout the 1830s. Indeed, manufacturing became so subordinated to commerce that even its record keeping deteriorated. The proudly detailed displays of industrial statistics in the 1810 and 1820 manufacturing censuses cannot be found for the 1830s. No census of manufacturing was taken as part of the federal decennial census for 1830, and the census of manufacturing for 1840 aggregated the statistics by types of industry, and blended manufacturing in the city with that in the county. As a result, little is known about individual concerns. But other evidence suggests that the two directions in which manufacturing developed during the 1820s—the large-scale, steam-powered textile factories in the surrounding countryside, producing for overseas and overland markets; and the in-town iron manufacturers and small-scale handicraft shops, whose master craftsmen-turned-"manufacturers" produced mainly for the local market—became further differentiated during the 1830s and did not share the same response to the deflation from 1837 to 1843.[24]

Generally speaking, the thirties were not a prosperous period for steam-powered textile manufacturing. Two of the large-scale, out-of-town factories failed in the recession of 1829, and only one new one was built between 1829 and the early 1840s, when it was believed the China markets would be opened to Americans. Also, one such factory was constructed in town in 1829. This stabilization of textile manufacturing was mainly due to its dependence upon "foreign" markets (as opposed to the domestic market, which included Baltimore and its vicinity) in the Southern United States, the West Indies, South America, and the Far East. Fluctuating economic and political conditions in these markets combined with the banking problems at home discouraged the general expansion of this trade. Moreover, the domestic market for their products did not expand because their technology remained virtually unchanged, and the tariff policy of the federal government favored their technologically superior competitors. The productions of Baltimore's factories were crude by European standards, and the community imported most of its finer goods from abroad.[25]

The area of greatest manufacturing growth continued to be the new metals industry, which provided various products for Baltimore's expanding internal improvements system. Three new iron foundries and an iron-rolling mill were established, as were three new chemical factories, two copper-refining works, and another steam-powered sawmill. Other Baltimoreans became interested in Pennsylvania and Maryland coal mines to fuel the new establishments. Like their textile counterparts, these establishments were "Big Business," requiring large capitals and credits, and, though they were not dependent upon selling to foreign markets, they were subject to the same force in the international buying market: superior European technology. They shared, therefore, a certain interest in the tariff with the large-scale textile manufacturers.[26]

The small-scale shops of master craftsmen-turned-"manufacturers" were in a completely different, and far more vulnerable, position. These handicraft producers of goods for local consumption were more dependent upon local business conditions than were the larger-scale industries. They apparently prospered until the panic of 1837; but during the long deflation that followed, they were more affected by the depression than were the large-scale operators. For example, only a few textile factories around Baltimore appear to have curtailed their operations to half time; flour millers worked only sporadically, as did soap, candle, brick, furniture, cordage, and tanning factories; but breweries, distilleries, bakeries, and slaughterhouses do not appear to have shut down. Shipyard and residential construction was virtually stopped. Sugar refiners, like most iron and copper manufacturers, as well as chemical factories, appear to have continued operations. The manufacturers most affected by the deflation were those in small shops—tailors, boot and shoe makers, and millinery producers (makers of bonnets, caps, hats, and ready-made clothing of various kinds).[27]

Modernization and a New Consciousness about Business

In a variety of ways, the long deflation from 1837 to 1843 accelerated the industrial revolution by effectively discrediting eighteenth-century business mores and emphasizing new (meaning nineteenth-century) business methods and values. For one thing, almost everyone now understood that business must be governed strictly by financial considerations. The individual businessman could look back and see how he had become enmeshed in the depression through his cash-flow problem. The suspension of specie payments gave him merely temporary relief in his exchange operations; as the years of deflation extended after October of 1839, domestic and international exchanges grew increasingly disproportionate; and this, too, contributed to his cash-flow problem. He watched his selling markets gradually close as buyers, when there were any, either wanted very low credits or offered depreciated Southern and Western bank notes in payment. Unable to sell his goods for money and unable to borrow money from the banks to pay his own debts, the businessman had but three choices. He could ask his friends to aid him, he could ask his creditors for extensions of his debts, or he could fail. Caught in such a position, or later looking back upon himself in such a position, a businessman could see little sense in the argument that confidence and integrity would solve the difficulties of panic and deflation. How could a man have confidence in bank notes that fluctuated in value and were not refundable in specie? How could he have confidence in businessmen as a class when failures were frequent and unpredictable, even among those whom he had known and done business with for years? Above all, how could he have confidence in the business system itself when fluctuations were sudden, disjointed, and at times cataclysmic; when traditional landmarks—values and ways of doing things, as well as business firms—were suddenly erased and nothing was substituted for them; and when the system was seemingly destroying itself? But what most weakened the eighteenth-century businessman's faith was the visible disintegration of the concept of integrity. By destroying the businessman's faith in integrity and confidence, the deflation from 1837 to 1843 furthered a general trend of the industrial revolution: the erosion of personalism. A man of integrity was a man of strict morality who could be trusted explicitly. The fact that he might not do well financially did not detract from his reputation or character: he was merely unfortunate. But so many men of integrity failed during the long deflation that integrity was proven to be no longer armor against adversity. And if spiritual devastation of the deflation was bad enough, its physical debilitation of Baltimore's society was even worse. Talk of confidence and integrity seemed out of place and unrealistic to bankrupt, starving, and destitute men. And when times became better after 1843, Baltimoreans were more disposed in favor of rational calculation than ever before.

In this respect, the deflation made Baltimore's citizens more conscious of their environment. By the late 1830s Baltimore's newspapers were talking about the "commercial revolution," which had reoriented business relationships, and were attributing this revolution to the bank war, to the removal of the deposits, and to the general return to specie as the basis of American currency. No matter its cause: this "commercial revolution" was significant in educating Baltimoreans to the fundamental changes that had occurred. By 1843 a greater proportion of Baltimoreans understood the world they lived in and how it operated than had previously been true; and because they were educated to it through the perceptions of the coming new order, they themselves became the most important part of the "commercial revolution."

This consciousness of what was happening and why marked another turning point in Baltimore's development. The decade of the 1830s was momentous because industrialization was further commercialized. The hopes of returning to Baltimore's "Golden Age" that arose during the early thirties were dashed forever by the panics and long deflation which followed. Though the lesson was painful, Baltimoreans generally learned that they could not escape the monetization of credit, social and economic specialization, and the increasing institutionalization of social and economic processes. They might better work with, instead of against, these historical forces. Once this consciousness pervaded Baltimore's leadership, the few reactionaries who refused to change had only two choices: to withdraw or to become increasingly desperate in their circumstances. Some will be found in both camps.

CHAPTER VII
The Passing of the Old Order

The ways in which Baltimore's social and political realities had begun to change during the twenties formed clear patterns during the 1830s, and the outline of the city's future new order became visible for the first time. Essentially, the accelerating pace of foreign immigration, industrialization, institutionalization, and other forces of modernization imposed a new, more utilitarian value system upon society, undercut traditional ways of making decisions, and even changed the physical appearance of the city. But perhaps the most important change was the functional failure of the eighteenth-century stake-in-society basis of social organization. The property owners' private and economic power over the society was broken, first, by the new forces and then by the economic adversity of 1837–43. And yet, the end of the domination of the public sector by the private did not result in the immediate triumph of "King Numbers" and "the public good" as many believed, for the transformation was not complete or absolute, nor would it ever really be.

A series of failures characterized the passing of the old order. Its private support of internal improvements no longer proved adequate; nor did its revenue policies or its half-hearted support of free public education; and it failed to preserve Baltimore's preindustrial villagelike character by keeping steam engines and railroads from spreading throughout the city. Such failures resulted in municipal financial aid to the railroads, a new taxation policy, greater support for public education, and the geoeconomic and geosocial stratification of the city. Moreover, all of these changes spurred the larger transition away from the private and individual basis of the old order toward the public and group basis of the new one, and helped to divorce political activities from economic and social ones. In short, such failures were a necessary part of the more general specialization of society that characterized the industrial revolution in Baltimore.

Curiously enough, at the same time that Baltimore became more fragmented than ever before, it became less isolated within the nation. What happened in Baltimore occurred elsewhere, of course, and these shared processes became links between them. Baltimoreans had always adapted institutions of other cities to their own circumstances, but now even that process was hastened by the new communication and transportation facilities that appeared, by the continuing financial revolution, and by the new two-party system. In particular, the last, imposed upon the community from the outside, was oriented to national rather than local events and issues. Viewed from Baltimore's perspective, the chief function of this second two-party system was its dissemination of information about the wider, developing public society; and for that reason it was, itself, an integral part of that larger development.

The optimism and triumphant faith of the new forces provided a powerful impetus to the success of such changes, of course, but the resurgence of cultural conservatism played an equally vital role. Indeed, it was ironic how the changes were accompanied by the creation of a mythical past of values and relationships that stood in sharp contradiction to the realities of the 1830s. Cultural conservatives applauded the idea of free trade and a "let-do" society, all the while working to bring about vigorous participation by the state and municipal governments in private economic matters. They praised the virtues of privatism and simultaneously supported the expansion of municipalized public services. They renounced industrialism at the very time that they employed steam power in every manner of activity. They cherished the idea of restoring themselves as their society's elite, and tried to do so not only by appealing to the electorate in the rhetoric of democracy, but even by organizing the working classes as a political force. In Baltimore's "Golden Age," the values of the private society had been essentially unconscious attitudes and assumptions about the nature of society, a way of life. Now, a reformulated version of the same notions became a consciously articulated set of values to which ritual obeisance could be paid, irrespective of their relevance to actual circumstances. The old values thus took on a vital existence over and above the realities of Baltimore's way of life: past and future became reconciled.[1]

What gave life to all of these developments was Baltimore's continuing metropolitan expansion and the growth of its domestic economy. Together with the city's increasing population, this development advanced the functional specialization and the proliferating socioeconomic diversity that undermined the old order. Indeed, Baltimore's burgeoning domestic economy urbanized the countryside. Land prices rose, and towns were created or enlarged, or they declined, depending upon their proximity to the new transportation routes, and the intimacy of their contact with the emerging metropolitan market economy. However, this metropolitan growth did not expand uniformly in all directions from the city. Rather, it followed along routes established by custom or dictated by geography. Like the spokes of a wheel, turnpikes, canals, railroads, and steamship lines radiated in all directions from the hub of Baltimore to connect the countryside with the city. And in the process, agriculture became more responsive to urban growth while the tempo of change accelerated.[2]

As might be suspected, Baltimore continued to expand toward its three traditional market areas: the Susquehanna Valley; western Maryland, Pennsylvania, and Virginia; and southern Maryland and the area around Washington, D.C. Although the Susquehanna Valley trade continued to be lucrative to Baltimore during the 1830s, Philadelphia was beginning to divert portions of that trade across the mountains separating the Susquehanna and Delaware rivers through a cumbersome system of roads and canals. Baltimoreans attempted to improve their own connection with the Susquehanna River trade by building the Baltimore & Port Deposit Railroad during the thirties. Port Deposit, in Maryland near the mouth of the Susquehanna, was the main terminal for the river trade. Toward the West, Baltimoreans tried to improve their contact through two turnpikes and the extension of the Baltimore & Ohio Railroad. This railroad reached Point-of-Rocks, Maryland, on the upper Potomac River, in 1831, but a right-of-way dispute with the Chesapeake and Ohio Canal Company, which was building a canal alongside the Potomac River in Maryland, led to litigation and a court judgment favoring the canal company. That decision, coupled with the railroad company's lack of capital to build over a different route, halted construction of the road until 1834. In that year Baltimore and Maryland began floating bond issues to finance the continued westward extension of the railroad. Toward the south, Baltimore expanded its connections through the Savage Railroad Company, which connected the city with the coal and iron deposits at the town of Savage about twenty miles to the southwest. Baltimoreans also improved their connection with Annapolis and southeastern Maryland on the Western Shore through the Annapolis & Elk Ridge Railroad.[3]

Baltimore's metropolitan growth over the surrounding countryside received much more publicity than did its application of steam power to shipping, but the latter was equally significant. Altogether, ten steamship companies were formed in Baltimore from 1831 to 1843. Most of the steamships were for Baltimore's trade with southern Maryland, Norfolk and its environs, and the Delmarva Peninsula. The latter area, low, flat, and fertile, had long been one of the richest agricultural sections in Maryland, and in it vast slave-manned plantations produced such crops as tobacco, wheat, corn, and vegetables. Steamboats regularized the Chesapeake Bay trade, speeded it up, and stabilized it. To a lesser extent, other steamboats linked Baltimore with New York, Philadelphia, and New Orleans, which helped regularize Baltimore's coastal trade.[4]

This expansion was enormously prosperous before 1837 and occurred in forms that were increasingly common to the future new order. Of the 625 acts of incorporation by Maryland from 1783 until the passage of a general incorporation law in 1852, for example, the largest number were passed from 1831 through 1843. Of these new corporations, one-third were for Baltimore. Among the sixty-nine new Baltimore corporations launched during the 1830s, eighteen were for manufacturing, fifteen for transportation companies, nine for banking, nine for savings institutions, ten for insurance companies, and the remainder for miscellaneous other activities. Eighteen, or more than half of the new manufacturing and transportation companies, were using steam power. Baltimore's expansion, especially in connection with steam power, thus relied upon the joint-stock company form of organization to a greater degree than ever before.[5]

In turn, this expansion of the city wrought new functional specializations within the social order. New, successful, and large-scale manufacturers who appeared in Baltimore during the 1830s included textile manufacturers Horatio N. Gambrill and James S. Gary, iron manufacturers Horace Abbott and the Hayward brothers, and railroad builder Ross Winans. Gambrill was the only native Marylander, Gary and Abbott were from Massachusetts, the Haywards from New Hampshire, and Winans from New York. Two others, Hugh A. Cooper of Maryland and Charles Reeder from Pennsylvania, became successful and well-known steamboat builders. In addition, merchants who adapted themselves to the city's metropolitan growth did so through the new transportation systems. Samuel Shoemaker, for example, came to Baltimore during the panic of 1837 and began his freight-forwarding business, a specialty function literally created by the "transportation revolution" because of its dependency upon the railroad. So, too, did William T. Walters who came to Baltimore in 1841 and whose wealth would establish one of the city's famous art galleries. Robert Garrett from Ireland via Pennsylvania, who had been in business on and off in Baltimore since the early nineteenth century, pursued the freight-forwarding business as Shoemaker did, and also acted as a wholesaler of groceries to the interior towns. This latter function, the importation of foodstuffs, reversed Baltimore's previous character as a foodstuff exporter and pointed toward a trend that would accompany the city's increasing industrialization. Two other of Baltimore's future philanthropists, Johns Hopkins and Enoch Pratt, also made their fortunes as wholesale grocers to the interior via the railroads. So dependent on the Baltimore & Ohio Railroad did Garrett's business become that he became a stockholder and eventually a director. His son, John Work Garrett, became its president in 1858.[6]

Actually, the new opportunities were but one reason for the appearance of new business leaders; another was the passing of a generation of Baltimore's older merchants and their business ways. Incredibly, the 1830s marked the deaths of such prominent builders of Baltimore as Alexander Brown; James A. Buchanan; Thomas Edmondson; Benjamin, George, and William Ellicott; Richard Gittings; Lyde Goodwin; Charles Gwinn; Hall Harrison; Peter Hoffman, Jr.; Samuel Hollingsworth; Talbot Jones; Jessee Levering; Alexander MacDonald; Alexander, Issaac, Samuel, and William D. McKim; Philip Moore; Robert Oliver; William Patterson; Samuel Smith; Henry Thompson; Luke Tiernan; Cumberland D. Williams; George Winchester; and Edward G. Woodyear. Their passing, and the retirement from active business of many of their contemporaries, not only vacated positions as corporate officers, merchants, and manufacturers that required replacement, but also ended the eighteenth-century style of personal business enterprise. The deaths of Brown and Oliver, in particular, curtailed—though Brown's son, George continued —the tradition of the international merchant lending his capital and credit to other, smaller-scale merchants on the basis of his personal knowledge of them. This made Baltimore's lesser merchants more dependent than ever upon institutional (i.e., banking) capital and credit, which restricted their flexibility and thereby accentuated the severity of the banking crises of 1837, 1839, and 1842.

Indeed, the plight of traditional merchants was even worse during the thirties than it had been during the twenties, for they were most vulnerable to the wide swings in Baltimore's overseas trade, and their business style could not be simply transferred to their city's expanding overland markets. Many, such as Harmanus Boggs, James Campbell, Martin Eichelberger, James Erskine, Samuel Harden, William Norris, Asa Taylor, and Philip T. Tyson, failed during the course of the decade. But they did have the alternative—providing they were not too financially tied to the marketplace—of retiring from active business and living off their capital investments as *rentiers*, as many of them did. In general, this social trend continued the pattern of the 1820s: the deficit financing of Baltimore's metropolitan growth provided the very means by which entrepreneurs could escape active involvement in the risky business world. In practice, however, the plethora of interest-bearing securities issued from the expanded number of private and public sources during the 1830s necessitated a more careful management of such investments. Indeed, it made such management nearly a full-time occupation, and therein lay the transformation of Baltimore's *rentiers* during that decade which set the city's social elite even further apart from the rest of society.[7]

Before the 1830s, most of Baltimore's *rentiers* simply imitated their

European counterparts, chiefly British and French, as fairly inactive investors and certainly not active businessmen. Managers of various kinds looked after their interests. But traditionalists who abandoned active business during the thirties, who circumscribed their activities to those of "society" and who appeared to be *rentiers*, really became active investors. They became the "capitalists" or "men of capital" that contemporaries referred to, and they found various kinds of business opportunities, carrying different degrees of risk, offered. Most of them were concerned about preserving rather than increasing their capitals; therefore, they sought safe, stable investments and willingly accepted lower interest rates. Generally speaking, such an investment strategy hurt them during the periods of inflation but worked in their favor during times of deflation; and, for this reason, the experience of most of the *rentiers* during the 1830s was almost exactly the reverse from that of active businessmen. During the first half of the decade, inflation eroded their fixed investments—except for ground rents, which could be raised, providing the leases were short term, as the value of real estate rose. But the deflation from 1837 to 1843 worked in their favor. They were especially favored by the deflation if they invested in the new United States Treasury notes or other federal-government debt issuances, in municipal stocks that were backed by direct taxation, and if they invested at the beginning of the deflation when interest rates were higher. In other words, certain conditions of capital investments existed during the deflation, especially in connection with Baltimore and Maryland's deficit spending and with Jacksonian federal treasury policies, that made investment capitalism far more attractive (i.e. safe, stable, and profitable) than continuing in active business.[8]

This new environment for the employment of capital, the weakened power of the merchant class, and the attraction of a *rentier* life style were underscored by the continued growth and diversity of Baltimore's population, the changing urban geography of the city, and the rise of a new political party system. In the process, the cohesive base of the old order dissolved and the new cohesive elements of the future order slowly continued to take shape. That is, Baltimore's metropolitan expansion continued to sustain and even stimulate the development of a sedentary, enormously diversified and specialized society during the thirties as it had during the twenties, but it was not yet generating its own cohesion. Consequently, the new elements were a mixture of ongoing institutions and values from the immediate past, brand new ones introduced from outside of Baltimore's experience, and a few that were generated during the thirties. Taken as a whole, these institutions provided a framework that filtered and interpreted the dynamic processes of the community, and because this framework became ever more common to everyone, it eventually became the community itself.

Some of these developments, particularly in relation to socioeconomic diversifications and specialization, are illustrated by the patterns of Baltimore's population growth during the thirties. The economic crises of the decade probably account for why the city's population increase of nearly 27 percent was its smallest rate of growth throughout the antebellum period. But the more important facts were that the town was able to support over one hundred thousand people by 1840 in spite of those crises, that this concentration of people was more diversely specialized and interdependent than ever before, and that their ethnic diversity had assumed the patterns that would characterize Baltimore for the remainder of the antebellum period. The new people were overwhelmingly white; the free black population had increased about 21 percent, and the steady decline of slavery was hastened for the remainder of the antebellum period.

But the most dramatic change was an increase of nearly 425 percent in the rate of immigration into Baltimore. Over 55,000 immigrants poured into the port during the thirties, compared to about 10,500 during the twenties. Most of the newcomers were Germans, the second-largest group were Irish, and much smaller numbers came from other areas of Great Britain and continental Europe, in that order. However, the non-English background of the mass of immigrants (Germans) presented Baltimoreans with a particular problem: though many were literate in German, they remained cultural aliens in Baltimore. In 1839 the German community, in a petition to the City Council, stated that they numbered about twenty thousand (or one-fifth of Baltimore's population), that about five thousand of them were not literate in English, and that the council should therefore print all municipal laws, resolutions, and legal documents in German. The council refused, thus giving greater force to the arguments of those who advocated free public education.[9]

Besides such ethnic diversity, several spatial and geosocial changes accompanied Baltimore's growth in sheer size. Essentially, the city continued to expand outward from its harbor toward the east and especially the north and west. Growth toward the south continued to be very slow. Annual new home construction reflected the economic fluctuations of the period, rising from 542 in 1830 to 607 in 1835, then plunging to 366 in 1838, and then rising again to 558 in 1842. But even more visible changes occurred in the urban geography of the city. The most significant in terms of magnitude was the Canton Company development. Incorporated in 1828 as a private development, the company purchased Columbus O'Donnell's twenty-five hundred-acre estate southeast of the city for $320,000 in 1831, and subsequently bought up three miles of additional coastline. The promoters built Baltimore's first planned and industrial community on this site, with warehouses hugging the commercial waterfront, the Baltimore & Ohio, Baltimore & Susquehanna, and Baltimore & Port Deposit railroads intersecting at that waterfront, and residential areas laid out in uniform rectangles along streets leading away from the docks. In addition to a steam-powered sawmill, forge, and triphammer works, Peter Cooper built an iron works, which he sold to Horace Abbott in 1836.[10]

Less spectacular, though equally significant, was the residential development around the Washington Monument, called Mount Vernon Square, approximately one mile north of Baltimore's commercial center. Beginning in the late twenties for the first time, Baltimore's wealthier citizens began to abandon the commercial center of the city and move into new, economically segregated residential neighborhoods, leaving the working classes clustered within their own ethnic and employment pockets. The Mount Vernon Square area was the first such neighborhood. A number of wealthier citizens—the Beatty, Buchanan, Gilmor, Smith, Swann, Taylor, and three Williams families—built large and costly residences there, and created Baltimore's first exclusive neighborhood. Almost immediately followed the development of "Howard Park" (part of the estate of John Eager Howard, who died in 1827), which was adjacent to the square as a continuation of Baltimore's most fashionable area of private residences. Together with Canton, Mount Vernon Square–Howard Park developments illustrated Baltimore's shift away from a loosely undifferentiated, mercantile-oriented eighteenth-century village toward a more differentiated nineteenth-century city.[11]

The movement of steam engines away from the docks into residential neighborhoods and the introduction of the railroads into the city demonstrated this trend even more graphically. Indeed, they wrought the most visible changes in Baltimore's urban geography associated with industrial revolution. The establishment of the Baltimore City Cotton Factory by Robert Buchanan in 1829 was followed by the construction of Howland and Woollens's steam-powered flooring factory in 1832, and the same firm's new steam-powered sawmill in 1833. The latter was particularly controversial: the owners of property in its immediate vicinity petitioned the City Council to prevent its construction, and the Jacksonians tried to organize the city's carpenters in opposition to it, but both failed and "progress" continued, and the City Council even refused to enact municipal regulations of steam engines.[12]

The most controversial issue, however, was the introduction of the

Baltimore & Ohio Railroad into the city, and this dispute occurred on three levels of vested interests. One involved the owners of property along the proposed route, from Mount Clare Station in the west-central part of Baltimore eastward along Pratt Street to the harbor, who opposed the city's granting a right of way to the railroad company without their consent. Another involved the opposition of certain sections of the city (its northwestern, western, and southwestern portions) to the extension of the Baltimore & Ohio from the station to the docks because the through-connection would destroy the Western trade interests in those parts of the city. And the third level of opposition by carters, draymen, and other freight haulers also objected to this extension, because it would end their own businesses of hauling freights between the two transit points. The property owners lost, the western sections of the city lost, and the freight haulers lost; the railroad and the city, in its corporate whole, won. And this triumph of an innovative public utility over established though particularized and private interests was a forerunner of what would come.[13]

In spite of its incompleteness, however, this triumph of the municipal public good over private and localized interests marked a milestone in the passing of the old order, for it succeeded in breaking the control of the property owners over the municipal government and in reversing the relationship between the public and private sectors on certain matters. Indeed, because it transferred political decision-making from an identifiable property-owning elite to the legal fiction of all adult, free, white, male residents of the city, probably no other single development pointed so directly to the future public society. Legally speaking, even this partial triumph of the municipality over its most formidable interest group was a major change in Baltimore's constitutional order.

Accompanying this change, but not causing it, was the rise of the second two-party system. True, the new party system expressed, and even strengthened and sustained, the new majoritarian style of politics; but the new system did not originate in Baltimore, and, while it did shape the general direction of municipal services, it proved largely irrelevant to a wide array of local issues. However, the new system provided a mechanism that was expandable and could be adjusted to the growth of Baltimore. It also helped to transform municipal politics from personal and private elitism toward the impersonal elitism and institutional dynamics of a new, mechanistic order common to everyone. And for these reasons, its effects were democratic.

The defeat of the property-owning elite's control over the municipality resulted mainly from the continuing financial revolution. Baltimore had reached a financial predicament by the early 1830s: was the city to expand its domestic economy, or even to sustain its growth, through the private sector or by increasing the deficit spending of its public sector? Given the maritime depression of the twenties and the relatively low rate of growth during the thirties, private investment was simply insufficient to support Baltimore's internal improvements program; consequently, the role of public-sector deficit finance expanded steadily. But as it did, an unforeseen problem emerged that became of crucial concern early in the decade: deficit spending had become so integral a part of the city's finance that it was even relied upon to furnish current expenditures. Clearly, the city's taxation policies would have to be reorganized to meet its expenditures out of current revenues. The conflict, then, pitted the holders of the largest amounts of property in Baltimore—who bore the largest tax burden because of the shift during the twenties from taxes on trade to taxes on property, and who opposed increasing the city's taxes in any form—against those who realized that the city's growth and prosperity could only be achieved through deficit finance, and that this necessitated new taxation policies.

The conflict became public and political in 1831 when it was revealed that eighty-five of Baltimore's largest holders of property, nearly every one of whom was a member of the city's mechant and *rentier* elite, had petitioned the state legislature to limit the city's property taxing power to $120,000 per year, or its total revenues to $210,000, and their petition was granted. Mayor Small resigned in March, and his successor, William R. Steuart, inaugurated a study of the taxation policies of Boston, New York, and Philadelphia by a joint committee from both branches of the City Council. Their report, submitted in April, concluded that the other three cities relied upon three principal sources of taxation: real estate, personal property, and income. The committee recommended that Baltimore establish a more rigid personal property tax, a new tax on incomes, and that a new assessment of real estate be undertaken. However, the City Council did not respond to the report and the issue carried over into the following administration.[14]

Then followed what would prove to be a characteristic development in the future: the city's financial problem transcended party politics; all were affected by it, but the political party that dominated the administration, the Jacksonians in this case, received credit for what was essentially a bipartisan achievement. Elected in 1832 and again in 1834, Mayor Jesse Hunt called attention to the city's fiscal problems and the need for changing its taxation system. A special joint committee of both branches of the City Council was charged with investigating and reporting on the city's finances. As the Committee was dominated by anti-Jacksonians, the substance of its reports in January and February of 1833 became municipal ordinances in February 1833, in April 1834, and in February 1835, when the Jacksonians sometimes dominated the council.[15]

Essentially, the new taxation system reversed the approach to real-estate taxation of the twenties and added a personal property tax. With respect to real property taxes, the new policy departed from that of the 1820s by raising assessment valuations and lowering the rate of taxation. Between 1822 and 1835, for example, Baltimore maintained an almost uniform tax assessment on real estate but increased the rate of taxation. The result of such a policy was a decline in the total revenue from real-estate taxes but an increase of the tax burden on the individual property owner, which was what prompted the revolt of the property owners in 1831. Beginning in 1834 and 1835, however, Baltimore reversed this policy, as real property valuations were drastically and progressively increased while the rate of taxation was reduced. From 1835 to 1836, alone, property valuations skyrocketed from $3,787,762.00 to $42,931,960.00 and the rate of taxation per $100.00 fell from $3.33⅓ to $.50. Moreover, the rates for all specific levies were also reduced: the court tax from $.35 per $100.00 to $.04 from 1835 to 1836, the poor tax from $.47 to $.05¼, and the school tax from $.12½ to $.01⅛. Such a new policy stimulated two developments simultaneously. On one hand, property ownership became more desirable because taxes were lower, while on the other, prices of real estate spurted to contribute to the inflation of the mid-thirties. Both developments occurred mainly in the outlying wards whose representatives had voted for the new policy.[16]

This last fact indicates the real key to Baltimore's municipal politics during the thirties: party politics, while important at election time, played a negligible role compared to ward interests in the City Council voting on important local issues. Throughout the period, with but one exception in 1839, the number of Jacksonians in the City Council about equalled or exceeded their anti-Jacksonian counterparts. Yet neither political group took party positions on local issues; the Jacksonians were particularly oriented to national ones, and both groups usually split over local issues.[17]

A survey of such voting on the more important local issues shows how ward interests dominated municipal politics and undercut party differences. Wards one through four and six, ringing the basin and main harbor at Fell's Point and including the area of the city east of Jones's Falls, where the city's older commercial and shipping were concentrated, were

Baltimore in 1836 (courtesy of the Maryland Historical Society)

represented by Jacksonians during the first half of the decade and by anti-Jacksonians during the second half. Regardless of their political party affiliation, however, representatives from these wards voted consistently for bringing the railroads into the city, for tapping new sources of water supplies, against deficit spending, and against the new taxation policy that was inaugurated in 1834. Conversely, wards seven through twelve were generally represented by anti-Jacksonians during the first half of the decade, and by Jacksonians during the second half, and these representatives—again, no matter their party affiliations—voted relatively consistently against the water wards' representatives on these issues. Generally speaking, these wards embraced the fastest growing areas of the city, they were connected with the interior trade, and they changed rapidly as steam-power production was introduced into them. Though neither party voted consistently on municipal regulations, however, the Jacksonians tended, more than their opponents, to oppose regulating occupational pursuits—building contractors, chimney sweeps, and hack drivers, for example—but favored regulating the trade in anthracite coal.[18]

Such ward-interest politics helped to obscure the financial revolution that became even more acute during the middle and later thirties. Coincidentally, the need for financing internal improvements created a new set of conditions at the very time that Baltimore's new tax-assessment and collection machinery were created in conformity with the 1834 legislation. By December 1834, the Baltimore & Ohio Railroad had reached Harpers Ferry on the upper Potomac River, but the company was financially unable to continue building westward to Cumberland, Maryland, and on to Wheeling, Virginia; and it applied for further financial aid from both the city and state in 1835. In 1836 Maryland authorized Baltimore to loan an additional $3 million to the company and to impose new taxes to meet this loan. By resolution and ordinance of that year, and with both parties evenly divided on the issue, the City Council authorized a new 6 percent city stock redeemable in 1890, but stipulated that the city would pay the railroad company no more than $1 million in a given year. In the same fashion, Baltimore issued a 6 percent stock for $600,000, redeemable after 1870, for the support of the Baltimore & Susquehanna Railroad Company in 1837. A further stock issue of $150,000 in 5 percent stock redeemable after 1870 was made for the same railroad in February 1838, and the city also stipulated it would issue another $100,000 when the railroad was completed to York, Pennsylvania. But in November 1838, the terms of the latter loan were altered so that the company received the money in installments as the work progressed. Finally, in 1837 Baltimore issued $380,000 in 6 percent stock redeemable after 1870, which it authorized for the use of the Susquehanna Canal Company. Because such a huge increase in the city's indebtedness would result in a sharp rise in the annual interest payments and would impose severe demands upon Baltimore's treasury, the city was authorized by the state to levy an internal-improvement tax in 1838. This levy was another of those specific levies authorized by the state law of 1818 and under which Baltimore had already imposed a court levy in 1819, a poor tax in 1820, and a school tax in 1830. Now, in 1839, the anti-Jacksonian City Council imposed a tax of $.10½ per $100 of assessable property to pay for its support of internal improvements.[19]

In addition, the deflationary conditions that followed the panics of 1837 and 1839 eventually forced changes in the tax-collection policy of the old order. The problem of tax collections before 1841 was that payment of taxes was a moral duty only, and the city could merely proceed against tax delinquents as in cases of ordinary indebtedness. Moreover, the system of tax farming, whereby the collector bonded himself to the city for the amount to be collected, was cumbersome and inefficient. Tax arrears were carried forward from year to year until they were sold outright by the city to the collector. In 1829, for example, the collector was finally discharged from his liability for the tax collections of 1821, 1822, and 1823 by a payment of $225.00 to the city. Even in the prosperous year of 1836, the city collected a mere $153,230.00 of the total $295,244.24 in taxes owed it. Carrying tax arrearages like this forced the city to operate via deficit finance. And when the panic of 1837 turned into a long period of deflation, thus severely diminishing tax collections, the cumbersome system of tax collection portended financial disaster.[20]

By 1840 it was apparent to municipal officials that the city's method of tax farming would have to be altered to produce more current revenue. After repeated warnings to Baltimoreans to pay their taxes within the year for which they were assessed, the City Council copied an idea from banking practices that had originated during the panic of 1819 and applied it to tax collection. In the form of a resolution, the City Council asked the state that taxes upon property be made liens upon property and that the property itself should go toward the payment of taxes by its immediate sale instead of awaiting the long legal process of execution of court judgment, as in cases of ordinary indebtedness. Though the council was dominated by Jacksonians, the vote on this matter was evenly divided between the parties. The state legislature granted Baltimore's request in February 1841, and the city collector then enforced the prompt collection of taxes by threatening the public sale of property on which municipal taxes had not been paid. An ordinance did make such property sold redeemable by the delinquent taxpayer, however, if he paid all advances with interest, plus a penalty of 18 percent, within two years of the sale. Again, the public order triumphed over private interests.[21]

The city's experiences with deficit financing during the depression were much less successful than its experience with taxes. After 1837 Baltimore found the markets for stock issues had dried up. In 1838 and early 1839, for example, the city paid the installments to the internal-improvement companies it was helping to finance with money borrowed from the city's banks after giving them city stock for collateral. But after the second panic in the fall of 1839, when all banks south of New York suspended specie payments, even this source of money disappeared. At this point, the Baltimore & Ohio Railroad Company, the chief recipient of Baltimore's aid to internal improvements, proposed a novel scheme. The company would take the city stock at par directly, in lieu of money, as the installment payments in the city's pledged $3-million aid to the railroad. This stock would then be used by the company as money to pay its construction debts. For everyday expenditures and the payment of wages, the company would print up "stock orders" in denominations of $1, $2, $3, 5, and $100. These "stock orders" were then exchangeable for city stock at par in amounts not less than $100. Since the idea was merely to provide a circulating medium for Baltimoreans at a time when bank notes were disappearing, the company agreed that any profit that might arise from these "stock orders" circulating as money would go to the city. Delighted by such an opportunity to provide a circulating currency for Baltimore's working classes without further burdening the city's banking institutions, the City Council, with many Whigs supporting the dominant Jacksonians, authorized the city register in February 1841 to receive these "stock orders" in payment of debts and taxes to the city as well as to pay them out in discharging the city's debts.[22]

At first this scheme worked well. The railroad company issued the "stock orders" as payment for goods and services it required; and the amount in circulation almost trebled from $515,000 in October 1840 to $1,449,051 a year later. But after October 1841, they began to depreciate because of a state law that restructured Baltimore's tax system and which also required the banks to pay specie after May 1, 1842. By the spring of 1842 the "stock orders" had depreciated to twenty-five cents on the dollar; and in March the Jacksonian-dominated City Council repealed its ordinance, passed the previous year, that authorized the "stock orders" to be received in payment of taxes and debts due the city. By the summer of 1842 the "stock orders" had disappeared from circulation, most having been exchanged for city stock and the rest purchased outright. The

Jacksonians lost the fall elections, and this ended the municipality's provision of a monetary medium for the remainder of the antebellum
period.[23]

Jacksonians and Whigs as Modernists

Just as the forms of municipal revenue institutions were reversed during
the 1830s, away from their autonomous direction of the 1820s, so municipal services also changed. But the new two-party system played a much
more influential role in the latter than in the former instance. During
the thirties the Jacksonians pushed municipal services away from private
ownership or operation toward municipalization. Although this continued to be merely a trend and did not fully establish a system during the
thirties, it did condition the ways in which several services were expanded, making them more uniform, regular, and efficient. Insofar as the depression from 1837 to 1843 encouraged this, the depression played an
important role in shaping municipal services. By 1843 many of Baltimore's municipal services had followed the general tendency of its revenue institutions and taken the form they would assume for the remainder
of the antebellum period.

Such services as paving, repairing, and repaving the public ways, for
example, were modernized for the first time during the 1830s. These
services became matters of considerable public concern during the period, because physical expansion called attention to them and provision
for them assumed an increasing role in Baltimore's budget. In 1833 the
Jacksonian administration of Jesse Hunt adopted what was to become
the standard method of financing these services. No paving, repairing, or
repaving would be initiated by the city. When a petition asking for such
services from owners of property abutting the street reached the City
Council, the city commissioners would estimate the cost and notify the
owners that the city would undertake the service only after all the owners
of such property had deposited with the city two-thirds of the cost of the
estimate. The city would then pay the other one-third. By 1834, however,
it was realized that agreement of all property owners was rarely achieved;
and that the property owners could impede the progress of the city;
and this provision was changed to two-thirds of the owners of the property abutting the street needing such service. This was one more instance
of how the Jacksonians undercut the power of the property owners in the
name of the public good.[24]

The physical expansion of the city during the thirties also forced alterations in the municipality's handling of new street construction. Before 1836, Maryland controlled the extension of the city, because streets could only be extended into vacant land areas through special acts of the state legislature. Usually these acts were made conditional upon the assent of the mayor and City Council, and this gave the city the chance to make whatever modifications were thought necessary. But in 1836 the Jacksonian-dominated state legislature gave Baltimore complete power over street extensions and grading, and this power was reaffirmed by the state three years later. But another, tangential problem also confronted the municipality after 1836. Different commissioners were appointed for each separate case of street extension, and they were usually men with no qualifications or experience in such matters; they merely owned most of the land in the new street areas. In 1841, the Jacksonians corrected this procedure and laid the foundation for what was to be the future basis for extensions and reconstruction of streets. Three commissioners for opening streets were appointed annually. They had power to appoint assistants and were responsible for initiating street construction and reconstruction. The city paid none of the costs; all costs devolved upon the owners of the property abutting the street; and the triumph of the public order over the property owners seemed complete.[25]

Expansion of the police department was also necessitated by the physical expansion of the city, though here the Jacksonians followed the Whigs' lead in modernizing the city's police force. In his mayoral message in January 1835, Jesse Hunt called attention to the need both for employing additional night watchmen and for increasing the number of city bailiffs in the day police; but the Jacksonians did nothing toward these ends. Then, in 1838 the Whig-dominated City Council transformed the day police into the "city police," increased the number of bailiffs to thirty-six, and authorized the high constable to act as the chief of police. One-third of the "city police" received salaries; the others were paid from fines resulting from violations of city ordinances. And additional bailiffs to the "city police" were authorized by the City Council—again Whigs—in 1839.[26]

But the Jacksonians were mainly responsible for reorganizing Baltimore's fire companies. These private companies were loosely organized into the Baltimore Association of Firemen in 1831, which was then incorporated, in 1834, as the Baltimore United Fire Department. This organization was composed of seven representatives from each private company, plus one representative serving in a standing committee, and many of them were Jacksonian leaders. However, this fire department was a quasi-public institution at best; it tried to regulate the volunteer fire companies a little better, to settle disputes among them, and to provide a relief fund for injured firemen or their families. But the department was, speaking legally, a private corporation, not a municipal institution; consequently its decisions lacked the force of law. In spite of this, however, the Jacksonians linked the department with the city even more closely in 1842, when the City Council divided Baltimore into three fire districts and appointed for each a chief marshal, who was given complete authority over all companies present at any fire within the district. Thus, the politics of fire fighting pointed toward the next logical step: the municipalization of the service.[27]

The trend toward public control of municipal services can best be seen in the efforts to municipalize the Baltimore Water Company. The policies of this private company did not conform to the realities of Baltimore's physical expansion during the 1830s. Rather than tapping new, cheaper sources of supply, or even gradually expanding their current source, the company continued to operate from its traditional sources and to pass on its high water rates to consumers. In turn, high water rates limited its market, and the company's policy was to extend water service only into those sections of the city which were already well populated so that the company would realize an immediate return on its investment. Moreover, these were sections of the city whose residents could afford to pay the high water rates (of $10 per year). Such antisocial policies (regarded as such at the time) fostered efforts to municipalize the water company in 1830, 1833, and 1835. But the company's solid legal position and disputes about the value of the company prevented the city's purchase of it until 1854.[28]

Sundry other municipal services continued with but minor changes. With respect to public health, the Whigs abolished the office of consulting physician in 1839, and the City Council stipulated that one of the three commissioners of health appointed annually must be a physician and assume the duties of consulting physician. Two new markets were authorized by the Jacksonians in 1834 and in 1835, and permission was granted by the state legislature to levy special direct taxes to defray their costs. However, no significant changes were made in the administration of Baltimore's wharves and harbors, its court system, or its relief of the poor. Curiously, the state proposed one new social service that Baltimore did not support. In 1831 the state legislature authorized the creation of a children's House of Refuge in Baltimore: children convicted of criminal offenses, those committed as vagrants or street beggars, those whose parents asked their admission for incorrigible habits or vicious conduct, and those whose parents did not provide for them. Though the state appropriated funds for operating the House of Refuge, Baltimoreans did not aid the project and it did not become a reality until 1849.[29]

Obviously, Baltimore realities encompassed many developments and problems that politicians and party politics either ignored or even exacerbated. But a respectable democratic style came to characterize Baltimore society and politics during the 1830s. It was merely a style, however, a set of ideas and values that everyone could share in; it was not reality. Not everyone was a democrat nor wanted to be, but because its complex of ideals were so widely pervasive they functioned as community imperatives and thereby affected individuals. Though the effects of democracy were but partial during the thirties, and it remained for later generations to work them out in specific institutional forms, the important thing is that they appeared at all.

The real authority of the aristocratic, personal, private, and individual old order had been broken in the process. But its trappings would linger on in various ways even though the new commitment to the common good now took precedence in ever more numerous and greater ways. This was hardly tragic, for the new order taking shape was a means whereby Baltimore could be fragmentized almost endlessly and yet remain a coherent whole, for generations to come.

PART THREE

The New Order, 1843–1861

Introduction to Part Three

The economic, social, and political forms that had been generated and gathering force during the previous three generations emerged in Baltimore during the 1840s and 1850s as a nineteenth-century public society. Institutions and formal organizations now defined the life of the community and mediated between individuals, and between them and their community. Such formalism climaxed the transformation of Baltimore's eighteenth-century private society of personal and individual relationships, and future developments would spring from this new nature of the community. To be sure, elements of the private society lived on, particularly in business enterprise, but they did so as a subculture. For the community as a whole, its large size, its ethnic and economic diversity, and its social specialization made formal institutions the most practical and efficient means for dealing with people in aggregate.

The new order partly resulted from the verification of the ideas and values that evolved during the 1830s by the realities of the forties and early fifties. Much of what happened extended from the familiar processes of the continuing business revolution, but something else also occurred. Trying to maximize their opportunities in the new prosperity, entrepreneurs pushed industrialization into industrial revolution and transformed Baltimore's circumstances from its eighteenth-century base to a different and unfamiliar one. The traditional ideology surrounding commerce fit the new maritime prosperity and commercialism in general, but it was confusing, contradictory, and somewhat unintelligible amid Baltimore's new industrial realities. Indeed, industrial revolution and the community's development into an interregional economy created new economic, social, and political forms that demanded a different ideology, one whose elements were alien to Baltimore's dominant traditions. This made the situation all the more confusing and not a little frightening; and naturally, such conditions stimulated the culture's reliance upon institutions and organizations as integrating and self-protecting forms. In the end, the public society that appeared blended the new and the old, the contradictory and the continuous, and did not resolve them before Civil War engulfed Baltimore to force an artificial set of circumstances upon the community.

CHAPTER VIII

Industrialization and Triumphant Commercialism

Baltimore's physical environment and economy changed dramatically during the 1840s and 1850s. Commercial prosperity returned on a wave of expanded foreign trade, the city blossomed into an interregional economy, and industrialization assumed a new, more vital importance, because it underpinned the expansion and prosperity. Also, the "new Jacksonians" in the federal government created institutions that encouraged Baltimore's businessmen to expand their foreign and domestic markets. All of these changes hastened economic and social specialization, but the change in scale of Baltimore's economy had the greatest consequences, for the institutions that appeared now dealt with a wholly different set of circumstances than had hitherto existed. Thus, the new prosperity involved more than the simple return of profitable business conditions; it restored them within a new context. And for this reason commercial ideas and values merged with the new realities to continue traditional prejudices and habits of thought while scarcely noting those qualitative changes that accompanied them.

The Return of Prosperity

The return of maritime prosperity generally insured the success of commercial ideas and values, but several specific developments shaped Baltimore's new prosperity in peculiar ways. One was the opening of new foreign markets and the expansion of old ones. Another was the appearance of the upper Ohio-Mississippi Valley as a successful competitor to the Middle and Southern Atlantic states in the production of foodstuffs, and its link with the major Atlantic seaports by trans-Allegheny railroads. A third was the new institutional environment, established by the federal government, that aided businessmen. These developments constituted a watershed in Baltimore's history, because they completed the "commercial revolution" that contemporaries had referred to during the late 1830s.[1]

The single most important new foreign market for Baltimore was South America; by the late 1840s, this market had superseded the West

Indies in the city's long-established pattern of trade. Essentially, Baltimore exported the same kinds of commodities to South America as to the West Indies: beef, flour, grain, pork, staves, and textiles. But the older trade triangle between Baltimore, the West Indies, and continental Europe was gradually replaced by a new one with South America replacing the West Indies. For one thing, Baltimore-made brown sheetings were in great demand in South America (as well as in China) because of their greater durability in hot, humid climates than their European-made counterparts, and because of their low cost. For another, a new grade of flour—family flour—was developed in 1840, and this flour became Baltimore's largest export item to South America and southern Europe as well as to the West Indies. Of a higher grade than superfine, family flour was made from winter wheat, had better keeping qualities in warm and humid climates, and was thus better suited for southern markets than was flour from other American seaports. During the 1840s Baltimore shipped more flour to Brazil than did any other port in the United States, and coffee imports into Baltimore from South America climbed to almost a quarter of the total coffee imported into the United States. Baltimore also became the principal American port in the guano trade during this decade, and this trade continued to prosper during the 1850s.[2]

Though South American markets became the most important new markets to Baltimore in terms of the city's direct contact with them, the opening of the British corn and grain trade to Americans in 1846 had a more far-reaching effect upon the structure of international, American domestic, and, therefore, of Baltimore trade. Indeed, the opening of the British grain markets was part of a general shift in British society during the 1840s that accelerated the worldwide industrial revolution. Projected in terms of free trade and laissez faire capitalism, this shift furthered Great Britain's financial domination of world trade at the very time when the United States and other West European nations were beginning to apply steam power on a larger scale to enable them to compete with the British. The Bank of England Act of 1844 established tighter controls over the British national financial system; the abolition of the British corn laws in 1846 allowed cheaper foreign grain to be imported and thereby lowered food prices in Great Britain; and increased railroad construction accelerated the industrial revolution in Great Britain by stimulating urbanization and the proliferation of industry to the point where Britain became the "workshop of the world." Such major changes were accompanied by crises, and the transition away from agriculture toward industrialization, together with crop failures in several years, earned the decade the nickname, "the hungry forties."[3]

These British developments spurred American prosperity in two ways.

One was to intensify the British demand for both American cotton and foodstuffs. For America, expanding exports of American commodities to Great Britain gave the United States an increasing means of paying for British manufactured goods. For Great Britain, it freed British capital. Instead of paying specie for occasional imports of American commodities, British merchants and bankers now financed the American trade with China and the Far East on long credits backed by the imports of American cotton and foodstuffs. British capitalists also now invested in American enterprise, since such investments usually returned 5 percent more than comparable investments in Great Britain.[4]

The second way these British developments affected America's prosperity was by drawing the United States into the emerging international economy dominated by Great Britain. This eroded the national independence and self-sufficiency of the United States, which had been America's posture since the 1820s. Accordingly, in the 1840s and 1850s many Baltimoreans came to believe that free trade and laissez faire capitalism better fit reality than did national self-sufficiency and paternal capitalism. And for the city as a whole, these British developments rejuvenated its commericial character as a depot in the transit of trade. In response to the opportunities presented by the new British trade policies, Baltimore's merchants revived the old ways of trade in agricultural commodities, and commercialism flourished as never before. New interior lands were opened to agriculture and new transportation facilities built to tap them. In short, agricultural and commercial prosperity both depended upon and stimulated the expansion of the city into the countryside via an expanded internal-improvements program. And the new commercial prosperity thereby stimulated the application of steam power to transportation even more than it had been stimulated by the commercial depression before.

Two elements of Baltimore's internal-improvements program of the 1820s had been completed during the deflation from 1837 to 1843, and were poised to facilitate the city's expansion when foreign trade revived during the 1840s. One was Baltimore's tapping of Pennsylvania markets through two railroads and a canal. The Philadelphia-Wilmington-Baltimore Railroad was completed in 1838. Following the headwaters of the Chesapeake Bay and crossing the Susquehanna River near its mouth at Havre de Grace, Maryland, it connected Baltimore with Philadelphia, about one hundred miles to the northeast. Extending almost directly north from Baltimore was the Baltimore & Susquehanna Railroad. Completed in 1840, it reached fifty-seven miles upward through York, Pennsylvania, to Harrisburg, the capital of that state. The Susquehanna and Tidewater Canal also linked the Susquehanna River Valley to Baltimore when, in 1840, it overcame both the shallow mouth of the river and the flat, marshy land on either side of it, and funneled the trade of middle Pennsylvania for forty-five miles parallel to the river from Wrightsville, Pennsylvania, to Havre de Grace on the bay. The second element was of lesser economic but greater political importance. The Baltimore & Washington Railroad that connected Baltimore with the nation's capital, forty miles to the southwest, was completed in 1838; and from this track, a spur line, the Annapolis & Elkton Railroad, extended south-eastward to Annapolis, the state capital.[5]

The third and most important element of Baltimore's internal-improvements program, the city's connection with the trans-Allegheny West, did not succeed until 1853. Technological and financial problems, as well as political rivalry with the Chesapeake and Ohio Canal, prevented the Baltimore & Ohio Railroad from crossing the mountains before them. But the emergence of the Ohio-Mississippi Valley area as a rival to the Middle and South Atlantic states as a foodstuff-producing region during the late thirties and early forties convinced Maryland's agriculturalists that they must support the Baltimore railroad. The richer soil and flatter land of the interior, on which McCormick's reaper could be used, gave greater yields, which reduced the prices of wheat and corn in Eastern markets. Maryland grain farmers could no longer compete with the lower-priced Western produce in the New York and Philadelphia markets or in a few of the foreign markets. Indeed, the wheat and corn lands in western and northern Maryland around the head of the bay, and on the Eastern Shore, appeared "exhausted" in contrast to the higher yields of the Western lands. Consequently, Maryland farmers diversified their agricultural productions, mainly into the more salable—because more perishable—fruits and vegetables. As farmers understood these trends and concluded that their agricultural future lay in a diversification that was dependent upon urban growth, they supported, through state aid, the completion of the Baltimore & Ohio Railroad to Wheeling, Virginia, on the Ohio River in 1853.[6]

The expansion of foreign trade and Baltimore's development into an interregional economy were but two of the general causes of the city's maritime prosperity; a third was the new role of the federal government in the American economy and society. A new national institutional framework was created during the 1840s and 1850s which conformed to the new national and international realities, and which sought to profit from them. Mainly through the efforts of the commercial men—the new Jacksonians in general and Robert James Walker, secretary of the treasury from 1845 to 1849, in particular—the new institutional framework followed two directions. First the federal government abjured direct and positive involvement in American society except as an arbiter, and to a lesser extent as a regulator, of economic activities. Second, the federal government moved to standardize and institutionalize certain entrepreneurial activities. Through such legislation as the Bankruptcy Act of 1841, the Warehousing Act of 1842, the Independent Treasury Act in 1846, Walker's Report on the Treasury in 1845, and the subsequent Tariff Act of 1846, the debates over the Rivers and Harbors Improvement Bill in 1848, and the general shift in financing the federal government through treasury notes instead of bonded debt, the federal government helped to rationalize business practices and make them more uniform. Indeed, such uniformity of procedures helped to standardize local markets and thereby nationalize them. In turn, this facilitated the new interregional trade that the communication and transportation revolutions were creating.[7]

The trend toward standardization and uniformity in the national market system, and its importance for Baltimore's development, was most visible in finance. The return of prosperity demanded an expansion of money and credit, which could occur either one of two ways or by a mixture of both. Either the circulation of paper money issued by the state-chartered banks could be expanded fictitiously, and therefore carefully regulated by the state, or the stock of specie had to be enlarged so as to expand the circulation of paper money. These ideas conformed to the two traditional beliefs about money: it was either liquid credit or it was liquid wealth. The former view prevailed during the 1820s, but the necessity of regulating the supply of paper money by the second Bank of the United States, a creation of the federal government, was part of the paternal capitalism that gave rise to its opposition. Being believers in the theory of the "natural" economy, these opponents insisted that paper money be liquid wealth, meaning that one dollar in paper be equal to one dollar in traditional gold or silver, instead of liquid credit. The opposition thus insisted upon the alternative of enlarging the circulation of paper money by expanding the stock of specie, which is what occurred during the 1840s and 1850s.

Fortunately for the Jacksonians' theory, the amount of specie increased during the period because of the discovery of gold in California, expanded British investments in America, and the British financing of certain aspects of American international trade that required huge capital investments, such as that to the Far East. The expansion of American paper money naturally followed, but it was out of proportion to the supply of specie and therefore speculative. Significantly, the new institutional framework of the federal government encouraged this kind of response. Specifically, the new framework—especially the financing of the federal government by issuing treasury notes, the Warehousing Act, the Tariff, and the Independent Treasury Act of 1846—allowed businessmen to transact their business by maximizing their credit and minimizing their necessity to pay out specie. For example, the initial investment in treasury notes that was paid in gold could be continually renewed as the old ones came due, their interest paid in gold and left to accumulate, and new ones issued. The investor could watch his "hard money" capital literally grow over the years without having to touch it. Also, the new tariff system allowed importing merchants to store their imported goods in a government-designated warehouse for up to three years, and they did not have to pay the duties on the stored goods until they removed them from the warehouse. The federal government thereby maintained the merchant's inventory. Finally, what enabled the federal government to function in these roles was the Independent Treasury Act, which allowed all payments to the federal government to be made in either specie or treasury notes. It was obviously more profitable for importers to utilize the treasury notes. The Independent Treasury Act thus aided Baltimore's merchants by providing them with a new investment vehicle, the treasury notes, and then treating them as a new form of paper money.[8]

A new theory of money accompanied the new, more sophisticated financial policies of the United States Treasury. It applied supply-and-demand theory to currency levels. At long last, currency became a handmaiden of commerce, for here was embodied the eighteenth-century mercantile idea of money: it was neither fixed nor rigid but expanded and contracted according to the conditions of trade. Such a version of money was credit writ large. Precisely because it was flexible and represented opportunity, banking became more "public" and more subject to legal controls during the 1840s and 1850s. And, of course, banking in Baltimore expanded as a result of the city's booming prosperity.[9]

The expansion of banking followed various paths. Certain savings institutions were authorized by the state to issue notes; other savings institutions were transformed into banks by state law and thus acquired the power to issue bank notes; and new commercial banks were created. Perhaps because everyone remembered the three panics between 1837 and 1842, no new commercial banks were created between that time and 1854. Instead, two savings institutions were authorized by the state legislature to issue bank notes: the Fell's Point Savings Institution in 1844 and the Howard Street Savings Institution in 1849. A third institution, the Old Town Savings Institution, was authorized to issue notes in 1860. Directly following the booming mercantile economy, the mid-1850s were years of commercial bank expansion, the first since the inflationary period of the early and mid-1830s. The Howard Street Savings Institution became the Howard Bank in 1854; the Bank of Commerce was created in that year. In 1856, two other savings institutions, the Exchange and the People's, became commercial banks while another new commercial bank, the American, was founded.[10]

Unlike the expansion of Baltimore's banking system in earlier periods of prosperity, the expansion this time was remarkably conservative and stable. The ratios of specie to circulation, for example, ranged from a low of .60 (in 1844) to a high of 1.44 (in 1861), while those of specie to circulation plus deposits ranged from 1.72 (in 1844) to 5.58 (in 1861). Both sets of ratios rose over the decades because they reflected the return of prosperity and then, after 1857, the attempts to maintain the high level of Baltimore's economy. What happened to banking from 1851 to 1857, the height of the prosperity, is especially instructive about the financing of the boom: bank capital increased 60 percent, discounts 59 percent, circulation 49 percent, and specie merely 29 percent. Bank deposits increased 71 percent. Obviously, credit played a more important role in the boom than specie did. But perhaps the most interesting financial aspect of the boom was that the circulation of bank notes averaged merely 20 percent (ranging from 18 to 23 percent) of bank discounts. Memories of past panics probably decided Baltimore's bankers against circulating large amounts of bank notes that could be redeemed for specie when business conditions soured.[11]

The new consciousness and sophistication about the social and economic uses of money introduced by the new Jacksonians was partly responsible for this stability of Baltimore's banking system. For example, the new quantity theory of money helped to standardize banking principles and led to more uniform banking practices. Clearinghouses were established in most of the major urban centers (in Baltimore in March 1858), which made exchange processes easier, and also provided weekly reference records about the condition of the banks in the community. From 1838 to 1861, sixteen states passed "free banking" laws, and, though Maryland was not among them, the impetus they gave to standardized banking practices elsewhere helped to unify general American banking procedures. On the whole, this trend of consolidation, rationalization, and standardization provided the stability necessary to withstand the inflationary boom from 1848 through 1856 and the deflation after 1857. This process was doubly important in Baltimore's case because it facilitated the city's emergence as the center of an interregional economy.[12]

Though least known to contemporaries, probably the more important reason for Baltimore's banking conservatism was the city's declining share of the national market economy during the boom. In spite of the absolute position of Baltimore's export economy, its relative position in the nation declined by 2 percent among exports, by 4 percent of the tonnage engaged in foreign trade, and by more than 2 percent of new shipping tonnage built. Even more revealing is Baltimore's relative decline as measured by the nation's internal expansion. For the nation, a normal postdepression expansion occurred from 1844 to 1846, the boom followed from 1847 through 1856, and a depression set in from 1857 to 1861. Baltimore's position actually declined during the general boom from 1847 through 1856, and then its decline accelerated during the depression that began in 1857. Baltimore's banking conservatism thus reflected a very different kind of economic development from that of the nation at large, and the city thereby avoided several of the periodic liquidity crises which occurred in other cities that commanded a larger share of the national market, especially New York.[13]

Baltimore lost its share of the national economy relatively. That is, its market autonomy was lessened as it became subordinate to New York's expanding market system. The consequences were really far more serious than merely falling behind New York in the race for metropolitan leadership in the nation. Though a national economy, dominated by New York, was slowly evolving, several metropolitan interregional economies emerged during the 1840s and 1850s. This development inaugurated a new phase of the communication and transportation revolutions and changed the conditions of competition among the major seaports. Baltimore's traditional, meaning autonomous and local, ways did not work very well in this new context, and those Baltimoreans who operated in the burgeoning national market economy had to adapt themselves to the new realities. For these reasons, the finality which this development meant for their former way of life had a more profound impact upon the community than did its novelty.

Two examples illustrate how the communication and transportation revolutions subordinated Baltimore to New York. First, the telegraph reenforced the latter's domination of the nation's foreign-exchange markets. After 1845, rates for forcign exchange in Baltimore and other American seaports were set in New York because of that city's greater and more frequent access to foreign ports. In turn, this solidified the position of New York among world financial markets by making it the single most important American market for foreign exchange. Secondly, the railroads, which finally connected the major Atlantic seaports with the trans-Alleghany West during the 1850s, did not alter the relationship among the ports. Indeed, even though the railroads and canals undercut much of the traditional river trade to New Orleans, in returning Western produce to the Atlantic seaports they really furthered New York's already established domination of the general American export trade. For example, John Work Garrett, president of the Baltimore & Ohio Railroad Company, continually fought against attempts of New York and Pennsylvania railroad leaders to establish uniform freight rates between the Atlantic seaboard and the West during the late 1850s, arguing that such rates, even though prorated, would diminish Baltimore's natural geographic advantage of being two hundred miles closer to the West than New York. Yet, the Baltimore & Ohio could not compete against the combined interests of New York and Philadelphia railroads because they were more securely positioned and because the mainline of Baltimore's railroad connected with the southern portions of Ohio, Indiana, Illinois, and Missouri, and missed the more important grain-growing areas of the Northwest.[14]

Baltimore's relative decline in the national market system was also rooted in its historical pattern of foreign trade. The trade between America and Great Britain was the single most lucrative source of American commercial profits during the 1840s and 1850s. The enormous growth of American cotton exports to Great Britain, coupled with the ending of the British corn and grain laws in 1846, were the basis of this trade; but the cotton trade continued to be the most important. Unfortunately, Baltimore had never been heavily involved in either the British trade in general or the cotton trade in particular. In fact, the trade patterns that Baltimore had established in the eighteenth century were now, in the last two decades before the Civil War, partly responsible for the city's relative decline in the national maritime economy. Thus, no matter how intensive and profitable was Baltimore's trade with the West Indies, South America, China, or even the British grain markets, it declined in relative importance to the American cotton trade with England, a trade that Baltimore had largely abandoned during the 1790s and again during the 1820s.

Another crucial point about the cotton trade is that its enormous value to Great Britain overshadowed the value of other kinds of American exports to that country. Baltimore was caught in its traditional problem with respect to Great Britain: except for grain and tobacco, Maryland did not produce any goods for the English market. Almost all of Baltimore's tobacco went to the continent, and its grain exports were not sufficient to establish a firm export base that would, in turn, attract British imports. Baltimore was thus caught between New York's domination of the cotton- and grain-export markets (the two most important American exports to Great Britain) and its own inability to attract imports without a more adequate export base.

Baltimore's relative decline as a seaport was also due to the allocation of the city's resources for the expansion of its domestic rather than its foreign markets. This would prove beneficial in the long run, by the 1870s and 1880s, but in the short run it meant a slower growth rate for Baltimore relative to Philadelphia and New York. Even more importantly, it also meant that Baltimore was drawn into economic vassalage to New York. For example, the opening of the Chesapeake and Ohio Canal in 1851 and the completion of the Baltimore & Ohio Railroad to the West in 1853 made the West Baltimore's chief supplier of beef, grain, pork, and tobacco. Moreover, manufactured goods from the north increasingly filtered into and through Baltimore via the coastal trade. These latter two developments drew Baltimore into the orbit of New York's trade even more closely and lessened the city's autonomy as an export center. And Baltimore's relative decline accounts for why the panic of 1857 and subsequent depression were neither as devastating nor as long in Baltimore as they were in Philadelphia or New York.[15]

Even so, the panic of 1857 ended decisively the boom in Baltimore's maritime economy. Shipping activity fell off, and the balance of trade ran against Baltimore for the next two years. In combination with the industrial depression, the late 1850s were indeed grim in Baltimore. The number of business failures increased from fifty-eight in 1857 to seventy-six in 1858, and in October of 1858 the Association for the Benefit of the Poor classified 5,133 families, or about 18,600 people, as "poor"; this represented nearly 8 percent of Baltimore's population. The general depression and the high rate of unemployment during the winter of 1858–59 contributed to the politicocultural crisis in 1859 and 1860.[16]

The liquidity crisis in 1857 originated with the overextension of New York credit facilities in their effort to dominate the burgeoning national market system. Financing their city's export trade at its origins in the West, New York bankers also customarily furnished a six- or eight-month credit to purchasers of imported goods. Simultaneously, New Yorkers were increasingly financing the production of New England goods and the marketing of them in the South and West. By 1857, for example, most imported goods as well as American goods sold in Baltimore were financed by New York bankers on a six- or eight-month credit, and this paper was either discounted in New York or else held to maturity for payment by its Baltimore maker.

Specifically, the 1857 panic was a crisis in the credit structure that stemmed from a cash-flow problem. Having lent money against Western railroad securities whose market prices had fallen, the Ohio Life and Trust Company of Cincinnati and New York failed in August 1857. Financial repercussions in New York, where the Ohio Life and Trust Company was indebted to the American Exchange Bank for nearly half a million dollars, were instantaneous: the stock market declined and six private bankers failed. By the second week in September, the financial panic had spread to Baltimore. Businessmen who normally borrowed on their credit (their "business paper") at 9 or 10 percent interest found interest rates rising to 12 or 13 percent during the first week in September and then to 1½ to 2½ percent per month during the second week. As they were pressed for cash, New York bankers and merchants returned Baltimore business paper, selling it for whatever it would bring on Baltimore's open market, thus depressing the price of Baltimore business paper and raising interest rates accordingly. Though easing during the third week in September, when Baltimore banks stepped up their discounts, the suspension of specie payments by Philadelphia's banks on September 26 forced Baltimore's banks to suspend two days later in order to protect their own specie reserves. Suspension eased the money market: interest rates on first-class business paper immediately fell from 2 to 2½ percent per month to 1 to 1½ percent, and bank deposits increased. This situation continued until the first week in November, when financial conditions eased and the panic was over.[17]

Despite this, the depression and its consequences were just beginning. The optimism of the Baltimoreans began to flag, for the conditions that had sustained their maritime prosperity for the past decade suddenly dissolved. The adjustments of the British economy to peace following the Crimean War, together with its huge grain harvests from 1857 through 1860, drastically contracted the British demand for American foodstuffs, though not for cotton. In the Far East, the war waged by the British and the French against the Chinese from 1857 to 1858, followed by their military occupation of Canton until 1861, virtually closed the China market to the Baltimoreans. Moreover, the end of commercial prosperity within a burgeoning national economy dominated by New York had greater significance than merely ending prosperity. Reality and the rules governing behavior in it were changing.

Industrial Changes

The industrial transformation of Baltimore gained momentum because steam power underpinned the transportation system that was so vital to the city's expansion and prosperity. Moreover, steam-engine technology was virtually the same whether used in manufacturing or transportation: the engine required fuel, maintenance, and replacement parts; only the application was different. Thus, the burst of steam-powered manufacturing in the 1840s was a corollary of its successful application to commerce. Indeed, in 1850 the 110 steam-powered industries employing over 4,300 men that were in operation constituted the largest number in Baltimore throughout the entire antebellum period.[18]

Though industrialization continued its necessary but subordinate role to commerce, the increased use of steam power in manufacturing, the construction of a railroad system within the city, and depression among manufacturers developed Baltimore's industrial economy very differently from the city's general commercial prosperity. Industrialization expanded tremendously in response to the resurgence of foreign trade and the renewal of internal improvements during the 1840s, but once the momentum of restored commerce was established, a political reaction set in that forced manufacturers to consolidate; consequently, manufacturing became recessive during the 1850s. Yet, ironically, the peculiar form of the manufacturing depression of the 1850s had the opposite effect from what was intended, for it spurred the industrial transformation of Baltimore as much as the industrial growth of the 1840s had done.[19]

Specifically, the reopening of overseas markets, the renewal of railroad construction, and the protective tariff of 1842 stimulated the greatest growth of industrialization in and around Baltimore of the entire antebellum period. In Baltimore city and county as a whole, the per capita investment in manufacturing increased nearly 50 percent during the 1840s, productivity increased more than 25 percent, and the output value more than 50 percent. Steam power was applied in such diverse but existing industries as chemicals, flour milling, iron manufacturing, printing, tanneries, and textiles, and to a lesser extent to paper and leather production. A metals industry, producing machine tools, edge tools, and various copper implements flourished. Other new industries that became important included canning, packing, and preserving, activities which owed their importance as much to the city's extension into the countryside as they did to the expansion of Baltimore's overseas markets.[20]

Beginning in 1847, however, the conditions supporting this growth were dramatically changed by the effects of the new tariff law of 1846. This tariff substituted ad valorem for specific duties, which meant that a sliding-scale duty rate of from 20 to 30 percent of the foreign cost of goods was now charged at Baltimore instead of a fixed dollar amount. At first, the tariff's disastrous consequences for Baltimore's manufacturers were not felt because European prices were still high enough for the ad valorem principle to bar their importation. But as the British economy became industrially more efficient during the next fifteen years, and the speculation associated with the European "railway mania" ended, prices of European (particularly British) goods fell as did the American duties that they paid. The effect made Baltimore's different industries uncompetitive at different times—chemicals and textiles were immediately affected in 1847, for example, but iron products not until 1848 and 1849 —forcing industrialists to emphasize such cost efficiencies as consolidation, new technologies, wage reductions, and the like. Thus, the "free trade" tariff of 1846 tied Baltimore's manufacturers to the declining prices of European goods and thereby restricted their ability to compete with the superior products of Europe's more advanced technologies.[21]

The effect upon industrialization and the industrial revolution within Baltimore during the 1850s was devastating. The total number of steam-powered factories declined by 40 percent, and the employment of adult males within them declined nearly 14 percent. Again, the development was uneven. Where steam-powered production of iron, chemicals, and textiles suffered, the like production of leather and lumber products, and of agricultural equipment did not, while flour milling, printing, and stonecutting actually gained. Moreover, two important developments partially arrested the decline of iron manufacturing and other firms supplying a variety of metal products. One was the tapping of the bituminous coal fields of western Maryland and Pennsylvania by the Baltimore & Ohio and the Chesapeake and Ohio Canal, which enormously stimulated the market for coal-burning iron stoves, and the other was the construction of a railroad network with depots within the city. This latter development did not rescue the iron manufacturers, however, for the general conditions forced the railroads, particularly the Baltimore & Ohio, to pare expenses by restricting outside contracts and developing their own forges and boiler and repair shops. By 1860 the Baltimore & Ohio had built new facilities within Baltimore, which made the company the single largest employer among all iron-producing facilities within the city. Thus, among iron manufacturers at least, the depression of the fifties consolidated the industry by eroding the small-scale, specialty-produce manufacturers.[22]

Indeed, even generally speaking, the industrial transformation of Baltimore continued and moderately accelerated during the recessive industrialization of the 1850s. In spite of the absolute decline of industrial establishments and employment within them, the percentage of steam-powered concerns of all manufacturing establishments rose from less than 5 percent in 1850 to more than 6 percent in 1860, and their percentage of all employees engaged in manufacturing rose from 29 percent in 1850 to nearly 35 percent in 1860. But the more telling statistic was the greater rate of persistence for steam-powered manufacturers than for handicraft producers: it was over 27 percent for steam-powered concerns but merely 6½ percent for handicraft producers. The greater stability of industrialization in the midst of a manufacturing depression demonstrated its greater economic efficiencies in meeting the new conditions than traditional and more costly handicraft producers. Obviously, it was the trend of the future.[23]

An even better illustration of Baltimore's continuing industrial transformation lay with its flourishing industries. Generally speaking, and disregarding their source of power, these industries manufactured goods used by the growing population market that was tapped by Baltimore's expansion into an interregional economy. Steam power thrived among the construction industries, for example, as did handicraft producers of cigars, boots and shoes, as well as tailors and clothiers. However, these handicraft producers shared an approach to cost efficiencies that other crafts and trades did not: they engaged in mass, assembly-line production, they employed cheaper immigrant labor, and they usually paid wages by the piece rate. Probably the best example was the ready-made-clothing industry, for it reflected Baltimore's growing population as industrialized, specialized, and interdependent. By 1860, over 43 percent of the clothiers employed 6 or more adult males; one shop had 30 such employees, and seven others had 40, 55, 60, 70, 113, 200, and 211, respectively. The market positions of the largest employers were further enhanced by their using the new sewing machines; and the group as a whole had driven the milliners out of existence.

The pattern of industrialization seems clear. Handicraft producers who could consolidate, standardize parts and procedures, and make even more cost efficiencies through new technology and cheaper labor, resembled the steam-powered concerns. Indeed, together they constituted a new order of manufacturing. In circular fashion, large-scale production lowered per-unit costs, which simultaneously created and required demand markets for more-uniform products. The expansion of Baltimore into the interior, its growing population, and the expansion of its overseas markets provided the impetus for their initial growth during the 1840s. But, unfortunately, high profits locked them into a style of production that they could not change when conditions reversed themselves during the 1850s; they could only intensify cost efficiencies and hope for a revival of market demand. Handicraft producers who could not reduce costs became less competitive and were driven from the marketplace, a marketplace that was increasingly defined in monetary rather than social terms. Though the small shops having a few craftsmen each did not disappear, they lost, on the whole, their competitive edge to industrial concerns and to those craft firms that could be organized for mass production. Finally, both of the latter required a huge capitalization, which inhibited small entrepreneurs.

The effect of Baltimore's renewed commercial prosperity upon industrialization was to bring an important qualitative change in the city's social economy. Commercial success was purchased by dependence upon steam power, which made Baltimore a nineteenth-century industrial economy. An era ended when the city's eighteenth-century commercial base became dependent upon industrialism, and when its local economy was transformed into an interregional economy that undercut Baltimore's market autonomy. Such a new economic order was fraught with dilemmas for commercial men, the most serious of which involved their relationship to the new and crucial forces of steam power and their traditional sociopolitical leadership roles within the community. How these dilemmas developed was itself part of the process of the industrial revolution.

CHAPTER IX

An Industrial Society

Profound social changes accompanied the transformation of Baltimore's economy, and a new social order appeared. Superficially, the changes were one-dimensional and linear: the expansion of Baltimore's economic scale forced changes in the city's social and political organization. But the new society also reflected the city's qualitative development into a more complex system that embraced industrialism as well as commercialism. In addition, the new geographic and functional specializations introduced even greater complexities, and a huge population growth, especially through foreign immigration, fragmented Baltimore's previous unities as never before. The new social order thus appeared as an adaptive response to the new realities.

But the social changes were also part of a long historical process that was coming to an end. Baltimoreans had begun institutionalizing democratic opportunities during the business revolution, when organizations for expanding opportunities proliferated during the city's prosperous involvement in the wars of the French Revolution. The entire process then unfolded in a succession of stages. The next surge came after economic and social complexity was introduced by the paternal development of industrialization during the wartime crisis from 1807 to 1815, and during the maritime depression that followed. A reaction to paternalism set in during the long depression, when Baltimoreans changed their institutions to reflect indigenous ideas and values common to the culture, made them easier to understand, and called the entire process democratic. Now, in the midst of restored commercial prosperity during the forties and fifties, what had become familiar institutional responses were broadened to preserve the democratic opportunity that was alleged to be Baltimore's way of life. Individual opportunities were maximized, alien cultural elements were socialized, and conflicting or potentially conflicting elements were harmonized through institutional procedures. So familiar had the process become that it was now itself a Baltimore tradition.

During the 1840s and 1850s, however, Baltimoreans gradually discovered that they could no longer trust their familiar responses, for their actions produced different and unpredictable results amid their city's new realities. Before the 1840s, the city had been able to assimilate economic changes, because its circumstances remained essentially the same. Indeed, the effects of such developments as a huge foreign immigration and population growth, expansion of political democracy, and industrialization had been more evolutionary than revolutionary. However, an expanded economic scale, particularly the appearance of distant markets and the absolute necessity of industrialization to them, truly revolutionized the social order. Imbalances in the social structure appeared, traditional prejudices and habits of thought, as well as new ones, were magnified, and older social unities suddenly crumbled. The resulting new social order became more fragmented and more dependent upon institutional procedures than ever before. In fact, so important and pervasive did institutions become to Baltimore on the eve of the Civil War that they now defined the community itself. And when this happened, Baltimore had made the transition from an eighteenth-century private society to a nineteenth-century public one.

The Industrial Revolution in Baltimore

Baltimore's new circumstances changed society in two broad ways. First, commercial prosperity and geographic specialization completed the fragmentization of the city's traditional leadership. In a purely quantitative way, prosperity attracted many new men who called themselves merchants but who had neither the capital nor the connections to function as traditional merchants did. Internal divisions became more acute and the group became less powerful and articulate as a whole. In a qualitative way, Baltimore's development into an interregional economy created new geographic specializations among businessmen marked by differences of capital and credit. Only merchants having large capitals and lines of credit could afford the new opportunities created by the interregional economy, and when they pursued them they usually abandoned local markets to new entrepreneurs with smaller resources. And, finally, the new circumstances generally constricted businessmen to economic pursuits, thereby shifting their leadership roles in the political and social life of the community from active to passive and influential, and opening up these other kinds of opportunities to new men. Just as the economy became too large and complex to be dominated by any one group, so, too, did its society, as illustrated by the strengthening of multiple elite groups and the divorce of business from political and social activities. Baltimore was democratized on a wholly new scale.

As early as 1850, the traditional leaders, the merchants, no longer wielded the socioeconomic power they once did. Individually, they were not poor: the mean value of the real property that they reported in the 1850 federal population census was $20,414; and this in a year when a skilled tradesman might make $400, if he were lucky. But the group as a whole accounted for merely 12 percent of all property holders in the city, and, within the group, merely 20 percent of the merchants owned real property. Obviously, wealth had become highly concentrated.[1]

The merchants had also become a bloated group: 1,544 reported themselves as "merchants" in the 1850 census, or else prefixed one of seventeen different kinds of specialities such as "commission merchant" or "liquor merchant" in listing their occupation; and 80 percent listed no property holdings though most were between the ages of the early thirties and the early fifties. Nearly 80 percent of them were native Americans, and almost 71 percent were born in Maryland. Germans constituted the largest foreign-born group (though they were less than 10 percent of the total), Irish the second largest (less than 6 percent of the total), and other nationalities were scattered and tiny in number. Most of the listed 317 property owners were native Americans; only 19 percent of them were foreign born. According to ethnic origins, 27 percent of the Maryland-born merchants owned property, 24½ percent of the other American born, 17½ percent of the Germans, 40 percent of the Irish, and 20 percent of the English. The remaining groups were very small. Though great wealth was present it was concentrated, and, though the group as a whole still symbolized the traditional, individual entrepreneur in mid-nineteenth-century Baltimore, the majority had apparently become specialized caricatures of the eighteenth-century originals.[2]

In contrast to the swelling presence and declining force of the merchants was the rising importance of directors of business corporations. About four hundred Baltimoreans served in this capacity, and, though some were new to Baltimore, most were either members of old families or else had lived in the city for several years. Unlike the merchants, most directors were property owners, despite the fact that the mean value of their property holdings, $3,000, was much less, and had widely diverse occupations. Interlocking directorates took a subtle form. None existed between the commercial banks, for example, but many of these directors also served on the boards of savings banks and of insurance, manufacturing, real estate development, and transportation companies. Interlocking directorates between the boards of insurance, manufacturing, transportation, and real-estate development companies were virtually nonexistent, for only a few men served on more than one board. Apparently, then, financial contacts, rather than occupational affiliation or industrial domination, were the most important consideration in the evolution of the new business organizations. Also, the corporation continued to be mainly a financial device for business activity and to be democratic in its attraction of capital, though corporate stability, as measured by the low rate of turnover among the directors and the succession of sons to their fathers' positions, undoubtedly made them seem undemocratic in the society at large.[3]

Apart from the atrophy of the merchant class and the new importance of corporate businessmen, Baltimore's economic leadership was fragmented by geographic specialization. About one hundred of the wealthiest, most prominent, and most active businessmen spearheaded and then maintained their city's development into the new interregional trade. Many in this group, or members of their families, had long been involved in international trade, representing Baltimore to world markets as well as to other American seaports. Consequently, they were more responsible than those of any other business group for continuing and even institutionalizing the traditional antipathy of commercial men toward manufacturers. Even more importantly, they were responsible for promoting the industrialization of commerce, which increased their profits but did so at the expense of destroying their older social order.

The irony of how this commercial elite undermined the traditional social order when attempting to preserve it was demonstrated by two institutions that they created. One was the Corn and Flour Exchange. Organized in 1851 and incorporated in 1854, the purpose of the exchange was to facilitate the export of foodstuffs from the Midwest through Baltimore to other markets. Establishing product standards as well as their various price ranges, the exchange represented a return to the old exchange of 1816 and its way of merchandising produce in a central location where all traders met to conduct business and who knew one another. The second institution was the Board of Trade that was revived and reorganized in 1849 and incorporated in 1852. Membership was expressly restricted to traders and presidents of institutions, such as banks, which facilitated trade. Manufacturers were specifically excluded. One irony was that Baltimore's manufacturers had made the city's tapping of the Midwestern markets possible, and another was that incorporation indicated the importance which institutionalization now played in Baltimore's new economy. Indeed, the commercial elite understood how the corporate form could be used to encourage private and voluntary controls over trade, and how valuable the limited-liability feature of corporations was in this connection. Moreover, they understood how the financial requirements of a corporation preserved and created class lines, and how such a device could circumvent municipal regulation by members of the City Council who knew nothing of interregional or international trade. Preserving the old ways thereby led the commercial elite into business specialization as an extension of the private society, and into using incorporation as the primary form for preserving the old ways.[4]

Obviously, great changes were afoot if the commercial elite were finding it necessary to institutionalize and distinguish their social and economic roles from other groups in the city. Yet few of them knew precisely how their power was fragmented by other, larger and more inclusive developments. For one thing, as the front rank of Baltimore's commercial leaders focused their attention upon the new interregional economy and prosperous overseas markets, they abandoned positions in the local and even the regional markets. Also, new subsidiary positions opened up as the entire social economy expanded. Accordingly, new men moved into these positions. Though opportunities abounded at this secondary level as much as they did at the first, they were more limited. Consequently, the men who moved into the secondary level tended to operate in conventional and traditional ways, through partnerships or individual proprietorships in business, and as merchants or owners of "manufactories." And because their market horizon was Baltimore, and possibly the adjacent countryside and satellite towns, they bore the brunt of industrial revolution more directly than did their counterparts in the front rank. Moreover, this new generation of businessmen operated through received institutions, which they affirmed as responsible for their success. They were cultural conservatives who usually lacked the creativity and imagination of the men of the first rank, and their success was usually owing to a combination of luck, skill, and opportunity.[5]

Both ranks of business leaders shared the traditional commercial man's point of view, and the differences between them merely reflected their different market orientations, scale of business, and capital and credit resources; but this was not true of a third group of leaders, the merchant-manufacturers. Most merchant-manufacturers used steam power to produce industrial goods used in the interregional economy, such as steam engines and boilers, or consumer goods which they wholesaled, or else they processed agricultural commodities. They conducted their own marketing and associated and identified with the interregional and international trading merchants; some even intermarried with the purely commercial families. Prosperity and the new importance of industrialization gave them their socioeconomic importance and affirmed their own values of commercialism by strengthening their productive base. But their position became increasingly incongruous in the new order for two reasons: one was the new importance of steam power, which produced a group who were more concerned with technology than were the merchant-manufacturers, and the other was the traditional commercial men's prejudice against all manufacturers, a prejudice that became an institutionalized part of Baltimore life during the 1850s.[6]

The appearance of this second group of manufacturers, concerned more with production and technology than distribution or marketing, points to the second broad way that Baltimore's new economy fractured its social order: through industrial revolution. Industrial revolution did not simply reshape society in greater conformity with industrial technology, nor did it immediately redistribute power to a new social group; rather, it changed the quality of society by reshaping existing forms and conventions of social activities. Generally speaking, it specialized society by divorcing business from political and from social activities, by intensifying the fragmentation of traditional leadership groups, by creating diverse opportunities whereby new men who better understood the new social order could rise to power, and by standardizing established social patterns to accommodate population growth and diversity. The new importance of industrialists was the most visible example of industrial revolution.

The new manufacturers were business specialists who wielded enormous socioeconomic power as employers of thousands. Mainly engaged in various aspects of iron manufacturing, they called themselves boilermakers, engineers, iron founders, iron manufacturers, iron masters, machinists, and millwrights. Others used steam power in the building trades as stonecutters and saw millers, and still others (such as distillers and tanners) used steam power in processing commodities. Most of them were native Marylanders, the others coming mainly from New York and New England. Two of them—Horace Abbott, an iron-plate and rolling-mill manufacturer from Massachusetts, and Charles Reeder, Jr., steamboat-engine builder and native Baltimorean—acquired national reputations during the 1850s. Though having vital skills, capital, and business influence, however, the new manufacturers continued to be regarded as mere craftsmen by the commercial elite and the merchant-manufacturers. Consequently, they remained politically and socially mute until the Civil War cloaked their special talents with political importance.[7]

The new necessity of industrialization to Baltimore's economy wrought other kinds of changes as well. Some were part of, and continued, a long historical process. Occupational diversity proliferated, for example, in new forms connected with the metals industries, such as car builders, chemists, engineers, iron molders, machinists, pyrotechnists, and wire workers. Also, industrialism continued to erode the guild system and employer paternalism, but in ways peculiar to the 1840s and 1850s. The industrial stagnation from the late forties through the fifties combined with a large pool of available labor provided by a huge immigration to

Baltimore to raise the employers' awareness of the cost of labor. Wage relationships were typical of the industrial factories. The preindustrial guild system and employer paternalism continued, however, in the highly specialized crafts and among such handicraft manufacturers as boot- and shoemakers, cigar makers, clothiers, and tailors. However, even these employers were forced by economic circumstances to adopt assembly-line methods and to hire the cheaper labor of women and immigrants to reduce costs. Such cost-saving measures contributed to the general trend toward wage relationships between all employers and employees.[8]

The depression that engulfed industrialism specifically eroded the guild system and employer paternalism by eliminating the independent, small-shop craftsmen. Less than 8 percent of all manufacturers in Baltimore in 1850 remained in business ten years later, and the traditional handicraft manufacturers bore the brunt of this industrial consolidation. For example, the number of blacksmith establishments declined from 71 in 1850 to 10 in 1860; carpenters from 180 to 3; coach makers from 25 to 12; coopers from 60 to 17; curriers from 21 to 6; milliners from 45 to 2; saddlers from 36 to 6; shipsmiths from 16 to 5; silversmiths, jewelers, and watchmakers from 39 to 1; upholsters from 14 to 0; and wheelwrights from 21 to 8. Other traditional occupations declined less dramatically but in the same fashion. Together with the consolidation and concentration movements among steam-powered producers, the decline of these kinds of manufacturing activities transformed the traditional personal relationship between employers and employees into a more formal, ritual relationship governed by the employers' economic circumstances.

The emphasis upon wage relations was particularly evident in the large-scale industrialized facilities, and indicated the future social basis of manufacturing. Indeed, the new necessity of industrialization to Baltimore's new economy gave it a sedentary and uniquely cohesive social character, which became the basis for its new and vital social role. In 1850, for example, Baltimore's 110 steam-powered facilities employed 4,316 men, or 29 percent of all males engaged in manufacturing. An average facility employed about 39. In 1860 there were merely 66 such establishments employing 3,723 men, but which now represented nearly 35 percent of all male laborers in manufacturing, and each facility averaged about 56 employees. Their large capitalizations, together with the general trend of consolidation over the 1850s, made them the most stable, and therefore socially important, source of employment. Their rate of persistence, for example, was over 27 percent, compared with less than 7 percent for nonsteam-powered producers.

Following the normal tendency to rationalize production and reduce costs, steam power was applied where products could be standardized. They included agricultural implements, beer and whiskey, candles, china, flour, plaster, soap, building stone and marble, sugar, and wooden ware —buckets, tubs, washboards and the like. In addition, steam power had been used since the 1830s in cutting lumber and therefore standardizing and speeding up both house and ship construction. However, the increasing emphasis upon steam-powered production continued to fall upon transportation systems and reproducing itself rather than upon consumer products. Indeed, this emphasis even increased slightly during the 1850s. For example, though the percentage of steam-powered units producing castings, engines, machine parts, and nuts and bolts rose very little over the 1850s, from less than 31 percent to more than 37 percent, the number of men employed in such production increased from less than 45 percent to nearly 60 percent of the male labor force for all steam-powered facilities. The social effects of this change were paradoxical: on the one hand, increasing numbers of men employed in steam-powered units produced goods that they as consumers did not use, and, on the other hand, such employment was crucial to their existence. Consequently, many contemporaries found it easy to continue divorcing industrialization from its social context at a time when industrial stagnation intensified the view of labor as a cost of production.

At least these were the effects that produced Baltimore's first industrial conflict between labor and employers. The occasion was a massive, city-wide strike within Baltimore's iron industry that lasted from February 12 to April 2, 1853. At the time, the iron industry was the second largest industrial employer in the city. There were six iron furnaces and thirteen major foundries, and their best customers were the railroads, especially the Baltimore & Ohio and the Baltimore & Susquehanna. The industry as a whole employed nearly four thousand men, or about one-quarter of Baltimore's male force employed in manufacturing; and on February 12, the great majority of these workers struck for a 15 percent increase in wages. The two railroads and five of the foundries immediately agreed to the increase, but the other employers refused to raise wages unless the railroads increased their contracts with the foundry operators. The latter were, of course, the most marginal operators and wanted to pass on their increased costs immediately to their customers. Five days later, almost half of the strikers returned to work with those employers who granted the raise, agreeing to share one-fourth of their wages with those workers remaining on strike. At the end of February, about two thousand workers were still on strike, though financial pressures were beginning to thin their ranks by forcing several workers to return to work at the old wage

An Industrial Society

rates. In early March however, the strikers received financial aid from mechanics in other cities as well as from several of Baltimore's craft unions, which enabled them to continue their stike through March. By the first of April the strike was a success. Almost every worker had returned to work at advanced wages, though some were reported not to have received the wage increase.[9]

The strike was important for several reasons. For one thing, the strikers advanced a sophisticated theory of the rights of industrial labor against what the employers argued were the "immutable laws of supply and demand" in determining wage rates. Going beyond the argument that their wages were insufficient for their cost of living, the workers challenged the very authority and logic of employers being the sole judge of such wages. And this created a dilemma for them. Though they argued an older, communitarian tradition of workers sharing in the profits of the employer, they couched their demands in a formal rhetoric of "the struggle between labor and capital," which assumed a logic that could only result in a victorious battle amidst a lost war:

> We discountenance all agrarian doctrines, and fully acknowledge that capital has its rights as well as labor, and that our employers have deserved well of the community for their enterprise and perseverance—but we have served them faithfully—have placed our labor against their capital, and in this, their day of prosperity, we merely ask for a fair equivalent for our labor in the same ratio that all other marketable commodities have risen.

The strikers were hardly revolutionaries; all they desired was a larger slice of the economic pie; and to the extent that higher wages were forthcoming, they were successful. But such success was offset by the loss of labor's general thrust. That is, workers remained a cost of production (though now a more expensive one), industrial manufacturing continued to play a growing role in Baltimore society, traditional antiindustrial values and ideology remained dominant and culturally overwhelming in this first confrontation with the forces of the new order, and the labor movement was itself divided for a variety of reasons.[10]

However, the chief importance of the strike was political, for the strike demonstrated to Baltimore's workers that the existing political mechanism was used to support the employers and not themselves. In 1853 the majority of Baltimore's workingmen were Democrats; yet the employers did not hesitate to exert pressure on the strikers through the established Democratic party clubs and politicians whose political careers were built upon their image as the "workingmen's candidate." When the leaders of the strike tried to form a "pure" workingmen's political movement, separated from established parties, their inexperience and lack of cohesion, but especially the opposition of the Democratic party, ensured their failure. Thus, Baltimore's social forms moved against the workers' broader cultural interest in political ways that had become traditional since the Jacksonians. But Baltimore realities during the 1850s were qualitatively different from what they had been during the 1830s, and the workers did have another political choice. In short, the antiindustrial manufacturing values that dominated the Democratic party, the weakness of the Whigs, and the strike leaders' affiliation with the Order of United American Mechanics, the national, nativist, and secret workingmen's association whose executive council was headquartered in Philadelphia, set the stage for the emergence of the Know-Nothing party in the following year.[11]

Apart from social-interest relationships, industrialization also transformed Baltimore in two broad ways. One concerned the urban geography of the city. Generally speaking, the geographic pattern of all manufacturing within the city depended upon a variety of factors: transportation routes and costs, when steam power was adopted by different industries, and population growth and its directions; and one general result was to locate producers according to social function rather than by industry group. For example, manufacturers who provided the most direct and everyday retail goods and services—bakers, blacksmiths, boot- and shoemakers, cabinet (furniture) makers, carpet manufacturers or weavers, cigar makers, clothiers and tailors, and wheelwrights—were scattered throughout the city. Also, those independent craftsmen, producers, and retailers who flourished during the depressed 1850s did so in the fastest-growing wards. Likewise, construction occupations such as brickmakers and builders, transportation-connected occupations such as harness makers and wagon makers, and retailers as diverse as confectioners, fancy-dry-goods-store owners, and potters were located in the same growing wards. The more highly rationalized handicraft producers such as clothiers and tailors were located in the same wards as the largest employers among the steam-powered establishments. Large-scale employers such as flour millers and shipbuilders apparently did not change their locations when they adopted steam power. Shipbuilders were an obvious exception because of their necessary access to the harbor, but otherwise producers were not concentrated by industry. Within the livestock industry, for example, butchers were concentrated in the outlying wards 7, 8, and 19, meat packers in wards 9 and 10, curriers in 12 and 14, tanners in ward 11, and hide and tallow makers in wards 8 and 11. Like most retailers, retail users of leather such as boot- and shoemakers, saddlers, and harness makers were scattered throughout the city. Finally, the iron industry was as dispersed as the livestock industry. Foundries were concentrated in wards 1, 4, 8 and 16, locomotive works in wards 16 and 18, and machinists in wards 2, 4, and 15.[12]

However, a comparison of the 1850 manufacturing census with that of 1860 reveals a distinct geographic pattern underlying the decline and consolidation of steam-powered establishments. In each census, the six wards having the largest number of such units remained the same (wards 1, 2, 4, 9, and 10, 11, and 15). Also, they contained twenty-six of the thirty steam-powered establishments that persisted in business over the decade, and ten of the twelve units that produced such integral parts of industrialization as castings, engines, machine parts, and nuts and bolts. Industrialization thus concentrated and stabilized in a core group of wards. In contrast, the least persistent steam-powered producers were in wards that formed an outer arc around this core (wards 5 and 6, 7, 8, 12, 14, 16, 18, 19, and 20).[13]

The other aspects of Baltimore's changing urban geography concerned housing and the introduction of the railroad into the city. The more subtle of the two was the boom in new house construction, for such prosperity in the residential building trades directly reflected the economic boom of the 1840s, obscured the industrial stagnation of the 1850s, but clearly paralleled Baltimore's burgeoning population and domestic economy. From the annual new construction rates of 583, 607, and 412 during the height of the prosperous 1830s—1834 through 1836, respectively—the numbers of new housing units ballooned to over 2,000 in 1847, more than 1,900 in 1848, and nearly 1,900 in 1849. By 1850, there were over 24,000 single-family dwelling units within the city, each having an average occupancy rate of 1.21 families and 7.04 persons. Though declining from their height during the 1840s, annual new construction rates continued during the 1850s to run about two and a half times the highest rates of the 1830s. By 1852, the average occupancy fell to 5.81 persons per house, and in 1860, when there were 40,169 houses in the city, it fell to 5.29.[14]

Generally speaking, housing patterns conformed to the population movements within the wards. That is, the general citywide pattern of a population increase, a housing increase, and an increase in the number of families was followed in twelve of the twenty wards (wards 1, 3, 6 through 8, 11 and 12, and 15 through 20) which were the same wards that experienced heavy inflows of foreign immigrants, free blacks, and slaves. Only one of the immigrant wards (ward 2) deviated significantly from this norm. It experienced a decrease in both population and hous-

Baltimore in 1853 (courtesy of the Maryland Historical Society)

ing. Residential construction tradesmen thus had a very different experience from that of industrial workers, and especially the foreign immigrant, during the 1850s.

The form of housing also changed, for the massive demand for housing produced the innovative "row house" during the 1840s. Though the two-story red-brick house continued to characterize Baltimore's residential architecture, several blocks of the more cheaply constructed row houses had been built by 1850 to accommodate working-class families. These were "town houses," built of brick, three stories high, measuring fifteen feet in width, and were separated from one another by a single brick wall. Though working-class families commonly bought these homes, they leased the land on which they were built, usually for ninety-nine years, but renewable forever. Given this traditional arrangement, a throw-back to old English systems of quitrents, it was obviously advantageous to landowners that tenants in possession of a property were liable for two-thirds of its taxes under Maryland law. The workers who inhabited these homes were mainly skilled tradesmen who earned, on the average, nine dollars a week when they worked; but most of them worked seasonally or were subject to layoffs when business was slack; consequently, very few of them earned as much as four hundred dollars in one year.[15]

The other change in Baltimore's urban geography was the enlarged presence of the railroad into the city. By 1860 the Baltimore & Ohio Railroad had completed or was constructing four depots in wards 2, 16, 18 (which was its main terminal, the Mount Clare station), and 20, and the Pennsylvania Railroad had constructed or was completing three depots in wards 8 and 11. The Baltimore & Ohio was particularly important, because it linked Baltimore's water-borne and overland trades. Its tracks ran along the docks at the northern end of the harbor and basin in wards 1, 2, and 9, and continued west into ward 18, while branches ran northward from various points along the way. Businesses would, of course, cluster along the tracks, particularly around the terminals.[16]

The second broad way that industrialization transformed Baltimore involved the relation of Baltimore's growing population to all of these patterns; and here the result was mixed. For example, the population generally decreased or increased very little in the stable industrial wards but expanded greatly in the outlying, perimeter wards, particularly in the north and west. This pattern was also true of free blacks and slaves. However, foreign-born immigrants increased in both the industrial core and the perimeter wards.[17]

For Baltimore's population as a whole, the importance of industrialization apparently lay in its social diversity and sedentary effects. The city's population increased tremendously, by 110,105 or over 107 percent, from 1840 to 1860, in spite of the fact that available goods and services declined, as measured by both production and its producers. In 1860 Baltimore was able to support more than 212,000 people. In comparison with the Baltimore of the 1790s, what had changed was the city's capacity as a social economy to support a population during the 1850s that was about ten times larger than it had been during the former decade. Moreover, the new public society merely seemed more fluid and loose than during the 1790s because of the greater numbers and diversity of everything; for it is doubtful that the rate of transiency among heads of households during the 1850s exceeded the 17 percent of the 1790s. Moreover, the persistence of the eighteenth-century legal system of property ownership mainly accounts for the fact that real property ownership declined from a 10 percent rate in 1798 to less than 2 percent in 1850. Industrialization contributed to the diversity that made Baltimore's growth possible.[18]

So did foreign immigration. Like industrialization, foreign immigration had been a continuing part of Baltimore's development; but between 1840 and 1860, it reached flood tide when nearly 170,000 foreign immigrants poured into the city. During the 1850s, alone, nearly 100,000 entered Baltimore and the number of alien residents increased nearly 50 percent. Apart from their numbers, however, a qualitative change in their ethnic origins also occurred. Over 97 percent of the foreign immigrants who landed in Baltimore throughout the antebellum period came from Europe, with Germans making up the largest ethnic nationality. But during the late 1840s, the number of Irish immigrants suddenly ballooned to nearly half of the yearly immigration before falling off again in the mid-1850s. This sudden influx of thousands of Roman Catholic Irish, many of whom were illiterate, unskilled, and of rural origins—and were not, therefore, immediately assimilable into a commercial, industrial, and urban way of life—created tensions and conflicts between the Germans and Irish as well as between these immigrants and native-born Americans. Depressed industrial conditions sharpened these tensions.[19]

The settlement of the foreign immigrants in relation to industrialization also affected the residential patterns of other groups within the city. Generally speaking, the foreign-born concentrated in the water wards ringing the harbor and basin (wards 1, 2, and 17, but not 9 or 15), in wards 3 and 4, in the heavily Roman Catholic wards 8 and 12, and in ward 19, which was rapidly expanding in connection with the Western trade.

Otherwise, they were scattered. In 1850, before industrial consolidation and stagnation worsened, over 51 percent of the foreign-born lived in these eight wards, and, during that decade, the number of industrial establishments within these wards increased over 19 percent, employment in those industries declined nearly 24 percent, the number of free blacks declined more than 13 percent, and the number of slaves declined nearly 23 percent. Foreign immigrants thus bore the brunt of the industrial consolidation and unemployment.[20]

Having no political status and being the most vulnerable nonslave group in Baltimore, free blacks left the immigrant wards and apparently even the city. The group as a whole increased by less than 1 percent during the 1850s, the number of males declining, though that of females increased. Working at the most marginal and least paid traditional occupations, they gravitated toward the cheapest living areas within the city. They abandoned their former locations in the industrial and commercial wards and moved to the perimeters (their most significant increases, 30 percent or more, occurred in the outlying wards 7, 18, 19, and 20). Here, they probably followed or found the white population who traditionally served as their patrons, employers and protectors, and who themselves disliked the foreign immigrants. Moreover, the general life style in the perimeter wards was more traditional (i.e., nonindustrial) than in their former wards. Lacking political power and, of lesser significance, manufacturing skills, free blacks could not hope to compete with their white immigrant socioeconomic rivals for commercial and industrial jobs; and racism continued as part of the new social order.[21]

The movement of slaves within the city was virtually identical to that of the free blacks. The only wards in which slavery increased during the 1850s were 11, 18, 19, and 20, along the western and northwestern perimeters of the city, farthest away from the basin and, except for ward 11, the industrial and immigrant wards along the water. Again excepting ward 11, previous patterns of slaveholding remained much the same. On the whole, the slaves were young and female; the largest group of slaves were females of childbearing age; more male slaveholders held these female slaves than female holders did; and the majority of all slaveholders were men. Ward 11 was peculiar, because the largest number of male slaves of any age group lived there, and their specific age group, twenty-one to forty-five, suggests that they were employed in the manufacturing industries in that ward. The usual trend toward young female slaves was most pointed in the immigrant and water wards, where slavery declined on the whole, but where the number of women slaveowners sharply increased over the decade.[22]

The use of slave labor apparently shifted away from commercial and industrial pursuits into domestic service. The number of slaves declined absolutely and the population became younger and increasingly female.

By 1860, there were twice as many female as male slaves. Indeed, economically productive males between the ages of ten and seventy constituted less than 1 percent of the total male labor force in that age range in the city (in contrast to free black males who represented one-third of the group), and nearly 55 percent of the males and 48 percent of the females were under twenty. In 1860, moreover, two-thirds of all slaveholders owned merely one slave.[23]

Slaveholding was also a source of rental income, especially for women owners. Slaveholders continued to be incredibly transient: their persistence was less than 10 percent during the 1850s, and those who remained were primarily women owners. Moreover, the proportion of male slaveholders declined from about 75 percent in 1850 to 60 percent in 1860. Male owners held the largest numbers of female slaves of childbearing age (twelve to forty) as well as male slaves, ages from twelve to forty-five; women held mainly females slaves, ages twelve to forty, and more females up to eleven years of age and from forty-one to sixty than they did male slaves. Moreover, a larger proportion of women owners hired out their slaves than male owners did.[24]

Continuing Institutionalization

Long before the 1840s, Baltimore's private society had learned to assimilate physical and social changes by elaborating its ongoing institutional structure. Now, confronted with the massive changes of the forties and fifties, this infrastructure was expanded on a huge scale to acculturate the new forces. In the process, Baltimore's private and voluntary society became less personal and more dependent upon institutions.

No fewer than twelve institutions were created during the forties and fifties to care for orphans, the sick, the poor, alcoholics, and men and women in various other kinds of distress. Virtually every one of these bodies, the sole exception being the General Workingmen's Sick Relief Union formed in 1851, was religious or religiously connected in origin. Nine, the great majority of them, were formed during the 1850s, the decade of industrial stagnation, consolidation, and the heaviest foreign immigration of the antebellum era. Also, eighty-one new church congregations were formed from 1843 to 1861, a greater number than had previously existed in the city. More than half of them were established during the 1850s. Altogether, they were overwhelmingly white, Protestant, and connected with the major established denominations. Two of the religious organizations directly reflected the ethnic backgrounds of new immigrants: four Jewish synagogues appeared for the first time in Baltimore, three of them during the 1840s, and eight Roman Catholic churches were established, seven during the 1850s.[25]

Within the major Protestant denominations, two important developments occurred. First, nearly half of these new churches were Methodist and another 20 percent were Episcopalian. Moreover, where nineteen Methodist churches had existed in Baltimore before 1843, twenty-nine new ones were formed afterward; for the Episcopalians, the number was six and twelve respectively. Such dramatic changes did not characterize the Baptist, Lutheran, or Presbyterian denominations, each of which formed the same number of churches during the forties and fifties as had existed previously. Second, the establishment of these new churches occurred mainly during the 1850s, except for the Methodists. That is, most of the new Baptist, Episcopal, and Presbyterian, and all of the new Lutheran churches were formed during the decade. About half of the new Methodist congregations were formed during each of the decades. If church formation was an index of religious activity, Methodists were the most active Protestant denomination, and religious activity was generally greater during the fifties than in the previous decade.[26]

Related to this remarkable church activity was the increasing impact of public schooling upon Baltimore society during the forties and fifties. Though more directly a creation of the public rather than the private society, and though it touched fewer lives than church activities (less than 3 percent of school-age white children attended the schools in 1830, less than 7 percent in 1840, less than 16 percent in 1850, and slightly more than 23 percent in 1860), the function of public education made it an increasingly important agent of acculturation in the private society. Indeed, secular public education even expanded in institutional sophistication. The first high school was opened in 1839, and two more were established in 1844. In 1848, grades, which had always characterized the primary schools, were introduced into the high schools. The number of teachers and students steadily expanded. In 1840, 16 teachers taught 14,156 students, the largest such numbers during the antebellum period. In view of its internal development at least, secular public education achieved an enormous success in the forties and fifties.[27]

The Civil War halted the further normal expansion of this infrastructure, but the society's reliance upon and identification with such institutions was now complete. Its accommodation of the massive and ethnically different population increase gave it a permanency and stability that defined the community, in part, to the large numbers of transients. Moreover, its facilitation of Baltimore's increasing socioeconomic specialization no doubt ameliorated many potential effects of the massive changes of the forties and fifties. Indeed, the proliferation of the structure in familiar ways covered over many tears, or potential ones, in the social fabric in much the same way as commercial prosperity obscured many implications of Baltimore's economic transformation.

Sheer size and complexity prevented the private society from ameliorating all cultural disparities; many problems were simply too large to be reached by the voluntary initiative of individuals. For these problems, Baltimore had already developed the public society, its municipal government. That, too, changed in response to the city's new material and social conditions of the forties and fifties, but in ways that were as traditionally novel as they were logical. And because it was the "public society" that touched all, its changes received most attention.

CHAPTER X
A Municipal Polity

The new economy and society that came into being during the forties and fifties placed enormous strains upon Baltimore's political organization. The expanded scale of the city's social economy generated a pervasive concern with maximizing the flow of goods and people by systematizing procedures and structures, and intensified demands for municipal services along the same mass lines that characterized other aspects of the new order. But the passing of the old order and its replacement by the new one did not occur all at once; instead, it happened in fragments over time, and contemporaries dealt with the new realities in piecemeal fashion. As a result, Baltimore nearly dissolved into a mosaic of various political forces that resisted some of the changes and encouraged others. No one group was able to control and stabilize Baltimore's political life in conformity with its new economic and social realities. And it was ironic that when the traditional elite finally did return to political power in late 1860, their efforts to restore order evaporated as the secession crisis gathered momentum and burst into Civil War.

Lacking the perspective of nonparticipants, the Baltimoreans did not perceive how their city's political life changed in the same ways that its economic and social life did, or how these political changes were connected with the economic and social changes that surrounded them. The political party system collapsed; new men, carrying radically democratic ideas, replaced traditional and less specialized officeholders; the trade unionism of the new industrial workers stimulated their new conception of politics; and the huge foreign immigration presented enormous problems of political acculturation. Such developments, and the interplay among them, produced both a public society and the Know-Nothing political movement of the 1850s.

The new public society broke from Baltimore's eighteenth-century moorings by reifying society above its individual members, vesting it with its own rules of behavior, and establishing its legal authority through the municipal government. Ideologically speaking, the concept more fully articulated the "public-good" idea from the 1830s; on a more practical level, it resulted from the common assumption of both political parties that the general good ought to prevail over private interests. In the course of its evolution, government acquired much greater status, separate and independent from the society that it governed; its authority and presence became more widely effective through the enforcement of its laws; and public services were either publicly regulated or owned. At the same time, privatism became more restricted and no longer functioned alone to define Baltimore society. Privatism continued, of course, especially in the form of private interests using government to accomplish their aims, but it could no longer be in the name of self-serving aggrandizement. In theory at least, the municipal government became the instrument of the people as a whole rather than merely of the private elite, and in that name it took up such new ideas as mass transit, recreational facilities, and more efficient land utilization. In practice, however, the government usually broadened its functions within a more restricted sphere, because various private, elitist interests had learned to use the rhetoric of the public society to further their own ends. Moreover, the new interregional economy reenforced the state's constitutional power over the city. In short, the new public society provided a frame of government whose functions were more democratic in the sense that they affected greater numbers of people and in new ways. But its actions were hampered by the turmoil of change and then cut short by the Civil War.

The confusion surrounding the appearance of the public society prevented contemporaries from understanding it as a sharp break with Baltimore's past. Though many traditionalists opposed its innovations, habits of thought focused public attention upon the sudden, surprising success of the Know-Nothing party and its violence, and away from the more fundamental changes in Baltimore's circumstances. The poverty and unemployment that surfaced during the depression which followed the panic of 1857 and again during the secession winter of 1860–61 reemphasized the tradition of private charity rather than public welfare. Moreover, the general commercial prosperity prior to 1857 made the changes seem less profound than they really were. If these were not enough, contemporaries disagreed over what the form of the public society should be. That is, almost everyone recognized that the new conditions demanded the extension of public services, but few agreed how this was to be done. Consequently, the public society was made up of a hodgepodge of forms, some representing a compromise with tradition and others radical change, whose viability made it Baltimore's frame of government for the remainder of the nineteenth century.

Because the public society achieved expression through the expanded role of the municipal government, it was mainly a political and an administrative phenomenon. In both cases, however, much of its development was curious and even contradictory. No single political party was more responsible for its appearance than the others. Political fortune merely accounted for the Know-Nothings' being in power when many of the municipal government's important features were enacted, and the Whigs and Democrats had equally supported public-society measures before them. Municipal ownership replaced private ownership of important municipal services in some cases, and public regulation of privately owned ones in others. Moreover, the public society evolved in Baltimore partly as a result of the city's contact with developments in other metropolitan centers. By 1860 the transportation and communication revolutions had broken down the eighteenth-century isolation of the major eastern seaboard cities and had created a network of common metropolitan experiences that Baltimore could tap almost instantaneously. To a certain extent, then, the appearance of Baltimore's public society during the forties and fifties coincided with the evolution of a national public society that was urban and industrial, though both were still in the process of forming at the time of the Civil War.

Nevertheless, the new public society fit Baltimore realities so well that political agreements on its issues proved more important than differences did. The public society was not precisely defined and adopted by a majority vote; it evolved in bits and pieces, because it was a process of articulating the consensus of the community. All parties, for example, responded to the demands of continuing internal improvements and population growth, in spite of doing so for different reasons and at different times. More specifically, between 1843 and 1855 the city steadily expanded its municipal services while the Democratic party usually outnumbered the Whigs on the City Council, and while three of the six mayors were Democrats. Yet, on several occasions and over a variety of issues, the Whigs carried the vote because they were joined by Democrats, and Whig party issues were passed in spite of that party's minority status. Moreover, though the momentum of the developing public society was clearly evident by 1854 when the rise of the secret Know-Nothing party marked the collapse of traditional party politics, the Know-Nothings accelerated its evolution during the later fifties, because they needed its institutions and immediately popular issues to remain in power. In addition, the more radical character of the Know-Nothing movement directed the public society into wider democratic channels, and the Civil War, coming when it did, introduced a new set of military and industrial concerns that solidified and reenforced the forms of the public society.

The issues making up the substance of the public society had been debated for a generation—the city's financing of internal improvements, its concern with raising revenues sufficient for its expenditures, providing various public-health and sanitation safeguards, and providing for a host of municipal services, such as fire and police protection, a new alms-house and jail, public parks, and water facilities—but the disputes were now over kinds and degrees rather than over the city's responsibility for providing them at all. No one seriously challenged that responsibility; on the contrary, the conflict was over who would fulfill it and how. The public society was characterized by the expanded role of municipal government activity in nearly all areas of Baltimore's social economy, and where such activity was not present, the public authority exercised final judgment because it was now believed to personify collective responsibility.

The Democratic party, which dominated Baltimore's administration when the depression lifted in 1843 and turned into the prosperity of the later 1840s, had little reason to inaugurate political and administrative innovations. Returning prosperity allowed all three Democratic administrations to adjust to changes in traditional fashion. In spite of the naval station's being closed by the secretary of the navy in January 1844, for example, city revenues were increased by raising property assessments in 1846, establishing a new range of levies, and holding deficit spending to a minimum. Though Mayor Jacob G. Davies called for a reorganization of the police and additional appointments to the night watch, his cohorts on the City Council did not respond. They did investigate the almshouse, however, and recommended the separation of first offenders —particularly juveniles—from repeated offenders, a recommendation which eventually led to the creation of the House of Correction for juvenile delinquents. Democrats also recommended the city's purchase of park land between the downtown area and Fell's Point, and for Baltimore to establish more public squares so that the city would then more closely resemble Philadelphia. Also, members of both parties began supporting council controls over land use during the 1840s for the first time. The Democrats continued to deal with the fire departments as private organizations at first; but by 1848 the rioting and other misbehavior of the firemen, coupled with the enormous increase of new house construction—from annual rates of 515 in 1843 and 609 in 1844 to 1,508 in 1845, 1,118 in 1846, and 2,006 in 1847—pressured the Democrats on the council to divide the city into fire districts, assign one company to each district, and to confine that company's responsibility to that district. This marked a direct precedent for the municipalization of the fire departments in 1858.[1]

Though Democrats generally initiated and carried through these changes, many Whigs voted with, and a few Democrats against, the measures. Such ambivalence was also apparent in the formation of a municipal public-health program, for the first time, during the 1840s. Actually, the severe smallpox epidemics of 1845 and 1846, when death rates ran to 78 and 79 per 100,000, and the cholera epidemic of 1849 forced both parties to address the matter. In 1845, the offices of a commissioner of health and a city physician were created and they, together with an appointed health officer, constituted the city's Board of Health. Provision was made for an assistant to the commissioner of health in the following year, and he became, in practice but not in authority, a fourth member of the board. The City Council also established a permanent vaccine program under the general direction of the board. Each year one vaccine physician was appointed by the mayor within each ward. In addition to providing free vaccinations against smallpox, this physician also acted as a health warden to inspect sanitary conditions within his ward and to report instances of unsanitary conditions and contagious diseases to the Board of Health. This program of administering Baltimore's public health continued much the same throughout the remainder of the antebellum period. In addition, a Smallpox Hospital was built in 1847 and placed under the direction of the Board of Health. But in the following year its name was changed to the Marine Hospital, and its management was placed under another new officer, the Marine Hospital physician, who also became a member of the Board of Health. In addition, the Democrats on the City Council municipalized street cleaning in 1845 and thereby ended the old contract system which the Whigs voted consistently to preserve.[2]

Beginning in 1851, however, a new set of political and administrative priorities engaged Baltimore's political leaders, and they grappled with them as best they could until the Know-Nothing movement in 1854 again changed political conditions. To a large extent, Baltimore's political life during the first half of the 1850s, reflected its underlying socioeconomic realities. That is, the sudden and furious growth of the city during the late forties—the building boom, the sudden spurt of immigrants and particularly the influx of large numbers of Roman Catholic Irish—now diminished, leaving inflation and unemployment, which created another set of problems. Expanding internal improvements necessitated readjusting the city's finances once again; law-and-order problems introduced a new set of issues relating to the city's police power; the city municipalized the water company; the Democratic party was torn by several "independency" movements; and a Whig mayor (John H. T. Jerome) found himself jockeying against a Democratic-dominated City Council. The political confusion of the fifties did not begin with the Know-Nothings, it preceded and gave rise to that movement.

One fundamental problem of the decade was the city's financial situation. After remaining practically stationary from 1844 to 1850, the city's funded debt virtually tripled during the fifties. Indeed, the greatest absolute increase in Baltimore's indebtedness throughout the antebellum period occurred during this last decade.[3] True, the transition to the public society was responsible for much of this new debt, but the initial impetus to it came from the city's revived aid to internal improvements. From 1851 to 1853, the city helped to finance three new railroads: the Northwestern, a spur line of the Baltimore & Ohio extending southward in western Virginia to Parkersburg on the Ohio River; the Susquehanna, building from York, Pennsylvania, to connect with the Baltimore & Ohio at Cumberland, Maryland; and the Pittsburgh & Connellsville, which was also to link Pittsburgh with the Baltimore & Ohio at Cumberland. Baltimore extended a total of $3 million in aid to these railroad companies, but not in the traditional manner. Under the old method, the city directly assumed financial responsibility by issuing city stock and paid the monies received from its sale over to the internal-improvement companies, or the city gave its issues to the companies to sell. But during the 1850s, the city simply endorsed the corporate securities issued by the railroad companies. Baltimore thus guaranteed the payment of interest and principal of securities issued by the railroad companies, and the companies assigned liens upon their property and revenues to the city. In effect, the city became a mortgagee to them.[4]

Still another method of aiding internal improvements was used by the city in the case of the Baltimore & Ohio Railroad Company. This road was completed to Wheeling, Virginia, on the Ohio River, by January 1, 1853, but was financially unable to continue on into Ohio. In December and January 1853–54, Baltimore reverted to the old method of financing internal improvements and authorized a 6 percent municipal stock issue amounting to $5 million, redeemable in 1890, the sales proceeds of which were to be paid to the company. But the city required the company to execute a full mortgage against all its property and revenues and place it with the city as collateral. The railroad got into Ohio, and the city became its mortgagee.[5]

The second impetus to Baltimore's huge increase in indebtedness was its deficit financing of certain aspects of the public society, the largest being the acquisition and initial maintenance of the Baltimore Water Company. Agitation for either the municipalization of the company or its public regulation was hardly new, but conditions during the early 1850s facilitated the city's action on one or the other. True, the growth of Baltimore's population, particularly toward the northern and eastern outskirts of the city, and the tremendous increase in the number of houses constructed each year increased the demand for water; but the private company operated on the basis of maximizing profits and refused to construct additional mains into the newer areas of the city where the lowest rates for single dwellings prevailed. The Whig Mayor Jerome challenged his Democratic-dominated-council by calling for either public ownership or regulation of the water company, because "the privation of this necessary article is already seriously felt by the mechanic and labouring classes in the suburbs and other locations, where it will not pay a stock company to convey it."[6] But the Democrats on the council agreed; and in the summer of 1854, the city purchased the company for $1,350,000 and issued a 6 percent stock for that amount, redeemable in 1875, which it paid to the company. Under the management of a newly created City Water Board, water service nearly doubled, if measured by length of piping and number of consumers, in the last five years of this decade, though this, too, was achieved through deficit spending.[7]

In turn, the new needs for deficit spending necessitated administration changes in Baltimore's revenue structure. The Democrats on the council first responded by streamlining tax collections. They created a new financial officer in 1852, the city auditor, and made him solely responsible for auditing all municipal tax collections, a function formerly carried on by the city register. Such structural reform expanded municipal controls but did not provide sufficient cost savings, however, and in the following year the council raised the assessed valuation on real property and simultaneously lowered the rate of taxation. Indeed, one of the hallmarks of the emergent public society was the cheap cost of property ownership. Before 1835, the municipal tax rate on real property averaged $4.78 per $100.00 of assessed valuation; during the deflation of late thirties and early forties it averaged $.67; now it rose to nearly $1.00 during the 1850s. This property tax remained the single most important item in the city's revenue system, though other income continued to be derived from the levy system (the court tax, school tax, poor tax, internal improvements tax) and from licenses, fines, fees, gifts, and wharfage duties. The administration of these other sources of revenue changed very little in structure, however; and the rates of the levy system resembled those of the property tax during the fifties, both fluctuating in response to the municipality's needs.[8]

Perhaps the most revealing characteristic of the public society was its expansion of the city's police powers under the guise of social services and in relation to the broad theme of law and order. For nearly a generation, the ability of the old order to accommodate Baltimore's huge and diverse population growth had gradually declined, leaving more and more people without any "place" in society; but now, during the later forties and fifties, the magnitude of such problems gave them greater social significance. The huge immigration also contributed to both an increase in crime and a sense of lawlessness and violence, to the growing numbers of beggars, vagrants, and tramps who were different from the "virtuous poor," to the need for expanding the jail and building a workhouse as well as a separate facility for incarcerating juvenile offenders of the law, and to the need for extending the street-lighting system to make the city's streets safer at night. It was especially easy to link crime and lawlessness with foreign immigrants. The most direct measure of the city's expanded police power was, of course, its police force itself. Baltimore's expenditure for this service increased an enormous 270 percent, from $70,238.48 in 1845 to $259,962.33 in 1860; and between 1853 and 1857 the day police and night watch were reorganized into the municipal police that were characteristic for the remainder of the nineteenth century.[9]

The Democratic party administrations had responded to the increase in crime during the 1840s by simply expanding the number of day police and night watchmen in 1848, and, though their Joint Committee Report on the Almshouse in February 1845 found nothing wrong with the operations or the management of that institution, there really were simply too many paupers and vagrants to be adequately provided for by that facility. But the more forceful emphasis upon law and order followed the election of the Whig Mayor Jerome in November 1850. The fighting, rioting, and even murder that attended his election during the previous month precipitated his demand for more street lights, an increase in the number of night watchmen, an end to the watch box (the watchman's shelter, which would force him to walk his beat), an end to watchmen calling out each hour of the night, and an end to their carrying a truncheon for beating on the pavement as the signal for help. Additional police were appointed by the City Council in the following month, and in 1853 the council began the reorganization of its police force.[10]

It fell, however, to the Know-Nothing party to complete the reorganization of Baltimore's municipal police and other aspects of the public society. Unfortunately, the Know-Nothings have acquired a bad reputation because of their parochial and un-American values of anti-Roman Catholicism, antiimmigration, and violence, without any mention of their constructive achievements. Know-Nothing politics have been investigated but not their administrative accomplishments; and yet it was their administrations that brought the public society to fruition.

In Baltimore the Know-Nothing movement was a lower- and middle-class reaction to the socioeconomic events of the time and to the collapse of the traditional party system. Several circumstances, both general and specific, contributed to its appearance. One was the fragmentation of the social order, especially during the late forties and early fifties, under the impact of a heavy foreign immigration, prosperity, and Baltimore's blossoming into an interregional economy. Another was the continued appearance of social-reform political movements—such as antislavery, nativism, and temperance—which now, amid Baltimore's new realities, acquired a new significance. In addition, the splintering of the two major parties created the opportunity for the rise of new party structures. The Whigs declined because of their northern wing's association with abolitionism, and the Democrats were plagued by the proliferation of "independency" within their party. The Democratic organization survived, however, partly because its leaders invented the primary system in 1852 in order to compromise differences within the party and thus preserve the organization intact. Also, the first industrial strike in Baltimore in 1853, involving nearly four thousand ironworkers, played a pivotal role in the formation of the Know-Nothing movement. Citywide in scope, this strike received much publicity in the newspapers and was "won" by the workers in the sense that the wages of a few of them were raised. Many of the strike leaders were Know-Nothings, and the strike suddenly revealed the industrial nature of their society to most Baltimoreans, as well as the importance and meaning of the wage relationship between employee and employer. In the following year, the Know-Nothing party appeared so suddenly and secretly when it swept the municipal elections that many Baltimoreans thought the party a genuine expression of popular reaction against the two-party system.[11]

Though affected by all of these circumstances, Know-Nothingism was rooted in nativism, which was first institutionalized as a political party in Baltimore in February 1845. At that time, the politicization of nativism seemed to be part of a national effort to further splinter the Democratic party after the national elections of 1844. Almost completely confined to urban areas where antiimmigrant sentiment was strongest, the movement aimed at providing a nonsectional basis on which Americans could unite outside of the Democratic party. In addition to nativism, the new party (calling itself the American Republican party) advocated such conservative values as reforms of the electoral process and industry and utility as social virtues; it looked back to a purer, simpler, pre–War of 1812 America when patriotism, the Constitution, and Washington's Farewell Address were sufficient guides for life. At first this political movement was a general failure. In Baltimore it made a miserable showing in the fall elections of 1845, winning only one seat on the City Council. It did not run any candidates in the 1846 elections, and on January 1, 1847, the party's newspaper, the *American Republican & Baltimore Clipper*, shortened its name to *The Baltimore Clipper*, continued to educate its readers to nativism and American conservatism, and gradually shifted its political affiliations away from independency into the Whig party.[12]

Actually, the party's objection to immigrants was too vaguely focused during the 1840s and it did not have a sufficiently broad following. What was needed was to sharpen the focus on the danger posed by the immigrants to Baltimore's political order and to broaden this danger by lifting it out of its narrow political confines and projecting it as a fundamental crisis in the city's culture. This was only possible in the 1850s, after the new immigration of Irish Catholics had begun, when radical Protestant ministers attacked Roman Catholicism as a violation of Baltimore's way of life in various specific ways. Such an attack fell back, of course, upon the traditional fear of an established church. Also, the fifties witnessed the city's first real suburban development and the consequent erosion of established, and ethnic, neighborhoods. The development of omnibus lines, running chiefly east, north, and west from the commercial center of the city, together with the first construction of iron bridges across Jones's Falls, opened the city's peripheries to new development, increased Baltimore's tax base, and broke down existing neighborhood identities and inclusiveness. Economically successful ethnics could escape the old neighborhoods if they wished; recent immigrants could go directly to the new suburban areas under development where costs were cheaper (this was the case in Baltimore's famous "Irish Eighth" ward); and the different ethnic groups scattered throughout the city came into contact with one another on a more regular and massive basis than ever before. The city was becoming one, but it was a mechanical unity, and the transition aggravated existing ethnic antagonisms.[13]

Thus, while the rhetoric of nativism was directed against immigrants in general, it was specifically directed against the large number of Irish Catholics who had come into Baltimore during the late 1840s and early 1850s. Since 1820, at least, Baltimore's non-British immigrants had been mainly Protestant Germans from the northern and eastern Germanies, where the industrial revolution was highly advanced, and they somewhat understood the values and way of life in urban, industrial Baltimore. By contrast, the Roman Catholic Irish came from predominantly rural backgrounds and were unfamiliar with an urban industrial culture. Moreover, the Irish had a far higher incidence of illiteracy than did the Germans, which meant that they were far more difficult to assimilate into Baltimore's developing public society than were the Germans, who could at least be reached through their own literate culture.[14]

An equally important feature of nativism in Baltimore concerned the city's relationship with the planter-dominated state legislature. Most of the planters and slaveowners of southern Maryland and the Eastern Shore were Roman Catholics or Episcopalians who operated through the Democratic party. They disliked urban, industrial, and radical Protestant Baltimore, and they had long frustrated the unity of Baltimore by controlling the political vote of the Roman Catholic Irish in the city through the Democratic party. It was in their interest to nip the nativism movement in the bud, but they could do nothing until 1852 because the Whigs dominated the state legislature.[15]

Events from 1848 to 1852 turned out much better than these planters could have hoped. On one hand, the Whig party was weakened by its taint of abolitionism. Not only did the planters benefit politically by reducing the Whig majorities in the state legislature, but their proslavery attitudes were reaffirmed as cultural ideals in the process. On the other hand, a movement to revise the state constitution succeeded in a way that they could not have imagined. The movement to revise this constitution aimed at adjusting the political framework to new ideas and new socioeconomic realities. Most planters opposed the revision, because the changes would give greater power to northern and western Maryland, and especially to Baltimore, whose population had increased so greatly, and would curtail the representation of the counties of southern Maryland and the Eastern Shore. As it turned out, the new constitution of 1851 did precisely this. But it also compromised so many other issues and was so unsatisfactory in general that the Whigs, who played the leading role in the reform movement, lost in the elections of the fall of 1851 and the Democrats succeeded them as the majority party in the state legislature. The timing of these events was important, for the planters were now in a position to use the state legislature to widen support for their Democratic party in Baltimore city, whose representation in the state legislature was doubled from five to ten members under the terms of the new constitution. Such a course was logical, necessary, and potentially explosive.[16]

But two events in 1852 served to divorce nativism in Baltimore from Whiggery and set the stage for politicizing nativism in the following year. The first was the shattering of the Whig party. Because of their association with abolitionism, the Whigs received very little support from the Baltimoreans, and many of the most prominent members of the Baltimore's Whig party later joined the Democrats. The second event was the discussion of the Kearney bill in the state legislature. A Democratic-party measure, this bill proposed to reorganize Maryland's school system by financially aiding private, which is to say Roman Catholic, schools. In Baltimore, Roman Catholics and the Democratic party naturally supported the bill.[17]

Debate over the Kearney bill dragged on through the winter of 1852–53 and throughout 1853, thereby providing a continuing issue for nativist attacks. Meanwhile, another development dramatically stimulated the politicization of nativism in Baltimore from February to April. This was the citywide strike, involving thousands of workingmen, that was led by the Baltimore chapter of the Order of United American Mechanics (OUAM). Headquartered in Philadelphia, this secret, nativist organization had branches in several of the major American cities. Members aided one another in various ways, but their organization's aid to Baltimore's strikers was especially crucial. When the strike seemed to falter in March, for example, these groups introduced another nativist organization, the United Sons of America (USA), into Baltimore to aid the local chapter of the OUAM. The establishment of the USA was crucial to the subsequent appearance of the Know-Nothing party in the city. In August, the USA organized the first political meeting since 1845 of Baltimore nativists independent of both major parties, and they helped found another nativist organization, the Supreme Order of the Star-Spangled Banner (SSSB), in October. Baltimore's nativists thus worked through four organizations, the OUAM, the USA, the SSSB, and the Order of United Americans, the last formed in 1851, to create the Know-Nothing party in Baltimore in January 1854.

These nativist organizations had a number of things going for them. First and most important, the successful strike of 1853 proved to Baltimore's workingmen that they were able to organize themselves and act in concert. Second, the strike had also shown that the secret leadership of the OUAM was very effective. Third, the attempt in Baltimore in the summer of 1853 had been quashed by the regular Democratic party, which appealed to the workingmen not to leave the party framework on the ground that doing so would play into the hands of the Whigs. Though this ploy had often been used before, the resort to it now, in the wake of the workingmen's successful strike, convinced the workers that they could not pursue their own interests within the established organization. Fourth, as the Whig party disintegrated, Whigs looked for another political vehicle. Already, many Whigs had gone into the Democratic party because it represented, institutionally, the conservative party, and many more would follow them later. But those Whigs who remained within their party structure, the "Old-Line Whigs," offered a potential source of support for the growing nativist party. Fifth, the Democratic party was also in trouble because of the hardening of the southern attitude against all antislavery elements in the party. Supporting slavery was not in the interest of Baltimore's workingmen; and when the regular party's emphasis upon state sovereignty, the constitutional protection of slavery, and upon localism failed to bring the workingmen into line during 1854, the regular Democratic party newspaper turned against the workingmen and vehemently denounced the Know-Nothing party. Baltimoreans were culturally ethnocentric, there was anti-Roman Catholic and antiimmigrant feeling in the community, and it was altogether too easy to inflame these prejudices.[19]

Oddly enough, the surviving Democratic party was strengthened by this train of events. Because the successful strike and the activities of the nativist organizations among Baltimore's workingmen drew wide support for political nativism from the Democratic as well as from the splintered Whig party, the Democratic party leaders opposed the strikers and later the nativists. Such opposition polarized political choices for Whigs: either they joined hands with nativism (and many did in 1854–56, but later broke from them) or they joined with the Democrats. Many elitist Whigs joined the Democratic party. Though they may have been repelled by the secrecy, the mumbo jumbo rituals, and the cultural prejudices of the nativists, they understood that the Democratic party supported the employers during the strike and had tried to prevent the workingmen from bolting the party. The majority of Baltimore's elitist thus identified with the Democratic party from the mid-1850s until the upheavals of Grant's administration once again realigned the socioeconomic basis of Baltimore's politics in the very late 1860s.[20]

The Know-Nothings and the Public Order

The career of Baltimore's Know-Nothing party began with a sweeping victory in the municipal elections in 1854, when they won the mayorship and twenty-two of the thirty seats on the City Council. Some contemporaries referred to the election as a "political explosion" because of the party's secrecy, its striking differences from the other party structures, and its avoidance of traditional issues. Others considered the party suspect and sinister. But its sudden, overwhelming victory cloaked the party with an air of political spontaneity that gave the movement greater importance than a more conventional party development.[21]

Actually, the composition of the party changed over time, and the organization in 1860 was very different from what it had been in 1854–56. The early party was an amalgamation of newcomers to Baltimore, skilled and unskilled workers, retail-level tradesmen and businessmen, and a few professionals. After their victory and until the national elections in 1856, they were joined by a few elitist conservatives from the Democratic and Whig parties who tried to identify the local movement with similar ones in other metropolitan centers in America. But their failure in the 1856 national elections, followed by the panic and depression during the next year, returned the party to its formative social base. That is, the depression eroded the support of the skilled workers and businessmen, and they increasingly abandoned the party after 1856, leaving its leaders searching for a new constituency and dependent upon controlling the electoral process to remain in power. Indeed, the mob violence and illegal electoral activities associated with the Know-Nothings really characterized the party from 1856 through 1859.

Two other important characteristics of the party conformed more or less to this framework. One involved the ongoing antipathy between Roman Catholics and Know-Nothings. Wards in which large numbers of Roman Catholics lived refused consistently to support the Know-Nothings. The thrust of Baltimore nativism was as much an ethnocultural movement as it was a class reaction to the organization and distribution of goods and services in the society. Consequently, Know-Nothing leaders who were Protestant clergymen, whether Methodist-Episcopal, Methodist, or Presbyterian, played equally influential roles as the party's working-class leaders did. Another feature of Baltimore's nativism was that some of its supporters were foreign born. Not surprisingly, this support diminished considerably after 1856 when elitist conservatives abandoned the party. In wards 2 and 8, for example, whose foreign-born population comprised 80 and 61 percent of the residents respectively, the percentage of the Know-Nothing-vote which ranged between 25 and 50 percent from 1854 through 1856 dropped to a range between 17 and 3 percent from 1857 through 1859.[22]

These characteristics, plus the fact that the Know-Nothing leaders were new to politics and inexperienced at making communitywide decisions, account as much for their furthering the municipal controls of the public society as did their notion of Baltimore as a democratic society. The Know-Nothing administrations of Samuel Hinks in 1855 and 1856 and of Thomas Swann from 1857 to 1860 stepped into an ongoing stream, as it were, of swelling demands for services provided through the auspices of the municipal government. Because those demands reflected their own needs and values, and because their party would benefit politically from satisfying them, their votes completed the transition to the public society. In the process, however, the Know-Nothings introduced an innovation in the long history of patronage politics. In circular fashion, their control of the municipality was necessary to the control of patronage, and controlling patronage was vital to maintaining their control of Baltimore's administration. Thus, patronage politics became one of the props of public-society politics just as it had been for private-society politics. In the final analysis, the larger cultural importance of Baltimore's Know-Nothings was less their violence and flagrantly illegal activities than it was their municipalization of the fire companies, the police force, the water company, and their expansion of the court system of the city, among other things, for these elements of the public society inaugurated a new era in Baltimore's history as a municipality.[23]

The Hinks administration expanded water facilities enormously during 1855 and 1856. They organized a municipal water department, headed by a three-man board (doubled in 1857), appointed by the mayor for staggered three-year terms. This board, which exercised almost absolute control over the department, extended water mains throughout the city and enlarged water-supply sources by tapping Jones's Falls. As a result, the number of houses supplied with water tripled, from fewer than five thousand in 1850 to about sixteen thousand by the end of the decade, and the city's expenditure for water service rose from $18,136.89 in 1850, to $78,920.93 in 1855, and to an enormous $704,094.66 in 1860.[24]

The Hinks administration also reorganized the city's police into a more efficient municipal police department. The administration did away with the old distinction between day police and night watch, consolidated the department under one marshal, divided the city into four police districts, and provided for the annual appointment of 350 policemen by the mayor. Because many of the policemen were recruited from the Know-Nothing clubs, Baltimore's new municipal police force became a valuable patronage machine. But it was increasingly expensive: it cost the city $110,102.99 in 1850, $232,629.57 in 1855, and $259,962.33 in 1860.[25]

Changes were also made in the city's correctional and court systems. A new municipal institution for juvenile delinquents, the House of Refuge, was built in 1855, and construction of a new city jail was begun in 1856. Three new courts—the Court of Common Pleas, the Superior Court, and the Criminal Court—were also created, each having a judge and clerk popularly elected and salaried by the state, but with the city bearing all other expenses of the court. The Know-Nothings used this new judicial process to achieve immunity from prosecution for criminal actions, for Criminal Court Judges Henry Stump and Erasmus ("Ras") Levy, Justice of the Peace Malcolm Mearis, and bail bondsman John Hinesly were themselves notorious Know-Nothing partisans.[26]

Coming into power on the heels of these changes, the Swann administrations slightly shifted the focus of the municipality's public services. The change most consistent with what Hinks's administration had begun occurred in 1858 when Baltimore municipalized all fire-protection services by replacing the volunteer, private companies with a salaried fire department. Five persons were appointed by the mayor to constitute an unsalaried Board of Fire Commissioners. This board was to serve for five years and was so arranged that one member was replaced each year. They were empowered to appoint all members of the new city fire department, purchase the equipment of the volunteer companies, and introduce the new fire-alarm telegraph. This latter innovation was probably responsible for the extraordinary and immediate decline in the number of fire alarms, from 428 in 1858 to 267 in 1859. By 1860, the new municipal fire department had proved much more efficient than the older volunteer system, though the cost of such efficiency more than quadrupled from $30,331.21 in 1855 to $137,030.25 in 1860.[27]

But the most dramatic municipal innovation during the Swann administrations related to urban planning: public parks and squares, and a boulevard ringing the city to distinguish it from the countryside. Prior to 1850, the acquisition of parks and squares was by gift, as in the case of Patterson Park in 1829, or, more rarely, by purchase, as with Franklin Square in 1844. But the spurt in growth of Baltimore's population during the late forties and early fifties, especially in the eastern, northern, and western portions of the city, caused city leaders and concerned residents to take greater interest in regularizing and planning Baltimore's development. In 1846, Union Square was given to the city, as was Eutaw Square in 1853, and the city purchased Federal Hill in 1852 and Madison Square in 1853. In 1851, the City Council first began discussing the notion of ringing the city with a large boulevard, but after years of discussion, surveys and debate, the plan was abandoned as impractical. In 1856, however, Mayor Swann announced that he would not support a pending ordinance to enfranchise a streetcar company unless one-fifth of the company's gross income was applied to either the construction of the boulevard or to the purchase and maintenance of a system of municipal parks. Swann succeeded in having this provision written into the enfranchisement act.[28]

The income from this franchise tax accumulated from 1857 until 1860 when the City Council established an unsalaried Public Park Commission, which was to select and purchase sites for municipal parks. Their first purchase was Druid Hill Park, a site of over five hundred acres that surrounded Druid Lake, one of the city's reservoirs, immediately northwest of the city. Their second purchase was land adjacent to Patterson Park in the eastern portion of the city, relatively near the Canton Company's development. To pay the initial costs of these purchases and reconstruction, the City Council issued $553,966.25 worth of special city stock called Public Park Stock, redeemable at the end of thirty years, and whose interest payments were to be met from the streetcar company's franchise tax. Though the boulevard was never built and the expense of Baltimore's parks and squares program exceeded all previous estimates— in 1860, municipal expenditures for them reached $57,764.45; in 1855, the expenditures had been $6,763.95—the city had acquired a new public responsibility.[29]

The added financial burdens caused by the increase in public services, coupled with Baltimore's ongoing internal-improvement program, forced Swann's administration to institute certain financial changes to raise municipal revenues. For over a generation, Baltimore's leaders had been experimenting with credit to improve the life of their city. Basically, they learned to expand municipal debt by increasing the city's current revenues. By financing new public services through debt serviced by current revenues, future generations were left to pay for the expansion of current services. Such a system began in the late twenties and gained momentum during the early and mid-thirties. But the panic of 1837 and long depression that followed forced retrenchment and scared the city's leaders sufficiently to prevent them from resorting to it during the 1840s. Now, however, a different set of conditions prevailed during the 1850s. In the fifteen years from 1845 to 1860, Baltimore's expenditures ballooned by 318 percent: from $687,972.96 in 1845 to $806,504.06 in 1850, to $1,672,140.62 in 1855, and to $2,875,774.39 in 1860. But while Swann's administrations were as concerned with efficient tax collections as previous administrations were, previous ones did not have to reckon with the panic of 1857 or the subsequent depression.[30]

Swann, himself, understood the necessity for financial controls, and in 1857, his first year in office, his administration created the office of city comptroller to supervise Baltimore's financial affairs in their entirety. The comptroller's office coordinated the activities of the city collector and register, the auditor's office was abolished, and the collection of municipal revenues was streamlined as never before. For example, the assessment of real and personal property was separated in 1861; larger discounts were offered for the prompt payment of taxes on personal property than for payment of those on real estate; persons who did not pay their personal property taxes within five months after they were assessed were prosecuted by the city; and taxes on real estate that fell into arrears became liable to penalties and legal processes after the end of the fiscal year. In addition, a reassessment of property within the city was made in 1858, and the state legislature raised the ceiling by 60 percent, from $500,000 to $800,000, on the amount of revenues that the city could derive from such property taxes in that same year.[31]

Swann made other administrative reforms along lines similar to the function of the new city comptroller. Essentially, he changed previous municipal bureaucratic procedures whereby department heads reported to the City Council. One by one, they began reporting to the mayor's office. Swann thereby strengthened the power of the executive office by extending its authority over the workings of the municipal bureaucracy in opposition to the City Council, and the mayor's office no longer functioned merely to make appointments and to authorize payments from the city treasury. Ingeniously, he argued that strengthening the executive office in this manner was an integral part of the necessary reorganization of the municipal government in order to meet the lawlessness and "great political excitement."[32]

In spite of depression conditions being bad enough to cause Mayor Swann to declare in favor of a protective tariff to shield Baltimore's industrial workers from cheap foreign products, it was the Know-Nothings' violence and illegal activities, rather than Swann's nonresponse to the depression, that eventually turned the community against them. Municipal elections became murderous affairs and an outright sham in the closing years of the decade. Fourteen were killed and 300 wounded in the 1856 elections; a Know-Nothing policeman was killed in the 1857 election and polling stations were flagrantly abused by both the Democrats and the Know-Nothings. But the Know-Nothings' outrageous frauds in the 1858 election that resulted in the "triumph" of twenty-nine Know-Nothing candidates for the thirty positions on the City Council, as well as the reelection of Mayor Swann, finally crystallized public sentiment. In November, immediately following that election, a "City Reform Association" was formed to rid the city of Know-Nothing corruption. Composed of Baltimore's elite, remnants of the old mercantile-landed gentry, former Whigs and Democrats, the reformers rallied public sentiment in 1859 against the Swann administration's granting a franchise to Philadelphia businessmen to form the Baltimore City Passenger Railway Company. The reformers made a determined effort to defeat the Know-Nothings in the fall elections; but, again, Know-Nothing fraud, intimidation, and violence prevailed. This led the reformers to invoke the state's power over the municipality, which severed the link between Baltimore's semiautonomous status and the public society. Specifically, the reformers petitioned the state legislature during its session of 1859–60 to void the 1859 elections, to administer future elections in Baltimore, and to transfer the appointment and control of the police away from the city to the state. County representatives in the state legislature were not averse to accepting the invitation to assert state authority over the municipality, and the legislature accordingly fulfilled the reformers' petitions prior to the fall elections in 1860. This made possible the reformers' sweeping victory in those municipal elections, and George William Brown, former Whig and one of the early organizers of the Reform party, was elected mayor.[33]

But reforming Baltimore would have to wait, for the larger events of the secession crisis and the looming Civil War almost immediately engulfed the city. Financial panic struck in late October and then turned into a deepening depression throughout the winter of 1860–61. In spite of mounting unemployment, hundreds of workingmen joined the majority of Baltimore's manufacturers and most of its commercial leaders to affirm unionism and reject secession in a series of citywide meetings during December and January. Private charities, such as the Association for the Improvement of the Condition of the Poor, did what they could, and Mayor Brown's administration created a make-work program by hiring the unemployed to work on the city's new Druid Hill Park. But the political experience of the workingmen during the 1850s had educated them to a different, less passive role in, and view of, their political society. During the last two weeks before the firing upon Ft. Sumter, several hundred of them met on four different occasions and demanded that the city provide them with greater public employment: to build a new city hall, a new almshouse, extend the streets, and engage in other municipal improvements. They also objected to working at Druid Hill Park because it was far away from many of their homes, and its pay of $4.50 per week was insufficient to maintain their families. In spite of the crisis, or perhaps because of it, Baltimore's workingmen felt less reluctant to voice their expectations of what their society, through its government, should do for them. Such demands had been inconceivable sixty years before.[34]

In contrast, the state-sovereignty arguments of the secessionists held little appeal for the workingmen. Though the secessionists were numerous, dominated by merchants, young professionals, and appointees to the various federal offices in the city, and held several citywide public meetings during February and March, after the unionists did, they were divided amongst themselves, consequently indecisive, attracting little support from either municipal leaders or workingmen. However, President Lincoln's mobilization of the federal war machine on April 15 and Virginia's secession two days later gave their movement the momentum that was lacking, and they now argued for the specific preservation of Maryland's rights against the invasion of federal troops. This tapping of the traditional reservoir of localism and cultural conservatism was responsible for the riots against federal troops passing through Baltimore to Washington, and influenced the election of Baltimore's ten-man delegation to the extraordinary session of the state legislature. Naturally, every one of these representatives advocated states rights and secession.[35]

But the movement for secession was too late. The state militia finally organized and quelled the mob rule that was reminiscent of the Know-Nothings during the last week in April, and federal troops entered and occupied the city on May 13. Outside forces now directed Baltimore realities.

EPILOGUE

In Retrospect

Baltimore was more than a city or even a cultural entity: it was a process as well. Its intertwining economic, social, and political forms evolved unevenly, for one or another usually lagged behind a third. Certainly, economic and technological changes did not merely produce instantaneous social and political adjustments to the new realities. Cultural inertia, especially in the form of commitments to anachronistic values that symbolized a past and better, because more perfectly understood, way of life also contributed to the lag, and so, too, did a few of the economic changes themselves. The most important one, for example, the ongoing financial revolution, created private and public debts that made possible a *rentier* elite, who became carriers of former values; and as such debt became an integral part of Baltimore's development, it touched ever larger numbers of individuals. This same financial process, together with Baltimore's large immigration and steadily improving transportation systems, also eroded guild controls and shaped the development of a group of free, day-laboring, wage-earning workingmen. Interactions between society and economy such as these wrought certain kinds of democratic effects upon Baltimore's eighteenth-century class structure, slowly refashioning it into its mid-nineteenth-century forms.

Superficially, at least the differences between the Baltimore of 1860 and that of 1790 related to motion, size, and technology. Mid-nineteenth-century Baltimore seemed in constant motion. Indeed, so pervasive had the values of economic, geographic, and social mobility become that two of their most expressive institutions were newspaper reports of how men acquired wealth and the passanger railroad depots. Upward and outward, the entire society seemed to be in transit. Actually, a web of institutional developments enabled Baltimore to grow from thirteen and a half thousand in 1790 to nearly a quarter of a million people by 1860, and it would support even further expansion into the future. Correlated with these institutions were technological changes that touched everyone and that changed social realities and perspectives. Steam-driven ships, iron buildings, bridges and horses, shortened distances, and opened new vistas to the Baltimoreans, while the telegraph hurried decisions and brought their city into more immediate contact with other urban centers.

These and other technological changes on a smaller scale altered the everyday life of the Baltimoreans and made it faster paced and more intense. Simultaneously, an emerging ideology of the greatest good for the greatest number introduced a standardization and uniformity that replaced the more colorful and individual character of eighteenth-century Baltimore. Yet, such leveling-down tendencies permitted greater numbers to level up, and the new public society that resulted was archetypical of the mass society of the future.

Beneath this surface, however, the very definition of society had changed. By 1850, Baltimore included all individuals residing within its political-geographic boundaries. Ever since its origins, Baltimore had been evolving from a typical eighteenth-century and traditional social order of family units and status elites. Though its very newness and the changing circumstances of its growth made Baltimore traditionally urban in different ways than, say Boston was, Baltimoreans conformed, outwardly at least, to the general social forms of other contemporary urban orders. Those orders commonly presented a fairly sedentary, deferential, and hierarchic order where the elites who dominated the economies and polities constituted what was known as society. Because it was the preserve of only a few, such a society was aristocratic, exclusive, monolithic, and private in comparison with what would come.

Another change was more material: Baltimore became an industrial city by 1860, a generator of goods and services used within and without its political-geographic boundaries. Indeed, its variety of economic and social specializations and enlarged scale of activities created such enormous local complexities that the city itself constituted an economy. No longer was Baltimore merely a preindustrial depot for trade, a commercial center whose main function was the exchange of commodities, and whose growth was in direct ratio to its volume of trade. It was now a producer of goods for trade as well. So subtle and qualitative was this change that it nearly obscured the attendant social changes that altered eighteenth-century Baltimore's private, status society in the direction of more democratic forms. The economic and social changes occurred together, however; each contributed to and reinforced the other's development; and in spite of certain lags and internal strains and conflicts, Baltimore's social economy developed as a whole. The great irony of the process was that many of these social forms associated with industrialization and later called industrial revolution actually predated the appearance of the new technology. In short, industrialization encountered a very receptive social economy, one that already knew how to facilitate its use.

The new social forms originated with Baltimore's, and Maryland's,

Epilogue

independence from Great Britain, and the community's response to varying circumstances during the following generation. The American Revolution unleashed the forces of Baltimore's already dynamic social economy by removing British mercantile restrictions without imposing new ones, and presenting opportunities to Baltimoreans that enabled them to expand in both scale and specialization. Their expansion continued after the war, owing to the town's overseas trading patterns, the commodities it offered for trade, and the dynamic leadership of its merchants. But the adoption of protective mercantile policies by several of the new sovereign American states in response to contracting market conditions during the 1780s inhibited Baltimore's expansion and threatened its future growth. The town's merchant elite understood that the proposed Constitution of 1787 would prohibit such developments by creating an interstate market economy, and for this and other reasons they supported the new federal system.

The new conditions of freedom, together with the enlarged scale of activities, encouraged Baltimoreans to innovative business practices from 1775 through the War of 1812 that were part of the American business revolution. The overthrow of the colonial order presented Baltimoreans with greater magnitudes of operations and specializations that involved greater costs and new complexities connected with distant and unfamiliar market conditions. To solve them, they and other Americans telescoped their English heritage of business experiences and practices that had accumulated over nearly two centuries, and adapted them to their own situations. Though the results were uneven and quite mixed, they provided a workable institutional framework, which the Baltimoreans subsequently altered and refined as they applied its components to fit their changing circumstances. That framework shaped the direction and character of Baltimore's future development.

Essentially, the Baltimoreans adopted the joint-stock-company form of enterprise, gradually combined it with the legal status of the corporation, which they took from English municipal law, and occasionally added limited liability to the mixture. By 1815, the corporate joint-stock company was commonly used by private groups who furnished public services and characterized the larger, private-sector business enterprises in Baltimore. Though a few of them carried limited liability, the new hybrid organization was used in such diverse private and public undertakings as banks, bridge, insurance and manufacturing (regardless of means of power of the latter), trading and turnpike road companies, and the Baltimore Water Company. The fact that this form was mainly a function of the private sector, and that this sector provided most public services, reflected their distrust of government that had been accentuated during the American Revolution, as well as their belief in the efficacy of the form for dealing with conditions of large scale and magnitude. Indeed, their compromise between the English private joint-stock form of organization and public corporate status in English municipal law enabled them to preserve the English tradition of the private provision of public services. That generation of Baltimoreans did not really break from their British heritage as much as they adapted certain elements of it to their own circumstances.

The Baltimoreans' sense of government was reflected in the charter that transformed their town into a city in 1797, and especially in their implementation of that charter's provisions. That government also reflected their notions about society. To begin with, only adult free white male property owners were permitted to participate in its administration or decision making. That minority, including their families, constituted the broadest definition of Baltimore's society. Naturally, those urban yeomen who were closest to the everyday functioning of the marketplace (such as mechanics and tradesmen) exercised leadership roles in determining the policies of the political economy. Moreover, because it was *their* political economy, they managed it for their own interest. Their municipal government functioned to regulate the marketplace, not to provide social services, and the few public services were furnished by the private sector (which were themselves). Self-interest precluded their changing such arrangements, but events forced them to when Baltimore was swept up in a momentous event that altered their historical development, the international wars of the French Revolution.

Essentially, participation in politics was democratized. As Baltimore's marketplace became better regulated through inspection laws, taxes, marketing licenses, and other restrictions of various sorts, which also contributed to the city's general prosperity, small-property owners demanded participation in government decision making. In the early 1800s voting procedures were changed from viva voce to ballot, and the property qualifications for voting and holding public office were reduced enormously. Underlying these changes was the fact that the very definitions of wealth and property were changed by Baltimore's prosperity, and especially by the monetization of debt. Wealth was becoming more fluid, because it became money and socially diffuse amid inflationary conditions. Consequently, more Baltimoreans either became qualified to participate in city politics or recognized their potential to do so. The Republican advocacies of the new banking system and reduced property qualifications for participation in politics fit together hand in glove.

But Baltimore's inflated prosperity ended when the European war turned in favor of the British, and the Americans lost their neutral status in the transatlantic trade. Jefferson's administration then tried to escape America's overseas problems through its embargo policy, and encouraged domestic industry and internal improvements. Eventually, Jefferson's heirs even advocated rechartering of the Bank of the United States. For most Baltimore Republicans, however, this about-face occurred too abruptly: merchants of every political hue were hurt by the embargo policy, and, though no one foresaw the potential new economic and social order, they did understand profits and several grasped the opportunities presented. Their joint-stock corporations readily adopted the cost-saving new technology of steam power to manufacturing (textiles), the processing of agricultural commodities (flour milling), and to transportation (steamboats). Moreover, the first applications of steam power to manufacturing and processing occurred outside of the city, and they did not change Baltimore's existing social structure. In these terms, and those of urban geography and the nature of its economy, Baltimore during the 1810s remained much the same as it had been during the 1790s. Only the political constituency had changed, though not by much. But then Baltimore entered the war that made the new technology necessary and brought it into the city. Still, industrialization did not cause the social changes that occurred; rather, the wartime circumstances did. The military crisis suspended normal peacetime activities while the mustering of the militia and the opportunities presented by privateering weakened peacetime social controls, particularly the guild system. This was a very subtle development for two reasons. One was the Baltimoreans supported the conflict as a "Second War for American Independence." That is, following the mob violence against the Federalist opponents of the war in 1812, most Baltimoreans wholeheartedly supported the war and gave nearly all their attention to it. The other was that the men who brought industrialization into the city were not prominent merchants and did not publicize what they were doing. Indeed, the men who introduced steam power into the city were relatively obscure manufacturers who had had long experience in manufacturing. Their obscurity, together with the absence of industrial revolution and the focus of everyone's attention upon the war, marked one of the more important material changes in Baltimore's development. Most Baltimoreans continued to perceive their city as a commercial depot for trade, the new technology as a novelty, and everyone was caught up in their successful defense against the British that produced "The Star-Spangled Banner."

For these reasons, 1815 marked a turning point in Baltimore's development. Never again would the city enjoy the reputation that it then had in the nation. Moreover, its experience since the Revolution had laid the foundation for its future development. Industrialization was part of this foundation, of course, but even more importantly the Baltimoreans had established a style for dealing with reality. They had learned to institutionalize procedures and practices to further their private and public interests. But such an education carried two inherent faults. One was that such behavior was invented under conditions of prosperity, and, though times would change, Baltimoreans would continue to behave in the only ways they knew, because these once resulted in enormous prosperity. Secondly, prosperous conditions caused the Baltimoreans to define behavior in such ways as to make it more predictable and rational; that was the commercial thrust of the age. But such predictability and rationality also made for rigidity and inflexibility. Except for the years from 1798 to 1800, the rigidity of such institutions never posed a problem because the general conditions of prosperity supported them. Naturally, the twenty-year-old men who fought in the Revolution, who then created these institutions, and who participated in the "Second War for American Independence" as fifty-year-olds, thought that the wartime crisis was merely a temporary aberration, and they looked forward to the postwar period as a time of restored prosperity. Little did they know what was in store for them, or, worst of all, how ill-equipped they were to deal with the new realities.

The Transitions

For nearly two generations following the war, Baltimore was caught in a reversal of conditions from those that had enveloped and shaped its prewar development. And when several new developments occurred, Baltimoreans responded in ways that they had learned under different circumstances. Not only did such responses produce very different results from what they anticipated, but the more they tried to solve their problems the more they changed their society in completely new ways. Moreover, because customary responses no longer worked well, new men whose entrepreneurial and political styles better fit the times rose to power and stamped Baltimore's institutional responses with their own values. Boldly imaginative, yet incredibly cautious and attentive to detail by eighteenth-century standards, these new leaders pioneered the technological and social changes that constituted the heart of industrial revolution. They presided over Baltimore's transition from an eighteenth to a nineteenth-century society, and later generations would merely specialize and improve upon what these innovators did.

The new realities that underpinned Baltimore's transformation during the 1820s and 1830s originated with the reimposition of mercantile controls and other peacetime adjustments by the West European nations following the French Revolution. Baltimore's merchants immediately confronted curtailed trade, contracting markets, increased shipping competition, and one huge wave after another of European imported goods that had been inventoried during the war. All of these developments were accompanied by disturbances in the American economy, especially in the agricultural sector, which broke down the chain of national and international trade, and produced distortions of prices. This culminated in the panic of 1819, a liquidity crisis that shocked Baltimoreans into modifying their business practices to better fit the new realities insofar as they perceived them. But as the panic lengthened into a long maritime depression, they came to understand that their situation was due to more fundamental, long-range, and structural problems, an understanding that became dramatically clear when New York completed the Erie Canal in 1825. This event galvanized the Baltimoreans into a major policy decision affecting their community's entire way of life: they concentrated upon expanding their overland markets. Unfortunately, no one understood at the time that these efforts would not succeed for another generation, or that the society would become an industrial one in the process.

From Baltimore's perspective, the transformation of the community began with the panic of 1819, for its origins also lay in the stock speculations of a group of bankers, most of whom were officers of the branch Bank of the United States. It was their failures that led to the first major alterations in banking and bankruptcy procedures. Also, and on a broader scale, the panic and subsequent economic distortions produced major changes in the American financial system as a whole, changes that operated against Baltimore in its race against Philadelphia and New York for metropolitan leadership. Under the new direction of Nicholas Biddle, the BUS established a federal banking system that rivaled the preponderant influence of the urban banks in the nation's monetary system, and that offered a more secure monetary system to country buyers. Given this new more stable financial institution in conjunction with the downward tendency of nearly all prices, a pricing system simultaneously replaced the traditional credit system between the country merchant and his city wholesale supplier. The pricing system and the more stable federal banking system operated to the advantage of country buyers by making them freer to purchase in markets offering lower prices. Being closer to Liverpool, the center of nineteenth-century industrialization, New York City had lower prices than Baltimore, and its tapping of the Western markets via the Erie Canal catapulted its lead over Baltimore in the national and international chain of trade.

Baltimoreans responded to these developments by launching one of the boldest enterprises of that generation, and one that was to have fateful consequences for their community, the Baltimore & Ohio Railroad. The technological feature of this innovation was startling enough, but its social implications were even more so. Overland expansion via steam power reordered Baltimore's society and economy in several ways. It turned the city away from the sea toward overland, Western markets, made Baltimore's access to them dependent upon the railroads, and expanded the social specialization of the community in such ways as to generate entirely new urban forces. For one thing, the importance of the railroad to the well-being of the community insured the development, and consequent social importance, of an iron industry that would literally transform the material nature of Baltimore's social economy. For another, by reaching out into the hinterland for new markets, those merchants connected with the railroad would be abandoning Baltimore's local market to new men, and the technology of the railroad would add an entirely new group to Baltimore's social structure. And, finally, the success of the railroad would exert a sedentary effect upon Baltimore's social economy in connection with the new urban forces. Thus, in their effort to restore Baltimore's prewar commercial prosperity, the merchant elite adopted a technology that undermined the prewar social order which they knew and understood. And that was one more reason why the 1820s and 1830s were a time of profound, bewildering and, in many ways, immeasureable transitions.

As these developments unfolded during the course of the 1820s, Baltimore's social structure began to change visibly for the first time. The old order fragmented into multiple elites as functional and status elites divided and the new conditions promoted new social specializations. Also, increasing foreign immigration and the changing status of free blacks noticeably altered previous social patterns. As these and other socioeconomic landmarks shifted, Baltimore's politics and administration also changed. Certain ideas about and ways of governing the municipality ended, and new policies and institutional concerns were introduced that heralded the beginning of a new political order. Thus, in terms of transforming one set of economic, political and social arrangements into another, the 1820s were the pivotal years in Baltimore's case.

These changes were direct responses to the new conditions. The devastating panic of 1819 altered social relationships precisely because the adjustments made within the city's financial and economic institutions and practices were meant to enforce new standards of behavior. A new functional elite arose as carriers of these new standards; they were Baltimore's new business leaders; and businessmen who did not follow their lead retired into the reputable status of the community's social elite. Remembering and representing the old ways, this latter group mythologized Baltimore's past and readily responded to the continuing financial revolution, especially to the municipality's adoption of deficit funding of its services, because such monetized debt provided safe alternative investments to continuing their capitals in trade.

These shifts at the top of Baltimore's social hierarchy were accompanied by a more fundamental shift affecting the entire community: Baltimore's population was increasing at the very time that the city's preindustrial economic base, its maritime trade, was declining. Contemporaries did not understand that Baltimore's expanding population faced decreasing traditional opportunities, or that such a situation offered a potential social and economic crisis on a grand scale. They did see, however, that increasing demands sustained high prices for food and housing, that the number of free blacks was increasing and that fewer of them were living in white households where they were subject to the head of the household's control, that slavery was decreasing and foreign immigration increasing, and that all of these things were breaking down customary practices between employer and employee. Indeed, Baltimoreans discovered "workingmen" during the 1820s and cast them into a new, socially specialized role just as they did "businessmen." Though relatively inarticulate, their time severely limited by work and family circumstances, workingmen demanded or were given such social and political changes as savings institutions, public education, and a mechanic's lien law. And, because they were so numerous, they gradually acquired political importance.

Politics, itself, became more specialized. Essentially, the municipal government expanded its public-service functions and began supporting the city's new westward and overland expansion. The change had important consequences: Baltimore shifted its taxation base away from trade to property and deficit spending; its administrative bureaucracy expanded and decision making was somewhat decentralized; and the city's ordinances, regulations, and inspection laws were codified. Such modernization was accompanied by antagonisms between political interests in which property owners and manufacturers opposed commercialism: Irish Catholics and German Lutherans opposed Scotch-Irish, Quakers, and Presbyterians; and the northwestern, western, and southwestern portions of the city opposed the business section, Old Town, and Fell's Point. Commercialism triumphed in this contest, partly because of the emergence of the second-American-party system and the Jacksonians' subordination of local issues to national ones, and partly because the property owners all too easily fit the stereotype of antidemocratic aristocrats. Unfortunately for the immediate future, Baltimore's circumstances during the 1820s compelled Jacksonian commercial men—heirs of the Jeffersonian Republican ideology of balanced budgets and a minimal public debt—to accept deficit finance as sound municipal fiscal policy. Such events had enormous consequences during the 1830s. The Jacksonian commercial men triumphed in the municipal elections. Then, after a decade of failing to escape their circumstances, the old-fashioned ways suddenly seemed to work again. Everything seemed to come together for the Baltimoreans during the early and mid-1830s: prosperity appeared to return; the Jacksonians created a "commercial revolution," which popularized an ideology of commerce and local controls in opposition to the national planning of industrialization; they brought the railroad into the city, which altered the face of the community forever; they equated democracy with individualism and encouraged private-sector, opportunistic solutions to social problems at the very time that they encouraged public-sector expansion; and they unconsciously presided over Baltimore's subordination to New York's expanding metropolitan economy. To many Baltimoreans, the Jacksonians provided progressive, new directions that pulled them out of the depression of the 1820s.

Despite this, nearly everyone misread the signs of the times. Partly out of ignorance and partly out of their desire to return to the good old days, they misjudged what was happening in the developing national and international markets. They did not really understand the appearance of an international economy or the creeping British domination over it. Nor did they understand the ramifications of the new American financial relationship with Great Britain and the inflation that was borne of it. Moreover, though they saw their own market increasingly subordinated to New York's expanding one, they refused to acknowledge their inferior position. In short, the Baltimoreans shut their minds or failed to perceive the implications of the new realities of the 1830s, and they continued to respond to them in the old ways. Indeed, most Americans did—with devastating results. In Baltimore's case, not only did the inflated and uneven conditions from 1831 to 1837 produce immediate social and political disturbances, but they also constituted the sources for the severe economic adjustments from 1837 to 1843 that played an even greater role in hastening the transition to the nineteenth-century public society.

Specifically, Baltimoreans made the most of opportunities arising from the demise of the second BUS, President Jackson's reopening of America's trade with the British West Indies, and the tariff of 1832; but they did not understand the effects of the 1832 European crisis or that their shipping trade reached its nadir from 1834 to 1836, when inflation raged at its worst. Indeed, the inflation obscured important developments. For example, the influx of British capital that vitalized internal improvements via public-deficit finance promoted commercial or transportational industrialization but not Baltimore's overseas trade nor its industrial expansion except for the spinoffs from the steam engine, steamboat, and railroad building. Consequently, the liquidity crisis and long deflation that set in after 1836 hurt the small-scale, retail businessmen much worse than the large-scale manufacturers and commodity processors who were oriented to foreign markets, and to urban and other American ones in the south.

Such economic developments were accompanied by the first visible changes in Baltimore's urban geography and sociopolitical character that pointed to its future shape, and that followed the changes in the city's social structure during the 1820s. The Canton Company, Baltimore's first large-scale, planned real-estate development, deliberately located residences in reference to transportation and productive facilities; railroad tracks were built into the city to reach the business section and the docks; the city's first geo-economic specialization into neighborhoods occurred; and the routing of steam engines began to fan outward, away from the docks.

These changes started Baltimore's material transformation into an industrial city, but equally important, they were attended by the first triumph of the public sector over private interests. Indeed, the defeat of the property owners by the Jacksonians in the name of the public good ended the eighteenth-century linkage of economics with politics and its domination by a monolithic merchant class. That issue, the public versus the private good, divided the merchant leadership, specialized politics from business, and occasioned the rise of a new group, the workingmen, to power. A new public order dimly appeared for the first time, one whose origins and compositions indicated the future trends of democratic impersonalism and public institutional dynamics in opposition to the personal and private elitism of the old order. That this new order occurred in conjunction with the rise of the new Jacksonian party insured its appearance beyond the confines of Baltimore.

The emergent new public order reified politics above economic interests in a uniquely important way: the power of the property owners was now subordinated to the municipal government, but the interests of the workingmen as a class were not enhanced. That is, the old group was not replaced by the new one. Initially, at least, government and politics were specialized and separated from the economic interests of all private groups. Except for a few political-patronage appointments, workingmen received no real benefit from the new political order. Moreover, the potential for upward mobility was certainly no effective substitute for reality, and wage earners were whipsawed by inflation during the first half of the decade and by unemployment during the second. And though the new ideology of the public good spurred attempts to modernize municipal tax-collection procedures, the city police, the fire companies, and street construction and reconstruction, legislative proposals for the regulation of steam-engine operations, the zoning of activities, construction of various kinds, or occupations in general were defeated. The public good was more than the sum of private goods, but it had yet to be defined more accurately.

The new order was promoted as much by the efforts of the elite (considering the different ones collectively) to preserve their own status and leadership as it was by the majoritarian demands of the lower orders. Indeed, confronted by drastically changing circumstances, the elite blended the public good with the enhancement of their own status through broadly construed social reforms and a variety of voluntary associations. Moreover, the elite reaped the economic and social benefits from the general process of democratic development. As Baltimore became more democratic in the sense of reflecting greater complexity and participation by various new groups, the elite moved away from the rest of society. What helped to obscure this latter development was that the rich became richer at the same time that socioeconomic conditions allowed for greater individual social mobility, and individual mobility received all the attention.

The long deflation that followed the false prosperity of the early 1830s also proved a turning point in Baltimore's development. *Rentiers*, who lived off of interest and dividend income from various debt issues that continued to be paid, benefited from the deflation of the late thirties and early forties, as did anyone who remained employed at constant wages or salaries. But most importantly, nearly everyone came to appreciate better the social role of money and banking, and to understand better the need for careful planning before deficit spending. In a departure from similar crises in the past, Baltimoreans were educated to a new concern: public finance. The sources of government revenues, the need for more efficient tax-collection machinery, and the tailoring of government spending to its financial resources became important public concerns. The long deflation proved a giant step in the ongoing financial revolution, because it forced Baltimoreans to assess themselves and their potential more accurately, and to compare what they found with their chief metropolitan rivals, Philadelphia and New York. And as they did so, the flamboyant boasting that had long characterized Baltimore gave way to a more subdued optimism during the 1840s and 1850s. Actually, this new consciousness about finance was part of the age of the economists that was just beginning. Statistics and tables, maps and plats, became increasingly important indicators of reality. Indeed, they would become so integral a part of the new order that some Baltimoreans would mistake them for reality itself.

The New Order

The new order really came into being during the 1840s and 1850s when industrialization and industrial revolution made their first full impact upon Baltimore. Many of its components—its technology, social patterns, and its democratic politics—had appeared at different times and under different circumstances over the course of the previous three generations, but Baltimore's peculiar circumstances during the forties and fifties precipitated their rapid and sudden maturity. Economic growth continued during those decades, as Baltimore's population became larger, more heterogeneous, specialized, and diversified, and the city area expanded—outward via iron bridges and improved roadways, and upward via iron girding. New citywide omnibus services linked the whole together. But such growth alone did not induce the emergence of the new order with its public society; the peculiar prosperity of the period also caused its appearance. In the renewal of prosperity following the deflation, Baltimore's commercial men adopted steam power with unusual vigor, and the forties were a time of solid industrial expansion. Then, however, beginning later in that decade, prosperity skewed as industrial production declined but commerce continued to thrive. Yet even in that context, the new technology was utilized wherever its investment would save costs that would pay for it. Its diffusion had reached the point by the 1850s that it was now necessary for business survival, and businessmen knew it. Ironically, while industrialization thus transformed Baltimore's economy and society, many business leaders, especially the most prominent ones connected with overseas and overland markets, remained carriers of preindustrial values.

In part, the irony grew out of Baltimore's new circumstances. Though th⸱ city developed into a trans-Allegheny interregional economy, it actually lost its market autonomy and became more subordinate to New ʹork than ever before. The uniformity and standardization of business ⸱ustoms and practices that reduced market differences to functions of price, together with the march of communication and transportation improvements, enabled New York to triumph over its metropolitan rivals. Indeed, the emerging American national economy developed in tandem with New York's expanding market controls over it. By the early 1850s when Baltimoreans encountered this larger economy, they, too, found themselves following New York market rates and middlemen. And there was nothing that they could do about it.

The irony also grew out of the subordination of Baltimore's industrialists and manufacturers to the city's merchants and traders. Indeed, the community's mercantile values were strenghened by the renewal of commercial prosperity during those last two antebellum decades. New foreign markets opened, old ones expanded, the Northwest emerged as a major producer of foodstuffs shipped aboard the Baltimore & Ohio Railroad for export, and the federal government, dominated by commercial men, pursued policies which encouraged agricultural production and its exportation abroad in return for manufactured goods. In particular, the Warehousing Act of 1842, the Independent Treasury Act, and the tariff of 1846 stimulated Baltimore's overseas trade by establishing credit and storage facilities for importers, by providing a stable specie-based financial policy respecting payments made to the federal government, and by linking America's tariff rates to overseas prices. These and other federal laws, together with the particular policies of Secretary of the Treasury Robert James Walker, aimed at creating a mechanism that would promote trade on an orderly and regular basis, subject only to fluctuation of prices.

Actually, such policies flourished because they conformed to the most important international development of the forties and fifties: the British conversion from mercantile to free-trade policies. Great Britain opened its markets to American foodstuffs, concentrated upon industrialization, reduced prices, and undersold Baltimore manufacturers. From the midforties until the panic of 1857, commercial men flourished, especially after 1852 when the Baltimore & Ohio Railroad was completed to the Midwest, while industrialists suffered a wrenching adjustment of decline, consolidation, and almost frantic concern with cost savings. And this seeming contradiction of commercial prosperity and industrial decline accounted for many of the sociopolitical changes that occurred.

Pervading all of these developments, and especially correlated with the commercial character of Baltimore's prosperity, was the triumph of Jacksonian ideas about money. As was the case with other Jacksonian ideas and values, the circumstances of the forties and fifties "proved" their truthfulness. That is, a new quantity theory of money now characterized the private and public sectors. The Jacksonian notion of money as specie, and the impracticality of substituting specie for paper as the only circulating medium, had led to greater public regulation of banking institutions. But then the discoveries of gold in California and Australia increased the stock of specie and the paper issued thereon, and businessmen suddenly began following the ebb and flow of currency levels. They found that flow of funds expanded and contracted with the changing conditions of trade, and they now applied the same correlations between supply and demand to money that they applied to other commodities.

This notion of money as a commodity, the new consciousness about and sophisticated use of it, was accompanied by a carefully monitored expansion of banking institutions that fueled Baltimore's prosperity. Commercial and savings banking facilities proliferated, and the rising volume of transactions created such complications that a clearing house was established for exchanging the bank notes. For the first time since the 1790s and early 1800s, banking became a respectable way of life.

The banking expansion, the renewal of a prosperous foreign trade and of railroad construction, and the protective tariff of 1842 stimulated a sudden spurt of industrialization. Per capita investment, productivity, and output value grew in the range between 25 and 50 percent during the 1840s, and new industries of canning, packing, and preserving sprang up. But then, following the implementation of the free trade tariff of 1846, industrialization actually declined. The number of steam-powered factories declined by 40 percent and the number of adult males working in them declined nearly 14 percent. Here, again, the change was subtle and various: steam-powered production of iron, chemicals, and textiles declined, but commercially oriented facilities producing leather and lumber products and agricultural equipment did not, and flour milling, printing, and stonecutting even gained. Steam power changed the construction industry by standardizing parts, and new occupations such as engineers, iron molders, and machinists appeared. Railroad tracks proliferated throughout the city, depots were built in its various parts, and when the railroads reached the bituminous coal fields of western Maryland and Pennsylvania, coal-burning iron stoves became a common means of heating homes.

Large-scale, standardized production lowered per-unit costs, created demand markets for its uniform products, and changed society accordingly. Essentially, standardization of parts and procedures enabled manufacturers to translate units and subunits into financial terms and to seek ways to promote cost efficiencies. In the process, labor itself became standardized; workers became no more than a cost of production, and, because they constituted a large part of that cost in a period of industrial decline, employers sought to reduce it through technological innovation and maintaining wage rates. Wage earners were caught between rising living costs and declining employment opportunities in which an ever-increasing number of foreign immigrant competitors appeared. For such workers, the 1850s were grim.

The guild and employer paternalism continued in pockets of highly specialized crafts and among certain handicraft manufacturers, but most labor relationships with employers had shifted to wage-earning, free labor by 1860. The industrial stagnation and consciousness of costs stimulated the trend, because it resulted in a consolidation and standardization of manufacturing that eliminated the independent, small-shop craftsmen and led to fewer establishments with larger numbers of employees. Regimentation of the workplace and cost analysis were imperative in these larger establishments, and, on the eve of the Civil War, the majority of Baltimore's male labor force were employed in making things that they did not use. Socioeconomically, Baltimore's industrial workers occupied a status similar to that of the town's sailors in the eighteenth century. The nature of their work made them extremely vulnerable in society, because they were dependent upon the complexity, diversification, and specialization of the community to provide them with what they could not provide for themselves—nearly everything. Given the provision of various public services by private groups, Baltimore's industrial workers naturally supported the expansion of the municipal government's control over such services.

In broader perspective, the entire society bent in the direction of the new industrial, commercial, and social realities. Employment and lifestyles changed under the impact of industrial standardization and depression, and amidst larger magnitudes, greater complexity, and increasing numbers of foreign immigrants. Distant overland markets and the dependence on steam power to reach them undermined old social unities, promoted imbalances in the social structure, and aggravated existing social antagonisms. Baltimore became more fragmented and more reliant upon institutionalization than ever before. Only now, such institutionalization strengthened the widening gaps between economic, political, and social activities, and between groups within each sphere. Moreover, the power of the traditional group of authority, the merchants, was undermined by the new circumstances: they could no longer dominate the city's polity or society, and their specialization in business made their domination of Baltimore's economy dependent upon continued commercial prosperity. The group splintered itself when the wealthiest and most dynamic of them either led or followed Baltimore's expansion into distant overland markets, leaving others to focus upon the city and its nearby environs. Consequently, new men cropped up as important business, political, and social leaders; the merchant-manufacturers emphasized their marketing orientation and promoted their identification with the merchant tradition, while another groups of manufacturers, those who emphasized production and technological innovation, existed as a subculture. Weakened in these various ways, the merchants retreated all the more into business specialization, divorced it from the intellectual, political, and social life of their community, and followed the new laissez faire of free-trade ideology, which idealized the business realities.

The most visible signs of the new industrial order lay in the changing urban geography of the city. A core of heavily industrial wards appeared along the harbor, the Jones's Falls valley, and around the Mt. Clare station, the main terminus and maintenance area of the Baltimore & Ohio Railroad just west of the business district. Also, the railroads, which first entered the city during the early thirties, now crisscrossed the city in all directions and four passenger depots appeared for the first time in various parts of the city. Steam power did not change the location of flour millers, iron manufacturers, shipyards, or textile factories. But to the east, north, west, and, to a lesser extent, the southwest, Baltimore's population grew most quickly, and manufacturers of various consumer goods spread, outward from this core. New housing construction was the greatest industry in these areas, and its subsidiary functions prospered as well. Brick- and lumberyards were opened here, butchers and tanners set up shop, as did makers of saddles, harnesses, soap, and candles.

Indeed, an important development to the new industrial order was that Baltimore's population more than doubled from 1840 to 1860. Most of the increase was due to foreign immigration, and there were definite locational patterns to their settlement. Moreover, though one hundred and seventy thousand foreigners poured into the city, large numbers of them were Roman Catholic Irish instead of the usual Protestant Germans. Most of the newcomers settled in the industrial wards, where the numbers of slaves and free blacks decreased and where industrial stagnation and consolidation were at their worst. But the fact that the immigrants bore the brunt of the industrial depression during the 1850s was obscurred by their displacement of native Americans.

This massive influx of people virtually necessitated the enlarging and extension of institutional activities. Several new ones sprang up to care for alcoholics, orphans, the poor, and the sick, and more new church congregations were started from 1843 to 1861 than had previously existed in the city. Most of the new churches were Protestant and white, and there were elements of reaction to the threat of Roman Catholicism and the novelty of the Jewish synagogues. The effect upon public schooling was equally dramatic: the percentage of school-age white children attending public schools rose threefold from 7 percent in 1840 to 16 percent in 1850 and to 23 percent in 1860. Schooling also became more specialized with the introduction of the high school, grades in the high schools, and larger numbers of better-trained teachers. The very operations of this entire web of institutions, invented as a means of acculturating newcomers to life in Baltimore, allowed for the city's continued growth in size and complexity and accommodated ever larger numbers of transients. By 1860, it had become the city itself.

The impact of institutionalization in the public sector and the attendant new powers of the municipal government were what really characterized this new conception of the city. The new socioeconomic circumstances of the forties and fifties necessitated changing the city's political organization in the direction of systematizing and standardizing procedures and structures to maximize the flow of public services, and to enlarge the scope of public services. As a result, the municipal government acquired greater power and responsibilities than it had ever had and the municipality now embodied the principals of the public society that had dimly appeared during the 1830s. The new public society of the 1850s sharply differentiated the spheres of economics, politics, and society, reified society as a whole above its individual members, vested this artificial construct with its own rules of behavior, and established its legal authority through the municipal government. The general good thus triumphed over private interests, and this triumph marked the overall transition of Baltimore from an eighteenth-century private society to a nineteenth-century public one.

The transition occurred because the traditional groups in authority were fragmented, and every group that came into political power claimed they acted for the public good, even when this meant the advancement of their own private interests. The public society was created in piecemeal fashion, largely because political responses during the forties and fifties were themselves fragmented. No one group could control politics or make over the municipal administration to conform to the new socioeconomic realities. Moreover, the traditional party system collapsed, which allowed new men, the Know-Nothing carriers of public society ideas mixed with self-interest ones, to replace traditional officeholders and to make the administration more amenable to their own notions of society and government. Though the Know-Nothings restricted privatism and ushered in Baltimore's nineteenth-century public society, however, their expansion of the role of the municipal government in providing public services was not without broader community support. Indeed, the issues comprising the public society had been debated for a generation: the municipality's financing of internal improvements, establishing a tax-collection system sufficient to meet increasing expenditures, public health and sanitation measures, municipalized fire, police, and water services, public recreational facilities, and expanded government responsibility for poor relief. Political fortune cast the Know-Nothings in political office at the time of most of the legislation, but the transition was also due to Baltimore's contact with other seaport metropolitan centers. They shared similar urban, industrial, and commercial experiences, which the railroads, telegraph, and continuing foreign immigration made ever more common.

The restored prosperity of the 1840s brought demands for small- rather than large-scale changes: additional appointments to the night watch, improving conditions at the almshouse, and the city's purchase of park land and creation of more public squares. The few real changes that were made were a permanent municipal vaccine program in response to the smallpox and cholera epidemics, the municipalization of street cleaning and abolition of the contract system, and the creation of fire districts and assignment of individual fire companies to them. The Democratic-party administrations received credit for these changes, though some Whigs voted for, and some Democrats against them. But then, from 1851 until the Know-Nothings came into power in 1855, Baltimore changed dramatically. Inflation and commercial prosperity combined with industrial depression, new foreign immigrants—Roman Catholic Irish—entered the city in record numbers, law-and-order problems pervaded election campaigns, the Democrats were splintered by a variety of insurgency movements, a Whig mayor jockeyed against a Democratic-dominated City Council, and the city vastly increased its financial aid to the railroads and municipalized the water company. In response to outcrys about the increasing number of beggars, tramps, and vagrants, the city expanded its street-lighting system and began the construction of a new jail and almshouse. A proposal for a municipal workhouse was debated but defeated. Thus, such problems preceded the Know-Nothings, and certain adjustments of them were made before 1855.

Essentially, the Know-Nothing movement was a lower- and middle-class reaction to these socioeconomic events. Though rooted in nativism and first appearing in 1845 in opposition to the large foreign immigrant constituency of the Democratic party, it failed in the municipal elections of that year. But then came the huge Roman Catholic Irish immigration and a mounting series of attacks against them by Protestant ministers. Other immediate circumstances contributing to the rise of the Know-Nothings included the collapse of the traditional two-party system (the abolitionist tinge of the northern wing of the Whig party was not acceptable to Baltimore's slave society), the various independency movements within the Democratic party, that party's support of the Kearney bill, which would give state financial aid to Roman Catholic schools, and Baltimore's first citywide industrial strike in 1853, which was led by nativist organizations.

Suddenly and secretively, the Know-Nothings swept the fall 1854 municipal elections, winning the mayor's office and twenty-two of the thirty seats on the City Council. The winners were newcomers to politics, skilled and unskilled workers, retail tradesmen, businessmen, and a sprinkling of professionals. But during the course of 1855 and 1856, they were joined by professional politicians and elitist conservatives from both the Whig and Democratic parties, who were trying to broaden the movement into a national one for the presidential election of 1856. Following their failure, the party gradually returned to its original social base, and the period from 1857 to 1860 marked the greatest violence and illegal electoral victories in the annals of that party.

Apart from their political style, the Know-Nothings were important in a direct, positive, and administrative way. They were in power when demands for enlarged and more-efficient public services were already important issues in municipal politics; satisfying those demands gave them the community support and legitimacy they needed; and implementing such programs meant making patronage appointments, which strengthened the party all the more and provided sources of employment for their supporters. The Know-Nothings municipalized the fire company, the police force, and the water company; they expanded the court system; and they systematized the city's parks and squares through a Public Park Commission.

But the public society was very expensive, being financed through deficit spending. Municipal leaders had begun using deficit finance during the 1820s and increased it enormously during the thirties; but then the panic of 1837 and subsequent deflation scared them so that they scarcely resorted to it during the 1840s. During the fifties, however, the city's indebtedness soared by three and a half times. Unfortunately, the panic of 1857 and the subsequent slowdown of the commercial economy curtailed the city's revenue but increased the demand for certain municipal services, namely, poor relief. In response, the Know-Nothings first tried administrative reforms: they created the office of city comptroller and made all department heads answerable to the mayor rather than the City Council. Simultaneously, the tempo of election frauds increased. The elections became such outrageously illegal and murderous affairs that a City Reform Association was founded after the 1858 elections to reform the electoral procedures. Made up of Baltimore's "best men," this antebellum progressive movement failed in the 1859 elections but then asked for the state to nullify those elections and intervene through its police powers in special elections in 1860. Under the supervision of the state militia, the reformers won, but before they could implement their program they were engulfed by the events leading to the Civil War.

The legacy of the Know-Nothings has been a lasting reputation for murder, mayhem, and blatant election frauds. These things were true and have been well documented. But less well known is the Know-Nothings' role in culminating a historical process. It was unconscious on their part, for they acted as a catalyst in the larger whole. Nevertheless, they left Baltimore with a municipal government that functioned according to the ideology of the public good, that provided a variety of public services which characterized the municipality for the following two generations, and that separated government from private interests, though remaining subject to its influences. Their more important legacy, then, was to preside over Baltimore's becoming a modern society.

NOTES
BIBLIOGRAPHY
INDEX

NOTES

Abbreviations of Historical Repositories Used in Notes

BCH	Baltimore City Hall, Department of Legislative Reference
BHC	Burton Historical Collection, Detroit Public Library
DU	Duke University, William R. Perkins Library
EI	Essex Institute
EPL	Enoch Pratt Library, Baltimore
GPI	George Peabody Institute
HSP	Historical Society of Pennsylvania
LC	Library of Congress
MdHR	Maryland Hall of Records
MdHS	Maryland Historical Society
MdSL	Maryland State Library
NA	National Archives
NMAS	Norfolk Museum of Arts and Sciences
PAC	Public Archives of Canada
PIL	Peabody Institute Library, Baltimore
SC	Swarthmore College, Friends Historical Library
SCHS	South Carolina Historical Society
UM	University of Michigan, William L. Clements Library
UNCL	University of North Carolina Library, Southern Historical Collection
UV	University of Virginia Library

Prologue: The Promise of Baltimore

1. Evarts B. Greene and Virginia D. Harrington, *American Population before the Federal Census of 1790*, pp. 22, 23, 31, 40, 41, 46, 65–70, 95–105, 117–20, 133 note e, 146, 153, 155.

2. Herbert C. Bell, "West Indies Trade before the Revolution," pp. 272–87; Rudolph C. Blitz, "Mercantilist Policies and the Pattern of World Trade, 1500–1750," pp. 39–55; Michael Kammen, *Empire and Interest*, pp. 45–94; Richard Pares, *Yankees and Creoles*, passim; Richard Pares, *War and Trade in the West Indies, 1739–1763*, passim; Frank W. Pitman, *The Development of the British West Indies, 1700–1763*, passim; Basil Williams, *The Whig Supremacy, 1714–1760*, pp. 290–304; Charles M. Andrews, *The Colonial Period of American History*, vol. 4, chaps. 10 and 11; James F. Shepherd and Gary M. Walton, *Shipping, Maritime Trade, and the Economic Development of Colonial North America*, passim; George Rogers Taylor, "American Economic Growth before 1840," pp. 427–44; William B. Weedon, *Economic and Social History of New England, 1620–1789*, vol. 2, chaps. 13, 14, 16, and 17; Robert G. Albion, "Colonial Commerce and Commercial Regulation," pp. 44–59.

3. Paul H. Giddens, "Trade and Industry in Colonial Maryland, 1753–1769," pp. 512–39; Clarence P. Gould, "The Economic Causes of the Rise of Baltimore," pp. 225–51; Clarence P. Gould, *Money and Transportation in Maryland, 1720–1765*, passim; Keach Johnson, "The Baltimore Company Seeks English Markets," pp. 37–60; Frank W. Porter III, "From Backcountry to County," pp. 324–49; Carl D. Bell, "The Development of Western Maryland, 1715–1753," passim; David Klingaman, "The Significance of Grain in the Development of the Tobacco Colonies," pp. 268–78; Aubrey C. Land, "A Land Speculator in the Opening of Western Maryland," pp. 191–203.

4. Though Baltimore represented the forces of modernization in the Old Line state, the town was never able to dominate Maryland politically or culturally throughout the antebellum period. The antagonism between urban, commercial, and eventually industrial Baltimore on the one hand, and agrarian, rural Maryland on the other, persisted and even worsened through the years. Baltimore was like Philadelphia in this respect, and both were the opposite of Boston and New York, and Charleston and New Orleans: cities which provided the leadership within their respective states. Tradition and the constitutional system of Maryland allowed the landed interest continually to frustrate Baltimore's demand for a greater voice in state policies long after Baltimore surpassed Annapolis in economic power. For the role of Annapolis as Baltimore's economic rival in the eighteenth century and its political rival in the nineteenth century, see Edward C. Papenfuse, *In Pursuit of Profit*, passim; and John Hemphill II, "Annapolis," vol. 1, pp. 3–28. Robert A. East captured the spirit that was Baltimore in "The Business Entrepreneur in a Changing Colonial Economy, 1763–1795," pp. 16–27, and *Business Enterprise in the Revolutionary Era*, pp. 164–73.

5. Scotch-Irish, Germans, and Protestants shaped Baltimore's early traditions. In addition to the sources cited in note 3, see Clarence P. Gould, *The Land System of Maryland, 1720–1765*, passim; Beverly W. Bond, Jr., "The Quit-Rent in Maryland," pp. 350–65; Aubrey C. Land, "Economic Base and Social Structure," pp. 639–54; Aubrey C. Land, "Economic Behavior in a Planting Society," pp. 469–85; Aubrey C. Land, "The Tobacco Staple and the Planter's Problems: Technology, Labor and Crops," *Agricultural History* 43 (January 1969): 69–81;

Edward C. Papenfuse, "Planter Behavior and Economic Opportunity in a Staple Economy," *Agricultural History* 46 (April 1972): 297–312; Edward T. Schultz, *The First Settlements of Germans in Maryland* (Frederick, Maryland: D. H. Smith, 1896), passim; James G. Leyburn, *The Scotch-Irish*, passim; Jacob M. Price, "The Rise of Glasgow in the Chesapeake Tobacco Trade, 1707–1775," *William & Mary Quarterly* 11 (April 1954): 179–99; Charles A. Barker, *The Background of the Revolution in Maryland* (New Haven: Yale University Press, 1940), passim; Daniel W. Nead, *The Pennsylvania-Germans in the Settlement of Maryland* (Lancaster, Pennsylvania: Press of the New Era Printing Co., 1914); and Vertrees J. Wyckoff, *Tobacco Regulation in Colonial Maryland*, passim.

6. Baltimore's eighteenth-century private society is treated in more detail in Gary L. Browne, "Baltimore in the Nation, 1789–1861," chap. 1. The mercantile character of this society was similar to that of Benjamin Labaree's Newburyport, John G. Clark's New Orleans, Frederick Tolles's Philadelphia, and even Bernard Bailyn's seventeenth-century New England; cf. Labaree, *Patriots & Partisans: The Merchants of Newburyport, 1764–1815* (New York: W. W. Norton & Co., 1975); John G. Clark, *New Orleans, 1718–1812: An Economic History* (Baton Rouge: Louisiana State University Press, 1970); Frederick B. Tolles, *Meeting House and Counting House: The Quaker Merchants of Colonial Philadelphia, 1682–1783* (New York: W. W. Norton & Co., 1963); Bernard Bailyn, *The New England Merchants in the Seventeenth Century* (New York: Harper Torchbook, 1964); Bernard Bailyn, "Kinship and Trade in Seventeenth Century New England," pp. 197–206.

7. B. L. Anderson, "Money and the Structure of Credit in the Eighteenth Century," pp. 85–101. Ronald Hoffman, *A Spirit of Dissension*, and Philip A. Crowl, *Maryland During and After the Revolution*, specifically touch upon the merchants' problems.

8. Ronald Hoffman, "Economics, Politics, and the Revolution in Maryland," pp. 34–124.

9. In addition to sources cited in notes 7 and 8, see Paul S. Clarkson and R. Samuel Jett, *Luther Martin of Maryland*, pp. 55–6; Bernard C. Steiner, "Maryland Privateers in the Revolution," pp. 99–103; wartime opportunities pervade the Woolsey & Salmon Letterbook, 1774–84; also see George Lux to Nathaniel Greene, May 26, 1778, November 29, 1780, November 3, 1781, December 3, 1782, Mordecai Gist to George Washington, September 6, 1781, and Nathaniel Greene to Mordecai Gist, January 23, 1781, Nathaniel Greene Papers. George Lux succeeded his father, William, on the Baltimore County Committee of Safety after William died in early May 1778. A merchant connected with the Bowly family before the Revolution, William became the Baltimore agent of the Marine Committee of the Second Continental Congress. The future first mayor of Baltimore, James Calhoun, was also a member of the Baltimore Committee as well as deputy quartermaster for the Southern Army. Baltimore Town briefly housed the Continental Congress from December 1776 to March 1777, and is described in Edmund C. Burnett, ed., *Letters of Members of the Continental Congress*, 2: 178–297.

10. The Cheston, Ellicott, Hollingsworth, Pennington, Stump, Taggert, and

Tyson families were the more prominent ones. The importance of this expansion of flour milling lay in the qualitative changes it introduced into the social economy. Flour milling necessitated subsidiary, spin-off industries such as the making of hoops, staves, and barrels. East, *Business Enterprise*, pp. 164–73; Gould, "Rise of Baltimore," pp. 225–51; Charles Byron Kuhlman, *The Development of the Flour-Milling Industry in the United States*, p. 39. John Hayes, editor of the *Maryland Gazette or the Baltimore Advertiser*, published in Baltimore during the 1780s and 1790s, was an early champion of manufacturing. Many of his self-sufficiency arguments later appeared in Hezekiah Niles' *Weekly Register*. See the *Maryland Gazette*, August 20, 1784, August 15, September 26, 1786, January 9, April 17, July 13, 1787, and July 18, 1788, especially.

11. Merrill Jensen, *The New Nation: A History of the United States During the Confederation Period, 1781–1789* (New York: Vintage Books, 1950), pp. 115–16, 182, 192, 219–27, 283–98; Rhoda M. Dorsey, "The Pattern of Baltimore Commerce During the Confederation Period," pp. 119–33; Mary Jane Dowd, "The State in the Maryland Economy, 1776–1807," pp. 90–132, 229–58.

12. *Maryland Gazette or Baltimore General Advertiser*, September 19, 26, October 24, November 7, 28, 1786, January 2, 16, February 13, 1787.

13. Bernard C. Steiner, "Maryland's Adoption of the Federal Constitution," pp. 22–44, 207–24; Dorothy Marie Brown, "Politics of Crisis," pp. 195–209; Dorothy Marie Brown, "Maryland and the Federalist, pp. 1–21; Jackson T. Main, "Political Parties in Revolutionary Maryland, 1780–1787," pp. 1–27; J. R. Pole, "Constitutional Reform and Election Statistics in Maryland, 1790–1812," pp. 275–92; Clarkson and Jett, *Luther Martin*, chaps. 7 and 16; *Maryland Gazette or Baltimore General Advertiser*, April 11, 15, 22, May 2, October 10, 24, November 28, December 30, 1788, January 2, 30, 1789; Crowl, *Maryland During the Revolution*, chap. 4; Kathryn L. Behrens, *Paper Money in Maryland, 1727–1789*, chap. 8.

I. The Business Revolution

1. The role of individuals in traditional societies, such as eighteenth-century Baltimore, was one-dimensional or multifunctional. Individuals played a variety of roles because the social structure of premodern societies was undifferentiated. For example, occupation was a social definition denoting the status of an individual among the social orders; it did not refer to an individualized and economically specialized function. Calvin Goldscheider, *Population, Modernization, and Social Structure*, pp. 93–96; Neil J. Smelser, *Social Change in the Industrial Revolution*, passim; Neil J. Smelser, *The Sociology of Economic Life*, chaps. 1 through 3, and 5; Bert F. Hoselitz, "Main Concepts in the Analysis of the Social Implications of Technical Change," in Bert F. Hoselitz and Wilbert E. Moore, eds., *Industrialization and Society*, pp. 11–29; Browne, "Baltimore in the Nation," pp. 1–80.

2. Joseph Gregory Blandi, *Maryland Business Corporations, 1783–1852*, pp. 93–4.

3. Much of my discussion about monetized credit follows from the insights of P. G. M. Dickson, *The Financial Revolution in England*, passim; and Fritz Redlich, *The Molding of American Banking*, 1: 7–23.

4. See, for example, the exchanges in the Baltimore *Federal Gazette and Daily Advertiser*, July 19, 21, August 10, 15, 24, 1797, in reference to the East Indies trade. Baltimore remained capital-poor throughout the antebellum period, as countless newspaper editorials reiterated; indeed, their growth in sophistication of presentation itself marked the financial revolution—cf. the Baltimore *American*, January 31, 1839, with the former citation; also see Abraham Van Bibber to Anthony Manguin, July 22, 1792, Corner Collection, MdHS.

5. James Kent, *Commentaries on American Law*, 3: 86–181; Sir John Barnard Byles, *A Practical Compendium of the Law of Bills of Exchange*, passim; Joseph Story, *Commentaries on the Law of Bills of Exchange*, passim.

6. General discussions about banking in Baltimore are found in Dowd, "The Maryland Economy, 1776–1807," pp. 90–132, 239–51; Alfred Cookman Bryan, *History of State Banking in Maryland*, pp. 1–133; and John Thomas Scharf, *History of Baltimore City and County*, pp. 449–50.

7. For information about Robert Gilmor and Robert Oliver, see Eugene L. Didier, "The Social Athens of America," pp. 20–36; Robert C. Alberts, *The Golden Voyage*, pp. 114–15, 123, 131–32, 138, 160, 221, 224–28, 241, 264, 273, 308, 312, 364, 415–19, 423, 426, 494, 514; [Robert Gilmore, Jr.], "The Diary of Robert Gilmor," pp. 231–68, 319–47; and Stuart Bruchey, *Robert Oliver*, pp. 109–31.

8. No records of these early banks exist, to my knowledge. My ideas are derived from the various merchants' records cited and from Redlich, *Molding of American Banking*, 1: 7–23; Bray Hammond, *Banks and Politics in America from the Revolution to the Civil War*, pp. 40–226; Bruchey, *Robert Oliver*, pp. 43–51, 109–22; James O. Wettereau, "The Branches of the First Bank of the United States," pp. 68–69, 75, 89, 95–96, 98; John Thomas Scharf, *The Chronicles of Baltimore*, p. 260; East, *Business Enterprise*, pp. 303–4; Richard Caton to James McHenry, October 11, 1794, James McHenry Papers, UM; a tabular statement about these early banks is printed in *Niles' Weekly Register*, December 27, 1817, p. 281.

9. A fuller discussion of these early banks is found in Gary L. Browne, "The Panic of 1819 in Baltimore," pp. 212–27.

10. Frank Lee Benns, *The American Struggle for the West Indian Carrying Trade, 1815–1830*, passim; Gordon C. Bjork, "The Weaning of the American Economy," pp. 549–60; Laura Bornholdt, *Baltimore and Early Pan-Americanism*, passim; Bruchey, *Robert Oliver*, pp. 29–35; Charles Lyon Chandler, "U. S. Merchant Ships in the Rio de la Plata," pp. 26–54; Charles Lyon Chandler, "United States Commerce with Latin America at the Promulgation of the Monroe Doctrine," pp. 466–86; John H. Coatsworth, "American Trade with European Colonies in the Caribbean and South America, 1790–1812," pp. 243–66; Dorsey, "Pattern of Baltimore Commerce," pp. 119–34; East, *Business Enterprise*, passim; Roland T. Ely, "The Old Cuba Trade," pp. 456–58; William Freeman Galpin, *The Grain Supply of England During the Napoleonic Period*, passim;

Jane N. Garrett, "Philadelphia and Baltimore, 1790–1840," pp. 1–13; Giddens, "Trade and Industry in Colonial Maryland," p. 515; Dorothy Burne Goebel, "British Trade to the Spanish Colonies, 1796–1823," pp. 288–320; Dorothy Burne Goebel, "British-American Rivalry in the Chilean Trade, 1817–1820," pp. 190–202; Gould, "Rise of Baltimore," pp. 225–51; Thomas Waters Griffith, *Annals of Baltimore*, pp. 81–82; Herbert Heaton, "The American Trade," in C. Northcote Parkinson, ed., *Trade Winds*, pp. 194–226; Lucy Frances Norsfall, "The West Indian Trade," in Parkinson, ed., *Trade Winds*, pp. 157–93; Alice B. Keith, "Relaxations in the British Restrictions on the American Trade with the British West Indies, 1783–1802," pp. 1–18; James W. Livingood, *The Philadelphia-Baltimore Trade Rivalry, 1780–1860*, passim; Alan K. Manchester, *British Preeminence in Brazil*, passim; Roy F. Nichols, "Trade Relations and the Establishment of the United States Consulates in Spanish America, 1779–1809," pp. 289–313; Edwin J. Pratt, "Anglo-American Commercial and Political Rivalry on the Plata, 1820–30," pp. 302–35; Lowell Joseph Ragatz, *The Fall of the Planter Class in the British Caribbean, 1763–1833*, pp. 286–383; James Fred Rippy, *British Investments in Latin America, 1822–1949*, pp. 17–26; James Fred Rippy, *Rivalry of the United States and Great Britain over Latin America (1808–1830)*, passim; J. Holland Rose, "British West India Commerce as a Factor in the Napoleonic War," pp. 34–46; Vernon G. Setser, *The Commercial Reciprocity Policy of the United States, 1774–1829*, passim; Robert Sidney Smith, "Shipping in the Port of Veracruz, 1790–1821," pp. 5–20; Steiner, "Maryland Privateers in the American Revolution," pp. 99–103; Arthur P. Whitaker, *The United States and the Independence of Latin America, 1800–1830*, passim. A small group of Baltimore merchants, the Samuel Smith faction and the Oliver-Pringle-Gilmor connections out of Philadelphia, also benefited from the war in the Pacific, which enabled them to move into the East Indies trade. For accounts of Americans moving into this trade during the wars of the French Revolution, see Seward W. Livermore, "Early Commercial and Consular Relations with the East Indies," pp. 31–58; C. Northcote Parkinson, *Trade in the Eastern Seas, 1793–1813*, passim; and G. Bhagat, *Americans in India, 1784–1860*, chaps. 2 and 3.

11. The controversy over Jay's Treaty in 1796 redirected Baltimore's political interest away from Federalism toward Republicanism in national politics. The turning point came when the dominant McHenry wing of the Federalists attempted to dictate Samuel Smith's (Baltimore's representative in Congress) vote in favor of Jay's Treaty. Piqued at the attempt, and desiring to assert his independence, Smith aligned himself with Baltimore's mechanics and tradesmen, the old political base of the Ridgely-Sterret-Chase faction of the 1780s, in opposition to the dominating clique among Baltimore's merchants. Himself a merchant, Smith of course voted for Jay's Treaty; but the split within Federalist ranks in 1796 led to Smith's identification with the burgeoning Democratic-Republican party after that year. The socioeconomic makeup of this new political party remained essentially unchanged from the 1780s until the late 1840s when industrial revolution then changed the entire nature of politics by changing the cul-

ture in which it operated. For Samuel Smith's role during the Jay Treaty crisis, see Jerald A. Combs, *The Jay Treaty; Political Battleground of the Founding Fathers*, pp. 178–79, but especially Frank A. Cassell, *Merchant Congressman in the Young Republic: Samuel Smith of Maryland, 1752–1839*, pp. 66–72.

12. For how the renewal of war stimulated Baltimore's economy, see John Hollins to Wilson Cary Nicholas, August 5, 1803, Wilson Cary Nicholas Papers, UV; Thomas and Samuel Hollingsworth to Levi Hollingsworth, August 18, November 16, 1803, Hollingsworth Family Papers, HSP; Alex Brown & Sons to William Cumming, October 12, 1803, to John Foster, July 2, 1803, Alex Brown & Sons Papers, LC; George Salmon to Sylvanus Bourne, August 25, September 30, October 12, 1803, February 28, April 7, 19, 21, June 14, 17, August 10, September 11, October 14, 24, 1804, and William Taylor to Sylvanus Bourne, February 13, June 15, September 12, 1804, Sylvanus Bourne Papers, LC. For the contraction of Baltimore's West Indies shipping, beginning in 1805, see Thomas and Samuel Hollingsworth to Levi Hollingsworth, October 10, 1805, March 6, June 4, July 15, September 30, October 3, 1806, February 12, 1807, Hollingsworth Papers, HSP; Barker & Annesley to John Cunningham & Co., July 18, 1805, Thomas P. Cope Papers, HSP. For the momentous events of 1807–8, see the Baltimore *American*, June through August, 1807, and December, 1807, through January, 1808; Thomas and Isaac Edmondson to Hall, Northage & Co., July 2, 1808, to York & Sheepshanks, September 28, 1808, Edmondson Letterbook, MdHS; Frederick Brune to John Reynolds, November 6, 1807, Von Kapff & Brune Papers, MdHS; Thomas and Samuel Hollingsworth to Levi Hollingsworth, June 29, July 25, October 1, November 17, December 30, 1807, March 1, October 31, 1808, Hollingsworth Papers, HSP; Robert & John Oliver to Baring Brothers & Co., May 11, 1808, Oliver Record Books, MdHS; William Freeman Galpin, "The American Grain Trade Under the Embargo of 1808," pp. 71–100; Libero Marx Renzulli, "Maryland Federalism, 1787–1819," pp. 316–20; John S. Pancake, "Baltimore and the Embargo, 1807–1809," pp. 173–87; Louis Martin Sears, "The Middle States and the Embargo of 1808," pp. 152–69; Walter Wilson Jennings, *The American Embargo, 1807–1809*, passim.

13. After the wars began, the demand for foodstuffs in the French West Indies sent the prices of Baltimore flour and wheat soaring. The British consul in Baltimore, Edward Thornton, objected to what he regarded as the town's merchants "taking advantage" of the situation, and he went so far as to label William Taylor, one of Baltimore's most prominent merchants, a "known agent" of Fauchet, the French minister. The naive and impressionable Thornton was confusing business arrangements with political ideology—perhaps deliberately so; but if the British ministry received these kinds of reports from their other consuls in America during 1794 and 1795, then misinformation may have played a larger role than previously assumed about their decision to seize all American ships trading with the French West Indies. See Edward Thornton to Lord Grenville, July 11, 12, November 15, 1794, and September 14, 1795, British Consular Reports, PAC. Baltimore's rivalry with Annapolis contributed to the misinformation when

the *Maryland Gazette and State Register*, published in Annapolis, reported on April 10, 1795, that almost fifty Baltimore vessels were serving as privateers in the French navy, a report without foundation.

Before February 1803, data about Baltimore's markets must be pieced together from the correspondence of merchants and haphazard reports published in the newspapers. But in that month and year Joseph Escaville began publishing his weekly *Price Current*, and this has been a crucial source of my information about Baltimore's economy until the 1830s. Howard Irving Chapelle, *The Baltimore Clipper*, passim, and Jerome R. Garitee, *The Republic's Private Navy*, passim, are the best works on their subjects.

14. Samuel and Thomas Hollingsworth to Levi Hollingsworth, November 20, 1799, Hollingsworth Papers, HSP. Actually, the seizure of Baltimore ships by the British and French occurred in successive stages. The British seizures began in 1794 and continued after 1796 in spite of Jay's Treaty. The French seizures began in 1797 and led to the undeclared naval war between France and the United States from 1798 to 1800. The Hollingsworth Papers, the Smith & Buchanan Letterbooks in the Smith Papers, MdHS, and the Sylvanus Bourne and William Taylor Papers, LC, contain numerous references to the seizures of Baltimore ships. The most succinct overview of Baltimore's shipping problems in connection with the French Directory is found in Samuel Smith to Jonathan Dayton, July 4, 1797, Gratz Collection, HSP.

15. Robert & John Oliver to Thomas & Henry Lynch & Co., December 4, 1797, Oliver Record Books, MdHS; Mark Pringle to Colt, Baker, Day & Co., January 6, 1798, to James J. Ullmann, April 26, 1798, to Barber, Palmer & Co., Samuel Thompson, Robert Stewart, and Joseph Thomas Brown, April 28, 1798, Pringle Letterbook, 1796—1798, MdHS.

16. Four manuscript collections of planter families illustrate this transition from tobacco to wheat: the Lloyd Papers, the Carroll Papers, and the Ridgely Papers, all in the MdHS, and the William Henry Hall Papers, DU. The Carrolls and Ridgelys went from tobacco into wheat even before the American Revolution. Because wheat was not as labor-intensive as tobacco, one effect of this transition was to contribute to the decline of slavery. This situation continued until the early 1820s when the drastic decline in European demand for Baltimore flour caused an attempted reversion to tobacco. But this reversion failed for two reasons: (1) European tobacco prices were too low to permit the investment in additional slaves for the new production; (2) soil conditions were too poor to compete with the yields of the new trans-Allegheny lands and it was cheaper to move west with one's current slaveholdings. Between the two, slaves and land, land was the cheaper variable. Throughout the 1820s, it was more economic for planters to move west and set up on the relatively cheaper lands than it was to stay east, purchase additional slaves, and try to improve production. But a new agricultural opportunity also presented itself during this decade: as the foreign wheat market just about disappeared and prices in general plummeted, British demand for American cotton steadily increased; and, though cotton was as labor-intensive as tobacco, the planters discovered that they could grow cotton at its lowest postwar price, seven cents a pound, and still make a profit. The agricul-

tural reforms that became so popular in this decade were responses to these new marketing exigencies, and to the lower prices and reduced demands for traditional commodities. Baltimore was caught in these circumstances because it was not a cotton port; and the Baltimoreans did the only thing possible: they tried to tap new foreign markets in South America for their flour and wheat. Mark Pringle to Lubbock, Colt & Co., February 14, 1797, Pringle Letterbook, 1796–1798, MdHS; Robert & John Oliver to Richard Forster, June 26, 1797, Oliver Record Books, MdHS; Hamilton Owens, *Baltimore on the Chesapeake*, chaps. 5 and 6; Hoffman, "Economics, Politics and Revolution," pp. 181–302; Griffith, *Annals of Baltimore*, pp. 128–29; Scharf, *Chronicles of Baltimore*, pp. 277–78; E. Emmet Reid, "Commerce and Manufactures of Baltimore," in Clayton C. Hall, ed., *Baltimore*.

17. The details of this depression have been pieced together from a variety of sources: the Oliver Record Books, Wessels & Primavesi Papers, Smith Papers, Edward Hall Papers, Bentalou Journal, all in the MdHS; Cope Papers, Gratz Collection, Etting Collection, Hollingsworth Papers, all in the HSP; Ogden, Day & Ferguson Papers, Grinnan Papers, Wilson Cary Nicholas Papers, all at the UV; Sylvanus Bourne Papers, William Taylor Papers, both at the LC; and the Baltimore *American* from 1799 through 1803.

18. Robert & John Oliver to Landi & Constantine, May 6, 1797, Oliver Record Books, MdHS; T. H. Backer to John F. F. Wessels, April 29, 1802, Wessels & Primavesi Papers, MdHS; Barker & Annesley to Sutcliff & Hodgson, July 27, 1802, to Edward Wilson, March 24, 1803, and to Abraham Binns & Co., May 30, 1803, Cope Papers, HSP; Owens, *Baltimore on the Chesapeake*, pp. 138–57.

19. McDonald & Hollingsworth to Levi Hollingsworth, December 5, 1799, Thomas and Samuel Hollingsworth to Levi Hollingsworth, December 5, 1799, January 11, 31, March 21, 1800, June 17, December 29, 1801, Hollingsworth Papers, HSP; George Salmon to Sylvanus Bourne, June 29, 1799, February 17, 20, 1800, to Rebecca Bourne, December 29, 1799, January 31, February 20, June 30, 1800, Bourne Papers, LC; Thomas Cope to Israel and Jasper Cope, March 28, 1802, Cope Papers, HSP; Robert & John Oliver to Samuel Brown, February 8, 1800, to John Cummingham, February 8, 1800, Oliver Record Books, MdHS. The social significance of these mercantile failures was enormous. Adrian Valck, the Willinks's agent in Baltimore, failed and thereby curtailed one of the town's most important sources of credit and capital; David Stewart & Sons, one of the leading firms in the West Indies trade, also failed; so did John Smith, Samuel and Robert's elder brother; and John Hollins, the Smith's brother-in-law, also failed. Edward Hall to David Stewart & Sons, March 15, 1800, Letterbook, 1798–1800, Edward Hall Papers, MdHS; Bentalou Journal, October, 1799, through 1801, MdHS; Samuel Smith to Wilson Cary Nicholas, June 24, 1800, Smith Papers, LC; Archibald Campbell to Thomas Willing, February 26, 1800, and William Bingham, Samuel Breck, Isaac Wharton to Thomas Willing, January 28, 1800, Etting Collection, HSP. Editorials in the Baltimore *American* on June 18, November 4, 1799, and August 18, 1800, illustrate how the anti-Federalist and anti-British editor, Alexander Martin, erroneously assigned

the cause of the depression to British and French depredations upon Baltimore shipping. The merchants knew better.

20. Archibald Campbell to Thomas Willing, January 21, February 26, 1800, and John Swan to Thomas Willing, March 18, 1800, Etting Collection, HSP.

21. Alex Brown & Sons to William Cumming, March 14, 1804, to John Brown, May 4, 1804, Brown Papers, LC; John Muir to William Thomas, August 4, 8, December 10, 1806, Thomas Family Papers, MdHR; Baltimore *American*, September 13, November 6, 20, 21, 23, 26, 29, 1804, June 27, 28, 29, July 1, 8, October 7, 1805.

II. Emergence of the City

1. Professor Jean Baker suggested this apt characterization.

2. Browne, "Baltimore in the Nation," pp. 1–25; Didier, "The Social Athens of America," pp. 20–36; Ruthella Mory Bibbins, "The City of Baltimore, 1797–1850," vol. 1, pp. 71–147; Clayton Colman Hall, "Baltimore Town, 1730–1797," vol. 1, p. 56.

3. Sam Bass Warner, Jr., also refers to the privatism of this type of society when he describes late eighteenth-century Philadelphia in *The Private City*, pp. 3–45. Baltimore's right of eminent domain was implicit from 1796 to 1817 because (1) it was not explicit in its charter; (2) it only partially appeared in particular instances such as in cases involving the construction of sewer lines where the town commissioners were empowered to enter upon private property "to regulate, make or repair" them (*Ordinance*, April 10, 1797); and (3) the state retained the right within the city, though the city could, and did, petition the state to allow the city to exercise the right in specific cases. All of these cases grew out of the fact that the city's charter did not allow the city to build new or change old streets without the consent of the affected property owners. As Baltimore grew, so did the number of state laws granting such petitions: *Laws of Maryland*, 1797, c. 64; 1798, c. 19; 1799, c. 31; 1800, c. 56; 1801, c. 18; 1803, c. 68; 1810, c. 153; 1811, cs. 24, 133; 1812, cs. 34, 40, 118, 171; 1813, c. 97.

4. Browne, "Baltimore in the Nation," pp. 25–38; *Laws of Maryland*, 1796, c. 68, "An Act to erect Baltimore Town, in Baltimore County, into a City, and to Incorporate the inhabitants thereof."

5. In addition to the sources cited in note 13 of the Prologue, see William Bruce Wheeler, "The Baltimore Jeffersonians, 1788–1800, pp. 153–68; Cassell, *Samuel Smith*, pp. 73–102; John S. Pancake, *Samuel Smith and the Politics of Business, 1752–1839*, pp. 44–50; Bernard C. Steiner, editor, *The Life and Correspondence of James McHenry, Secretary of War Under Washington and Adams* (Cleveland: The Burrows Brothers Company, 1907), pp. 144–451; Renzulli, "Maryland Federalism," pp. 18–320; Cary Howard, "John Eager Howard: Patriot and Public Servant," *Maryland Historical Magazine* 62 (September 1967): 300–17; Malcolm C. Clark, "Federalism at High Tide," pp. 210–30.

6. Thaddeus Peter Thomas, *The City Government of Baltimore*, pp. 1–22; *Laws of Maryland*, 1796, c. 68; 1797, c. 54.

7. Several sources deal directly with Samuel Smith: Cassell, *Samuel Smith*; Cassell, "General Samuel Smith and the Election of 1800," pp. 341–59; John S. Pancake, *Samuel Smith and the Politics of Business*; and "Samuel Smith," *Dictionary of American Biography*, vol. 17, pp. 337–38. My story of Smith has been stitched together from these sources and, more importantly, from the Samuel Smith Papers at the LC, MdHS, UV; the Wilson Cary Nicholas Papers and Edgehill-Randolph Papers, both at the UV; the Otho Holland Williams Papers, the William & Robert Smith Papers, and the Smith & Buchanan Letterbooks, all in the MdHS. The Dielman, Genealogical, and Vertical Files at the MdHS were also helpful, as was Scharf, *History of Baltimore*, pp. 76–111.

8. See citations in Prologue, note 13, and note 3, above. The intimate information comes from the Hollingsworth Papers, HSP, the Wilson Cary Nicholas Papers, UV, the Patterson, McHenry, Bayard, and Howard Papers, all at the MdHS, the *Maryland Journal and Baltimore Advertiser* to 1797, and the Baltimore *Federal Gazette* and *Daily Advertiser* from 1799*ff*.

9. The mechanics and tradesmen were organized into the "Baltimore Society for the Promotion of Manufacturing and the Useful Arts," and several served as officers under Smith in the state militia. David Harris to James McHenry, March 3, 1796, James McHenry to Robert Oliver, April 7, 1796, James McHenry to James Winchester, March 24, 1798, James Winchester to James McHenry, April 18, 1798, William Mathews to James McHenry, October 11, 1798, James McHenry Papers, UM.

10. This information has been compiled from *The Baltimore Directory, for 1799, Containing the Names, Occupations, and Places of Abode of the Citizens, Arranged in Alphabetical Order*, compiled by John Mullin; *The Baltimore Directory for 1810*, compiled by William Fry; *The Baltimore Directory, corrected up to June, 1819*, compiled by Samuel Jackson (Baltimore: Richard J. Matchett, 1819); the Republican party newspaper, the Baltimore *American and Daily Commercial Advertiser*, and the Federalist party newspaper, the Baltimore *Federal Gazette*; and the federal "Assessment Lists of All Dwellings, Lands, Wharves and Slaves in Baltimore City, 1798," microcopies 604 and 605, MdHS. Lists of the yearly membership of the City Council can be found in Scharf, *History of Baltimore*, pp. 187–90, 192–93; a list of the mayors of Baltimore can be found in the Maryland Vertical File, in the Maryland Room, Enoch Pratt Free Library.

11. Only three property assessments were made from 1796 to 1818, but all were made at the direction of the state because the city could not act without state authorization. *Laws of Maryland*, 1797, c. 89; 1803, c. 92; 1812, c. 191. The rate of taxation was changed from shillings to dollars in the 1812 reassessments.

12. *Ordinances and Resolutions of the Mayor and City Council* (hereafter *Ordinances*), March 27, 1797; March 9, 1804; March 6, 1812; March 24, 1813; March 18, 1814; March 4, 1815.

13. *Ordinances*, April 11, 1797; March 2, 1804; March 25, 1805; March 13, 1816.

14. The city's three public wharves were built in 1797, 1803, and 1806. *Ordinances*, March 19, April 24, 1797; February 26, 1799; March 15, 1800; May 21, 1801; March 8, 15, 1803; March 14, 1806; April 8, 1807; March 22, 1809; March 24, 1813. The controversy between the city and state over the city's regulation of its public wharves can be followed in *Ordinances*, March 24, 1813; *Laws of Maryland*, 1813, c. 118; *Ordinances*, March 21, 1814; March 25, July 27, 1815.

15. *Ordinances*, April 10, June 18, 1797; February 20, 26, 27, 1799; March 15, April 7, 1800; March 14, 1806; March 19, 1807; March 22, 1809; March 25, 1814. For new street construction, Baltimore had to apply for state authorization that was cast into legislation such as *Laws of Maryland*, 1797, c. 64; 1798, c. 19; 1799, c. 31; 1800, c. 56; 1801, c. 81; 1803, cs. 68, 82; 1810, c. 153; 1811, cs. 24, 133; 1812, cs. 34, 40, 118, 171; 1813, c. 97.

16. The city's first direct grant of money to volunteer fire companies was made in 1800; see *Ordinances*, March 6, 1800; March 8, 1803; March 2, 1804. For Baltimore's water service, see *Ordinances*, March 10, 1798; February 26, 1799; March 25, 1803; March 8, 1804; February 14, 1806; March 11, 1809; February 10, 1810; and Griffith, *Annals of Baltimore*, p. 171; Scharf, *Chronicles of Baltimore*, pp. 296, 303; and Nelson Manfred Blake, *Water for the Cities*, pp. 69–77, 220–21.

17. *Laws of Maryland*, 1805, c. 94; Griffith, *Annals of Baltimore*, p. 145; *Ordinances*, February 20, 1798; February 20, 1799; November 18, 1800; June 25, 1808; March 24, 1813; March 21, 1814.

18. *Ordinances*, April 7, 1797; March 20, 1801; March 22, 1803; March 18, 1807.

19. *Ordinances*, March 19, April 24, 1797; May 21, 1801; March 8, 1803; March 14, 1806; March 22, 1809; March 24, 1813.

III. Industrialization and the Crisis of War

1. Baltimoreans regarded manufacturing as a necessity not only because trade was curtailed, but also because British manufacturers gradually ceased operations after the American embargo. See Louis Martin Sears, "British Industry and the American Embargo," pp. 83–113; and George W. Daniels, "American Cotton Trade with Liverpool under the Embargo and Non-Intercourse Acts," pp. 276–87. For Baltimore's situation, see Escaville's *Price Current* for 1808 and 1809; Robert & John Oliver to Baring Brothers & Co., May 11, 1808, Oliver Record Books, MdHS; Thomas and Isaac Edmondson to Hall, Northage & Co., July 2, 1808, to York & Sheepshanks, September 28, 1808, Edmondson Letterbook; MdHS; Thomas and Samuel Hollingsworth to Levi Hollingsworth, January 4, 1808, Levi Hollingsworth, Jr., to Levi Hollingsworth, June 21, December 12, 1808. On March 28, 1808, Thomas and Samuel Hollingsworth wrote to their brother, Levi, in Philadelphia: "Our Mills are all Idle here[.] We stoped grinding in Decr. & have only abt 500 Barls flour on hand. Millers discharged & One Team of Horses sold to reduce the expence. Crews discharged & Our Vessels

Three now *laid up in Dry Dock*—in Jeffersonian Style." Hollingsworth Papers, HSP.

2. Robert & John Oliver to Robert Montgomery & Co., October 17, 1809, to Baring Brothers, October 25, 1809, to Duncan McIntosh, September 20, 1810, to Benjamin Weir & William B. Hight, January 10, 1811, Oliver Record Books, MdHS; Thomas and Samuel Hollingsworth to Levi Hollingsworth, February 4, 11, 13, March 13, 17, April 3, 13, 21, 26, July 23, August 22, 25, October 14, 1809, August 4, 27, September 6, October 28, December 14, 18, 28, 1810, January 5, 24, 27, April 3, May 4, 12, 20, June 4, 17, September 6, 7, November 17, 1811, Hollingsworth & Worthington to Levi Hollingsworth, April 3, 29, May 10, 27, October 30, 1809, Hollingsworth Papers, HSP; Samuel Smith to John Spear Smith, March 24, 1811, Smith Papers, LC; William Taylor to Sylvanus Bourne, August 8, 1809, Bourne Papers, LC; Alex Brown & Sons to John Potter, December 17, 1810, to John McKee, December 18, 1810, to Silas E. Weir, December 29, 1810, Brown Papers, LC; Liverpool *Price Currents* of firms Robert & Alexander Slater, William & Richard Rathbone, and Martin, Hope & Thornely for 1809–11, all at the HSP. Samuel Breck of Philadelphia visited Baltimore in September 1809, for the first time since 1793 and was astonished, not at the city's maritime depression but at how much the city had grown; Breck, *Recollections of Samuel Breck with Passages from His Note-Books (1771–1862)*, pp. 266–67.

3. The problems of the closing of the Bank of the United States cannot be divorced from the creation of four new banks in Baltimore in 1810. These banks were created in an atmosphere of "Republicanism" surrounding the reelection of Samuel Smith to the United States Senate in 1809. Samuel and Robert Smith were feuding with Albert Gallatin, the secretary of the treasury, and could not count upon support from the regular Republican party. Samuel was reelected with Federalist aid as an independent Republican in spite of Gallatin's and Madison's opposition; John S. Pancake, "The Invisibles: A Chapter in the Opposition to President Madison," pp. 17–37; James McHenry to James Ross, April 6, 1811, James McHenry Papers, UM; Baltimore *American*, March 5, 12, 16, 19, 21, 24, April 9, June 5, December 20, 1810, January 5, 9, 1811; Thomas and Samuel Hollingsworth to Levi Hollingsworth, August 4, 27, September 6, October 28, December 14, 18, 28, 1810, January 5, 24, 27, 1811, Hollingsworth Papers, HSP; Alex Brown & Sons to James Gibbon, December 22, 1810, Brown Papers, LC; speech of Samuel Smith in the United States Senate on February 16, 1811, *Annals of Congress*, 11th Cong., 3rd sess., 1811, pp. 240–42, 256–59, 322–23; Cassell, *Samuel Smith*, pp. 144–52, 161–70.

4. The infamous riot of 1812 occurred in this context; see Frank A. Cassell, "The Great Baltimore Riot of 1812," pp. 241–59.

5. An important stimulant to the appearance of textile manufacturing around Baltimore was the continuing need for sailing duck (canvas for ships' sails). The embargo and then the war itself virtually halted the importation of linen duck (usually from Holland), which had traditionally been used for ships' sails. The technological innovation in the years from 1809 to 1815 was the appearance of cotton duck, which was found comparable by some users, and superior by others,

to linen duck. For some of the early manufacturers, sales of cotton duck were extremely lucrative because of the wartime demand; gradually the manufacturers made cotton duck one of their established lines, and by the 1820s, almost every textile manufacturer in and around Baltimore had a line of cotton duck. William R. Bagnall, *The Textile Industries of the United States*, 1: 325–26; Victor S. Clark, *History of Manufactures in the United States*, 1: 549. The first application of steam power to textile manufacturing in Baltimore was the Hamilton Cotton Factory, built by Robert and Alexander McKim in 1814. In 1812, William Barker built the first foundry in Baltimore where iron castings were made for steam engines. In 1813, Job Smith built the first steam-powered sawmill; William McDonald operated the first steamboat; and Charles Gwinn built the first steam-powered flour mill. Griffith, *Annals of Baltimore*, pp. 190–91, 203–5; Scharf, *Chronicles of Baltimore*, p. 302; J. Leander Bishop, *A History of American Manufactures from 1608 to 1860*, 2: 131–32, 140, 198; in his "Report on Manufactures" of April 17, 1810, Albert Gallatin listed two cotton-spinning factories in operation near Baltimore that increased their number of spindles from 1,100 in 1809 to 6,000 in 1810. He also noted another cotton-spinning factory being built to accommodate 5,000 spindles; *American State Papers*, Class 3, *Finance*, 2: 432. Several previous attempts were made in the late 1780s and early 1790s to establish large-scale cotton-spinning factories, but they were unsuccessful because of poor technology and the opposition of the trading merchants; East, *Business Enterprise*, pp. 310–11; Joseph S. Davis, *Essays in the Earlier History of American Corporations*, 2: 267–68. Clive Day sharply distinguishes between factories built prior to 1812 and those built afterward by reasoning that those built after 1812 must have been better equipped and had more capital because they did not fail as rapidly as those built before 1812. Moreover, he argues that their technological and financial strength was more important than the postwar tariff protection for establishing America's domestic industry. In Baltimore's case, however, the protective tariff saved many of these "infant industries," and, indeed, several of the better capitalized and more technologically advanced factories succumbed to the depression of the 1820s in spite of the protection. See Clive Day, "The Early Development of the American Cotton Manufacture," pp. 450–68. An excellent factual description of manufacturing in Maryland is Richard W. Griffin, "An Origin of the Industrial Revolution in Maryland," pp. 25–32.

6. Examples of the first type of generalist, those living in a manufacturing enclave outside the city, were the Ellicott, Moore, Pennington, Stump, and Taggert families. Examples of the second type of generalist, the merchant-millers, were the Gwinn, Hollingsworth, McKim, and Tyson families. In 1800, there were about fifty flour mills in the vicinity of Baltimore, five of them within the city; in 1810, there were sixty-five mills in and around the city, and in 1822 there were about sixty. A new industry that appeared during the 1790s was the manufacture of gunpowder. The danger from explosions necessitated isolating this industry outside of the town, and only two such powder mills appear to have been built before 1812. Griffith, *Annals of Baltimore*, p. 133; Arlan K. Gilbert, "Gunpowder Production in Post-Revolutionary Maryland," pp. 187–201; Reid,

"Commerce and Manufactures," p. 509; Scharf, *History of Baltimore*, pp. 373–76; Tench Coxe, comp., *A Statement of the Arts and Manufactures of the United States of America, for the Year 1810*, pp. 79–87; United States Department of Commerce, Bureau of the Census, *Fourth Census of the United States, 1820: Manufactures*, microcopy 279; and John W. McGrain, "Englehart Cruse and Baltimore's First Steam Mill," pp. 65–79.

7. Many of these master craftsmen were conservative—whether Federalists or Gallatin-Republicans—many were Germans, and some were Roman Catholics. From 1793 to 1812, they seemed to oppose consistently the Smith-Republican-party faction who were, on the whole, Scotch-Irish, Protestant—mainly Presbyterian and Quaker—and who constituted a majority of the "Baltimore Mechanical Society," another institutional prop of Smith's political support. *Maryland Journal and Baltimore Advertiser*, October 2, 1792, December 13, 1793, July 28, 1794, December 3, 1795, April 21, 22, 27, May 4, 1796, August 18, 1798; and the Baltimore *American*, October 6, 1801, July 7, 14, August 1, 1804, July 2, October 5, 1805, May 22, 27, June 21, 27, 30, July 2, 3, 4, 5, 7, 14, 15, 1806, October 6, November 19, 1807, January 1, 29, February 6, October 3, 7, 1808, January 31, 1809, March 12, 16, 19, 24, 1810, January 3, April 15, May 7, 1811, January 7, 1814.

8. The six most important industries, in terms of their output values, were in this order: tanneries, shoes and boots, cabinet making, tobacco manufacturing, rope walks, and hatters. The output value of all six amounted to $1,256,000. In contrast, the five most important industries in Baltimore County were those, except for rope walks and distilleries, that were not found in the city: rope walks —15 in the county, 3 in the city; flour mills; gunpowder mills; distilleries—122 in the county, 1 in the city; and iron forges. The county contained 65 flour mills, 26 sawmills, 4 fulling mills, 4 carding machines, and 3 gunpowder mills. Coxe, *Manufactures for the Year 1810*, pp. 79–87.

9. This and the subsequent few paragraphs are based upon an analysis of Fry, ed., *Baltimore Directory for 1810*.

10. Mullin, comp., *Baltimore Directory, for 1799*; Fry, comp., *Baltimore Directory for 1810*.

11. Scharf, *History of Baltimore*, pp. 84–98; Scharf, *History of Maryland*, 3: 40–80; Scharf, *Chronicles of Baltimore*, pp. 306–86; Annie Leakin Sioussat, *Old Baltimore*, chaps. 17 and 18; Matthew Page Andrews, *Tercentenary History of Maryland*, 1: 716–32; William Marine, *The British Invasion of Maryland, 1812–1815*, passim; Frank A. Cassell, "Response to Crisis: Baltimore in 1814," pp. 261–87; however, the best source for understanding how the war crisis rent Baltimore's social fabric are the "Minutes of the Committee of Vigilance and Safety" edited by William D. Hoyt, Jr., and found in Hoyt "Civilian Defense in Baltimore, 1814–1815," *Maryland Historical Magazine* 39 (September 1944): 199–224, (December 1944): 293–309; ibid., 40 (March 1945): 7–23, (June 1945): 137–232. Also see *Niles' Weekly Register* and the various Baltimore newspapers from June 1812 to February 1815. Roger H. Brown's thesis, that the war was a matter of the American nationality and Republicanism, and not of self-interest, was true in Baltimore's case. Contrast Brown's *The Republic in*

Peril, with Norman K. Risjord, "1812: Conservatives, War Hawks, and the Nation's Honor," pp. 196–210.

12. Baltimore *American*, August 17, 1813.

13. "Baltimore. This city has grown to its present size within a few years, and contains a more various and mixed population than any other city in the U. States. It is in a great measure made up of adventurers from other parts of this country, of foreigners, FUGITIVES FROM JUSTICE, the OUTCASTS OF SOCIETY AND THE DISGRACE OF IT; with very little of that solid character which is the result of a great variety of moral and phsical causes. *It may in the course of a century attain to a* DECENT REPUTATION; but it will more probably continue like the city of Marseilles, always to have a bad one." Baltimore *American*, September 3, 1812, quoting from the Boston *Repertory*.

The numbers and value of these British prizes has always been a matter of estimation. The 126 privately armed Baltimore vessels capturing 556 British vessels was estimated by John Phillips Cranwell and William Bowers Crane, *Men of Marque*, p. 82. The 1,341 total British prizes is from George Foster Emmons, *The Navy of the United States, from the Commencement, 1775 to 1853*, pp. 56–75, 198–301; but historians have disagreed about the exact number of British prizes taken by the Americans. For example, Ruthella Mory Bibbins thought there were 1,634 British prizes (Bibbins, "Baltimore, 1797–1850," p. 100); James Schouler, 1,750 (*History of the United States of America, Under the Constitution*, 2: 455); George Coggeshall, over 2,000 (*History of the American Privateers*, p. 395); and Charles Jared Ingersoll estimated the largest number at 2,425 (*History of the Second War Between the United States of America and Great Britain*, 2: 117). The glossary of privateering terms on pp. 163–69 of Donald B. Chidsey, *The American Privateers*, is very helpful. The values of the prizes taken by the Baltimoreans were estimated by Bibbins, "Baltimore, 1797–1850," p. 105. Also see Jerome R. Garitee, *The Republic's Private Navy*, pp. 210–12; the Baltimore *American*, August 18, 1812; and *Niles' Weekly Register*, 7: 112, for the Baltimoreans' equation of privateering with patriotism, and New England's condemnation of the city for it.

14. *United States Statutes at Large*, 2: 755–59, 3: 81, 105, contain the relevant federal laws respecting privateers. One of Baltimore's most famous privateers, Henry Fulford, described the arrangements that were made for fitting out two privateers, the *Transit* and the *Patapsco*, in a letter dated November 21, 1813. The *Transit* was to carry flour to Puerto Rico, exchange it for coffee, and then proceed to New York. The *Patapsco* was to carry flour and navy bread to Havana, exchange it for white sugar, go to France, and then return to New York. Captain Kelly of the *Patapsco* received $60 per month in wages and two bonuses: $300, when he arrived in Havana, and another $300 when he landed in New York. Ordinary seamen were paid $30 per month or about 50 percent higher than ordinary seamen's wages were before and after the war. Marine, *British Invasion of Maryland*, pp. 19–20. The *Transit* made no captures, but the *Patapsco* made three. Bibbins, "Baltimore, 1797–1850," p. 102.

15. The problem of runaway apprentices can be followed in the Baltimore *American*, July 15, 29, August 11, 19, September 11, 19, 23, 1812, June 22, 27,

July 2, September 30, November 17, 1814. Advertisements to hire apprentices, laborers, and journeymen can be found in the *American*, July 14, 1812, December 14, 1813, January 18, February 8, June 20, August 3, November 3, 19, 1814.

16. In and around Boston, by contrast, the war stimulated household industry but not steam-powered production; Oscar and Mary Flug Handlin, *Commonwealth; a Study of the Role of Government in the American Economy*, pp. 182–84. But Philadelphia followed the same pattern as Baltimore: Rolla Milton Tryon, *Household Manufacturers in the United States, 1640–1860*, pp. 281–83. Other comparative patterns are found in the wholesale price indexes of American-made goods during the years from 1810 through 1819. For Baltimore, this index began high, bottomed at 91 in May 1812, topped at 161 in November 1814, and bottomed at 88 in August 1819. Baltimore thus followed Philadelphia's manufacturers, whose prices also bottomed in May 1812 at 93, topped at 144 in January 1815, and also bottomed in August 1819 at 87. However, the price pattern in New York was similar to that of Boston, and both were different from Baltimore and Philadelphia. Before the War of 1812, New York and Boston led Baltimore and Philadelphia; after the war they fell behind the two Southern cities. For New York, the price index bottomed at 92 in July 1811, peaked at 155 in January 1815, and bottomed at 91 in December 1819. New York manufacturers thus found their prices bottoming out ten months sooner than Baltimore's during the war, peaking two months later than Baltimore's during the war, and bottoming out three months later than Baltimore's during the depression of 1819: all of which suggests New York's greater involvement in the international economy than Baltimore's. Walter B. Smith, "Wholesale Commodity Prices in the United States, 1795–1824," p. 181.

17. Because of its partisanship, *Niles' Weekly Register* must be treated carefully. But Niles did comment upon postwar Baltimore's growth: 8: 234, 290; 10: 217, 334–36, 338; 16: 259; [Jared Sparks], "Baltimore," pp. 99–138. The literary nationalism that accompanied Baltimore's heady atmosphere in 1815 is treated in Marshall W. Fishwick, "*The Portico* and Literary Nationalism After the War of 1812," pp. 238–45.

IV. Economic Crisis and New Directions

1. Thomas P. Martin, "Some International Aspects of the Anti-Slavery Movement, 1818–1823," pp. 137–48; Benns, *American Struggle for the West Indian Carrying Trade*, passim; Setser, *Commercial Reciprocity Policy*, passim; Bradford Perkins, *Castlereagh and Adams*, pp. 220–325. Isaac McKim, prominent merchant and manufacturer, member of the Smith faction, and Jacksonian congressman, wrote to John Forsyth, secretary of state, on November 17, 1834: "Our Treaty with Bremen has turned out most unfortunately for the U.S., we put their vessels on the same footing as ours, and gave them the Entry of all our ports to the extent of 1500 miles of coast, whereas all they have got to offer us in return, is the port of Bremen, and which during the fall and winter months is not accessible and full of danger at the best of times.—the Consequence is we are

over run with Bremen Vessels who bring Passengers and carry Tobacco at 15/ or 20/ Stg. pr. Hhd to the great injury of our shipping interest—this Reciprocating Treaty Business is not well understood—it will only answer to have those kind of Treaties with the first rate powers, because they have extent of coast and vessels to interfere with ours, and then it acts in some measure equally, but small powers must take care of themselves—the Bremen Treaty has 5 or 6 years yet to run before we can get rid of it, and you may rest assured, that they are annoying us at a great rate." U.S. Department of State, Letters of Application and Recommendation During the Administration of Andrew Jackson, 1829–1837; also see the *Commercial Chronicle & Daily Marylander*, February 26, July 3, September 20, November 30, December 4, 1820, January 16, 1821; Baltimore *Federal Gazette*, August 3, December 11, 1821, July 24, 1823, January 5, July 27, 1824, February 1, 1825; Baltimore *Patriot*, July 16, 26, 31, August 26, 1822, April 22, September 22, October 4, 18, December 10, 29, 1824; Baltimore *Gazette*, December 14, 21, 1826, February 21, June 27, November 21, 1827, April 25, May 8, August 27, 29, 1828; *Federal Republican* and Baltimore *Telegraph*, January 2, 1816; and the Mayor's Annual Message, 1836. The data about Baltimore's markets from January 1816 through December 1830 can be found in Escaville's Baltimore *Price Current*.

2. George Rogers Taylor, *The Transportation Revolution, 1815–1860*, pp. 334–38; Walter Buckingham Smith, *Economic Aspects of the Second Bank of the United States*, pp. 26–28, 40–41, 75–78, 99–133; Douglass C. North, *The Economic Growth of the United States, 1790–1860*, pp. 182–88; George Dangerfield, *The Awakening of American Nationalism, 1815–1828*, chap. 3; and Frederick Jackson Turner, *The Rise of the West, 1819–1829*, chap. 9. Also see note 19.

3. News of the Treaty of Ghent reached Baltimore on Monday, February 13, 1815. One week later, prices of European manufactured goods had fallen 50 percent. Baltimore *Patriot*, February 23, 1815; Baltimore *Federal Gazette*, October 15, 1815, June 6, September 10, 12, December 18, 1816, August 5, 7, 1817, November 27, 1818; Thomas and Samuel Hollingsworth to Levi Hollingsworth, February 20, March 16, 18, October 9, 20, 23, 26, November 26, 1815, March 6, July 22, September 5, 1816, January 2, February 3, 13, 18, March 27, July 4, September 2, 10, October 31, November 5, 1817, October 30, November 23, December 14, 1818, Hollingsworth Papers, HSP; R. Crane to James Cox, April 27, 1815, Alexander Lanier to James Cox, October 26, 1817, Corner Collection; MdHS; Matthew Smith to James Potts, January 12, 1816, to John Wyld, November 27, 1818, Matthew Smith Letterbook, MdHS; William and Richard H. Douglass to R. Richardson, January 6, 1817, Douglass Letterbook, MdHS; James Robinson to Benjamin Clap, October 11, 1817, Clap Papers, BHC; Alex Brown & Sons to William Gihon & Son, December 15, 1818, Brown Papers, LC; Thomas Bond to Major James Thomas, May 21, 1817, Thomas Family Papers, MdHR; *Niles' Weekly Register*, 15: 283; also see the Baltimore *Patriot*, October 13, 1818.

4. Isaac and Thomas Edmondson to Mayson, Grave & Co., November 5, 1816, to John Roberts, November 6, 1816, to John and Jacob Wakefield, No-

vember 8, 1816, to Richard Blackstock & Co., November 8, 1816, September 30, 1817, October 12, 1818, to James Schofield, November 12, 1816, September 27, 1817, to John W. Adam & Co., November 14, 1816, May 17, 1817, March 23, 1818, to John Horsburgh, November 15, 1816, June 10, 1817, Edmondson Letterbook, MdHS; Matthew Smith to James Potts, September 4, 26, 1815, April 18, 1816, February 26, November 26, 1818, to John Wyld, October 17, November 28, December 15, 1815, July 20, October 8, November 16, 1816, February 28, 1818, to William Redhead & Co., April 18, 1816, Matthew Smith Letterbook, MdHS; William and Richard H. Douglass to Staniforth & Blunt, September 10, November 1, December 2, 1816, April 28, June 14, July 18, 1817, to W. & A. Maxwell, September 7, October 31, 1816, Douglass Letterbook, MdHS; Thomas and Samuel Hollingsworth to Levi Hollingsworth, March 6, 18, 1815, March 6, 1816, January 2, May 10, 1817, Hollingsworth Papers, HSP. A list of the produce dealers who refused country bank notes is published in the Baltimore *Patriot*, November 27, 1818. An excellent editorial about the nature of Baltimore's economy being a "chain of Credit that needs to be reaffirmed" is in the *Commercial Chronicle & Daily Marylander*, December 15, 1820.

5. Baltimore's banking capital was nearly 80 percent of that for all of Maryland. See the Baltimore *Federal Gazette*, March 6, September 6, 7, 9, 10, December 12, 1816, February 3, 6, 12, 26, April 26, May 28, July 16, 1817; *Niles' Weekly Register*, 15: 285; Baltimore *Patriot*, October 15, 16, December 5, 1818; Donald Chester to John Myers, October 4, 1817, August 29, December 3, 1818, April 15, 1819, Myers Family Papers, NMAS; Robert & John Oliver to John & Thomas H. Perkins, August 29, 1815, Letterbook, 1809–1817, Robert Oliver Papers, MdHS; William and Richard H. Douglass to John Cullen, October 1, 1816, to S. & J. G. Hollingsworth, December 19, 1816, Douglass Letterbook, MdHS; Matthew Smith to James Potts, December 29, 1815, January 12, April 18, 1816, to William Redhead & Co., April 18, 1816, to John Wyld, December 12, 1816, Matthew Smith Letterbook, MdHS; Thomas and Samuel Hollingsworth to Levi Hollingsworth, October 9, 26, November 10, 1815, July 22, September 5, 26, 1816, February 13, 18, 22, July 4, September 2, 10, 1817, October 30, November 23, December 14, 1818, Hollingsworth Papers, HSP; Henry Didier to John D'Arcy, March 7, 1815, and on March 27, 1815 Didier wrote to D'Arcy: "The last was on the 7th Inst since which time the Schooner Burrows has arrived at this port from St. Iago with a cargo of sugars, she will not do so well as formerly, having sold her sugars for only 16 $ which brought in time of war 30 to 33 $. We have loaded her with a cargo of gun powder & muskets, & she will sail in a day or two for Carthagena, where I expect she will make a good voyage; the Spanish admiral has declared all the ports along the main in a state of Blockade, so that none but fast sailing Balto Schooners will attempt to go there." And on May 5, 1815, Didier wrote to D'Arcy: "You must not be uneasy at our business in this country; our fast sailing Vessels are always useful and particularly now at present to South America, the last accts from Carthagena, muskets were selling for $30 and plenty of silver to pay for them." Henry Didier Letterbook, 1809–1817, MdHS.

6. Thomas and Samuel Hollingsworth to Levi Hollingsworth, November 10,

1815, July 22, August 1, 12, September 5, 1816, February 3, 5, 6, 13, 18, 22, July 4, September 2, 10, 1817, October 30, December 14, 1818, Hollingsworth Papers, HSP; Baltimore *Federal Gazette*, July 16, August 5, 7, 1817; William H. Crawford to William Jones, February 8, 1817, William Jones Papers, HSP; *Niles' Weekly Register*, 12: 262–63, 13: 97, 14: 4, 22, 110; Hammond, *Banks and Politics*, chaps. 9 and 10; Leon M. Schur, "The Second Bank of the United States and the Inflation After the War of 1812," pp. 118–34; Thomas P. Govan, *Nicholas Biddle*, pp. 51–9.

7. Baltimore *Patriot*, January 11, February 10, 24, 27, March 25, May 27, 31, June 4, 7, 21, 25, 1819. The story of the Baltimore branch of the Bank of the United States has been pieced together from the following sources: the Jonathan Meredith Papers, LC and DU; Langdon Cheves Papers, SCHS; Records of the Baltimore Branch of the Second Bank of the United States, LC; Samuel Smith Papers, MdHS, LC, and UV; John White Papers, MdHS and DU; Nicholas Biddle Papers, LC; Uselma C. Smith Papers, HSP; Hollingsworth Papers, HSP; Etting Collection, HSP; Lyde Goodwin Diary, MdHS; Gratz Collection, HSP; Brown Papers, LC; William H. Crawford Papers, LC and DU; Ralph C. H. Catterall, *The Second Bank of the United States*, pp. 39–53, 64–69, 78; Govan, *Nicholas Biddle*, pp. 57–58; Smith, *Economic Aspects of the Second Bank*, pp. 99–116; Bray Hammond, *Banks and Politics*, pp. 260–62.

8. Raymond Walters, Jr., "The Origins of the Second Bank of the United States," pp. 120–29, mentions the roles played by Dennis A. Smith and Henry Payson—both Baltimoreans, Smith was president of the Mechanics Bank and Payson of the Union Bank—in the early movement; and by John Jacob Astor, David Parrish, Stephen Girard, and Jacob Barker in 1814 in establishing a national bank. Walters's account should be balanced by Kenneth L. Brown, "Stephen Girard, Promoter of the Second Bank of the United States," 2: 125–48.

9. McCulloh's name was spelled incorrectly in the original Supreme Court case. Baltimore *Patriot*, June 7, 18, 1819; Samuel Hollingsworth was president of the City Bank; Thomas and Samuel Hollingsworth to Levi Hollingsworth, Janaury 14, February 13, 27, March 27, April 2, 8, 10, 12, March 3, 29, May 20, 1819, Hollingsworth Papers, HSP; Langdon Cheves to John White, who replaced McCulloh as cashier of Baltimore's branch of the Bank of the United States, May 18, 22, 26, 27, June 9, 12, 16, 23, 28, July 19, 24, August 3, 5, October 17, 1819, John White to Langdon Cheves, May 20, 23, June 28, July 3, 12, 18, 21, 22, 26, August 9, 13, September 15, 20, 29, October 4, 6, 8, 14, 1819, R. L. Colt to John White, August 4, 1819, Richard B. Magruder to John White, September 7, 1819, John White Papers, MdHS; Thomas and Isaac Edmondson to Richard Blackstock & Co., April 17, 1819, to Rathbone, Hodgson & Co., April 20, 1819, Edmondson Letterbook, MdHS; Alex Brown & Sons to William Gihon, April 3, 30, to John Cumming, April 6, to Robert Dickey, April 6, 26, to James Carruthers, April 22, 1819, Brown Papers, LC.

10. Charles Francis Adams, ed., *Memoirs of John Quincy Adams*, diary entry for May 30, 1819, 4: 382–83; James Robinson to Benjamin Clap, May 26, June 1, 9, 16, 23, July 12, 1819, Clap Papers, BHC; Ann C. Smith to Francis Blackwell, June 5, 1819, Mayer Family Papers, MdHS; entries for May 28, 29,

1819, Henry Thompson Diaries, MdHS; John McHenry to John McHenry, May 23, June 23, 1819, Anna Boyd to John McHenry, July 12, 26, August 2, 23, 1819, McHenry Papers, MdHS; on August 6, 1819, Anna Boyd wrote to her brother, John McHenry: "I think John, one of the most provoking parts of the business is, that these destroyers of Widows, and Orphans, affect to Consider themselves as persecuted men. McCulloh for example struts about in all the pride & gaiety belonging to an honest heart, and unspotted name boasting as it were; that he is stript of his feathers, that they were determined to bring him down & have succeeded." Also see John Hastings to John Myers, June 17, 23, July 1, September 1, 23, 1819, Myers Papers, NMAS.

11. *Laws of Maryland*, 1805, c. 110; 1806, c. 98; 1816, c. 221; 1819, c. 84; 1820, cs. 108, 182; 1821, c. 250; 1822, c. 102. In 1820, creditors were made liable for the support of their imprisoned debtors—c. 186.

12. This change from endorsement to collateral as loan security can be followed in the papers of the Baltimore branch of the Bank of the United States, LC; the Jonathan Meredith Papers, LC; the John White Papers, MdHS; and to a lesser extent in the Langdon Cheves Papers, SCHS. The cashier of the branch, White, apparently began requiring mortgages on property, instead of endorsements, in early November 1819. As late as October 30, 1819, White's policy was to require two endorsers instead of one (White to John Donnell, October 30, 1819, Cheves Papers, SCHS), but the letter of John T. Keppler to the president and directors of the Baltimore branch, November 15, 1819, (in Baltimore Branch of the Bank of the United States Papers, LC) clearly specifies that White had asked for a mortgage on Keppler's property for double the amount of the prospective loan in lieu of an endorser.

13. Redlich, *American Banking*, 1: 43–66, 96–162; Govan, *Nicholas Biddle*, pp. 60–111; Hammond, *Banks and Politics*, chap. 11; Catterall, *Second Bank*, pp. 38–113; several studies have dealt with the functions of the country merchant: Lewis E. Atherton, *The Pioneer Merchant in Mid-America*; Lewis E. Atherton, *The Southern Country Store, 1800–1860*; Gerald Carson, *The Old Country Store*; Thomas D. Clark, *Pills, Petticoats and Plows*; Lawrence A. Johnson, *Over the Counter and On the Shelf*; Fred M. Jones, *Middlemen in the Domestic Trade of the United States, 1800–1860*; Harold D. Woodman, *King Cotton & His Retainers*, pp. 3–195; and Richardson Wright, *Hawkers & Walkers in Early America*. Lewis E. Atherton also has two articles that relate to the points in the text: "Itinerant Merchandising in the Ante-Bellum South," pp. 35–59, and "Predecessors of the Commercial Drummer in the Old South," pp. 17–24.

14. How the functions of the national bank affected the operations of Baltimore's interregional merchants can be seen in the Brown and Riggs Papers, LC; and in the Matthew Smith Papers, Riggs & Gaither Papers, Robert Oliver Papers, and J. Hall Pleasants Papers, all in the MdHS.

15. The institutional arrangements of marketing were also altered by these changes. The shift from a sellers' to a buyers' market necessitated the seaport merchants' solicitation of business from the country merchants. Before the mid-1820s country merchants came to the seaports; afterward, a few continued to do so, but the seaport merchants now sent salesmen into the interior to solicit busi-

ness. The "drummer," a traveling salesman, first appeared in the American marketing structure during the 1820s. As an institutional device, the American "drummer" descended from the British "commercial traveller," a method of merchandizing that had become common in Great Britain during the very early nineteenth century. Before "commercial travellers," the younger partners of mercantile firms carried their goods from town to town, selling them as they went along. As manufacturing became more complex in the late eighteenth century, "commercial travellers" were hired by the merchants to sell their goods, thereby freeing them to concentrate upon production and distribution. "Commercial travellers" did not carry the goods of the merchant; they merely carried samples which customers ordered from after inspection. Though Americans increasingly substituted the term *commercial traveller* for *drummer* after the 1820s, the English thought no better of the former than Americans did of the latter. As one English historian remarked in 1823: "These travellers are a body of men exhibiting intelligence and acuteness, combined, in many instances, with self-conceit and the superficial information acquired by reading newspapers." Richard Guest, *Compendious History of the Cotton-Manufacture*, p. 11. In America, prices were beginning to become standardized during the 1820s; see Lee M. Friedman, "The Drummer in Early American Merchandise Distribution," pp. 39–42; James D. Norris, "One-Price Policy Among Antebellum Country Stores," pp. 455–58. For reactions to the new "drummer" way of conducting business, see Stanley C. Hollander, "Nineteenth Century Anti-Drummer Legislation in the United States," pp. 479–500.

16. The behavior of Baltimore's merchants suggests that changes in the American national marketing system led to alterations in the international marketing system, and that changes in both marketing systems acted to stabilize the price structure and to thus prolong the lowered price levels. Walter B. Smith hinted at this when he said that the canal-building boom of the 1820s and 1830s was a response to the panic of 1819, because canals provided the cheapest means of transporting bulk goods (Smith, *Economic Aspects of the Second Bank*, p. 26). The point is that the "depression" of lowered price levels really opened society by creating new opportunities for new men to fill. At least, this was what lay behind the antiauction controversy of the 1820s. The auction system of granting licenses to selected firms, who then legally monopolized such sales, was an extension of the eighteenth-century private society. Moreover, it answered the enormous prosperity of the 1790s and early 1800s. But during the depression of the 1820s, most of the importing merchants in each of the major seaports moved against this vestige of more prosperous days, in the name of antimonopoly. Of course, they themselves wanted to import goods and to auction them, a sales method that fit the era of declining prices, but goods must have been forthcoming in order for this change to occur, and importers wanted greater freedom of access to these goods. See Taylor, *Transportation Revolution*, pp. 11–12; Norman S. Buck, *The Development of the Organization of Anglo-American Trade, 1800–1850*, pp. 135–50; Emory R. Johnson, et al., *History of Domestic and Foreign Commerce of the United States*, 2: 37–41; Ray Bert Westerfield, "Early History of American Auctions—A Chapter in Commercial History," pp. 159–310;

Jones, *Middlemen in Domestic Trade*, pp. 30–45; Arthur H. Cole, *The American Wool Manufacture*, 1: 156–60; Lewis E. Atherton, "Auctions as a Threat to American Business in the Eighteen Twenties and Thirties," pp. 104–7; Ira Cohen, "The Auction System in the Port of New York, 1817–1837," pp. 488–510; Ralph W. Hidy, "Organization and Function of Anglo-American Merchant Bankers, 1815–1860," pp. 53–66.

17. The manufacturers were listed as members of the newly formed "Society of American Manufacturers"; Baltimore *Patriot*, March 16, 1819.

18. Alexander Brown, one of Baltimore's new men, perfectly understood that the days of credit had been replaced by the new emphasis upon money: "Business is not likely to be what it used to be in this Country, formerly industry and credit enabled an intelligent Merchant to get forward, we do not see how any person who has a family to support can get forward, if they have Interest to pay for all their Money employed in Business. It requires some known capital to give confidence and credit." Alex Brown & Sons to William & James Brown & Co., January 4, 1821, Brown Papers, LC. Govan, *Nicholas Biddle*, pp. 63–67, 84–87, discusses the stabilization effects of the Bank of the United States upon the domestic exchange markets.

19. Three studies treat the effect of the panic of 1819 upon American society in general: Samuel Rezneck, "The Depression of 1819-1822, A Social History," pp. 28–47; William W. Folz, "The Financial Crisis of 1819," passim; and Murray N. Rothbard, *The Panic of 1819, Reactions and Policies*, passim. Other studies that focus upon particular localities include Dorothy Baker Dorsey, "The Panic of 1819 in Missouri," *Missouri Historical Review* 29 (January 1935): 79–91; Thomas H. Greer, "Economic and Social Effects of the Depression of 1819 in the Old Northwest," pp. 227–43; Joseph H. Parks, "Felix Grundy and the Depression of 1819 in Tennessee," *Publications of the East Tennessee Historical Society* 10, no. 10 (1938): 19–43; and Malcolm J. Rohrbough, *The Land Office Business*, chap. 7. Livingood, *Philadelphia-Baltimore Trade Rivalry*, p. 18, captures what happened in Baltimore, but see Browne, "The Panic of 1819 in Baltimore," pp. 212–27. Benns, *American Struggle for the West Indies Carrying Trade*, pp. 75–81, describes how bitterly Baltimore's commercial interests fought the American navigation bills that became law in 1818, which prohibited British ships from being employed in the American trade to the British West Indies unless American ships would be granted reciprocal trading privileges in the trade between British possessions. But Benns does not elaborate upon the fact that for Baltimore, and American southern seaports in general, the British West Indies were a large, lucrative market in which to sell foodstuffs and naval stores. Scarcely any of the shipping interests in Baltimore and the southern seaports were involved in the trade from the British West Indies direct to Great Britain, as were the shipping interests in the seaports north of Baltimore. Benns does call attention to this commercial sectionalism by quoting (on p. 79) from the *New England Palladium and Commercial Advertiser*, February 8, 1822: "The citizens of seaports North of Baltimore appear to be in favor of the continued exclusion of British vessels from their colonies, unless American vessels are admitted to those colonies. The citizens of seaports South of Baltimore seem to be in favor of an

admission of British ships without the other condition." The Southerners were right, of course; the attempts of the Eastern shippers to dominate the American carrying trade, which first appeared in 1785, now succeeded in the 1820s, and the Southern shipping interests sank in depression because of the American navigation system. Tables 2, 3, 8, 11–13, 16–17, in Appendix B of Browne, "Baltimore in the Nation," illustrates Baltimore's maritime trade during the 1820s.

20. Alex Brown & Sons to William & James Brown & Company, April 12, 1822 (but also see the letters dated December 8, 20, 1821, February 7, March 22, 28, May 13, June 12, 17, December 27, 1822, to ibid.) and to John A. Brown, March 29, 1822, to Milnes, Holdsworth & Co., April 12, 1822, to William Goddard, March 17, 1824, to William Gihon & Son, April 16, 1824, Brown Papers, LC; Thomas P. Cope & Son to William & James Brown & Company, August 20, 1822, Cope Papers, HSP. Several secondary works discuss various aspects of Baltimore's internal improvements: Balthasar Henry Meyer, et al., *History of Transportation in the United States Before 1860*, pp. 395–413, 588–92; Taylor, *Transportation Revolution*, pp. 8, 23, 43, 77, 80–1, 94, 98–100; Walter S. Sanderlin, *The Great National Project*, pp. 13–212, 282–94; Julius Rubin, "Canal or Railroad? Imitation and Innovation in the Response to the Erie Canal in Philadelphia, Baltimore and Boston," pp. 1–78; Carter Goodrich and Harvey H. Segal, "Baltimore's Aid to Railroads," pp. 2–35; Edward Hungerford, *The Story of the Baltimore & Ohio Railroad, 1827–1927*, vol. 1, passim; Alvin F. Harlow, *Old Towpaths, the Story of the American Canal Era*, pp. 113–14, 169–76, 230–40; Milton Reizenstein, *The Economic History of the Baltimore and Ohio Railroad, 1827–1853*, passim; Livingood, *Baltimore-Philadelphia Trade Rivalry*, passim; Roger L. Ransom, "Interregional Canals and Economic Specialization in the Antebellum United States," pp. 12–35; Frederick A. Cleveland and Fred W. Powell, *Railroad Promotion and Capitalization in the United States*, pp. 15–16, 62–69, 74–82, 117–24, 202–13, 240; Joseph Austin Durrenburger, *Turnpikes*, pp. 13, 20–23, 66–69, 128, 134–39; and perhaps the best account of the race for metropolitan leadership among the major Atlantic seaports is Robert Greenhalgn Albion, *The Rise of New York Port [1815–1860]*, chap. 18. Contemporary newspaper accounts include Baltimore *Federal Gazette*, September 11, 25, October 3, 4, 5, November 29, 1821, February 12, 13, 14, 18, 28, April 3, 4, August 15, September 17, October 20, November 11, 12, December 16, 22, 26, 29, 31, 1823, January 23, December 14, 16, 24, 1824; Baltimore *Gazette*, November 15, December 15–20, 1825, January 25, February 22, April 11, 12, 25, 1826, December 26, 1828; Baltimore *Republican*, August 7, 1827; Baltimore *Patriot*, March 13, April 3, 11, June 6, 10, 11, July 16, 1822, January 7, May 29, June 9, August 7, 1824.

21. Baltimore's losing out to New York in tapping the trans-Allegheny Western markets after 1825, coupled with the relative decline of Baltimore's maritime economy during the 1820s and 1830s, invites a comparison between New York and New Orleans during the following generation. During the 1840s and 1850s, the New Yorkers diverted much of New Orleans trade from the upper Mississippi Valley area to New York via the new railroad network; see Harry A. Mitchell, "The Development of New Orleans as a Wholesale Trading Center,"

pp. 933–63; and John G. Clark, *The Grain Trade in the Old Northwest*, chaps. 10 and 13.

22. Several studies have explored the rivalry between Baltimore and Philadelphia as a motivating force behind their expansion as metropolitan centers: Cleveland and Powell, *Railroad Promotion*, pp. 117–24; Livingood, *Baltimore-Philadelphia Trade Rivalry*, passim; Meyer, et al, *History of Transportation*, pp. 207–8, 210–14, 222–25, 234–37, 245–48, 394–96, 411–13; Rubin, "Canal or Railroad?" pp. 8–9, 13–24; and Garrett, "Philadelphia and Baltimore," pp. 1–13; also see the editorial, "The Rival Cities," Baltimore *Patriot*, May 2, 1822.

23. *Laws of Maryland*, 1797, c. 70; 1804, cs. 51, 91; 1813, cs. 126, 167; 1815, cs. 48, 99, 190; 1828, c. 193. The Baltimoreans tried to engineer a cooperative effort between the states of Maryland and Pennsylvania to tap this Western trade, but nothing came of it. Baltimore *Gazette*, December 20, 23, 1826.

24. In 1823, the major seaports tried to improve their trade by tapping their countryside through canals. Baltimore's efforts turned in two directions, westward via the Potomac Canal route and northeastward via the Susquehanna Canal route. Because the city was too far overland from the Potomac River—and because of the political power of the Potomac interest, the counties bordering the river, in the state legislature—Baltimore mainly pinned its hopes on the Susquehanna Canal route. But, of course, Pennsylvania stifled its plans.

Two articles, each entitled "The Baltimore and Ohio Railroad," were written by Peter Cruise and published in the *North American Review* in 1827 and 1829. Cruise was editor of the Baltimore *American*, probably the most influential newspaper published in the city at the time, and his articles reflect what Baltimoreans thought and hoped about their railroad.

"Going to New York" notices are in the Baltimore *Federal Gazette*, April 7, 8, 12, 15, 1824; Baltimore *Patriot*, April 12, 1824; also see Baltimore *Gazette*, June 27, July 9, August 7, 1827, January 3, 18, 29, February 15, April 29, May 3, October 27, December 26, 1828, February 16, 17, 18, 23, 24, March 10, May 9, 1829, July 24, August 16, 1830, June 15, 1831, July 6, 1832; Lyde Goodwin Diary, March 13, April 3, 1827, MdHS; Charles Howard to Benjamin C. Howard, January 27, 1830, Robert Gilmor to Benjamin C. Howard, January 17, 18, 19, 21, 27, 1830, Bayard Papers, MdHS.

25. William Mactier to Nicholas G. Ridgely, October 16, 1829, Ridgely Papers, MdHS; Baltimoreans also formed the Baltimore & Susquehanna Railroad Company (*Laws of Maryland*, 1827, c. 72), but soon encountered Pennsylvania's jurisdiction. Baltimore *Gazette*, September 6, 1831; *Laws of Maryland*, 1828, cs. 27, 147, 170, 171, 183; 1829, c. 42.

26. Like Baltimore, New York and Philadelphia were excluded from the carrying trade between the British West Indies and Great Britain during the generation following the War of 1812; but they moved into the cotton reexport trade. New York was most successful in this trade because of its attraction for Liverpool imports; it was closer to Liverpool than American seaports to the south; it had better harbor facilities; its auction law required that all goods put up for sale at

auction must be sold at the highest price bidded in; it had several packet lines; and it had the best potential as the major transshipment center for European and New England goods to the American West and South. In comparison, Baltimore had traded directly with the West Indies and with Europe in a double-V pattern, and did not trade with the West Indies and Great Britain in a triangular pattern. Producing no commodities for the English market to attract imported goods, Baltimore had no means of establishing itself in the cotton reexport trade. Instead, Baltimore shippers who were involved in the cotton trade usually shipped direct from the Southern cotton ports to British ports. The Alex Brown & Sons Papers, LC, spell out these difficulties during the 1820s quite clearly, but also see Tables 2, 3, and 11 to 13 in Appendix B. of Browne, "Baltimore in the Nation," which compares Baltimore's position with other American seaports.

27. Collamer L. Abbott, "Isaac Tyson, Jr., Pioneer Mining Engineer and Metallurgist," pp. 15–25; G. Terry Sharrer, "Patents by Marylanders, 1790–1830," pp. 50–9.

28. *The Baltimore Directory, for 1799*; *The Baltimore Directory for 1810*; *The Baltimore Directory for 1819*; and *Matchett's Baltimore Directory for 1829*. The depression was of greater significance in saving Baltimore's textile manufacturers than the protective-tariff system. The newspapers commented about textile importations on several occasions: Baltimore *Federal Gazette*, September 6, 1816, September 6, 1817; Baltimore *Patriot*, October 18, 1817, March 25, 1819 (letter to editor from "Franklin"); *Niles' Weekly Register*, 15: 418–19. The Baltimore *Federal Gazette*, November 26, 1816, editorialized about the inability of American textile manufacturers to purchase raw cotton. Two textile factories were offered for sale during the period from 1816 to 1820; the Linen Manufacturing Company (Baltimore *Federal Gazette*, June 20, 1816); and Robert and Alexander McKims' factory (Baltimore *Patriot*, January 30, 1819).

29. A tabular statement comparing the specific duties on approximately one hundred articles established by the tariffs of 1816, 1824, 1828, and 1832, can be found in *Hunt's Merchants' Magazine*, 6: 574–75. The Warren Factory, built in 1816, and owned and operated by the infamous James A. Buchanan, former business partner of Samuel Smith and former president of the Baltimore branch of the second Bank of the United States, failed in 1829. Buchanan's son, Robert S., built a new steam-powered cotton factory in town in the same year; Baltimore *Republican*, July 9, 1829.

30. The Passenger Lists of Vessels Arriving at Baltimore, 1820–1891, in the National Archives, are the only federal government records of immigration through the port. The records originated with a federal law of March 2, 1819, requiring, after January 1, 1820, every captain of a vessel to submit a list of his passengers to the collector of the port where he landed. This requirement was supplemented by a Maryland law of March 22, 1833, that required masters of vessels landing at Baltimore to submit lists of their passengers to the mayor of the city. These municipal records (available at the Department of Legislative Reference, BCH) also contain the age, occupation, and destination of the immigrants. But there are at least six problems involved in working with these records: (1) An immigrant's place of birth is frequently missing, (2) the occupation is

frequently missing, (3) the last residence indicated by the immigrant was usually the port he or she left from, and not their original home, (4) the destination indicated cannot be trusted, (5) many of these immigrants were really visitors and not immigrants, (6) the figures totaled at the bottom of the pages do not include immigrant children, (7) many pages of the lists (and sometimes months, and even the year, 1839) are missing.

Immigrant-aid societies had long been established in the other, older major American seaports; see Erna Risch, "Immigrant Aid Societies Before 1820," pp. 15–33. The information about Baltimore's immigrant-aid societies was gleaned from the newspapers, chiefly the Baltimore *American*, over the decade.

V. Fragmentation of the Old Order

1. *Niles' Weekly Register*, 8: 234; 10: 217.

2. *Laws of Maryland*, 1816, c. 251; *Ordinance*, June 17, 1816; *Commercial Chronicle*, May 30, June 3, 1820; Baltimore *Gazette*, January 11, 1826; Scharf, *History of Baltimore*, p. 437; Baltimore *Federal Republican*, August 7, 1816; Victor Sapio, "Maryland's Federalist Revival, 1808–1812," pp. 1–17.

3. Alex Brown & Sons to Gray & Pankey, August 18, 1826, Brown Papers, LC; Gary L. Browne, "Business Innovation and Social Change: The Career of Alexander Brown After the War of 1812," pp. 243–55.

4. Alex Brown & Sons to William Brown, October 27, 1819, Brown Papers, LC; when writing to their New Orleans' agent, Benjamin Story, on June 5, 1826, the Browns cautioned him about overadvances: "it is better to be without consignments in the general way than have to reclaim over advances still there are some good people that it would not do to be too close with on this point this must be left to your good judgment; it is better however to risk missing a consignment than to risk losing money." Brown Papers.

5. William and Richard H. Douglass to R. H. Windsor, December 4, 1816, Douglass Letterbook, MdHS; something of the immediate effect of the peace upon general market conditions is indicated by William Rodman to Elisha Riggs, May 5, 1815: "What effect the late astonishing news from Europe may have on the market is utterly impossible to tell—its first effect however is to prevent the holders [of produce] from being willing to sell at any price. I cannot therefore at present give you much definite information as to the price your Cargo will Cost." Riggs Family Papers, LC. The importance of South America to Baltimore's trade during the first third of the nineteenth century has been greatly exaggerated. Until the 1840s, Baltimore's trade with South America was relatively small and typical of that of other American seaports. In some cases, finished and semi-finished goods, especially flour and textiles, were sent to South America, where they were exchanged for coffee, cocoa, copper, and specie, which was returned to the United States. In other cases, Baltimore merchants shipped flour and textiles to South America, where they were exchanged for silver, which was then sent on to the Far East. Very few Baltimore merchants sold muskets and powder to the South American revolutionaries (D'Arcy & Didier, possibly Joseph Karrick, and

Lemuel Taylor). The Didier, Donnell, Oliver, Pringle, and the Riggs Family Papers, LC, demonstrate how small this trade was to Baltimore's general maritime economy; cf. Bornholt, *Baltimore and Early Pan-Americanism*, passim; Frank S. Rutter, *South American Trade of Baltimore*, passim; Goebel, "British-American Rivalry in the Chilean Trade, 1817–1820," pp. 190–202.

6. The new men criticized the traditionalists for investing their profits from trade in land and not concentrating their capitals in trade; Alex Brown & Sons to William & James Brown & Company, January 25, 1823, Brown Papers, LC. Though many Baltimoreans were acquainted with Adam Smith's ideas before the 1820s, that decade marks the first time that attention was called to those newspaper editors whose point of view was Smithian. Baltimore's former Federalist party organ, the *Federal Gazette*, edited by William Gwynn, changed its name to the Baltimore *Gazette* on July 1, 1825, and on February 25, 1826, announced that Mordecai Noah of the *National Gazette*, William Coleman of the New York *Evening Post*, and Thomas Ritchie of the Richmond *Enquirer* were disciples of Adam Smith.

7. As the Browns elaborated their financial controls, for example, they developed a "rating system" for assessing the credibility of the people who bought from them; see Browne, "The Career of Alexander Brown," p. 251, note 14.

8. *Commercial Chronicle*, September 26, 1820; Scharf, *History of Baltimore*, p. 439. Founded in 1820, Baltimore's new Chamber of Commerce was modeled after New York City's institution; its membership was restricted to shipowners, merchants, presidents of insurance offices, and marine insurance brokers, but it became defunct by 1830 because of the city's commercial decline. The new men were members of the Chamber of Commerce and served as directors of such internal improvement companies as the Washington & Baltimore Turnpike Road Co., the Baltimore & Yorktown Turnpike Road Co., the Baltimore & Havre de Grace Turnpike Road Co., and the Baltimore & Reisterstown Turnpike Road Co., the Susquehanna & Patapsco Canal Co., the Maryland Iron Co., the Baltimore & Pittston Mining Co., the Susquehanna Steamboat Co., the Maryland & Virginia Steamboat Co., the Pennsylvania, Delaware & Maryland Steam Navigation Co., the Baltimore & Potomac Steam Packet Co., and the Baltimore & Rappahannock Steam Packet Co.

The most prominent of the new men were Jacob Albert; Alexander Brown; Frederick Brune; James Cox; Joseph Jamison; Talbot Jones; Peter, Nathan, and John Levering; Philip Littig; William Lorman; Leonard and William Matthews; Alexander, Robert, John, Jr., Isaac, and William D. McKim; Philip Moore; John and Joseph W. Patterson; Joseph Todhunter; Joseph Townsend; William Wilson; Edward G. Woodyear; Abraham and Charles Worthington.

9. Before the War of 1812, Baltimore's social or status elite were true *rentiers* in the sense that merchants who retired from trade put their capitals in land. The Gilmors, Christopher Hughes, Sr., James McHenry, the Olivers, and William Patterson were the most prominent names. However, as issuances of debt, monetized debt, became safe, stable, and especially regular, they became alternative investments to land for the *rentiers*. Christopher Hughes, Sr., to Jane O'Brien, October 22, 1801, Christopher Hughes Papers, UM; James McHenry to Benja-

min Stoddert, January 9, 1801, James McHenry Papers, UM; "Preliminary Introduction to the will of William Patterson," August 20, 1827, William Patterson Papers, MdHS; Robert & John Oliver's letterbooks have various references to purchases of land; one example is to Daniel Carroll, May 16, 1822, Letterbook, 1817–35, Robert Oliver Papers, MdHS.

10. John H. B. Latrobe, "Reminiscences of Baltimore in 1824," pp. 113–24. Michael McBlair, a Scotch-Irish immigrant, merchant and partner of John Hollins, whose firm failed in 1819, induced his brother-in-law, Lyde Goodwin, and Goodwin's uncle, Charles G. Ridgely, to establish the Maryland Manufacturing Company in 1823. McBlair became its manager but did not manage it profitably. After an unsuccessful attempt to hire a New England foreman as manager, McBlair's concern went into bankruptcy. Michael McBlair Papers, MdHS.

11. Organized by craft and ethnic groups, Baltimore's workingmen continued to think of their status as entrepreneurial during the 1820s, the last decade they would do so. After 1830, their demands for higher wages would stem from their being caught in an inflationary situation. When the plight of the unemployed, starving, fuelless working classes was particularly bad, the city's newspapers usually carried accounts of what the community was doing to aid them. The names of the "Managers of the Poor" can usually be identified as master craftsmen, manufacturers, or employers of some kind. Baltimore *Patriot*, April 25, 1815, March 20, 1819; Baltimore *Gazette*, January 24, 25, 1827, February 26, 1829. Baltimore also had a "Society for the Prevention of Pauperism"; *Commercial Chronicle*, February 29, 1820.

12. Baltimore *Gazette*, January 11, 13, 17, February 12, 15, 16, September 28, October 1, 1825, September 2, 3, 10, 13, 18, 24, 1826, September 6, 1828, April 7, 1829; *Laws of Maryland*, 1818, c. 93; a second such savings institution, the Maryland Savings Institution, was formed in 1826—*Laws of Maryland*, 1826, c. 195; Lyde Goodwin Diary, September 11, 20, 1826, MdHS; Scharf, *History of Baltimore*, p. 225.

13. The legal status of free blacks was virtually obliterated. Indeed, their status in Maryland law would not be altered as much between 1810 and 1861 as it was from 1796 to 1810. The foundations for the subsequent status of free blacks in Maryland were set in this earlier period. In 1796 Maryland law forbade free blacks from testifying in freedom trials; also, the first vagrancy law was passed. After 1806 any free black found in a disorderly assembly was liable to be fined or imprisoned; also, free blacks were required to obtain a permit if they possessed a firearm or a dog. After 1807 nonresident free blacks were forbidden to remain in Maryland for longer than two weeks, and those who did so were subject to a fine of ten dollars per week. After 1801 slaves could testify against free blacks charged with certain crimes, and after 1808 against free blacks charged with any crime, but not against whites. Finally, in 1809, free blacks were barred from voting in any elections in the state. James M. Wright, *The Free Negro in Maryland, 1634–1860*, pp. 95, 106, 112, 118–21.

14. At least the payment of cash wages to weavers was unique. Apparently, they received wages partly in cash and partly in store credits. Baltimore *Republican*, July 8, 1829. The winter problems of the laboring poor are mentioned in

the Baltimore *Gazette*, January 24, 25, 1827, February 26, 1829; the long commercial depression probably contributed to the realization that poverty was a continuing problem which individual voluntarism could not resolve.

15. Ordinary seamen's wages were $16.00 per month in 1829, compared with $30.00 per month during the War of 1812. During the booming years of the mid-1790s, carpenter's daily wages fluctuated between $1.50 and $2.00. Baltimore *Gazette*, January 26, 1829; Thomas Truxton to James McHenry, February 8, May 20, 1798, McHenry Papers, MdHS.

16. First Census of the United States, 1790; Second Census of the United States, 1800; Third Census of the United States, 1810; Fourth Census of the United States, 1820; Fifth Census of the United States, 1830; all Population Censuses, Record Group 29, Bureau of the Census, Department of Commerce, NA. The 1790 figures are the total for that census; the 1800 sample represents 53 percent of that census; the 1810 sample, 40 percent; the 1820 sample, 17 percent; and the 1830 sample, a little more than 50 percent.

17. Baltimore *Federal Gazette*, February 27, 1823, comments about the large numbers of free blacks coming into Baltimore; *Laws of Maryland*, 1824, c. 87; 1825, c. 161; 1826, c. 229. Though the number of free blacks and slaves declined in Baltimore after 1830, Maryland was characterized by an increasing number of free blacks and a decreasing number of slaves. Maryland's situation thus resembled Delaware's and not that of Virginia or North Carolina. The latter two states experienced increasing numbers of both free blacks and slaves. Wright, *Free Negro in Maryland*, pp. 91–3; Jeffrey R. Brackett, *The Negro in Maryland*, pp. 175–262, but especially 178–80; Penelope Campbell, *Maryland in Africa*, pp. 16–17. Richard C. Wade's conclusions about the general decline of both slaves and free blacks in *Slavery in the Cities* should be tempered by Claudia Dale Goldin, *Urban Slavery in the American South, 1820–1860*.

18. David K. Sullivan, "William Lloyd Garrison in Baltimore, 1829–1830," pp. 64–79; John L. Thomas, *The Liberator, William Lloyd Garrison: A Biography* (Boston: Little, Brown and Company, 1963), pp. 101–13; Walter M. Merrill, *Against Wind and Tide*, pp. 26–39; P. J. Staudenraus, *The African Colonization Movement, 1816–1865*, pp. 38–9; Merton L. Dillon, *Benjamin Lundy and the Struggle for Negro Freedom*, pp. 144–65; Campbell, *Maryland in Africa*, passim; Walter M. Merrill, ed., *The Letters of William Lloyd Garrison*, vol. 1, *I Will Be Heard! 1822–1835* (Cambridge, Mass.: The Belknap Press of Harvard University Press, 1971), pp. 33–41: letters numbered 33 through 40 and dated May 12 to July 14, 1830, were written from the Baltimore jail. Garrison's case (*Francis Todd v. William Lloyd Garrison*, Baltimore County Court, October Term, 1830) was reported in the Baltimore *American*, October 20, 1830.

19. Blandi, *Maryland Business Corporations*, p. 14.

20. *Commercial Chronicle*, August 23, 1821; Scharf, *History of Baltimore*, pp. 592–605, 667; Charles Varle, *A Complete View of Baltimore*, pp. 43–5.

21. Scharf, *History of Baltimore*, pp. 517–92.

22. Mark H. Haller, "The Rise of the Jackson Party in Maryland, 1820–1829," pp. 307–26; Richard P. McCormick, *The Second Party System*, pp. 19–

31, 154–65, 327–56; Whitman H. Ridgway, "McCulloch vs. the Jacksonians: Patronage and Politics in Maryland," pp. 350–62; Whitman H. Ridgway, "Community Leadership: Baltimore During the First and Second Party Systems," pp. 334–48; Whitman H. Ridgway, "A Social Analysis of Maryland Community Elites, 1827–1836: A Study of the Distribution of Power in Baltimore City, Frederick County, and Talbot County," pp. 231–59; W. Wayne Smith, "Jacksonian Democracy on the Chesapeake," *Maryland Historical Magazine* 62 (December 1967): 381–93; 63 (March 1968): 55–67; Wilbur F. Coyle, *The Mayors of Baltimore*, pp. 19–45.

23. Thomas King, *Consolidated of Baltimore, 1816–1950*, pp. 1–60; Scharf, *History of Baltimore*, pp. 500–501; *Ordinances*, April 4, 1816, March 27, 1818, February 20, 1821, March 9, 1826.

24. *Ordinances*, February 2, 10, 29, 1820; Hollander, *Financial History*, p. 116.

25. Hollander, *Financial History*, pp. 114–15; Scharf, *History of Baltimore*, p. 197; *Laws of Maryland*, 1816, cs. 193, 227, 1817, cs. 190, 195, 1818, c. 209, 1821, c. 249, 1822, c. 167.

26. *Laws of Maryland*, 1818, c. 122, 1822, c. 167; *Ordinances*, March 16, 1821, April 7, 1826, April 2, 1827; *City Council Resolutions*, February 23, 1827, February 4, 1828. A group of Baltimoreans organized themselves into a "Board of Managers for the Prevention of Pauperism in the City of Baltimore," in 1822. Observing that they were following similar organizations in Philadelphia, New York, and the Massachusetts legislature, and that they were followers of the precepts of Thomas Chalmers and Thomas Malthus, they emphasized temperance, education, and self-help in general in preference to charity. Baltimore *Patriot*, January 12, 1822. Also see Douglas G. Carroll and Blanche D. Coll, "The Baltimore Almshouse: An Early History," pp. 135–72; and Blanche D. Coll, "The Baltimore Society for the Prevention of Pauperism, 1820–1822," pp. 77–87. Like the other major American seaports, Baltimore was changing into its later nineteenth-century social forms prior to industrialization; see Raymond A. Mohl, *Poverty in New York, 1783–1825*, passim; John K. Alexander, "The City of Brotherly Fear: The Poor in Late-Eighteenth-Century Philadelphia," pp. 79–90; and David Montgomery, "The Working Classes of the Pre-Industrial American City, 1780–1830," pp. 3–22.

27. Joseph L. Arnold, "Suburban Growth and Municipal Annexation in Baltimore, 1745–1918," pp. 109–28; *Votes and Proceedings of the House of Delegates of Maryland*, November Session, 1816, pp. 103–4.

28. *Laws of Maryland*, 1817, cs. 142, 148; 1826, c. 217.

29. *Biographical Directory of the American Congress, 1774–1961* (Washington, D.C.: Government Printing Office, 1961), p. 1,346; Coyle, *Mayors of Baltimore*, pp. 27–31.

30. *Laws of Maryland*, 1817, c. 148.

31. Baltimore *American*, August 14, 20, 21, 23, 24, 27, September 2, 5, October 3, 1822; Johnson's margin of victory is erroneously printed as 18.

32. See Map 2; Baltimore *Federal Gazette*, October 4, 1820, October 3, 1822, October 2, 1824, October 3, 1826.

33. Baltimore *American*, February 11, March 12, April 26, May 2, July and September, passim, 1823, January 22, July 1, 19, August 26, September 1, 10, 15, 1824; *Niles' Weekly Register*, 24: 161, 25: 145, and especially p. 257; Livingood, *Philadelphia-Baltimore Trade Rivalry*, pp. 54–65.

34. Baltimore *Federal Gazette*, October 2, 1824; Coyle, *Mayors of Baltimore*, pp. 19–34.

35. The most important ordinances that codified market regulations were passed on January 19, February 16, March 2, 5, November 20, 1825, January 28, February 9, April 7, 12, 1826; that regulated auctions, March 5, 1825, March 16, April 6, May 31, 1826; that regulated elections, January 26, 1826; that created the Commissioners of Finance, April 3, 1826; that defined the duties of various municipal officers, January 20, February 9, March 21, April 3, 8, 9, 1826; that used deficit finance to promote the city's interest, March 5, 1825, April 3, August 31, 1826; and that illustrate Montgomery's tax policies, February 9, 18, March 1, 1825, February 8, 1826. The number of appointed municipal employees rose from 120 in 1824 to 130 in 1826, and, under Small's first administration, to 178 in 1828, City Register's Annual Reports, Baltimore City Archives; T. Courtenay J. Whedbee, *The Port of Baltimore in the Making, 1828 to 1878*, pp. 35–6.

36. Baltimore *American*, September 22, 1826.

37. Ibid., August 24, 30, September 21, 22, 29, October 3, 1826.

38. Ridgway's work, cited in note 22, above, shows the enormous personnel changes within the Jacksonian party from 1827 to 1832.

39. *Laws of Maryland*, 1827, c. 183, 1831, c. 214; Baltimore *American*, October 12, 1832; *Journal of the Proceedings of the City Council of Baltimore* [hereafter cited *Journal of the City Council*], March 16, 1831, pp. 4–5.

40. *Ordinances*, June 26, 1828, June 25, 1830; City Council *Resolutions*, March 20, 1827; Hollander, *Financial History*, p. 380. The tariff of 1828 allowed railroad companies such as the B & O to import English-made rails duty-free, and the Maysville Road Veto in 1830, which forced railroad contractors to economize as much as possible, virtually forced them to import such rails.

VI. The Commercial Revolution, 1831–1843

1. Baltimore *Gazette*, December 9, 10, 16, 23, 26, 30, 1833, January 3, 15, 18, 28, February 5, 6, 11, 12, 13, 15, 17, 18, 21, 22, 26, March 1, 6, 13, 14, 15, 22, 1834, September 1, 1837; Baltimore *Patriot*, February 16, 1839, September 27, 1842, March 31, July 11, 1843.

2. Leland H. Jenks, *The Migration of British Capital to 1875*, p. 85, estimates the total British investment in America during the 1830s at $174 million. But also see Govan, *Nicholas Biddle*, pp. 269–73; Smith, *Economic Aspects of the Second Bank*, pp. 58–59, 278–79; John M. McFaul, *The Politics of Jacksonian Finance*, pp. 115–16; North, *Economic Growth*, pp. 69–71; Peter Temin, *The Jacksonian Economy*, pp. 59–112; Thomas D. Willett, "International Specie Flows and American Monetary Stability, 1834–1860," pp. 28–50; George

Macesich, "Sources of Monetary Disturbances in the United States, 1834–
1845," pp. 407–34; Jeffrey G. Williamson, "International Trade and United
States Economic Development, 1827–1843," pp. 372–83; Jeffrey Williamson,
American Growth and the Balance of Payments, 1820–1913, pp. 99–111; Guy
S. Callender, "Early Transportation and Banking Enterprises of the States in
Relation to the Growth of Corporations," pp. 143–46; Paul M. O'Leary, "The
Coinage Legislation of 1834," pp. 80–94.

3. Browne, "Baltimore in the Nation," Figures 8 and 9, Tables 2, 3, 5–9, 11–
17 in Appendix B. The information about Baltimore's market conditions from
January 1831 through March 1838 can be followed from the weekly market
reports found in the city's newspapers, particularly the Baltimore *American*; in
April 1838, the Baltimore *Price Current* again began publication and can be used
through 1843 (it continues to June 17, 1854).

4. Baltimore's trade to the West Indies did increase absolutely after October
1830, when the British opened their colonial possessions there to American
ships. The Baltimoreans cited this, of course, as evidence of their "astonishing
prosperity" (Baltimore *Gazette*, April 14, 29, 1831); however, nothing was said
when this trade fell off again in 1832, after the initial rush was over.

5. Until the opening of the British West Indies to Americans, British shippers
had the clear advantage of the triangular trade between Europe, the United
States, and the West Indies. By monopolizing their West Indies trade, British
shippers were guaranteed a back freight to England and could thus freight goods
from England to the United States more cheaply than could their American competitors, who had little back freight and who were excluded from the British
West Indies. Accordingly, American shippers looked upon the opening of the
West Indies to Americans as an attempt by the British to dominate the cotton
trade by making their West Indies possessions the reexport center for American
cotton, just as New York City was becoming. Ever since 1828, when the British
Parliament had reduced the duty on cotton hauled by a British ship from a British colony to England, British shippers had steadily increased their share of the
American cotton trade. They were, moreover, carrying the American cotton to
the British West Indies, where it was then reexported to England. American
shippers who carried cotton from American ports directly to England were not
able to compete with the British shippers, who paid far lower duties on American
cotton in England. The opening of the British West Indies to American shippers
was, in part, the effort of British shippers to have Americans haul cotton to the
British colonies, where it would then be reexported to England in British ships.
The British idea behind this policy was to revive the declining importance of its
West Indies possessions. Though this goal was not achieved, the policy did suc-
ceed in undercutting American shipping competition. Alex Brown & Sons to Wil-
liam & James Brown & Company, October 10, 1828, Brown Papers, LC; Jenks,
Migration of British Capital, p. 69; Timothy Pitkin, *A Statistical View of the
Commerce of the United States of America*, pp. 189–213; Benns, *American
Struggle for West Indian Trade*, pp. 185–88.

The passage of the Railroad Iron Bill on July 14, 1832, was extremely helpful
to the general railroad expansion in America during the 1830s. Under its pro-

visions, a state or corporation engaged in railway construction was allowed a drawback on the 25 percent ad valorem duty paid on imported (chiefly from Great Britain) iron, provided that the iron was used within three years of the time of importation. Since American iron manufacturers could not possibly furnish enough iron to the railroads—they furnished about one-third of the iron used by American railroads; besides, their products were far inferior to those of the British—American railroads had been forced to import their iron. But after July 1832, American railroads saved from $16.25 to $18.75 per ton duty on imported iron, depending upon its quality. This act, which amended section nine of the Tariff Act of 1830, was steered through Congress by Samuel Smith, then senator and chairman of the Committee on Finance; *Register of Debates in Congress*, 22nd Cong., 1st sess., May 31, 1832, pp. 990–91. British rails thus played a key role in the expansion of American internal improvements during the 1830s, as much as British credit and gold did. See Lewis H. Haney, *A Congressional History of Railways in the United States, 1850–1887*, 1: 132–51; Cleveland and Powell, *Railroad Promotion and Capitalization*, pp. 240–41.

6. The building boom of the middle thirties, the expansion of the city, and the increase in immigration fed the inflation of the decade as much as the sense of prosperity did after the West Indies were opened to American shipping.

7. The Franklin Woolen Factory did not make any profits in 1828–29 (Thomas Wilson to the President and Directors of the Bank of the United States, Baltimore Branch, May 19, 1829, Bank of the United States, Baltimore Branch, Papers, LC), and the Warren Cotton Factory, with an estimated net worth of $450,000, was broke in July 1829. Samuel Moele and Reverdy Johnson to [Jonathan Meredith?], July 13, 1829, Jonathan Meredith Papers, LC.

8. For Baltimore's response to the cholera epidemic, see the Baltimore *Gazette*, July 9, 10, 11, 18, August 8, 9, September 28, 1832.

9. Phillip E. Thomas to General James Thomas, January 9, 1834, Pike & Neale to General James Thomas, March 25, May 3, 1834, Thomas Family Papers, MdHR; William Hindman to Edward Lloyd, December 27, 1833, Lloyd Papers, MdHS; Frederick W. Brune to George C. Shattuck, March 21, May 3, 1834, Brune-Randall Papers, MdHS; Samuel H. Bell to James Martin Bell, March 26, 1834 [misdated 1833], James Martin Bell Papers, DU; Alex Brown & Sons to Benjamin Story, May 23, 1834, Campbell & McIlvaine to William Baxter, January 21, 1834, to Edelsten & Price, March 1, 1834, to Donald McIlvaine, March 20, 29, April 4, 14, May 5, 1834, to D. F. Manice, March 25, 1834, to Boorman, Johnston & Co., March 27, 1834, Brown Papers, LC; Baltimore *Gazette*, March 24, 25, 26, 27, 29, April 2, 3, 4, 8, May 7, 10, 23, June 6, 7, 11, 13, 16, 17, 19, 23, July 2, 5, 7, 8, 14, 21, 22, 24, 25, 30, August 6, 7, 1834.

10. The historiography of Andrew Jackson's "Bank War" is virtually equal to the war itself. Descriptions of the "Bank War" in Baltimore can be found in Hammond, *Banks and Politics*, pp. 414–15, 419–21, 431–32; Davis R. Dewey, *Financial History of the United States*, pp. 198–212; M. Grace Madeleine, *Monetary and Banking Theories of Jacksonian Democracy*, pp. 52–8, 69–70; Frank Otto Gatell, "Spoils of the Bank War: Political Bias in the Selection of Pet Banks," pp. 35–58; Frank Otto Gatell, "Secretary Taney and the Baltimore

Pets: A Study in Banking and Politics," pp. 205–27; Robert V. Remini, *Andrew Jackson and the Bank War*, passim; Carl B. Swisher, *Roger B. Taney*, pp. 160–290; Walker Lewis, *Without Fear or Favor: A Biography of Chief Justice Roger Brooke Taney*, pp. 129–201; McFaul, *Jacksonian Finance*, p. 24; Redlich, *American Banking*, 1: 162–77; Govan, *Nicholas Biddle*, chaps. 13–25; Smith, *Economic Aspects of the Second Bank*, chap. 10; Catterall, *Second Bank of the United States*, pp. 164–358; Harry N. Scheiber, "The Pet Banks in Jacksonian Politics and Finance, 1833–1841," pp. 196–214; Edward Pessen, *Jacksonian America*, pp. 328–36; Temin, *Jacksonian Economy*, chap. 2; Schlesinger, *Age of Jackson*, chaps. 7–10; Reginald C. McGrane, *The Panic of 1837*, pp. 70–90; and Stuart Bruchey, ed., "Roger Brooke Taney's Account of His Relations with Thomas Ellicott in the Bank War," *Maryland Historical Magazine* 52 (March 1958): 58–74, and (June 1958): 131–52.

A general treatment of the entire problem of "contractions" and "depressions" throughout the antebellum period is J. R. T. Hughes and Nathan Rosenberg, "The United States Business Cycle Before 1860: Some Problems of Interpretation," pp. 476–93; and Clark Warburton has investigated the business cycle in much the same way in "Variations in Economic Growth and Banking Developments in the United States from 1835 to 1855," pp. 283–97; and an excellent source of information about other general economic trends that encompassed the Jacksonian economy is the series of articles in *Trends in the American Economy in the Nineteenth Century*.

11. William McIlvaine to John White, April 21, 1832, John White to William McIlvaine, May 5, 1832, John White Papers, MdHS.

12. Alex Brown & Sons to Benjamin Story, May 23, 1834, Brown Papers, LC; John Spencer Bassett, ed., *Correspondence of Andrew Jackson*, 5: 49–52; and the most pertinent manuscript information is in the Morris, John M. Gordon, William P. Preston, and Perine Papers, all in the MdHS, and in the Brown, Jonathan Meredith, and Roger B. Taney Papers, all in the LC; Baltimore *Gazette*, March 24, 25, 27, 29, April 2, 3, 4, 8, May 10, 23, June 6, 7, 11, 13, 16, 17, 19, 23, July 2, 5, 7, 8, 14, 21, 24, 25, 30, August 6, 7, 1834, February 9, 10, 18, March 5, 19, 21, 25, June 18, 23, 24, 25, 27, 28, 29, 30, July through October 22, 1836; Baltimore *American*, July 25, 1834; *Commercial Chronicle*, August 17, 22, 24, September 2, 8, 11, 14, 1835, February 11, November 2, 1836; Baltimore *Republican*, March 14, 16, 24, 26, April 1, 9, 10, 11, 13, May 4, 5, 12, August 10, 1835; Baltimore *Patriot*, March 25, April 1, 21, July 15, 22, 26, August 4, 5, 6, 7, 8, 1834, August 4, 5, September 3, 7, October 1, 2, 3, 5, 14, 17, December 2, 17, 22, 1835.

13. The statistics of Baltimore's trade are charted in Browne, "Baltimore in the Nation," pp. 131–32, 213–14, 233, 319, and tabulated in Appendix B, pp. 481–517.

14. New Orleans *Price Current*, April 9, 1836, found in the Jackson, Riddle & Co. Papers, UNCL; Temin, *Jacksonian Economy*, pp. 33–36, 68–112; Jenks, *Migration of British Capital*, pp. 74–98; McGrane, *Panic of 1837*, pp. 12–64.

15. Thomas H. Benton, *Thirty Years View*, 1: 436–58; Jenks, *Migration of British Capital*, pp. 81–88; Smith, *Economic Aspects of the Second Bank*, pp.

58–59, 278–79 note 31; Temin, *Jacksonian Economy*, pp. 65–66; O'Leary, "Coinage Legislation of 1834," pp. 80–94; Reginald C. McGrane, *Foreign Bondholders and American State Debts*, pp. 12–14.

16. McGrane, *Panic of 1837*, chaps. 4, 6, 7; Govan, *Nicholas Biddle*, pp. 299–407; Hammond, *Banks and Politics*, pp. 451–99; Ralph W. Hidy, *The House of Baring in American Trade and Finance*, chaps. 9–12; Jenks, *Migration of British Capital*, pp. 65–125; Smith, *Economic Aspects of the Second Bank*, pp. 28–30, 35–36, 59–63, 89–96.

17. The effect of this new international alignment upon Baltimore was important. Dissatisfied with the stoppage of the Baltimore & Ohio Railroad at Harpers Ferry, many prominent Baltimoreans met in an "Internal Improvement Convention" in May 1836. Confronted with the facts that the Maryland Court of Appeals had already decided that the Chesapeake and Ohio Canal had the right of way over the railroad, and that the railroad had no more funds to continue construction, the Convention demanded that the community assume greater control over the railroad. The railroad thus became a quasi-public company when it was subsequently funded by the bonded debts of both the municipality of Baltimore and the state of Maryland. These bonds were sold in the British capital markets, and the railroad's board of directors was enlarged to accommodate appointments by the city and state. Naturally, an entirely new administration of the Baltimore & Ohio entered their offices in July 1836.

18. These six banks began operations almost immediately; but four others were also chartered in anticipation of the demise of the Bank of the United States; however, they could not raise sufficient capital to begin operations before the depression struck; *Laws of Maryland*, 1834, c. 210, 1835, cs. 251, 287, 289, 298, 313, 314, 315, 317, 320.

19. The following newspaper accounts detail the tightening money situation in general and describe how the panic spread toward Baltimore: *Commercial Chronicle*, March 22, April 5, 11, 19, 26, May 3, 1837; Baltimore *American*, March 29, 30, April 2, 5, 12, May 12, 1837; Baltimore *Patriot*, January 24, February 2, 13, 21, 22, 28, March 5, 29, May 8, 11, 16, 19, 23, June 4, 1838, April 10, 16, 1839; Baltimore *Gazette*, January 27, March 13, 27, April 1, 3, 8, 12, 13, 21, 22, 24, 27, May 1, 5, 6, 8, 10, 11, 12, 13, 20, 22, 23, 26, 30, June 21, 28, July 29, August 8, 24, September 1, 2, November 24, 25, 30, December 11, 28, 1837. Individual merchants' comments about the deflation from 1837 to 1843 are too numerous to list, but the most important collections that describe its progress in Baltimore are: the George Peabody Papers, EI; the Riggs Family Papers and the Brown Papers, LC; the Baring Brothers Papers, PAC; the Perine Papers, Brune-Randall Papers, Tyson Family Papers, Partridge Family Papers, Richard Dorsey Papers, Howard Family Papers, and John M. Gordon Diary, all in MdHS; the Richard Hallet Townsend Diary, EPL; the Robert Garrett & Sons Papers, LC; and the Thomas Family Papers, MdHR. Everyone seemed to remember the depression as one of the worst in Baltimore's history, probably because the suspension of specie payments by the banks dried up the small-denomination paper money, leaving society at large with no means of paying its everyday ex-

penses. Attempts were made by the city and the Baltimore & Ohio Railroad Company to print and circulate fractional currency, whose denominational values ranged from five cents to two dollars, but such currency quickly depreciated and only compounded the city's problems. Also see Jenks, *Migration of British Capital*, pp. 65–98; Govan, *Nicholas Biddle*, pp. 205–13, 244–74, 295–345; Hammond, *Banks and Politics*, pp. 326–495; Temin, *Jacksonian Economy*, passim; Smith, *Economic Aspects of the Second Bank*, pp. 34–36, 40–59, 76–96, 147–230; North, *Economic Growth*, pp. 189–203; McGrane, *Panic of 1837*, chap. 9; Hidy, *House of Baring*, part 2.

20. Statistics illustrating the revival of Baltimore's trade during the deflation are in Browne, "Baltimore in the Nation," pp. 481–517; United States Treasury Department, *Annual Report on the State of the Finances, 1837–1843*, 4: 1–647; the Franklin Bank failed on January 2, 1841, and was the city's only bank failure during the entire deflation; Baltimore *Clipper*, April 23, May 6, 9, 22, 26, June 5, 1840, January 8, 11, 17, 24, 26, 28, 31, February 1, 3, 8, 9, 1842; Baltimore *Patriot*, April 29, July 31, August 3, September 4, 10, 12, 23, November 26, 27, December 11, 1840, January 1, 9, 13, 14, 23, 25, February 1, March 9, October 21, 28, November 5, 6, 8, 11, 13, 16, 18, 29, 30, December 1, 10, 14, 17, 1841, June 10, September 10, 12, November 24, 1842, January 6, 7, March 15, 16, April 17, 26, June 1, 19, 28, 1843; Baltimore *Republican*, February 15, 17, 23, 28, 1842; Robert Garrett & Sons to George Wilson, January 2, 9, 23, June 1, 16, 1841, to C. C. Wolcott, January 2, 1841, to Henry J. Lippincott, January 8, 1841, to A. Reed, January 13, 1841, Letterbook B, Robert Garrett & Sons Papers, LC; John R. Ricards to George Peabody, August 13, September 10, 20, 22, 27, 1841, William C. Shaw to George Peabody, June 22, 1838, Tiffany, Duvall & Co. to George Peabody, June 22, 1838, Peabody, Riggs & Co. to George Peabody, April 22, March 6, 1837, February 14, 1838, January 30, 1839, February 15, March 16, 17, 28, April 28, May 7, 30, June 11, 17, 27, July 29, November 15, 28, December 5, 1840, January 11, 16, July 13, August 5, 28, September 11, 23, 28, October 28, November 20, 28, 1841, Samuel Riggs to George Peabody, October 12, November 12, 20, December 11, 1841, April 14, 1838, Henry T. Jenkins to George Peabody, July 12, 13, 17, 29, August 5, 1841, John R. Ricards to George Peabody, January 11, 1842, George Peabody Papers, EI.

An important dimension to the financial depression, especially with regard to the panic of 1839, was the appearance of the *means* of investment banking during the late 1830s. The issuance of Treasury Notes by the federal government and of Post Notes by Biddle's Bank of the United States allowed banks to shift slightly from commercial to investment banking which were safer investments. The United States Treasury Department, for example, had far more applications for Treasury Notes than were necessary. The importance of this was that the banks and financiers now purchased these paper issues instead of businessmen's paper and thus reduced the credit facilities available to businessmen. Such policies would extend the already depressed financial conditions. A key figure was William Wilson Corcoran, financier and private banker, whose path to millions lay through his friendships with the various appointed officials in the Treasury

Department from the mid-1830s through the 1850s. For specific references to the demand for Treasury and Post Notes by financiers and bankers, especially in reference to the developing panic of 1839, see W. W. Corcoran to Elisha Riggs, January 31, May 25, 29, 30, June 22, September 20, 23, October 19, 1839, Riggs Family Papers, LC.

21. Baltimore *Gazette*, November 15, 23, 1837; Baltimore *Patriot*, February 6, March 31, 1838, April 3, May 4, July 31, September 4, December 11, 1840, May 7, 11, 12, 15, November 20, 26, 1841, April 21, September 16, 1842. Altogether, eight savings institutions were created for Baltimore's workingmen; *Laws of Maryland*, 1831, c. 211, 1832, cs. 18, 33, 46, 90, 140, 1833, c. 27, 1838, c. 143.

22. The 1842 panic can be followed in the Baltimore *American*, the *Clipper*, the *Gazette*, the *Patriot*, and the *Republican* from January through June; but also see James Owings to Elisha Riggs, January 8, 1842, Samuel Riggs to Elisha Riggs, March 1, 3, 7, 9, 10, 11, 12, 15, 17, 18, 23, 26, 30, 31, April 6, May 17, 1842, Peabody, Riggs & Co. to Riggs, Aertsen & Co., May 30, 1842, Riggs Family Papers, LC; Samuel Riggs to George Peabody, January 28, December 3, 1842, Peabody, Riggs & Co. to George Peabody, January 10, February 5, 12, 26, March 5, 7, 12, 17, 29, April 4, 11, 26, May 7, 14, 28, June 28, July 13, 29, August 13, 27, 30, September 13, 27, October 11, 13, 29, November 15, 28, December 13, 28, 1842, Henry T. Jenkins to George Peabody, August 9, September 30, 1842, Peabody Papers, EI; Arthur L. Simms to Richard Dorsey, July 8, 1842, Richard Dorsey Papers, MdHS; William R. Steuart to General James Thomas, March 5, 1842, Henry W. Thomas to General James Thomas, April 9, 1842, Thomas Family Papers, MdHR; Alex Brown & Sons to William & James Brown & Company, January 4, 16, 17, 27, March 5, 16, 27, April 5, 1842, on March 11 they wrote to the same firm: "Every thing continues very gloomy and money matters getting worse daily. We view the times here far worse than in 1837 [.] failures are occurring and there must be many in the next 60 days." Also see Alex Brown & Sons to George Cleveland, Jr., January 3, May 7, 1842, to Southgate & Co., January 21, 1842, to Samuel Nicholson, February 9, March 9, April 12, 1842, to Maxwell, Wright & Co., February 24, 1842, to William Fowle & Son, March 7, 8, 1842, to James Birckhead, March 11, 1842, to George B. Cumming, March 30, 1842, Brown Papers, LC; John McTavish to the Earl of Aberdeen, August 10, 1842, British Consular Reports, PAC; Goodrich and Segal, "Baltimore's Aid to Railroads," pp. 8–9.

23. The reduction of bank notes in circulation was, of course, a hardship for the community, and curtailing the circulating medium upset existing social arrangements. The problem was remedied to a certain extent by the circulation of "shinplasters"—certificates issued by the Baltimore & Ohio Railroad Company in denominations from $.125 to $100.00, each bearing the inscription, "When presented in amounts of $100. and over, these certificates will be redeemed by the Baltimore & Ohio Railroad Company in Baltimore City stock, drawing six per cent." Over $500,000.00 worth of these certificates were issued from 1837 to 1838. Hungerford, *Baltimore & Ohio*, 1: 191.

24. Baltimore *Clipper*, January 3, 1842; a description of Maryland's manufacturers was not included in Louis McLane's report in 1832 (*United States
Treasury Department, Documents Relative to the Manufactures in the United
States, Collected and Transmitted to the House of Representatives, in Compli-
ance with a Resolution of January 19, 1832, by the Secretary of the Secretary of
the Treasury*). McLane had asked John Pendleton Kennedy, lawyer, novelist,
future Whig politician, and son-in-law of Edward Gray, owner of one of the largest textile-factory enclaves just outside of Baltimore, to compile such a report,
but, apparently, Kennedy never did; John Pendleton Kennedy to Elizabeth Gray
Kennedy, February 13, 1832, John Pendleton Kennedy Papers, GPI.

25. John H. O'Donnell, son of John O'Donnell, represented Baltimore's merchants on Caleb Cushing's mission to open the China trade up to Americans in
1843; Baltimore *Patriot*, May 29, 1843; also see citations in note 23.

26. They had such names as the Liberty Copper Company, the Maryland and
New York Iron and Coal Company, the Mineral Company of Baltimore, the Baltimore Print Company, the Baltimore Resinous Cloth and Carpet Manufacturing
Company, and the Baltimore & Chesapeake Steam Saw Mill Co. Baltimoreans
had formed the first mining corporation in Maryland's history in 1828 (William
Lorman, William Gwynn, and Ashton Alexander were behind the Baltimore and
Pittston Coal Company; *Laws of Maryland*, 1828, c. 57), and, after this, the
1830s witnessed a sudden growth of enterprises connected with the chemical
and mineral bases of industrialization. Probably in response to this flurry, Maryland passed its first incorporation law for manufacturing enterprises in 1838.
This law was very general—it did not specify, for example, limited liability or
nonlimited liability; that decision was left up to the incorporators—and mainly
aimed at establishing state authority over such corporate bodies. For example,
the state could now repeal or alter any charter; all charters were limited to a
thirty-year life; and the books and properties of such companies were subject to
inspection by the state legislature (*Laws of Maryland*, 1838, c. 267, particularly
sections 16 and 17). For the charters of companies formed during the 1830s, see
Laws of Maryland, 1831, c. 102, 110, 1832, c. 82, 1834, cs. 52, 144, 152, 243,
1835, c. 304, 1836, c. 96, 1837, cs. 61, 218, 221, 307, 1838, cs. 350, 408, 1839,
cs. 308, 338; also see the numerous letters between Roswell Lyman Colt and
James William McCulloh, on the one hand, and Duff Green, on the other, during
1836–39, in the Duff Green Papers, UNCL.

27. Richard Townsend Diary, 1: 198–200, 244, 246–83; John McTavish to
Lord Palmerston, May 12, 23, 1837, October 25, 1839, April 30, 1841, British
Consular Reports, PAC; Baltimore *Gazette*, May 30, June 28, July 21, 29, September 4, November 15, 23, December 28, 1837; Baltimore *American*, April 20,
1839; Baltimore *Clipper*, March 15, April 6, October 29, November 12, 22, 23,
December 4, 10, 1841, January 3, 1842; Baltimore *Republican*, February 22, 23,
1842; Baltimore *Patriot*, February 6, March 2, 31, May 8, 16, 1838, April 10,
1839, April 29, May 4, 20, June 3, July 31, September 4, November 26, 27,
December 11, 1840, April 7, 10, 12, 13, May 7, 11, 12, 15, November 20, 23,
26, 30, December 21, 1841, April 21, May 18, 20, 27, 31, September 13, 16,

October 25, November 26, 1842, March 16, 17, 31, April 5, 14, 17, 26, May 16, June 28, July 19, 1843; and William McConkey, Jr. to Christopher Hughes, February 4, 1843, Christopher Hughes Papers, UM.

VII. The Passing of the Old Order

1. The contradictions resulted mainly from the commingling of the dominant Quaker, Presbyterian, English Methodist, Scotch, and Scotch-Irish traditions of Baltimore's elite, together with their changing circumstances. Every society tries to overcome its changing realities by explaining them in terms of its own value system, and that is what happened in Baltimore during the 1830s. Laissez faire economy and society were simply self-help and self-reliant individualism writ large. Likewise, temperance and education were projected from the individual or particular to the universal or social—and, thus, from the private to the public.

2. Whedbee, *Port of Baltimore*, pp. 29−44.

3. *Laws of Maryland*, 1831, c. 288, 1834, c. 202, 1836, c. 298; Baltimore *Gazette*, July 2, 1832, September 3, 9−12, 15, 25, November 5, 6, 8, 10, 22, December 5, 8−12, 1834, March 4, 11, 12, 15, 16, 22, April 1, 2, 6, 13, 14, 16, May 2−5, 9−11, June 3, 4, 7−10, 13, 16, July 13, August 5, September 13, 1836; the Jacksonian city officials memorialized the state legislature to prevent the construction of the Baltimore & Ohio Railroad in the city, Baltimore *Republican*, March 19, 1835.

4. *Laws of Maryland*, 1831, cs. 148, 166, 1833, c. 95, 1835, cs. 40, 244, 1838, c. 83, 1839, c. 328, 1840, c. 167, 1843, cs. 158, 365; Alexander Crosby Brown, *Steam Packets on the Chesapeake*, pp. 8−36; Robert H. Burgess and H. Graham Wood, *Steamboats Out of Baltimore*, pp. xvii−xx, 1−40, 147−48, 159−60, 210.

5. Blandi, *Maryland Business Corporations*, pp. 11−12, 15, 32, 99−102, 314; the number of houses built in Baltimore each year from 1834 to 1840 was taken from the Mayor's Annual Messages; they were 583 for 1834, 607 for 1836, 412 for 1836, 368 for 1837, 366 for 1838, 465 for 1839.

6. Mayer, *Baltimore*, pp. 255−74, 511−16; Ferdinand C. Latrobe, *Iron Men and Their Dogs*, pp. 1−10.

7. William Hindman to Edward Lloyd, April 29, 1833, Lloyd Papers, MdHS; Joshua Bates to Henry Mildmay, May 13, 1841, Baring Bros. & Co., PAC; Henry Partridge to John Partridge, May 9, 1837, Partridge Family Papers, MdHS.

8. After Robert Oliver died in 1834, leaving an estate of about $2.3 million, David M. Perine, who had drawn up Oliver's will, asked Charles, one of Robert's two sons, if he intended to reside in America; Charles replied "that he intended to live abroad, because a man in this country who had no occupation was not favorably regarded, and, as his friends were usually business men, if he wanted to see them he would have to interrupt them at their offices; whereas, abroad numbers of men were men of leisure and could be found at their clubs or homes at almost any hours." W. P. memorandum, n.d., "Oliver Family," Perine Papers,

MdHS; David M. Perine to Robert Morgan Gibbes, March 11, 1841, Perine Papers; Samuel Smith to Christopher Hughes, June 25, 1833, William McConkey, Jr., to Christopher Hughes, February 4, 1843, January 20, February 23, March 27, December 26, 1844, Christopher Hughes Papers, UM; Samuel Riggs, on behalf of Peabody, Riggs & Co., to Elisha Riggs, January 1, 1838, February 1, 3, 5, 10, 19, 1838, December 10, 1839, January 1, 1841, James Owings to Elisha Riggs, January 8, 17, March 1, 3, 1842, Riggs Family Papers, LC; some Baltimoreans, like John Barney and Samuel Riggs, speculated in the new Treasury Notes (their premiums fluctuated with the price of gold). W. W. Corcoran to Elisha Riggs, December 10, 1837, April 11, September 20, 1838, May 30, 1839, Riggs Family Papers.

9. *Journal of the City Council*, March 14, 1839, pp. 329–30; Fisher, *Gazeteer*, p. 29.

10. Figures for annual new home construction come from the Mayor's Annual Messages; also see Royal Makepeace, *Report on the Objects, Condition and Prospects of the Canton Company of Baltimore*, passim.

11. Mayer, *Baltimore*, pp. 89–90.

12. *Journal of the City Council*, November 14, 1833, p. 3; April 17, 1834, pp. 328–30.

13. Ibid., March 24, April 21, 1831, pp. 179–81, 229–34; March 19, 27, July 2, 3, 1834, pp. 6–8, 228–32, 260; March 12, 16, 17, 18, 19, 26, 30, 31, April 6, 20, 1835, pp. 215–18, 223–26, 235–45, 251–53, 259–73, 298–99, 308–11, 318–19, 337–38, 368–71.

14. Ibid., April 4, 1831, pp. 151–53.

15. Ibid., January 24, February 22, March 26, 1833, pp. 78–79, 128, 188–90; April 24, 1834, pp. 341–42; February 16, 1835, p. 130.

16. This information has been compiled from the records of the City Assessor's Office, the City Register's Office, and the City Collector's Office, Department of Legislative Reference, BCH.

17. Scharf, *History of Baltimore City and County*, pp. 192–93.

18. *Journal of the City Council*, February 9, 19, 1835, pp. 108, 140; Mayor's Annual Message, 1835.

19. Milton Reizenstein, *Economic History of the Baltimore and Ohio Railroad, 1827–1853*, pp. 85–86; *Laws of Maryland*, 1835, c. 127; *Ordinances*, April 26, 1836, April 10, 12, 1837, February 24, April 11, May 19, November 4, 1838, August 28, 1839, April 18, 1840; *City Council Resolutions*, March 17, 1836, April 10, 1837, February 27, March 10, 1838; Scharf, *History of Baltimore*, p. 343; William Bruce Catton, "John W. Garrett of the Baltimore & Ohio," pp. 26–29.

20. *City Council Resolutions*, April 6, 1829, April 8, 1830, February 16, 1832, February 26, 1833, April 3, 1838.

21. *Laws of Maryland*, 1840, c. 63; *Ordinances*, March 9, 1841; *City Council Resolutions*, January 16, 1841.

22. *Fourteenth Annual Report* [October 1840] of *the President and Board of Directors to the Stockholders of the Baltimore and Ohio Railroad Company*;

City Council Resolutions, February 9, 1841; Reizenstein, *Economic History of the Baltimore & Ohio*, pp. 46–47; Baltimore *American*, October 20, 1840; *Journal of the City Council*, January 4, 1841, pp. 19–20.

23. *Fifteenth Annual Report* [October 1841] *of the President and Board of Directors to the Stockholders of the Baltimore and Ohio Railroad Company*; *City Council Resolutions*, March 17, 1842; Reizenstein, *Economic History of the Baltimore & Ohio*, pp. 47–48; Mayor's Annual Message, January 16, 1843; Baltimore *American*, March 5, 1842.

24. *City Council Resolutions*, April 24, 1833; *Ordinances*, April 19, 1834, February 20, 1835.

25. *Ordinances*, March 9, 1841.

26. Mayor's Annual Message, January 5, 1835; *Ordinances*, May 23, 1838, February 12, 1839, February 9, 1841.

27. *City Council Resolutions*, April 10, 1838, February 13, 1840; *Ordinance*, February 26, 1842; Scharf, *History of Baltimore*, pp. 240–1.

28. Scharf, *History of Baltimore*, pp. 216–17; Blake, *Water for the Cities*, pp. 223–33.

29. *Laws of Maryland*, 1830, c. 64, 1833, c. 35; *City Council Resolutions*, April 16, 1835; *Ordinance*, February 15, 1839.

VIII. Industrialization and Triumphant Commercialism

1. Richard Townsend Diary, 1: 336, 339, 344–46, 351, 361, 369, 375–78, EPL; Corcoran & Riggs to Elisha Riggs, January 2, March 30, April 14, August 6, 13, December 30, 1846, December 10, 1847, to John J. Palmer, March 30, 1846, Riggs Family Papers, LC; Samuel Ward to Joshua Bates, January 16, 1847, Prime, Ward & King to Baring Brothers & Co., February 28, 1846, March 31, 1847, Corcoran & Riggs to Baring Brothers & Co., November 26, 1849, Howland & Aspinwall to Joshua Bates, March 31, 1847, Ward, Campbell & Co. to Baring Brothers & Co., December 10, 14, 1853, Baring Brothers Papers, PAC; Clark, *Grain Trade in Old Northwest*, chaps. 8, 10, 13. The general proposition of this chapter is similar to that argued by Scott Gordon in "The London *Economist* and the High Tide of Laissez-Faire," pp. 461–88, which is that the economic expansion of the late 1840s and 1850s convinced English liberals of the "truth" of their ideas about business and economics.

2. Samuel Riggs to Elisha Riggs, December 31, 1846, January 23, March 8, 11, 15, 17, April 5, 6, May 4, 24, June 15, November 9, 1847, Riggs Family Papers, LC; Samuel Riggs to George Peabody, June 29, July 20, 1844, July 14, 1845, Henry T. Jenkins to George Peabody, June 29, July 30, August 15, 1844, January 8, 14, 31, 1845, Peabody, Riggs & Co. to George Peabody, October 31, 1844, February 17, 1845, Peabody Papers, EI; the Baltimore *Price Current* provides the most complete data about Baltimore's markets from January 1844 through June 1854. From June 1854 through 1860, this information can be found in the weekly market reports published in the newspapers (the Baltimore *American* and *Sun*

provide the best coverage), and annual reviews of the Baltimore markets were published each January by the *American* and the *Sun*.

3. John McTavish to Lord Palmerston, September 25, 1848, British Consular Reports, PAC; Oelrichs & Lurman to Thomas Wren Ward, September 20, 1844, Baring Brothers Papers, PAC; John Pendleton Kennedy to Elizabeth Gray Kennedy, December 12, 1844, Kennedy Papers, GPI; Alex Brown & Sons to Brown Brothers & Co., July 8, 1852, Brown Papers, LC; *Annual Report of the President and Directors of the Corn and Flour Exchange*, 1856; Baltimore *Patriot*, October 20, 1845, August 24, 26, September 30, 1846, February 18, March 2, 5, 16, June 1, August 7, September 18, November 8, 12, 1847; Baltimore *Sun*, January 5, March 3, August 5, 19, 1848, February 14, March 9, July 31, October 1, November 8, 1850, February 14, 28, July 4, August 8, October 6, December 28, 29, 1853; January 28, February 14, March 16, April 10, 21, 22, May 6, June 15, September 14, 1854, January 25, February 28, March 1, September 12, 27, 1855, March 14, 1856, January 2, February 28, May 21, 1857; Baltimore *Republican*, March 15, April 5, 26, 1849, April 3, May 17, 26, 1852. American-made textiles had long been out-competing British-made textiles in the Far East and South America; Clark, *History of Manufactures*, 1: 360–63, 550; John Montgomery, *A Practical Detail of the Cotton Manufacture of the United States of America*, pp. 194–95; on p. 125, Montgomery demonstrates how the cost of American cotton manufacturers was 3 percent less than the British cost of production, because the greater cost of handling to the British manufacturer more than offset his low cost of production, even though his cost of production was much lower than that of his American competitor. Such demonstrations made clear to American textile manufacturers at the time that they shared an interest with American shippers in maintaining this higher transportation cost to the British. The European, chiefly British, events of the period are discussed by H. G. Lewin, *The Railway Mania and Its Aftermath, 1845–1852*; Cecil Woodham-Smith, *The Great Hunger*; G. M. Young, *Early Victorian England, 1830–1865*; R. C. O. Matthews, *A Study in Trade Cycle History*; Checkland, *Industrial Society in England*, pp. 352–62; G. Kitson Clark, "The Repeal of the Corn Laws and the Politics of the Forties," pp. 1–13; and E. J. Hobsbawm, *The Age of Revolution, 1789–1848*, pp. 27–52, 168–216.

4. John McTavish to Lord Palmerston, September 25, 1848, January 9, 1850, to the Earl of Aberdeen, October 25, 1844, May 5, 1846, British Consular Reports, PAC; Richard Townsend Diary, 1: 320, 325, EPL; Oelrichs & Lurman to Baring Brothers & Co., August 13, 1844, January 4, May 13, November 25, 1850, September 26, 1853, January 30, 1854, April 17, June 12, November 27, 1855, November 7, 21, 1856, November 14, 1857, February 22, May 11, September 20, 1858, September 27, 1859, September 3, 1860, to Thomas Baring, February 7, 1859, Baring Brothers Papers, PAC; Baltimore *Patriot*, November 28, 1843, March 10, October 29, December 7, 1844; Foster Rhea Dulles, *The Old China Trade*, pp. 110–22, discusses the first full-rigged clipper ship, the *Ann McKim*, on pp. 118–19, but omits that the ship was built by Isaac McKim of Baltimore, merchant, political protégé of Samuel Smith, and representative to

Congress as a Jacksonian Democrat from 1823 to 1825 and again from 1833 to 1838. The ship was named after his wife, Ann Bowly McKim.

5. Samuel Riggs to Elisha Riggs, January 17, 19, February 10, March 14, May 8, November 28, December 11, 14, 1844, February 25, 26, April 19, 22, June 30, November 1, 25, 1845, April 18, 20, 30, 1846, April 17, August 18, September 9, November 5, 1847, Riggs Family Papers, LC; Baltimore *Clipper*, January 8, May 20, 22, 31, June 5, 7, 1851; Baltimore *Republican*, January 9, 31, February 6, 12, 25, March 24, 29, May 12, 27, 1852; Baltimore *Sun*, January 6, 24, February 8, 25, March 1, 10, 23, 24, 28, April 16, May 31, December 19, 1853, February 1, 2, 7, 10, 17, 18, September 4, October 14, November 3, 23, December 2, 7, 19, 1854, January 18, February 5, 6, March 10, 27, July 24, 1855, January 14, 31, February 9, March 26, 1856, January 23, May 11, December 7, 1857, Baltimore *Daily Exchange*, July 27, August 10, 1858; Redlich, *American Banking*, part 1, pp. 1–21, 45–59, 187–204, 209–30; Livingood, *Philadelphia-Baltimore Trade Rivalry*, pp. 74–80; and Edwin J. Perkins, "Financing Antebellum Importers," pp. 421–51.

6. John McTavish to the Earl of Aberdeen, March 15, 1845, May 5, 1846, to Lord Palmerston, September 25, 1848, September 10, 1850, September 30, 1851, British Consular Reports, PAC; Oelrichs & Lurman to Baring Brothers & Co., December 28, 1844, Baring Brothers Papers, PAC; Baltimore *Patriot*, October 20, November 22, 1845, January 10, 1846; Baltimore *Sun*, July 28, October 11, 1848, December 5, 1850, February 22, December 28, 1853, April 6, 20, September 20, 27, October 21, 1854, January 8, May 23, 1855, August 11, 14, October 29, 1856; Baltimore *Republican*, January 13, 23, June 6, 1849, January 21, February 24, March 22, 1852; Baltimore *Clipper*, March 19, 31, April 5, 17, 1851.

7. Baltimore *Sun*, April 5, 1850; Baltimore *Clipper*, February 1, 1851; Baltimore *Patriot*, May 27, 1847; United States, Department of the Treasury, *Annual Reports on the State of the Finances, 1845–February, 1849*, 5: 1–619; 6: 1–664; 7: 1–672; "Report of the Secretary of the Treasury for 1850," House of Representatives, 31st Cong., 2nd Sess., *Executive Document No. 11*, passim.

8. Henry Cohen, *Business & Politics in America from the Age of Jackson to the Civil War*, passim.

9. Freeman Hunt, editor and publisher of *Hunt's Merchants' Magazine*, was one example, and John Smith Homans, who edited and published *The Banker's Monthly*, first in Baltimore and later in New Orleans, was another.

10. Bryan, *State Banking in Maryland*, pp. 112–14; Robert W. Thon, *Mutual Savings Banks in Baltimore*, pp. 28–37.

11. Browne, "Baltimore in the Nation," pp. 341–42.

12. Matthew Page Andrews, "History of Baltimore, from 1850 to the Close of the Civil War," 1: 162; Charles A. Hales, *The Baltimore Clearing House*, pp. 6–12, 24–25.

13. Browne, "Baltimore in the Nation," p. 323; Baltimore *Clipper*, January 22, March 5, 1851; Baltimore *Patriot*, February 13, April 22, August 22, November 15, 1844, August 22, September 6, October 25, November 18, December 10, 1845, August 24, September 2, 1846, February 18, March 2, 5, May 17,

June 1, 23, September 1, 1847; Baltimore *Sun*, January 5, March 4, April 7, August 5, October 31, December 21, 1848, February 23, 24, November 8, 12, 14, 20, 27, 1850, November 30, 1853, January 3, 1854, March 8, August 28, 1855, June 26, November 14, 1856, January 2, 20, August 3, 1857; Baltimore *Republican*, March 15, April 5, August 17, October 16, November 19, 1849, August 18, 1851, February 2, 3, 4, March 16, April 13, 28, June 10, August 21, 28, November 16, 22, 24, 26, December 9, 1852, July 12, 1860; Baltimore *Daily Exchange*, June 28, September 7, October 15, November 1, 1858; "Baltimore," *Hunt's Merchants' Magazine*, 23: 34–52.

14. Baltimore *Republican*, March 15, April 5, 26, 1849, August 18, 29, November 14, 1851, March 16, April 13, 28, May 19, June 10, August 21, November 16, 24, 26, December 9, 1852; Baltimore *Clipper*, January 22, 1851; Baltimore *Sun*, February 23, 24, September 19, 1850, March 8, November 13, 1855.

15. "As the great commercial centre, New York is the *controlling power*, [*sic*], both in finance and trade, for nearly all the rest of the country. The action of her banks, as one of the instrumentalities of her trade with the interior, must always influence, to a considerable degree, that of like institutions in the cities having such large and direct relations with her as does the city of Baltimore." Baltimore *Sun*, October 1, 1857. The revival of commerce brought back the old 1820s arguments that Baltimore needed direct trade with Liverpool, and that Baltimore could become the "New York of the South"; unfortunately, some of the city's merchants appeared very much like New Yorkers to the Southerners who assembled at the Southern Commercial Convention in Baltimore in 1853, and Baltimoreans would not hear Southerners discussing their city's commercial leadership of the South again until the Secession Winter, 1860–61. Baltimore *Republican*, November 24, 26, December 4, 9, 17, 18, 20, 1852; Baltimore *Sun*, June 17, December 28, 1853; Robert Royal Russel, *Economic Aspects of Southern Sectionalism, 1840–1861*, pp. 128–31.

16. Baltimore's banks resumed specie payments on December 16, three days after banks in Albany, Boston, and New York did. Baltimore *Sun*, August 26, 27, 29, 31, September 1, 2, 3, 4, 5, 11, 12, 14–19, 23, 26, 28, 29, 30, October 1, 2, 3, 5, 6, 7, 8, 9, 10, 12, 13, 14, 15, 16, 17, 19, 22, 24, 26, 28, 31, November 6, 7, 9, 11, 12, 13, 14, 16, 18, 20, 23, 24, 28, December 3, 7, 14, 17, 29, 1857; Richard Townsend Diary, 2: 752, 754–56, 760, 767, 772, 774, 782, 791, EPL; Mayor's Annual Message, 1858, 1859; *Annual Report of the President and Directors of the Corn and Flour Exchange*, 1857, 1858; Smith & Atkinson to Hacklett & Dubber, September 5, 1857, to George Buffy, September 5, 1857, Richard M. Smith to Richard Smith, September 9, 26, October 1, 24, 30, 1857, Smith & Atkinson Papers, MdHS; Oelrichs & Lurman to Baring Brothers & Co., September 7, 27, October 7, 13, 19, 27, November 14, 30, December 22, 1857, Baring Brothers Papers, PAC; Robert Garrett & Sons to George Peabody, September 29, October 5, 13, 30, November 2, 10, 1857, Robert Garrett & Sons Papers, LC; Alex Brown & Sons to Brown & Bowen, August 25, September 2, 17, 25, October 28, November 3, 1857, to Brown, Shipley & Co., September 11, 15, 29, October 16, 27, November 2, 13, 27, 1857, Brown Papers, LC; Balti-

more *Daily Exchange*, October 26, 1858, January 14, 1859; Freeman Hunt's observations on the panic and recession can be found in *Hunt's Merchants' Magazine*, 37: 325–35, 452–61, 581–92, 711–20; 38: 70–80, 195–208, 326–36; other contemporary observations about the panic and recession include "The Commercial Crisis of 1857," *Hunt's Merchants' Magazine*, 37: 529–34; "An Exposition of the Crisis of 1857," *Hunt's Merchants' Magazine*, 38: 19–35; "Report of the Boston Board of Trade on the Causes of the Commercial Crisis," *Hunt's Merchants' Magazine*, 38: 722–24; "Causes of the Recent Commercial Distress," *Hunt's Merchants' Magazine*, 39: 553–62; G. L. W., "Causes that Produced the Crisis of 1857 Considered," *Hunt's Merchants' Magazine*, 40: 19–37; Edmund Dwight, "The Financial Revulsion and the New York Banking System," *Hunt's Merchants' Magazine*, 38: 157–63; [editorial] "Retrospective View of the Year 1857," *Bankers' Magazine*, 593–604; Thomas Hart Benton, "Letters to Editors of the *National Intelligencer* on Banks and Banking," *Bankers' Magazine*, 13: 417–28; James Sloan Gibbons, *The Banks of New York, Their Dealers, the Clearing House, and the Panic of 1857*, passim. Twentieth-century historians' views of the panic of 1857 are A. H. Cole, "The New York Money Market of 1843 to 1862," pp. 164–70; George W. Van Vleck, *The Panic of 1857; An Analytic Study*, pp. 60–104; Samuel Reznick, "The Influence of Depression upon American Opinion, 1857–1859," pp. 1–23. One indication of how New Yorkers suffered more than Baltimoreans from the panic was that nearly every New York tobacco merchant who traded with Virginia defaulted in their notes to the planters while none of Baltimore's merchants did; see Joseph Clarke Robert, *The Tobacco Kingdom*, pp. 227–28. An excellent article that traces the emergence of New York over Philadelphia and Boston as the financial center of the United States by its financing of American railroads is Alfred D. Chandler, Jr., "Patterns of American Railroad Finance, 1830–1850," pp. 248–63.

17. New York *Times*, August 25, 1857; Richard Townsend Diary, 2: 752–63, EPL; the Laurel Factory closed, adding to the already depressed iron industry.

18. United States Department of Commerce, Bureau of the Census, Seventh Census of the United States, 1850, Manufactures, Baltimore, Maryland, MdSL.

19. The rise and decline of industrial manufacturing can be followed in Baltimore's newspapers: Baltimore *Republican*, April 9, 1845, August 21, October 4, December 12, 15, 16, 1851; Baltimore *Patriot*, August 1, 1844, March 16, July 7, November 7, 1846, January 25, 1847; Baltimore *Clipper*, February 15, 1851. In 1846, the National Exhibition of American Manufacturers in Washington, D.C., received much attention in the Baltimore *Patriot*, March 23, 30, April 11, May 13, 26–8, and June 5, 1846. Also see chap. 9, note 2, and John McTavish to Lord Palmerston, September 25, 1848, September 10, 1850, September 30, 1851, British Consular Reports, PAC; John Pendleton Kennedy to John H. Done, April 29, 1852, John Pendleton Kennedy Papers, GPI; Richard Townsend Diary, 1: 479; 2: 480–81, 483, 499, 505–7, 509, 516, 540, 561, 585, 614, 737, 797, 801, 808; Alex Brown & Sons to Hargreaves Brothers & Co., June 17, 1850, Brown Papers, LC; Baltimore *Republican*, April 9, 1845, November 1, December 19, 28, 1849, October 4, February 10, March 7, July 26, 1848, January 5, March

20, October 31, 1850, January 14, 20, June 9, 15, August 22, October 29, November 11, 1853, March 31, September 1, December 28, 1854, May 3, 1856, December 2, 1857; Baltimore *Patriot*, March 16, July 7, November 7, 1846; Baltimore *Clipper*, March 8, 1851; Baltimore *Daily Exchange*, January 1, 1859.

20. The statistics of consolidation obscure the diversification of Baltimore's industries. Tapping the Western markets with the Baltimore & Ohio Railroad in the 1850s meant shipping fruits, vegetables, and oysters westward. The oyster-canning industry, for example, virtually doubled itself from eighteen establishments with 1,500 employees in 1856 to thirty establishments with 3,000 employees in 1860; A. J. Nichol, *The Oyster-Packing Industry of Baltimore*, p. 16; Rhoda M. Dorsey, "Comment [about Baltimore's foreign trade]," p. 67; Clark, *History of Manufactures*, 1: 485; United States Department of Commerce, Bureau of the Census, Sixth Census of the United States, 1840, Manufactures, pp. 142–53; Manufacturing Census, 1850, MdSL; *Laws of Maryland*, 1844, cs. 83, 231, 1845, cs. 270, 279, 1846, cs. 43, 320, 1849, cs. 52, 158; the return of general prosperity can be followed in the Baltimore *Patriot*, May 12, 16, August 5, 28, September 8, 27, 1843, April 10, 16, 22, December 7, 1844, August 22, September 6, October 20, 25, November 17, 18, 1845, July 11, August 24, 26, 1846, February 11, 18, March 1, 16, 23, 1847; the railroad boom is mentioned in the Baltimore *Sun*, August 11, September 18, October 10, 1848, the Baltimore *Republican*, April 7, July 1–3, 8–12, 14, 15, 1845, and the Baltimore *Patriot*, October 15, 16, 1844, September 30, October 7, 8, 13, November 8, 22, December 20, 1845, January 10, September 15, October 13, November 21, 27, 28, December 1–3, 5, 11, 12, 17, 28, 31, 1846, January 9, 19, 28, February 9, 23, 24, March 1, April 1, 2, 5, 6, 9, 14–16, 24, 26, May 14, 16, 22, June 1, 2, 9, 21–26, July 1, 7, 16, 17, August 24–26, 30, October 12, 1847, March 16–18, 1848.

21. Baltimore *Sun*, July 26, October 11, 1848, October 31, 1850, June 9, October 29, 1853, March 31, June 3, September 1, December 28, 1854, January 8, 29, February 28, March 8, August 28, September 12, 27, November 13, 1855, July 2, August 11, December 2, 1856, January 2, 20, February 28, March 31, May 23, 26, December 2, 31, 1857, June 12, 1858; Checkland, *Rise of Industrial Society*, pp. 36–37.

22. Manufacturing Census, 1850, MdSL; United States Department of Commerce, Bureau of the Census, Eighth Census of the United States, 1860, Manufactures, Baltimore, Maryland, UNCL; not only did the Baltimore & Ohio Railroad Company reach another financial bind by 1853, which required additional capital, but there were rumors about immoral if not illegal insider-speculations in its stock; the city loaned five million dollars to the railroad in 1853, and a new management, more representative of the city's and individual stockholders' interests, came into power a year later; John McTavish to Lord Palmerston, September 30, 1850, Henry George Kuper to Lord John Russell, March 16, 1853, British Consular Reports, PAC; Baltimore *Republican*, July 1–3, 8–12, 14, 15, 1845, April 28, May 1, 4, 10, 11, November 16, 1849, January 21, March 11, 12, 15, 22, 27, June 10, 25, July 12, 13, October 18, 19, November 13, 16, 20, 1852, January 13, 28, 1854; Baltimore *Patriot*, October 7, November 24, De-

cember 20, 1845, May 2, September 15, November 21, 27, 28, December 1–3, 11, 12, 28, 31, 1846, January 7, 9, 19, 28, February 8, 9, 11, 23, 24, March 1, April 2, 5, 6, 8, 9, 15, 16, May 14, June 1, 9, 11, 19, 21, 23, 26, 29, 30, August 24–26, 30, October 4, 1847; Baltimore *Sun*, March 16–18, August 11, September 18, 1848, February 14, June 13, 1850, January 11, June 17, July 14, 25, August 8, 11, 23, 26, September 7, 13, October 10, 12, 13, 21, 22, November 15, 18, 21–25, 29, December 1–9, 12–24, 17, 19, 1853, January 13, February 21, 24, 27, April 4, 6, 10, 13, 18, 22, May 5, 24, 30, June 12, 21, August 3, 22, October 2, 10, 17, 20, 30, November 7–9, December 4, 14, 23, 30, 1854, March 12, 15, 16, 19, April 3, 11, 12, May 10, 12, 19, 21, 22, 24, 25, June 22, July 3, 11, 12, August 6, September 13, 18, October 16, 18, 23, November 15, December 14, 1855, January 9, February 7, 21, 27, March 26, April 10, 14, 30, September 4–6, 11, 12, October 21, 31, December 2, 9, 11–13, 15–19, 22, 24, 27, 31, 1856, January 3, 8, 12, 13, 17, 22, 24, 28, 31, March 12, 16, 19, 24, 30, 31, April 9, 16, 20, May 1, 2, 4–8, 15, 16, June 15, July 9, August 10–15, 18, 20, 22, 27, 31, September 3, 1857; Baltimore *Clipper*, April 19, 24, May 13, 1851; John E. Snodgrass, "The Baltimore and Ohio Railroad and Its Western Connections," pp. 64–72.

23. Manufacturing Census, 1850, Baltimore, MdSL; Manufacturing Census, 1860, UNCL.

IX. An Industrial Society

1. United States Department of Commerce, Bureau of the Census, Seventh Census of the United States, 1850, Population, Baltimore, Maryland, Record Group 29, NA.

2. Merely twenty-six of the sixty-five Irish merchants reported their ownership of property.

3. Persons serving as officers of Baltimore's various corporations were identified in the newspapers and city directories. Corporations were important because they were a means of conducting business activities via monetized debt on their own, independent of the individual stockholders. Besides, their concentrations of capital made for economic and social stability. Yet they were not the predominant form of business enterprise. Indeed, they accounted for merely 1 percent of all enterprises (in comparison with nearly 12 percent conducted as partnerships and 84 percent as individual proprietorships) on the eve of the Civil War; G. Herberton Evans, Jr. and Walter C. Kanwisher, Jr., "Business Organizations in Baltimore, 1859," pp. 63–67.

4. A Provisions Exchange was also established; Baltimore *Republican*, October 8, 1849, October 7, 1851; Baltimore *Sun*, March 6, September 19, 1850; the Baltimore *Daily Exchange* [the organ of the Old Guard] editorial on March 10, 1858, refers to the exchanges as a return to the "ancient way" of doing business which, inferentially, was good, and another editorial on June 29 attacked the corporations because of their size; Annual Report of the President and Directors of the Corn and Flour Exchange, 1854–61; Scharf, *History of Baltimore*, pp.

439–41; annual reports of the Board of Trade were published in the newspapers in the first week in October each year—for example, the Baltimore *Sun*, October 3, 1854, October 2, 1855.

5. The secondary rank of merchants included the Bond, Cassard, Hamilton, Hooper, Lee, Lilly, MacGill, Norris, Rogers, and Whitridge business firms, and included a variety of occupations from dry goods to groceries, hardware, and pharmaceuticals. Indeed, commercial activities were becoming so complex during the return of prosperity that Lewis Tappan of New York could institutionalize a credit-rating agency (his "Mercantile Agency" founded in 1846), which proved useful and even necessary for doing business with unknown men. Of course, Baltimore's Old Guard disliked it; see the Baltimore *Republican*, December 23, 1851: "Mercantile Agencies—A System of Espionage." Roy Anderson Foulke, *The Sinews of American Commerce*, pp. 360–68; Lewis E. Atherton, "The Problem of Credit Rating in the Ante-Bellum South," pp. 534–56.

6. Ross Winans typified the merchant-manufacturer who identified with the commercial elite, as Adam Denmead did of the technology-oriented manufacturers. Denmead had descended from Baltimore's eighteenth-century craftsman tradition; Winans was originally from New York and came to Baltimore in 1832 to build locomotives for the Baltimore & Ohio Railroad; the two men carried on a long and heated newspaper exchange in the Baltimore *Sun*, August 10–15, 20, 22, 27, September 3, 1857; L. W. Slagle, "Ross Winans," pp. 7–21.

7. Besides Abbott and Reeder, other manufacturers in the craftsman tradition were the Ames, Bartlett, Bates, Benson, Blake, Bolster, Green, Hayward, Hazlehurst, Hunt, Murray, Page, Poole, and Scott firms. Reeder's father came to Baltimore in 1813 and built the first steamboat engine in the city; in 1831, Poole & Hunt established their firm for making castings and machine parts; in 1836, Horace Abbott purchased the "Cooper" or "Canton" Forges from Peter Cooper, and the new Abbott Iron Works specialized in turning out axles, cranks, and shafts; and in 1844, Hayward, Bartlett & Co. began manufacturing stoves but then specialized in architectural iron. Scharf, *History of Baltimore*, pp. 425–27.

8. The information in this and following three paragraphs is based upon a comparative analysis of the Manufacturing Census of 1850 with that of 1860, UNCL. Employer paternalism is inferred to have continued. For example, in 1860 William Finsley paid each of his twenty women employees $5.05 per month and Frederick Petrow paid his woman employee $4.00 per month, and, in contrast to these boot and shoe shops, clothiers James E. Stansbury and William Schloss each paid their individual women employees $7.50 per month. Wages of $5.00 per month in 1860 were common for domestic servants and were what many slaveowners figured was the cost of keeping a slave. Also, many employers made a point of noting that the wages they paid were "without board"; for example, Frederick K. Kramer, a cabinetmaker, paid each of his two men $16.00 per month "without board."

9. Richard Lemmon to William W. Glenn, June 24, July 15, October 28, December 22, 1848, Glenn Papers, MdHS; William P. Preston Diary, February 11, 12, 1853, William P. Preston Papers, MdHS; Baltimore *Sun*, January 14, Feb-

ruary 12, 14–19, 21, 23, 24, 28, March 2, 5, 7, 9, 12, 16–19, April 2, 1853. None of the several studies of Know-Nothingism mention this strike; because free blacks apparently were not among the strikers, they presumably did not work in Baltimore's iron industry; see M. Ray Della, Jr., "The Problems of Negro Labor in the 1850's," pp. 14–32.

10. Baltimore *Sun*, February 16, 1853; these fifteen employers—Denmead & Son; Murray & Hazlehurst; Poole & Hunt; Ames & Green; Whitman & Co.; Scott & Bolster; Hayward, Bartlett & Co.; B. S. Benson; Ross Winans; John G. Millholland; Joel N. Blake; Henry D. Lawrence; George T. Bassett; Charles Reeder; and Robert Sinclair—employed about 2,300 men, or about one-half of the labor force for the iron industry as a whole. All of the smaller shops were represented in this group. The strikers' answer to the employers' statement is printed in the Baltimore *Sun*, February 17, 1853. The employers who refused to grant wage increases were probably working a very close profit margin and, like their employees, were caught in the inflationary spiral of costs outstripping revenues. Their bind was caused by the fact that railroad construction stagnated throughout Maryland during the 1850s. From 1852 through 1856, for example, no new railroad construction occurred at all. Joseph C. G. Kennedy, "Preliminary Report on the Eighth Census, 1860," p. 234.

11. Several leaders of the strike—James B. Askew, James M. Clark, Edward J. Codd, James McMillan, Edward Norwood, and John H. Waters—were leaders of the movement to form a workingman's party, independent of the Democratic and Whig parties. They ran Clark, an ex-Democrat, for sheriff of Baltimore County and briefly published a newspaper, *The Workingmen's Daily Press*; see the Baltimore *Sun*, March 30, April 8, June 3, 7, 30, July 8, 1853. Examples of the Democratic party's opposition to the workingmen and nativism can be found in the Baltimore *Republican*, January 20, March 25, July 8, September 11, 26, 29, October 10, 19, 1854; Baltimore *Sun*, June 3, 4, 7, 13–15, 20–22, 24, 30, July 1, 6–8, 13–15, 18, 19, August 5, 6, 11–13, 23, 25–27, 30, 31, September 2, 5, 15, 17, October 13, 18, 20, 22, 25–27, November 1, 5, 9, 1853; the city convention of the Democratic party denounced the Know-Nothings as "contrary to the principles of the Constitution," Baltimore *American*, July 22, 1854.

12. Manufacturing Census, 1850, MdSL; Manufacturing Census, 1860, UNCL.

13. Ibid.

14. Mayor's Annual Message, 1835, 1836, 1837, 1844–60.

15. Population Census, 1850, RG 29, NA; Population Census, 1860; Baltimore *Republican*, February 3, 1854; Baltimore *Sun*, May 7, 1853; Joseph C. G. Kennedy, *History and Statistics of the State of Maryland According to the Returns of the Seventh Census of the United States, 1850*, passim; James Dunwoody Brownson DeBow, *The Industrial Resources, etc., of the Southern and Western States . . .*, 2: 52; James F. W. Johnston, *Notes on North America—Agricultural, Economical, and Social*, 2: 318. In addition to the architectural innovation, Baltimore's building contractors also incorporated themselves into building associations that were frankly ethnic. Such associations as the Baltimore German

Building Association <u>No. 3</u> [underlining added] and the St. James Building Association of Baltimore apparently met the housing demands of Baltimore's growing population in the midst of industrial stagnation; Baltimore *Clipper*, May 30, 1851; *Laws of Maryland*, 1849, cs. 129, 198, 200, 315, 430, 438, 467, 499, 541, 551, 552.

16. Baltimore *Clipper*, January 15, 1850, December 5, 1854; Baltimore *Sun*, January 11, 1853, November 7, 1854, January 4, 1855; the Northern Central Railroad was also constructed within the city, Baltimore *Sun*, May 24, 1854.

17. New house construction generally conformed to this population growth pattern as well, though it followed more closely the fluctuating pattern of family numbers. Indeed, the decrease or small increase of people in the industrial wards was offset in some cases by an increase in the number of families. For example, in ward 1, an industrial ward and Baltimore's shipping center, the population increased 2½ percent, the number of families nearly 75 percent, and the number of houses 55 percent; in ward 2, similar to ward 1, the population decreased about 1½ percent, the number of families increased nearly 7 percent, and housing decreased nearly 17 percent. Population Census, 1850, RG 29, NA; Population Census, 1860, RG 29, NA.

18. The decennial federal population censuses from 1790 through 1860 are all in Record Group 29, NA; Assessment Lists of All Dwellings, Lands, Wharves, and Slaves in Baltimore City, 1798, Microcopies 604, 605, MdHS; persistence rates in wards 9, 10, and 11 were averaging 10 to 12 percent during the 1850s, though these figures are suspect.

19. United States, Department of Commerce, Bureau of Customs, Baltimore Passenger Lists, Microcopy 255, Record Group 36, NA. The impact of the ethnic change is most dramatic in the comparison of the population censuses for 1850 and 1860: the total number of foreign-born residents of Baltimore increased from 35,617 in 1850 to 52,497 in 1860, or over 47 percent; but their percentage of the city's total population increased merely from 21.07 to 24.71 percent.

20. Population Census, 1850, RG 29, NA; Population Census, 1860, RG 29, NA.

21. Ibid.; Population Census, 1840, RG 29, NA; in 1840, free blacks accounted for 17.56 percent of Baltimore's population; in 1850, for 15.05 percent; and in 1860, for 12.09 percent; Alfred Pairpont, *Uncle Sam and His Country*, pp. 219–23.

22. United States Department of Commerce, Seventh Census of the United States, 1850, Slave Schedules, Baltimore, Maryland, Microcopy 432, roll 300, Record Group 29, NA; United States Department of Commerce, Eighth Census of the United States, 1860, Slave Schedules, Baltimore, Maryland, Microcopy 653, roll 484, Record Group 29, NA; the total number of slaves decreased from 3,394 in 1840 to 2,946 in 1850, to 2,218 in 1860, males declined from 1,164 in 1840 to 947 in 1850, to 667 in 1860; females decreased from 2,230 in 1840 to 1,999 in 1850, to 1,541 in 1860.

23. Ibid.

24. Ibid.; where the sex of the slaveowners in 1860 can be determined, 32 of

the 482 male owners (or 6.64 percent) hired out their slaves and 29 of the 322 female owners (or 9.01 percent) did; all of these owners were located in the water wards, not in the outlying, perimeter wards.

25. Scharf, *History of Baltimore*, pp. 517–605.

26. Ibid., pp. 517–92.

27. Ibid., pp. 225–29.

X. A Municipal Polity

1. *Journal of the City Council*, February 21, March 21, pp. 170–71, 323–25; March 10, 1848, pp. 276, 296–97; Mayor's Annual Message, 1844, 1845, 1846, 1847, 1848.

2. *Journal of the City Council*, March 20, 21, 1845, pp. 306–7, 317; *Ordinances*, March 1, 1844, May 2, 1845, February 17, 1846, May 27, 1847, May 20, 1849, February 28, 1861; *City Council Resolution*, May 25, 1846.

3. City Register's Annual Reports, Department of Legislative Reference, BCH.

4. *Ordinances*, December 14, 27, 1853; *City Council Resolution*, January 19, 1854; *Laws of Maryland*, 1853, c. 34; Reizenstein, *Economic History of the Baltimore & Ohio*, pp. 62–71.

5. *Ordinances*, December 14, 27, 1853, January 19, 1854; Baltimore *Sun*, November 15, 18, 22–25, 29, December 1, 9, 12, 17, 1853; Baltimore *Republican*, January 13, February 21, 1854.

6. Mayor's Annual Message, 1852.

7. *Ordinances*, July 29, 1854, October 19, 1855, May 13, June 25, July 17, 1856; *Laws of Maryland*, 1853, c. 376, 1858, c. 38, 1861, c. 20.

8. Ledger, 1836–1840, City Collector's Annual Report, Department of Legislative Reference, BCH; Hollander, *Financial History*, pp. 258–61.

9. *Ordinance*, January 1, 1857; Mayor's Annual Message, 1856.

10. Mayor's Annual Message, 1845, 1850; *Journal of the City Council*, February 21, 1845, pp. 170–71.

11. Carleton Beals, *Brass-Knuckle Crusade*, pp. 171–92; Sister Mary St. Patrick McConville, *Political Nativism in the State of Maryland*, pp. v–vi; on p. 127 Sister McConville summed up her version of Know-Nothingism in Baltimore: "There remain the annals of the reign of Know Nothingism in Baltimore—one long record of vice, intrigue, and abomination." Few studies address the Know-Nothing movement in municipal politics, and those that do emphasize its political rather than its administrative character; see Michael Fitzgibbon Holt, *Forging a Majority*, passim; Louis Dow Scisco, *Political Nativism in New York State*, chaps. 2–4; Leon Cyprian Soulé, *The Know Nothing Party in New Orleans*, passim; William J. Evitts even titles his chapter on the Baltimore Know-Nothings, "Baltimore and the Politics of Violence," in his *A Matter of Allegiances*, pp. 89–117; Jean H. Baker does the same, though her focus is really upon state politics during the 1860s, *The Politics of Continuity*, pp. 4–6, 19–45, and her *Ambivalent Americans*, passim.

12. Henry W. Thomas to General James Thomas, November 10, 1844, Thom-

as Family Papers, MdHR; Bernard C. Steiner, *Life of Henry Winter Davis*, p. 80; McConville, *Political Nativism*, pp. 1–13; Beals, *Brass-Knuckle Crusade*, p. 173; Arthur C. Cole, *The Whig Party in the South*, p. 309; William D. Overdyke, *The Know-Nothing Party in the South*, pp. 1–15.

13. Mayor's Annual Message, 1859. Douglas Bowers's argument that Maryland's new constitution in 1851 settled the old political controversies and created an "issue-vacuum" that necessitated a new political environment deserves more serious consideration; "Ideology and Political Parties in Maryland, 1851–1856," pp. 197–217.

14. Irish illiteracy is manifest in the population censuses for 1850 and 1860. In 1852, Martin J. Kearney estimated from the 1850 census that 2,500 adult, white males were illiterate, or about 10 percent of the electorate. Baltimore *Republican*, April 28, 1852. Kearney wished the state to extend financial aid to Roman Catholic schools; also see note 33 below.

15. Evitts, *A Matter of Allegiances*, pp. 5–23; Baker, *Politics of Continuity*, pp. 3, 6–16.

16. Evitts, *A Matter of Allegiances*, pp. 24–53.

17. Martin J. Kearney was chairman of the Committee on Education in the Maryland House of Delegates where he represented Baltimore; he was a Roman Catholic and later edited a Roman Catholic paper in Baltimore, the *Metropolitan*. Bowers, "Ideology and Political Parties," pp. 201–5; Beals, *Brass-Knuckle Crusade*, pp. 177–78; Overdyke, *Know-Nothing Party in the South*, p. 58; McConville, *Political Nativism*, pp. 21–44; Laurence Frederick Schmeckebier, *History of the Know Nothing Party in Maryland*, pp. 15–16; Baltimore *Clipper*, May through December 1852 (the reaction of the Baltimore *Republican*, the Democratic party organ, to these events is quite revealing, for the Democratic party, relying heavily upon Irish voters, had a vested interest in stifling the resurgence of nativism; see the *Republican*, April 28–30, May 11, 1852, particularly).

18. Baltimore *Sun*, February 12, 14–19, 21, 23, 24, 28, March 2, 5, 7, 9, 12, 16–19, 1853; Beals, *Brass-Knuckle Crusade*, pp. 178–79; Overdyke, *Know-Nothing Party in the South*, p. 58; Schmeckebier, *History of Know Nothing Party*, pp. 14–16.

19. The most prominent Baltimore Whigs who went into the Democratic party were Reverdy Johnson, John Christian Brune, James Alfred Pearce, Severn Teackle Wallis, and Enoch Pratt. The Whigs came out as free traders in Maryland in the spring of 1854 (Baltimore *Republican*, March 3, 1854). Apart from economic considerations, Roman Catholic Whigs left that party and went into the Democratic party in 1855 when they helped to elect Enoch Louis Lowe, a Roman Catholic Democrat, to the governor's chair; Steiner, *H. W. Davis*, pp. 81–82; Evitts, *A Matter of Allegiances*, pp. 54–88; Sister McConville, *Political Nativism*, pp. 51–72, discusses Know-Nothingism as antislavery and antipuritanism and made up of Methodists and political refugees from Germany. She also identifies abolitionism with anti-Catholicism. Also see Bowers, "Ideology and Political Parties," pp. 210–17.

20. John Pendleton Kennedy to J. H. Reynolds, November 18, 1854, to Robert

Charles Winthrop, February 21, 1856, John Pendleton Kennedy Papers, GPI; Augustus Rhodes Sollers, a Democratic representative to Congress from Calvert County, Maryland, in a speech on January 4, 1855, in the *Congressional Globe*, 33rd Cong., 2nd sess., p. 183; Harry J. Carman and Reinhard H. Luthin, "Some Aspects of the Know-Nothing Movement Reconsidered," p. 222.

21. The election results are tallied in the Baltimore *Sun* and the *American*, October 12, 1854; but also see George H. Steuart to Lieutenant George H. Steuart, September 26, October 13, November 17, 1854, James E. Steuart Papers, MdHS; the Baltimore *Sun*, March 28, July 18, 26, August 1, September 4, 8, 26, 29, 30, October 5, 7, 14, 1854; Beals, *Brass-Knuckle Crusade*, pp. 180–81; Overdyke, *Know Nothing Party in the South*, pp. 58–59; Schmeckebier, *History of Know Nothing Party*, pp. 18–19; Benjamin Tuska, "Know Nothingism in Baltimore, 1854–1860," p. 226.

22. Jean Baker, *Ambivalent Americans*, pp. 139–40.

23. The ideology, structure and operation of the Know-Nothing party was of one piece. Most of its members were culturally unsophisticated and relatively inarticulate; they were mainly industrial workers whose secrecy reenforced their identity, promoted intimacy and camaraderie, traits that had always characterized such social movements in the past. Their definition of Americanism—anti-immigrant, anti-Roman Catholic, and backward looking—merely reflected their situation and perspective, just as their open enunciation of such values reflected their tough-mindedness. The cadre of the party were the political clubs, violent and deferential, such as the Rip Raps: "The Rip Rap Club of the West End composed of operatives of Winans & the Depot gave their friends of Philadelphia the Shiffler Club an entertainment 4th July last which cost us nearly $200. We have in the Club & among our American friends raised & paid the debt with the exception of about 35 Dollars. The parties we owe it to are pushing us for it and we are compelled to go out among our friends to raise it—among others we have been induced to write to you not knowing when you would be home. We could have raised the money without trouble if we had gone among all classes. This we do not want to do—we do not wish our enemies to Know anything about it. Should you be pleased to give us a Mite towards it it will be kept a secret & greatfully received & properly appreciated by us." George Craig, Jr., Thomas Wilson, Robert R. Blake, Committee on Behalf of the Rip Raps, to [Anthony Kennedy?], August 23, 1855, Christopher Hughes Papers, UM.

24. *Laws of Maryland*, 1853, c. 376, 1858, c. 38, 1861, c. 20; *Ordinances*, April 13, 1844, May 15, 1846, July 22, 1852, March 19, April 18, 1853, July 29, 1854, October 19, 1855, May 13, June 25, July 17, 1856; Scharf, *History of Baltimore*, pp. 279–81; Blake, *Water For the Cities*, pp. 233–47; the extension of water service immediately after the city purchased the company was astonishing: the 50 miles of water pipe that honeycombed the city in 1854, when the city acquired the water company, increased to 127 miles by 1861, and the number of users increased from 8,750 to 16,300. Concern over the public-health consequences of the "water question" will be found in the Baltimore *Sun*, May 17, 20, 21, 1856.

25. *Ordinance*, January 1, 1857; Mayor's Annual Message, 1856.

26. Article IV, Maryland Constitution of 1851, in Francis Newton Thorpe, comp., *The Federal and State Constitutions*, 3: 1712–41; *Laws of Maryland*, 1848, cs. 77, 316, 1852, c. 200, 1853, c. 122; *Ordinances*, May 23, 1851, May 16, 1861; *City Council Resolutions*, February 23, 1848, April 12, 18, 1849, July 16, 1853; Scharf, *History of Baltimore*, pp. 201, 826; the new Maryland constitution in 1851 marked the first constitutional recognition of Baltimore city separate from Baltimore County, and the county seat was moved from Baltimore city to Towson in the county; Charles F. Mayer, *Laying of the Corner Stone of the Baltimore House of Refuge*.

27. *Ordinances*, April 3, 1843, March 23, 1848, April 13, 1849, December 29, 1854, April 14, 1857, December 10, 1858, June 24, 1859; *City Council Resolutions*, April 12, May 11, 1852, October 5, 1853, May 31, July 6, December 7, 1858; *Mayor's Annual Messages*, 1856, 1860; Scharf, *History of Baltimore*, pp. 216–18.

28. *Ordinances*, March 28, 1859, July 21, 1861; City Register's Annual Report, Department of Legislative Reference, BCH; Baltimore *American*, June 22, 1851; also see note 278.

29. Baltimore *American*, March 30, 1859, June 26, 1860; *Ordinances*, April 20, May 31, 1858, July 21, 1860; *Laws of Maryland*, 1858, c. 294, 1861, c. 41.

30. City Register's Annual Report, Department of Legislative Reference, BCH.

31. Mayor's Annual Message, 1860.

32. Mayor's Special Messages, November 19, 1856, November 15, 1858; Annual Messages, 1857, 1860.

33. Baltimore *Daily Exchange*, January 20, February 7, 17, 22, 27, March 3, 1860; Baltimore *Republican*, April 16, 20, June 7, 17, 20, 25, 27, July 1, 2, 14, 16, 28, August 26, September 8, 9, 15, 20, 21, October 8, 17, 22, 29, November 8, 1859, February 7, March 15, August 17, 27, 30, September 20, 1860. The *Daily Exchange* was the newspaper of the reform movement, which was rooted in the values of the Old Guard; it was founded and edited by Charles G. Kerr, Thomas W. Hall, Jr., Henry M. Fitzhugh, William H. Carpenter, and Frank Key Howard. All of these men were close friends of George William Brown, the reformers' mayoral candidate, and Brown's law partner, Frederick Brune II; see Brune's letters to his wife, Emily Barton Brune, during 1859 and 1860, for candid comments about the reformers' activities, in the Brune-Randall Papers, MdHS; Tuska, "Know Nothingism in Baltimore," pp. 239–40, 246–49; McConville, *Political Nativism*, pp. 126–27.

34. Oelrichs & Lurman to Baring Brothers & Co., November 20, 26, December 4, 18, 23, 1860, January 1, 1861, Gustavus W. Lurman to Thomas Baring, April 25, May 24, 27, 31, 1861, Baring Brothers Papers, PAC; Alex Brown & Sons to Brown Brothers & Co., October 31, November 22, 1860, April 15, 19, 20, 1861, to Brown, Shipley & Co., November 2, 6, 16, 23, 30, December 4, 7, 18, 31, 1860, January 1, 29, February 4, 15, March 1, April 19, 1861, to David Dunlop, April 22, 1861, Brown Papers, LC; Philip W. Thomas to Mamie [Mary] S. Gardiner, April 19, 1861, Gardiner Papers, MdHS; George Whitmarsh Diary, November 22, 1860, MdHS; Baltimore *American*, January 11, April 25, 1861; Baltimore *Clipper*, November 1, 24, 1860, January 11, April 15–17, 1861; Bal-

timore *Daily Exchange*, October 28, November 1, 22, December 28, 1860, January 10, 11, April 22, 24, 26, 1861; Baltimore *Sun*, October 6, 25, 27, 28, 30, 31, November 1, 3, 9, 10, 13, 15, 17, 21–24, 26, December 7, 8, 19, 23, 1860, January 4, 7, 11, 31, March 8, 11–13, 18, 26, April 2, 4, 6, 8–13, 15–17, 20, May 2, 1861; William Bruce Catton, "The Baltimore Business Community and the Secession Crisis, 1860–1861," pp. 43–88; Steiner, *H. W. Davis*, pp. 194–96; Carl M. Frasure, "Union Sentiment in Maryland, 1859–1861," pp. 210–24.

35. Baltimore *American*, February 2, 9, 20, 1861; Baltimore *Clipper*, February 2, 1861; Baltimore *Daily Exchange*, February 1, 4, March 14, 1861; Baltimore *Sun*, February 2, 4, 19, 20, March 14, 1861; Catton, "Baltimore in Secession Crisis," p. 70.

BIBLIOGRAPHY

Contemporary Sources

MANUSCRIPTS

Annapolis, Maryland
  Maryland Hall of Records
    Baltimore City Jail Records
    Thomas Family Papers
  Maryland State Library
    United States. Department of Commerce. Bureau of the Census.
      Seventh Census of the United States, 1850. Manufactures. Maryland.
Ann Arbor, Michigan
  William L. Clements Library, University of Michigan
    Thomas J. Chew Papers
    Thomas Gage Papers
    Nathaniel Greene Papers
    Christopher Hughes Papers
    James McHenry Papers
    Miscellaneous Papers
Baltimore, Maryland
  Baltimore City Hall, Department of Legislative Reference
    City Register, Ledgers: 1814–16, 1817–18, 1823, 1824–25, 1826–29
    Tax Assessment Records, 1818–61
  Robert Garrett & Sons Letterbooks
  George Peabody Institute
    John Pendleton Kennedy Papers
  Enoch Pratt Free Library
    Richard Hallet Townsend Diary
  Maryland Historical Society
    Assessment Lists of All Dwellings, Lands, Wharves and Slaves in Baltimore
      City, 1798, Microcopies 604, 605
    Bayard Papers
    Paul Bentalou Journal
    Brune-Randall Papers
    Carroll Papers
    Corner Collection
    Henry Didier Letterbook, 1809–17

Richard Dorsey Papers
Douglass Letterbook
Edmondson Letterbook
Glenn Papers
Lyde Goodwin Diary (in Lloyd Papers)
John M. Gordon Papers
Edward Hall Papers
Howard Family Papers
Lloyd Papers
Michael McBlair Papers
McHenry Family Papers
Morris Papers
Robert Oliver Papers
Robert & John Oliver Record Books
Partridge Family Papers
William Patterson Papers
Perine Papers
William P. Preston Papers
Mark Pringle Letterbook, 1796–98
Ridgely Papers
Matthew Smith Letterbook (in Tyson Papers)
Smith & Atkinson Papers
Smith & Buchanan Letterbook
William & Robert Smith Papers
James E. Steuart Papers
Henry Thompson Diaries
Tilghman Papers
Tyson Papers
Von Kapff & Brune Papers
Wessels & Primavesi Papers
John White Papers
George Whitmarsh Diary
Otho Holland Williams Papers
Chapel Hill, North Carolina
  Southern Historical Collection, University of North Carolina Library
    Duff Green Papers
    Hardee-Zacharie Papers
    Jackson, Riddle & Co. Papers
    MacKay-Stiles Papers
    Minor Family Papers
Charleston, South Carolina
  South Carolina Historical Society
    Langdon Cheves Papers
Charlottesville, Virginia
  Manuscripts Division, University of Virginia Library
    Edgehill-Randolph Papers

Grinnan Papers
Wilson Cary Nicholas Papers
Ogden, Day & Ferguson Papers
Samuel Smith Papers
Detroit, Michigan
Burton Historical Collection, Detroit Public Library
Clap Family Papers
Durham, North Carolina
William R. Perkins Library, Duke University
James Martin Bell Papers
Courtenay Family Papers
William Henry Hall Papers
John Knight Papers
Maryland, Colonial and Revolutionary Papers
Isaac McKim Papers
Purviance Family Papers
George Rust Papers
George Hume Steuart Papers
Francis Thomas Papers
John White Papers
Norfolk, Virginia
Norfolk Museum of Arts and Sciences
Myers Family Papers
Ottawa, Canada
Public Archives of Canada
Baring Brothers & Co. Papers
British Consular Reports
Philadelphia, Pennsylvania
Historical Society of Pennsylvania
Thomas P. Cope Papers
Etting Collection
Gratz Collection
Hollingsworth Family Papers
William Jones Papers (in Uselma C. Smith Papers)
Uselma C. Smith Papers
Salem, Massachusetts
Essex Institute
George Peabody Papers
Swarthmore, Pennsylvania
Friends Historical Library, Swarthmore College
Moses Sheppard Papers
Washington, D.C.
Library of Congress
Bank of the United States, Baltimore Branch, Papers
Nicholas Biddle Papers
Sylvanus Bourne Papers

Alex Brown & Sons Papers
J. Kelsey Burr Collection
Stephen Collins & Son Papers
Galloway-Maxcy-Markoe Papers
Jonathan Meredith Papers
Riggs Family Papers
Samuel Smith Papers
Roger B. Taney Papers
National Archives
United States
Congress
Record Group 217, "Records of the United States General Accounting
Office"
First Auditor's Reports to the Comptroller of the Treasury Department
Letters Sent by the Comptroller of the Treasury
Revenue Letters Received from Baltimore Customs Collector, 1796–
1843
Department of Agriculture
Record Group 16, "Records of the Office of the Secretary of Agriculture"
Letters, Reports, Essays of the Agriculture Section of the Patent Office,
1839–60
Department of Commerce
Record Group 29, "Bureau of the Census"
First Census of the United States, 1790: Population. Microcopy T-498,
Roll 1
Second Census of the United States, 1800: Population. Microcopy 32,
Roll 9
Third Census of the United States, 1810: Population. Microcopy 252,
Roll 13
Fourth Census of the United States, 1820: Population. Microcopy 33,
Roll 42
Fourth Census of the United States, 1820: Manufactures. Microcopy
279, Roll 16
Fifth Census of the United States, 1830: Population. Microcopy 19,
Roll 54
Sixth Census of the United States, 1840: Population. Microcopy 704,
Rolls 158–61
Seventh Census of the United States, 1850: Population. Microcopy 432,
Rolls 281–87
Seventh Census of the United States, 1850: Slave Schedules. Microcopy
432, Roll 300
Eighth Census of the United States, 1860: Manufactures. In manuscript
Eighth Census of the United States, 1860: Population. Microcopy 653,
Rolls 458–66
Eighth Census of the United States, 1860: Slave Schedules. Microcopy
653, Roll 484

Bibliography

Record Group 36, "Bureau of Customs"
  Baltimore Passenger Lists, 1820–61. Microcopy 255
  Correspondence of Baltimore Collector of Customs, 1806–1861
  Records of the Collector of Customs at Baltimore: Entrances and
    Clearances, 1782–1824. Microcopy T-257
Record Group 41, "Records of the Bureau of Marine Inspection and
Navigation"
  Baltimore, Bills of Sale, 1815–17
  Baltimore, Certificates of Enrollment, 1791–1841, 1848–61
  Baltimore, Certificates of Registry, 1789–1861
  Baltimore, Licenses for Vessels under 20 Tons, 1793–1831, 1837–39
Department of the Navy
Record Group 45, "Naval Records Collection of the Office of Naval
Records and Library"
  Letters Received by the Secretary of the Navy from Navy Agents and
    Naval Storekeepers, 1843–61
  Letters Sent by the Secretary of the Navy to Commandants and Navy
    Agents, 1808–61
  Letters Sent by the Secretary of the Navy to Officers, 1798–1861
  Miscellaneous Letters Received by the Secretary of the Navy, 1801–61
  Miscellaneous Letters Sent by the Secretary of the Navy, 1798–1861
Department of State
Record Group 59, "General Records of the Department of State"
  Letters of Application and Recommendation During the Administration
    of John Adams, 1797–1801
  Letters of Application and Recommendation During the Administration
    of Thomas Jefferson, 1801–9
  Letters of Application and Recommendation During the Administration
    of James Madison, 1809–17
  Letters of Application and Recommendation During the Administration
    of James Monroe, 1817–25
  Letters of Application and Recommendation During the Administration
    of John Quincy Adams, 1825–29
  Letters of Application and Recommendation During the Administration
    of Andrew Jackson, 1829–37
  Letters of Application and Recommendation During the
    Administrations of Martin Van Buren, William Henry Harrison, and
    John Tyler, 1837–45
Department of the Treasury
Record Group 50, "Records of the Treasurer of the United States"
  Correspondence, 1814–46
Record Group 53, "Records of the Bureau of the Public Debt
  Estimates and Statements by the Register of the Treasury, 1791–1858"
  Letters Received in the Offices of the Secretary, the Treasurer, the
    Register, and the Comptroller, 1836–61
  Letters Sent by the Register of the Treasury, 1816–28

Bibliography

Record Group 56, "General Records of the Department of the Treasury"
Correspondence of the Secretary of the Treasury with Collectors of
Customs, 1789–1833
Letters Received by the Secretary of the Treasury from Collectors of
Customs, 1833–61
Letters Sent by the Secretary of the Treasury to Collectors of Customs
at All Ports, 1789–1847, and at Small Ports, 1847–61
Record Group 104, "Records of the Bureau of the Mint"
Letters Sent by the Director of the United States Mint at Philadelphia,
1795–1817

NEWSPAPERS

Baltimore *American and Daily Commercial Advertiser*, 1799–1861
Baltimore *Clipper and General Advertiser*, 1839–61
Baltimore *Daily Exchange*, 1858–61
Baltimore *Federal Gazette and Daily Advertiser*, 1793–1838
Baltimore *Patriot and Commercial Gazette*, 1812–61
Baltimore *Republican*, 1827–61
Baltimore *Sun*, 1837–61
Commercial Chronicle & Daily Marylander, 1819–40
Federal Republican and Baltimore *Telegraph*, 1816–34
Liverpool *Mercury and Lancashire and General Advertiser*, 1813–40
Maryland Gazette or Baltimore General Advertiser, 1783–91
Maryland Gazette and State Register, 1745–1839
Maryland Journal and Baltimore Advertiser, 1788–98
New Orleans *Daily Picayune*, 1837–61
New York *Herald*, 1835–61
New York *Times*, 1851–61
New York *Tribune*, 1841–61
Washington *Daily Globe*, 1831–45
Washington *Daily Madisonian*, 1837–41
Washington *Union*, 1845–59

PERIODICALS

American Farmer, 1819–31
Banker's Magazine and State Financial Register, 1846–61
DeBow's Review, 1846–61
Hazard's United States Commercial and Statistical Register, 1840–42
Hunt's Merchants' Magazine and Commercial Review, 1839–61
Niles' Weekly Register, 1811–49
North American Review, 1815–61
United States Magazine and Democratic Review, 1837–59

Bibliography

PRICE CURRENTS

Baltimore: 1803–30, 1838–61
Charleston: 1828, 1835
Liverpool: 1806–13, 1815–16, 1818–21, 1824, 1826–30, 1836, 1839–40, 1842–43, 1859
London: 1826, 1829–30, 1850–51
Mobile: 1828, 1835–36, 1838–39, 1846, 1848, 1853
New Orleans: 1828, 1830, 1835–37, 1839, 1842, 1844, 1847, 1850

MUNICIPAL DOCUMENTS

Journal of the Proceedings of the First and Second Branches of the City Council. Baltimore, 1797–1861.
Mayor's Annual Message and Annual Reports of City Officers. Baltimore, 1797–1861.
Ordinances and Resolutions of the Mayor and City Council. Baltimore, 1797–1861.

STATE DOCUMENTS

Dorsey, Clement, comp. The General Public Statutory Law and Public Local Law of the State of Maryland, from the year 1692–1839 Inclusive. 3 vols. Baltimore: John D. Toy, 1840.
An Exhibit of the Losses Sustained at the Office of Discount and Deposit, Baltimore, under the Administration of James A. Buchanan, President, and James W. McCulloh, Cashier; Compiled by the President and Directors of the Office at Baltimore, in Pursuance of an Order from the President and Directors of the Bank of the United States: To Which is Appended a Report of the Conspiracy Cases Tried at Harford County Court in Maryland. Baltimore: T. Murphy, 1823.
Laws of Maryland. Published in annual and biennial volumes by the General Assembly, 1763–1861.
House of Delegates. Proceedings and Journal of the House of Delegates of Maryland, 1825–1861.
———. Votes and Proceedings of the House of Delegates of Maryland, 1739–1824.
Maryland Public Documents, 1832–1861.
Senate. Journal of Votes and Proceedings of the Senate, 1777–1861.

FEDERAL DOCUMENTS

American State Papers: Class 3, Finance. 5 vols.; Class 4, Commerce and Navigation. 2 vols.; Class 6, Naval Affairs. 4 vols.; Class 10, Miscellaneous. 2 vols. Washington, D.C.: Gales & Seaton, 1832–61.

Bibliography

Clarke, Matthew St. Clair, and Hall, D. A., comps. *Documentary History of the Bank of the United States: Including the Original Bank of North America.* Washington, D.C.: Gales & Seaton, 1832.

Compendium of the Enumeration of the Inhabitants and Statistics of the United States, as Obtained at the Department of State, from the Returns of the Sixth Census, by Counties and Principal Towns. Washington, D.C.: Thomas Allen, 1841.

Congressional Globe. Washington, D.C.: John C. Rives, 1834–61.

Coxe, Tench, comp. *A Statement of the Arts and Manufactures of the United States of America, for the Year 1810.* Philadelphia: A. Cornman, Jr., 1814.

Debates and Proceedings in the Congress of the United States . . . 1789–1824 [Annals of Congress]. 42 vols. Washington, D.C.: Gales & Seaton, 1834–56.

DeBow, J. D. B. *Statistical View of the United States, Embracing Its Territory, Population—White, Free Colored, and Slave—Moral and Social Condition, Industry, Property, and Revenue; the Detailed Statistics of Cities, Towns, and Counties; Being a Compendium of the Seventh Census.* Washington, D.C.: Beverley Tucker, Senate Printer, 1854.

[DeBow, J. D. B., comp.] *The Seventh Census of the United States: 1850.* Washington, D.C.: Robert Armstrong, Public Printer, 1853.

Digest of Accounts of Manufacturing Establishments in the United States, and of Their Manufactures. Washington, D.C.: Gales & Seaton, 1823.

Evans, Charles H. "Exports, Domestic and Foreign, from the American Colonies to Great Britain, from 1697 to 1789, Inclusive. Exports, Domestic and Foreign, from the United States to All Countries, from 1789 to 1883, Inclusive." *House Miscellaneous Documents.* 48th Cong., 1st sess. No. 49. part 2 (1884). Serial 2236.

Kennedy, Joseph C. G. "Preliminary Report on the Eighth Census, 1860." *House Executive Document.* 37th Cong., 2nd sess. No. 116. (1862).

Mayo, Robert. *A Synopsis of the Commercial and Revenue System of the United States, as Developed by the Instructions and Decisions of the Treasury Department for the Administration of the Revenue Laws: Accompanied with a Supplement of Historical and Tabular Illustrations of the Origin, Organization, and Practical Operations of the Treasury Department and Its Various Bureaus, in Fulfillment of that System: In Eight Chapters, with an Appendix.* Washington, D.C.: J. & G. S. Gideon, 1847.

———. *The Treasury Department and Its Fiscal Bureaus, Their Origin, Organization, and Practical Operations, Illustrated; Being a Supplement to the Synopsis of Treasury Instructions for the Administration of the Revenue Laws Affecting the Commercial and Revenue System of the United States; in Fourteen Chapters.* Washington, D.C.: William Q. Force, 1847.

"Papers Relating to Trade with the British Colonies." *Senate Documents.* 21st Cong., 2nd sess. No. 20. (1831). Serial 203.

Bibliography

Register of Debates in Congress, 1825–37. 29 Vols. Washington, D.C.: Gales & Seaton, 1825–37.

Statutes at Large of the United States of America, 1789–1873. 17 vols. Boston: Charles C. Little and James Brown, 1846–73.

Thorpe, Francis Newton, comp. *The Federal and State Constitutions, Colonial Charters, and Other Organic Laws of the State, Territories, and Colonies Now or Heretofore Forming the United States of America.* 7 vols. Washington, D.C.: Government Printing Office, 1909.

United States. Department of Commerce. Bureau of the Census. *Sixth Census of the United States, 1840: Manufactures.* Washington, D.C.: Thomas Allen, 1841.

———. Department of Commerce. Bureau of the Census. *Eighth Census of the United States, 1860: Agriculture, Compiled from the Original Returns of the Eighth Census, under the Direction of the Secretary of the Interior, by Joseph C. G. Kennedy, Superintendent of Census.* Washington, D.C.: Government Printing Office, 1864.

———. Department of Commerce. Bureau of the Census. *Eighth Census of the United States, 1860: Manufactures. Compiled from the Original Returns of the Eighth Census, Under the Direction of the Secretary of the Interior.* Washington, D.C.: Government Printing Office, 1865.

———. Department of Commerce. Bureau of the Census. *Ninth Census of the United States, 1870: Population.* Washington, D.C.: Government Printing Office, 1871.

———. Department of Commerce. Bureau of the Census. *Tenth Census of the United States, 1880.* Vols. 2, 3, 7, and 20. Washington, D.C.: Government Printing Office, 1883–86.

———. Commissioner of Patents. *Annual Report on Agriculture.* Washington, D.C.: n.p., 1840–60.

———. Department of the Treasury. Commerce and Navigation. *Annual Reports.* Washington, D.C.: n.p., 1821–60.

———. Department of the Treasury. Comptroller of the Currency. *Annual Report, 1876.* Washington, D.C.: n.p., 1876.

———. Department of the Treasury. *Reports of the Secretary of the Treasury of the United States, 1801–49.* Washington, D.C.: Blair & Rives, 1837–51.

———. Department of the Treasury. *Statistics of the Foreign and Domestic Commerce of the United States.* Washington, D.C.: Government Printing Office, 1864.

SOURCES IN PRINT

[Adams, John Quincy.] *Memoirs of John Quincy Adams.* Edited by Charles Francis Adams. 12 vols. Philadelphia: J. B. Lippincott, 1874–77.

Address of the Maryland Ten Hour Association to the Working Men of the State. Ellicotts Mills: Howard Gazette Office, 1852.

Bibliography

Annual Report of the President and Directors to the Stockholders of the Baltimore & Ohio Railroad Company. N.p., 1829–61.

Annual Report of the President and Directors of the Corn and Flour Exchange. N.p., 1854–61.

Baily, Francis. *Journal of a Tour in Unsettled Parts of North America in 1796 and 1797.* London: Baily Brothers, 1856.

"Baltimore." *Niles' Weekly Register* 8 (June 3, 1815): 234.

——. *Niles' Weekly Register* 10 (June 1, 1816): 217.

——. *Hunt's Merchants' Magazine* 23 (July, 1850): 34–52.

Bancroft, George. "Bank of the United States." *North American Review* 32 (1831): 32–64.

Bankers' Magazine. [Editorial] 12 (February 1858): 593–605.

Beach, Thomas J. *A Full and Authentic Account of the Rise and Progress of the Late Mob, in the City of Baltimore.* Baltimore: W. G. Warner, 1835.

Benton, Thomas Hart. "Letter to Editors of the National Intelligencer on Banks and Banking." *Bankers' Magazine* 12 (January 1858): 559–65.

——. *Thirty Years View; or, A History of the American Government for Thirty Years, from 1820 to 1850.* 2 vols. New York: D. Appleton & Co., 1854–56.

Bernard, John. *Retrospections of America, 1797–1811.* Edited by Mrs. Bayle Bernard. New York: Harper & Brothers, 1887.

Biddle, Nicholas. *The Correspondence of Nicholas Biddle Dealing with National Affairs—1807–1844.* Edited by Reginald C. McGraine. Boston: Houghton Mifflin Co., 1919.

Bischoff, James. *A Comprehensive History of the Woollen and Worsted Manufactures, and the Natural and Commercial History of Sheep, from the Earliest Records to the Present Period.* 2 vols. New York: Augustus M. Kelley, 1968 [1842].

Boardman, James. *America and the Americans.* London: Longman, Rees, Orme, Brown, Green, & Longman, 1833.

Brackenridge, Henry M. *Recollections of Persons and Places in the West.* Philadelphia: James Kay, Jun. & Brother, 1834.

Breck, Samuel. *Recollections of Samuel Breck with Passages from his Note-Books (1771–1862).* Edited by H. E. Scudder. Philadelphia: Porter & Coates, 1877.

Buckingham, James S. *America, Historical, Statistic, and Descriptive.* 3 vols. London: Fisher, Son, & Co. [c. 1841].

Byles, Sir John Barnard. *A Practical Compendium of the Law of Bills of Exchange, Promissory Notes, Bank Notes, Bankers' Cash-Notes, and Checks.* London: S. Sweet, 1829.

Carroll, C. H. "New Views of the Currency Question." *Bankers' Magazine* 13 (May 1859): 833–42.

Carroll, Charles (of Carrollton), and Carroll, Charles (of Doughoregan). *Unpublished Letters of Charles Carroll of Carrollton and of His Father, Charles Carroll of Doughoregan.* Edited by Thomas M. Field. New York: n.p., 1902.

Bibliography

"Causes of the Recent Commercial Distress." *Hunt's Merchants' Magazine* 39 (November 1858): 553–62.

Cobden, Richard. *The American Diaries of Richard Cobden.* Edited by Elizabeth Hoon Cawley. Princeton: Princeton University Press, 1952.

Coke, Edward T. *A Subaltern's Furlough: Descriptive of Scenes in Various Parts of the United States, Upper and Lower Canada, New Brunswick, and Nova Scotia, During the Summer and Autumn of 1832.* London: Saunders & Otley, 1833.

"Commercial and Industrial Cities of the United States—Baltimore, Maryland." *Hunt's Merchants' Magazine* 42 (May 1860): 563–75.

"Commercial and Industrial Cities—Baltimore," *Hunt's Merchants' Magazine* 38 (April 1858): 417–37.

"Commercial Cities—Baltimore in 1850–51." *Hunt's Merchants' Magazine* 26 (February 1852): 172–84.

"The Commercial Crisis of 1857." *Hunt's Merchants' Magazine* 37 (November 1857): 529–34.

[Cruise, Peter.] "Baltimore and Ohio Railroad." *North American Review* 25 (July 1827): 62–73.

[Cruise, Peter.] "The Baltimore and Ohio Railroad." *North American Review* 28 (January 1829): 166–86.

Dallas, Alexander James. *Life and Writings of A. J. Dallas.* Edited by George Mifflin Dallas. Philadelphia: n.p., 1871.

Darby, William, and Dwight, Theodore, Jr., comps. *A New Gazetteer of the United States of America, Containing a Copious Description of the States, Territories, Counties, Parishes, Districts, Cities and Towns—Mountains, Lakes, Rivers, and Canals—Commerce, Manufactures, Agriculture, and the Arts Generally, of the United States; . . . With the Population of 1830.* Hartford: Edward Hopkins, 1833.

DeBow, James Dunwoody Brownson. *The Industrial Resources, etc., of the Southern and Western States: Embracing a View of their Commerce, Agriculture, Manufactures, Internal Improvements: Slave and Free Labor, Slavery Institutions, Products, etc., of the South, Together with Historical and Statistical Sketches of the Different States and Cities of the Union—Statistics of the United States Commerce and Manufactures, from the Earliest Periods, Compared with Other Leading Powers—The Results of the Different Census Returns Since 1790, and Returns of the Census of 1850, on Population, Agriculture, and General Industry, etc.* 3 vols. New Orleans: Published at the Office of DeBow's Review, 1852.

[Douglass, Frederick.] *Narrative of the Life of Frederick Douglass an American Slave.* Cambridge, Mass.: Harvard University Press, 1960.

Duncan, John M. *Travels Through Part of the United States and Canada in 1818 and 1819.* 2 vols. Glasgow: Andrew & John M. Duncan, 1823.

Dwight, Edmund. "The Financial Revulsion and the New York Banking System." *Hunt's Merchants' Magazine* 38 (February 1858): 157–63.

Eddis, William. *Letters from America, Historical and Descriptive: Comprising Occurrences from 1769, to 1777, Inclusive.* Edited by Aubrey C. Land.

Bibliography

Cambridge, Mass.: Belknap Press of Harvard University Press, 1969.

Ellicott, Thomas. *Bank of Maryland: Conspiracy as Developed in the Report to the Creditors.* Philadelphia: n.p., 1839.

"An Exposition of the Crisis of 1857." *Hunt's Merchants' Magazine* 38 (January 1858): 19–35.

Fearon, Henry Bradshaw. *Sketches of America: A Narrative of a Journey of Five Thousand Miles through the Eastern and Western States of America; Contained in Eight Reports.* London: Longman, Hurst, Rees, Orme, & Brown, 1818.

Fisher, R. S. *Gazetteer of the State of Maryland, Compiled from the Returns of the Seventh Census of the United States, and Other Official Documents.* Baltimore: James S. Waters, 1852.

Fithian, Philip Vickers. *Philip Vickers Fithian, Journal, 1775–1776.* Edited by Robert G. Albion and Leonidas Dodson. Princeton: Princeton University Press, 1934.

Foster, B. F. *The Merchant's Manual, Comprising the Principles of Trade, Commerce and Banking; with Mercantile Accounts; Inland and Foreign Bills; Par of Exchange; Equation of Payments, etc.* Boston: Perkins & Marvin, 1838.

Fry, William, comp. *The Baltimore Directory for 1810, Containing the Names, Occupations and Residences of the Inhabitants Alphabetically.* Baltimore: G. Dobbin & Murphy, 1810.

Gilmor, Robert. "Recollections of Baltimore." *Maryland Historical Magazine* 7 (September 1912): 233–42.

[Gilmor, Robert, Jr.] "The Diary of Robert Gilmor." *Maryland Historical Magazine* 17 (September 1922): 231–68, 319–47.

[Gilpin, Henry D.] "A Glimpse of Baltimore Society in 1827: Letters by Henry D. Gilpin." Edited by Ralph D. Gray and Gerald E. Hartdagen. *Maryland Historical Magazine* 49 (fall 1974): 256–70.

Gobright, John C. *The Monumental City, or Baltimore Guide Book.* Baltimore: n.p., 1858.

Guest, Richard. *Compendious History of the Cotton-Manufacture, with a Disapproval of the Claim of Sir Richard Arkwright to the Invention of Its Ingenious Machinery.* New York: Augustus M. Kelley, 1970 [1823].

Hall, Basil. *Travels in North America in the Years 1827 and 1828.* 3 vols. 3rd ed. Edinburgh: Robert Cadell, 1830.

Hall, Francis. *Travels in Canada, and the United States, in 1816 and 1817.* London: Longman, Hurst, Rees, Orme, & Brown, 1818.

Hall, Margaret Hunter. *The Aristocratic Journey: Being the Outspoken Letters of Mrs. Basil Hall Written During a Fourteen Months' Sojourn in America, 1827–1828.* Edited by Una Pope-Hennessy. New York: G. P. Putnam's Sons, 1931.

[Hamilton, Alexander Dr.] *Hamilton's Itinerarium, Being a Narrative of a Journey from Annapolis, Maryland, through Delaware, Pennsylvania, New York, New Jersey, Connecticut, Rhode Island, Massachusetts and*

New Hampshire, from May to September, 1744. Edited by Albert B. Hart. St. Louis: n.p., 1907.

Hamilton, Thomas. *Men and Manners in America*. Philadelphia: Carey, Lea & Blanchard, 1843.

Harriott, John. *Struggles Through Life, Exemplified in the Various Travels and Adventures in Europe, Asia, Africa, and America*. 3 vols. London: Longman, Hurst, Rees, Orme, & Brown, 1815.

[Harwood, James, and Ridgate, Benjamin C.] *Reply to a Pamphlet Entitled a Brief Exposition of Matters Relating to the Bank of Maryland with an Examination into Some of the Causes of the Bankruptcy of that Institution*. Baltimore: n.p., 1834.

Hewitt, John Hill. *Shadows on the Wall or Glimpses of the Past: A Retrospect of the Past Fifty Years*. Baltimore: Turnbull Brothers, 1877.

[Hone, Philip.] *The Diary of Philip Hone, 1828–1851*. Edited by Allan Nevins. 2 vols. New York: Dodd, Mead & Co., 1927.

Houstoun, Matilda Charlotte Jesse. *Hesperos; or, Travels in the West*. 2 vols. London: John W. Parker, 1850.

Howitt, Emanuel. *Selections from Letters Written During a Tour Through the United States in the Summer and Autumn of 1819*. Nottingham: J. Dunn, 1820.

Jackson, Andrew. *Correspondence of Andrew Jackson*. Edited by John Spencer Bassett. 7 vols. Washington, D.C.: Carnegie Institution, 1926–35.

Johnson, Reverdy. *Reply to a Pamphlet Entitled "A Brief Exposition of Matters Relating to the Bank of Maryland" with an Examination into Some of the Causes of the Bankruptcy*. Baltimore: n.p., 1835.

Johnston, James F. W. *Notes on North America—Agricultural, Economical, and Social*. 2 vols. Edinburgh and London: William Blackwood & Sons, 1851.

Jones, John Beauchamp [Luke Shortfield]. *The Western Merchant, A Narrative, Containing Useful Instruction for the Western Man of Business Who Makes his Purchases in the East; also, Information for the Eastern Man Whose Customers Are in the West; Likewise, Hints for Those Who Design Emigrating to the West. Deduced from Actual Experience by Luke Shortfield*. Philadelphia: Gregg, Elliot & Co., 1849.

Kemble, Fanny [Frances Anne Kemble Butler]. *Journal*. 2 vols. Philadelphia: Carey, Lea & Blanchard, 1835.

[Kendall, Amos.] *Autobiography of Amos Kendall*. Edited by William Stickney. Boston: Lee & Shepard, Publishers, 1872.

Kennedy, Joseph C. G. *History and Statistics of the State of Maryland According to the Returns of the Seventh Census of the United States, 1850*. Washington, D.C.: Gideon & Co., 1852.

———. *Statistics of American Railroads, Prepared by J.C.G. Kennedy at the U. S. Census Office, at the Request of the French Department of Public Works*. Washington, D.C.: Gideon & Co., 1852.

Kent, James. "A New Yorker in Maryland: 1793 and 1821." *Maryland Historical Magazine* 47 (June 1952): 135–45.

Bibliography

Klinckowström, Axel Leonhard, Friherre. *Baron Klinckowström's America, 1818–1820.* Translated from the Swedish and edited by Franklin D. Scott. Evanston: Northwestern University Press, 1952.

La Rochefoucault Liancourt, Francis A. F., Duc de. *Travels Through the United States of North America, the Country of the Iroquois, and Upper Canada, in the years 1795, 1796, and 1797.* 4 vols. 2nd ed. London: T. Gillet for R. Phillips, 1800.

Latrobe, Charles Joseph. *The Rambler in North America: MDCCCXXXII– MDCCCXXXIII.* 2 vols. London: R. B. Seeley & W. Burnside, 1835.

Latrobe, John H. B. "Reminiscences of Baltimore in 1824." *Maryland Historical Magazine* 1 (June 1906): 113–24.

Lawrence, William Beach. "Bank of the United States." *North American Review* 32 (1831): 524–63.

Levin, Alexandra Lee. "Two Jackson Supporters: Roger Brooke Taney and William Murdock Beall of Frederick." *Maryland Historical Magazine* 55 (September 1960): 221–29.

Lyford, William Gilman. *The Baltimore Address Directory: in Which Are Alphabetically Arranged the Vocations and Names of Many of the Most Prominent Business Men, of the City: to Which is Prefixed, a Statistical Article, Developing Some of the Resources of Baltimore.* Baltimore: J. Robinson, 1836.

Mackay, Alexander. *The Western World: or, Travels in the United States in 1846–47: Exhibiting Them in the Latest Development, Social, Political, and Industrial, Including a Chapter on California.* 2 vols. 2nd ed. Philadelphia: Lea & Blanchard, 1849.

Mackay, Charles. *Life and Liberty in America; or, Sketches of a Tour in the United States and Canada in 1857–58.* 2 vols. London: Smith, Elder & Co., 1859.

Mackinnon, Lauchlin B. *Atlantic and Transatlantic Sketches, Afloat and Ashore.* 2 vols. London: Colburn & Co., Publishers, 1852.

Makepeace, Royal. *Report on the Objects, Condition and Prospects of the Canton Company of Baltimore.* Baltimore: Pechin & Boothby, 1835.

Matchett's Baltimore Director for 1819, 1824, 1827, 1829, 1831, 1833, 1835, 1835/36, 1837/38, 1840/41, 1842, 1847, 1849, 1851, 1853, 1855/56. Baltimore: Richard J. Matchett, 1819–1856.
    The title varies: *The Baltimore Directory, Corrected up to June 1819,* compiled by Samuel Jackson; for the years 1824, 1827, 1845, *Matchett's Baltimore Directory*; for the years 1829–42, 1847–55, *Matchett's Baltimore Director.*

Mayer, Charles F. *Laying of the Corner Stone of the Baltimore House of Refuge: and the Address Upon the Occasion.* Baltimore: James Lucas, corner of Calvert Street and Lovely Lane, 1852.

Melish, John. *Travels Through the United States of America in the Years 1806 & 1807, and 1809, 1810, & 1811; Including an Account of Passages Betwixt America & Britain and Travels Through Various Parts of Britain,*

Bibliography

Ireland, and Canada, With Corrections and Improvements till 1815. Philadelphia: By the Author, n.d. Belfast: Jos. Smith, 1818.

Montgomery, John. *A Practical Detail of the Cotton Manufacture of the United States of America and the State of the Cotton Manufacture of that Country Contrasted and Compared with That of Great Britain.* New York: Augustus M. Kelley 1969 [1840].

Moreau de St. Méry, Médéric-Louis-Elie. "Baltimore as Seen by Moreau De Saint-Méry in 1794." Translated and edited by Fillmore Norfleet. *Maryland Historical Magazine* 35 (September 1940): 221–40.

———. *Moreau de St. Méry's American Journey, 1793–1798.* Translated and edited by Kenneth Roberts and Anna M. Roberts. Garden City, New York: Doubleday & Co., 1947.

Mullin, John, comp. *The Baltimore Directory, for 1799, Containing the Names, Occupations, and Places of Abode of the Citizens, Arranged in Alphabetical Order.* Baltimore: Warner & Hanna, 1799.

Murray, Henry Anthony. *Lands of the Slave and the Free; or, Cuba, the United States, and Canada.* 2nd ed. London: G. Routledge & Co., 1857.

Naff, John H. "Recollections of Baltimore; Thrown Together, as They Were Collected, at Different Times, from Conversations Had with the Elders of the City." *Maryland Historical Magazine* 5 (June 1910): 104–23.

Neal, John. *Wandering Recollections of a Somewhat Busy Life: An Autobiography.* Boston: Roberts Brothers, 1869.

Nichols, Thomas Low. *Forty Years of American Life, 1821–1861.* New York: Stackpole Sons, 1937.

Opdyke, George. "New Views of the Currency Question." *Bankers' Magazine* 13 (December 1858): 417–28.

Pairpont, Alfred. *Uncle Sam and His Country; or, Sketches of America in 1854–55–56.* London: Simpkin, Marshall, & Co., 1857.

Palmer, John. *Journal of Travels in the United States of North America, and in Lower Canada, Performed in the Year 1817.* London: Sherwood, Neely, & Jones, 1818.

Pickering, Joseph. *Inquiries of an Emigrant: Being the Narrative of an English Farmer, from the Year 1824 and 1830.* London: Effingham Wilson, 1831.

Pitkin, Timothy. *A Statistical View of the Commerce of the United States of America.* New York: Johnson Reprint Corporation, 1967 [1835].

Power, Tyrone. *Impressions of America During the Years 1833, 1834, and 1835.* 2 vols. London: Richard Bentley, 1836.

Prospectus of the Canton Company of Baltimore to Which Is Prefixed a Map of the Company's Ground; Together with the Act of Incorporation and an Explanation of the Designs of the Company and Some Views of the Local Advantages of Baltimore. Baltimore: n.p., 1829.

"Report of the Boston Board of Trade on the Causes of the Commercial Crisis." *Hunt's Merchants' Magazine* 38 (June 1858): 722–24.

"Retrospective View of the Year 1857." *Bankers' Magazine* 12 (February 1858): 593–604.

Bibliography

Scott, Joseph. *A Geographical Description of the States of Maryland and Delaware; also of the Counties, Towns, Rivers, Bays and Islands, With a List of the Hundreds in Each County*. Philadelphia: Kimmer, Conrad, & Co., 1807.

Semmes, Raphael. *Baltimore as Seen by Visitors, 1783–1860*. Baltimore: The Maryland Historical Society, 1953.

Snodgrass, John E. "The Baltimore and Ohio Railroad and Its Western Connections." *Hunt's Merchants' Magazine* 29 (January 1853): 64–72.

[Sparks, Jared.] "Baltimore." *North American Review* 20 (January 1825): 99–138.

[Stansbury, Elijah.] *The Life and Times of Hon. Elijah Stansbury, An "Old Defender" and Ex-Mayor of Baltimore; Together with Early Reminiscences, Dating from 1662, and Embracing a Period of 212 Years*. Baltimore: John Murphy & Co., 1874.

"Statistics on the Trade of Baltimore in 1860." *Hunt's Merchants' Magazine* 45 (August 1861): 131–36.

Stockbridge, Henry. "Commercial Cities and Towns of the United States—Baltimore." *Hunt's Merchants' Magazine* 23 (July 1850): 34–52.

Stockbridge, Henry, Sr. "Baltimore in 1846." *Maryland Historical Magazine* 6 (March 1911): 20–34.

Story, Joseph. *Commentaries on the Law of Bills of Exchange, Foreign and Inland, as Administered in England and America*. C. C. Little & J. Brown, 1843.

Sturge, Joseph. *A Visit to the United States in 1841*. Boston: n.p., 1842.

[Taney, Roger Brooke.] "Roger Brooke Taney's Account of His Relations with Thomas Ellicott in the Bank War." Edited by Stuart Bruchey. *Maryland Historical Magazine* 52 (March, June 1958): 58–74, 131–52.

Tanner, Henry Schank. *A Description of the Canals and Railroads of the United States, Comprehending Notices of All the Works of Internal Improvements Throughout the Several States*. New York: Augustus M. Kelley, 1970 [1840].

"Letters of Toussaint Louverture and of Edward Stephens, 1798–1800." *American Historical Review* 16 (October 1910): 64–101.

Thornton, Edward. "A Young Englishman Reports on the New Nation: Edward Thornton to James Bland Burges, 1791–1793." Edited by S. W. Jackson. *William and Mary Quarterly* 18 (January 1961): 85–121.

———. "Edward Thornton to James Bland Burges: Letters Written from Baltimore in the Eighteenth Century." Edited by S. W. Jackson. *Maryland Historical Magazine* 57 (March 1962): 16–28.

"Trade and Commerce of Baltimore in 1853." *Hunt's Merchants' Magazine* 30 (February 1854): 177–91.

Tudor, Henry. *Narrative of a Tour in North America; Comprising Mexico, the Mines of Real Del Monte, the United States, and the British Colonies: with an Excursion to the Island of Cuba in a Series of Letters, Written in the Years 1831–2*. 2 vols. London: James Duncan, 1834.

Bibliography

Varle, Charles. *A Complete View of Baltimore*. Baltimore: n.p., 1833.
W., G. L. "Causes That Produced the Crisis of 1857 Considered." *Hunt's Merchants' Magazine* 40 (January 1859): 19–37.
Welby, Adlard. *A Visit to North America and the English Settlements in Illinois with a Winter Residence in Philadelphia; Solely to Ascertain the Actual Prospects of the Emigrating Agriculturalist, Mechanic, and Commercial Speculator*. London: J. Drury, 1821.
Weld, Charles Richard. *A Vacation Tour in the United States and Canada*. London: Longman, Brown, Green, & Longmans, 1855.
Weld, Isaac, Jr. *Travels Through the States of North America and the Provinces of Upper and Lower Canada, During the Years 1795, 1796, and 1797*. London: John Stockdale, 1799.
Woods' Baltimore City Directory, Containing a Corrected Engraved Map of the City. Baltimore: John W. Woods. [1860].

Secondary Sources

Abbott, Collamer L. "Isaac Tyson, Jr., Pioneer Mining Engineer and Metallurgist." *Maryland Historical Magazine* 60 (March 1965): 15–25.
Adams, Donald R., Jr. "Wage Rates in the Early National Period: Philadelphia, 1785–1830." *Journal of Economic History* 28 (September 1968): 404–26.
Adams, Henry. *History of the United States*. 8 vols. New York: Antiquarian Press, 1962.
Alberts, Robert C. *The Golden Voyage: The Life and Times of William Bingham, 1752–1804*. Boston: Houghton Mifflin Co., 1969.
Albion, Robert Greenhalgn. "Colonial Commerce and Commercial Regulation." in *The Growth of American Economy*, edited by Harold F. Williamson, pp. 44–59. New York: Prentice-Hall, 1951.
———. *The Rise of New York Port [1815–1860]*. Hamden, Connecticut: Archon Books, 1961.
———. *Sea Lanes in Wartime: The American Experience, 1775–1942*. New York: W. W. Norton & Co., 1942.
Alexander, John K. "The City of Brotherly Fear: The Poor in Late-Eighteenth-Century Philadelphia." In *Cities in American History*, edited by Kenneth T. Jackson and Stanley K. Schultz, pp. 79–97. New York: Alfred A. Knopf, 1972.
Anderson, B. L. "Money and the Structure of Credit in the Eighteenth Century." *Business History* 12 (July 1970): 85–101.
Andrews, Charles M. *The Colonial Period of American History*. 4 vols. New Haven: Yale University Press, 1938.
Andrews, Ethan Allen. *Slavery and the Domestic Slave Trade, in a Series of Letters Addressed to the Executive Committee of the American Union for the Relief and Improvement of the Colored Race*. Boston: Light & Stearns, 1836.

Bibliography

Andrews, Matthew Page. "History of Baltimore, from 1850 to the Close of the Civil War." In *Baltimore: Its History and Its People*, edited by Clayton Colman Hall, vol. 1, pp. 151–237. 3 vols. New York: Lewis Historical Publishing Co., 1912.

———. *Tercentenary History of Maryland*. 3 vols. Baltimore: S. J. Clarke Publishing Co., 1925.

Arnold, Joseph L. "Suburban Growth and Municipal Annexation in Baltimore, 1745–1918." *Maryland Historical Magazine* 73 (March 1978): 109–28.

Atherton, Lewis E. "Auctions as a Threat to American Business in the Eighteen Twenties and Thirties." *Bulletin of the Business Historical Society* 11 (December 1937): 104–7.

———. "Itinerant Merchandising in the Ante-Bellum South." *Bulletin of the Business Historical Society* 19 (April 1945): 35–59.

———. *The Pioneer Merchant in Mid-America*. The University of Missouri Studies, vol. 14. Columbia: University of Missouri Press, 1939.

———. "Predecessors of the Commercial Drummer in the Old South." *Bulletin of the Business Historical Society* 21 (February 1947): 17–24.

———. "The Problem of Credit Rating in the Ante-Bellum South." *Journal of Southern History* 12 (1946): 534–56.

———. *The Southern Country Store, 1800–1860*. Baton Rouge: Louisiana State University Press, 1949.

Bagnall, William R. *The Textile Industries of the United States, Including Sketches and Notices of Cotton, Woolen, Silk and Linen Manufacturers in the Colonial Period*. 2 vols. New York: Augustus M. Kelley, 1971 [Cambridge, 1893].

Bailyn, Bernard. "Kinship and Trade in Seventeenth-Century New England." *Explorations in Entrepreneurial History* 6 (May 1954): 197–206.

Baker, Henry F. "History of Banking in the United States." *Bankers' Magazine* 9 (July 1854): 1–16; 11 (September 1856): 161–76; 11 (October 1856): 241–56; 11 (November 1856): 321–41; 11 (December 1856): 417–30; 12 (September 1857): 161–79.

Baker, Jean H. *Ambivalent Americans: The Know-Nothing Party in Maryland*. Baltimore: Johns Hopkins University Press, 1977.

———. *The Politics of Continuity: Maryland Political Parties from 1858 to 1870*. Baltimore: Johns Hopkins University Press, 1973.

Baldwin, Benjamin R. "The Debts Owed by Americans to British Creditors, 1763–1802." Ph.D. dissertation, Indiana University, 1932.

Bancroft, Frederic. *Slave Trading in the Old South*. New York: Frederick Ungar Publishing Co., 1959.

Beals, Carleton. *Brass-Knuckle Crusade: The Great Know-Nothing Conspiracy, 1820–1860*. New York: Hastings House, 1960.

Behrens. Kathryn L. *Paper Money in Maryland, 1727–1789*. Baltimore: Johns Hopkins University Press, 1923.

Beirne, Francis F. *The Amiable Baltimoreans*. Hatboro, Pa.: Tradition Press, 1968.

Bibliography

Bell, Carl D. "The Development of Western Maryland, 1715–1753." Master's thesis, University of Maryland, 1948.

Bell, Herbert C. "British Commercial Policy in the West Indies, 1783–1793." *English Historical Review* 31 (July 1916): 429–41.

————. "West Indies Trade Before the Revolution." *American Historical Review* 22 (January 1917): 272–87.

Benns, Frank Lee. *The American Struggle for the West Indian Carrying Trade, 1815–1830.* Bloomington: Indiana University Press, 1923.

Bernard, Richard M. "A Portrait of Baltimore in 1800: Economic and Occupational Patterns in an Early American City." *Maryland Historical Magazine* 69 (winter 1974): 341–60.

Bhagat, G. *Americans in India, 1784–1860.* New York: New York University Press, 1970.

Bibbins, Ruthella Mory. "The City of Baltimore, 1797–1850; The Era of the Clipper, the Turnpike, Mill, and Railroad: An Epoch of Commerce and Culture." In *Baltimore: Its History and Its People*, edited by Clayton Colman Hall, vol. 1, pp. 63–147. 3 vols. New York: Lewis Historical Publishing Co., 1912.

Bishop, J. Leander. *A History of American Manufacturers from 1608 to 1860.* 3 vols. 3rd edition, revised. New York: Augustus M. Kelley, 1966 [Philadelphia: Edward Young & Co., 1868].

Bjork, Gordon C. "The Weaning of the American Economy: Independence, Market Changes, and Economic Development." *Journal of Economic History* 24 (December 1964): 549–60.

Blake, Nelson M. *Water for the Cities: A History of the Urban Water Supply Problem in the United States.* Syracuse: Syracuse University Press, 1956.

Blandi, Joseph G. *Maryland Business Corporations, 1783–1852.* Baltimore: Johns Hopkins University Press, 1934.

Blitz, Rudolph C. "Mercantilist Policies and the Pattern of World Trade, 1500–1750." *Journal of Economic History* 27 (March 1967): 39–55.

Bohner, Charles H. *John Pendleton Kennedy: Gentleman from Baltimore.* Baltimore: Johns Hopkins University Press, 1961.

Boles, John B. *The Great Revival, 1787–1805: The Origins of the Southern Evangelical Mind.* Lexington: University Press of Kentucky, 1972.

Bolles, Albert S. *The Financial History of the United States from 1789 to 1860.* 3rd edition. New York: D. Appleton & Co., 1891.

Bond, Beverly W., Jr. "The Quit-Rent in Maryland." *Maryland Historical Magazine* 5 (December 1910): 350–65.

————. *The Quit-Rent System in the American Colonies.* New Haven: Yale University Press, 1919.

————. *State Government in Maryland, 1777–1781.* Baltimore: Johns Hopkins University Press, 1905.

Boorstin, Daniel. *The Americans: The National Experience.* New York: Random House, 1965.

Bornholt, Laura. *Baltimore and Early Pan-Americanism: A Study in the*

Bibliography

Background of the Monroe Doctrine. Northampton, Massachusetts: Smith College Press, 1949.

Boulden, J.E.P. *The Presbyterians of Baltimore: Their Churches and Historic Graveyards*. Baltimore: Wm. K. Boyle & Son, 1875.

Bourne, Edward G. *History of the Surplus Revenue of 1837: Being an Account of Its Origin, Its Distribution among the States, and the Uses to Which It Was Applied*. New York: B. Franklin, 1968 [1885].

Bowers, Douglas. "Ideology and Political Parties in Maryland, 1851–1856." *Maryland Historical Magazine* 64 (fall 1969): 197–217.

Brackett, Jeffrey R. *The Negro in Maryland: A Study of the Institution of Slavery*. Freeport, New York: Books for Libraries Press, 1969.

Bridner, Elwood L. "The Fugitive Slaves of Maryland." *Maryland Historical Magazine* 66 (spring 1971): 33–50.

Brown, Alexander Crosby. *Steam Packets on the Chesapeake: A History of the Old Bay Line*. Cambridge, Maryland: Cornell Maritime Press, 1961.

Brown, Dorothy Marie. "Maryland and the Federalist: Search for Unity." *Maryland Historical Magazine* 63 (1968): 1–21.

———. "Politics of Crisis." *Maryland Historical Magazine* 57 (September 1962): 195–209.

Brown, John Crosby. *A Hundred Years of Merchant Banking: A History of Brown Brothers and Company; Brown, Shipley & Company; and the Allied Firms*. New York: Privately printed, 1909.

Brown, Kenneth L. "Stephen Girard, Promoter of the Second Bank of the United States." *Journal of Political Economy* 2 (November 1942): 125–48.

Brown, Roger H. *The Republic in Peril: 1812*. New York: W. W. Norton & Co., 1971.

Browne, Gary L. "Baltimore in the Nation, 1789–1861: A Social Economy in Industrial Revolution." Ph.D. dissertation, Wayne State University, 1973.

———. "Business Innovation and Social Change: The Career of Alexander Brown After the War of 1812." *Maryland Historical Magazine* 69 (fall 1974): 243–55.

———. "The Panic of 1819 in Baltimore." In *Law, Society, and Politics in Early Maryland*, edited by Aubrey C. Land, Lois Green Carr, Edward C. Papenfuse, pp. 212–27. Baltimore: Johns Hopkins University Press, 1976.

Bruchey, Stuart. "The Inadequacy of Profit Maximization as a Model of Business Behavior." *Business History Review* 34 (winter 1960): 495–97.

———. *Robert Oliver: Merchant of Baltimore, 1783–1819*. Baltimore: Johns Hopkins University Press, 1956.

———. *The Roots of American Economic Growth, 1607–1861*. New York: Harper & Row, 1965.

———. "Success and Failure Factures: American Merchants in Foreign Trade in the Eighteen and Early Nineteenth Centuries." *Business History Review* 32 (autumn 1958): 272–92.

———, ed. "Roger Brooke Taney's Account of His Relations with Thomas Ellicott in the Bank War." *Maryland Historical Magazine* 52 (March 1958): 58–74; (June 1958): 131–52.

Bibliography

Bryan, Alfred Cookman. *History of State Banking in Maryland*. Baltimore: Johns Hopkins University Press, 1899.

Buck, Norman Sydney. *The Development of the Organization of Anglo-American Trade, 1800–1850*. New Haven: Yale University Press, 1925. 1925.

Burgess, Robert H., and Wood, H. Graham. *Steamboats Out of Baltimore*. Cambridge, Maryland: Tidewater Publishers, 1968.

Burnett, Edmund C., ed. *Letters of Members of the Continental Congress*. 8 vols. Washington, D.C.: Carnegie Institution, 1921–36.

Calderhead, William. "How Extensive Was the Border State Slave Trade?" *Civil War History* 18 (March 1972): 42–55.

Calhoun, Daniel H. *Professional Lives in America: Structure and Aspiration, 1750–1850*. Cambridge, Massachusetts: Harvard University Press, 1965.

Callender, Guy S. "Early Transportation and Banking Enterprises of the States in Relation to the Growth of Corporations." *Quarterly Journal of Economics* 17 (1902/1903): 111–62.

Campbell, Penelope. *Maryland in Africa: The Maryland State Colonization Society, 1831–1857*. Urbana: University of Illinois Press, 1971.

Carman, Harry J., and Luthin, Reinhard H. "Some Aspects of the Know-Nothing Movement Reconsidered." *South Atlantic Quarterly* 39 (April 1940): 213–34.

Carroll, Douglas G., and Coll, Blanche E. "The Baltimore Almshouse: An Early History." *Maryland Historical Magazine* 66 (summer 1971): 135–72.

Carson, Gerald. *The Old Country Store*. New York: Oxford University Press, 1954.

Cassell, Frank Allen. "General Samuel Smith and the Election of 1800." *Maryland Historical Magazine* 63 (December 1868): 341–59.

———. "The Great Baltimore Riot of 1812." *Maryland Historical Magazine* 70 (fall 1975): 241–59.

———. *Merchant Congressman in the Young Republic: Samuel Smith of Maryland, 1752–1839*. Milwaukee: University of Wisconsin Press, 1971.

———. "Response to Crisis: Baltimore in 1814." *Maryland Historical Magazine* 66 (fall 1971): 261–87.

Catterall, Ralph C. H. *The Second Bank of the United States*. Chicago: University of Chicago Press, 1960 [1903].

Catton, William B. "The Baltimore Business Community and the Secession Crisis, 1860–1861." Master's thesis, University of Maryland, 1952.

———. "John W. Garrett of the Baltimore & Ohio: A Study in Seaport and Railroad Competition, 1820–1874." Ph.D. dissertation, Northwestern University, 1959.

Chandler, Alfred D., Jr. "Patterns of American Railroad Finance, 1830–1850." *Business History Review* 28 (September 1954): 248–63.

Chandler, Charles Lyon. "United States Commerce with Latin America at the Promulgation of the Monroe Doctrine." *Quarterly Journal of Economics* 38 (May 1924): 466–86.

———. "U. S. Merchant Ships in the Rio de la Plata (1801–1808) as Shown by

Bibliography

Early Newspapers." *Hispanic American History Review* 2 (February 1919): 26–54.

Channing, Steven A. *Crisis of Fear: Secession in South Carolina.* New York: Simon & Schuster, 1970.

Chapelle, Howard Irving. *The Baltimore Clipper: Its Origin and Development.* Salem, Massachusetts: Marine Research Society, 1930.

Checkland, S. G. "American versus West Indian Traders in Liverpool, 1793–1815." *Journal of Economic History* 18 (June 1958): 141–60.

———. "Economic Attitudes in Liverpool, 1793–1807." *Economic History Review* 5 (1952): 58–75.

———. "An English Merchant House in China After 1842." *Bulletin of the Business Historical Society* 27 (September 1953): 158–89.

———. *The Rise of Industrial Society in England, 1815–1885.* London: Longmans, Green & Co., 1964.

Chidsey, Donald B. *The American Privateers.* New York: Dodd, Mead, 1962.

Clark, Dennis Rankin. "Baltimore, 1729–1829: The Genesis of a Community." Ph.D. dissertation, The Catholic University of America, 1976.

Clark, G. Kitson. "The Repeal of the Corn Laws and the Politics of the Forties." *Economic History Review* 4 (1951): 1–13.

Clark, John G. *The Grain Trade in the Old Northwest.* Urbana: University of Illinois Press, 1966.

Clark, Malcolm C. "Federalism at High Tide: The Election of 1796 in Maryland." *Maryland Historical Magazine* 61 (September 1966): 210–30.

Clark, Thomas D. *Pills, Petticoats and Plows: The Southern Country Store.* Indianapolis: Bobbs-Merrill, 1944.

Clark, Victor Selden. *History of Manufacturers in the United States.* 3 vols. New York: McGraw-Hill, 1929.

Clarkson, Paul S., and Jett, Samuel R. *Luther Martin of Maryland.* Baltimore: Johns Hopkins University Press, 1970.

Cleveland, Frederick A., and Powell, Fred W. *Railroad Promotion and Capitalization in the United States.* New York: Longmans, Green and Co., 1909.

Coatsworth, John H. "American Trade with European Colonies in the Caribbean and South America, 1790–1812." *William and Mary Quarterly*, 3rd Series, 24 (April 1967): 243–66.

Cochran, Thomas C. "The Business Revolution." *American Historical Review* 79 (December 1974): 1449–66.

Coggeshall, George. *History of the American Privateers, and Letters of Marque, During Our War with England in the Years 1812, '13, and '14.* New York: By the author, 1856.

Cohen, Henry. *Business & Politics in America from the Age of Jackson to the Civil War: A Career Biography of William Wilson Corcoran.* Westport, Connecticut: Greenwood Press, 1971.

Cohen, Ira. "The Auction System in the Port of New York, 1817–1837." *Business History Review* 45 (winter 1971): 488–510.

Cole, Arthur Charles. *The Whig Party in the South.* Washington, D.C.: American Historical Association, 1913.

Cole, Arthur Harrison. *The American Wool Manufacture: A History and Analysis.* 2 vols. Cambridge, Massachusetts: Harvard University Press, 1926.

Cole, Arthur Harrison, and Smith, Walter Buckingham. *Fluctuations in American Business, 1790–1860.* Cambridge, Massachusetts: Harvard University Press, 1935.

Cole, Arthur Harrison, and Williamson, Harold F. *The American Carpet Manufacture: A History and Analysis.* Cambridge, Massachusetts: Harvard University Press, 1941.

Cole, A. H. "Cyclical and Sectional Variations in the Sale of Public Lands, 1816–60." *Review of Economic Statistics* 9 (January 1927): 41–53.

———. "Evolution of the Foreign Exchange Market of the United States." *Journal of Economic and Business History* 1 (May 1929): 384–421.

———. "The New York Money Market of 1843 to 1862." *Review of Economic Statistics* 11 (November 1929): 164–70.

———. "Seasonal Variations in Sterling Exchange." *Journal of Economic and Business History* 2 (November 1929): 203–18.

———. "Statistical Background of the Crisis, 1837–1842." *Review of Economic Statistics* 10 (November 1928): 182–95.

Cole, A. H., and Frickey, Edwin. "The Course of Stock Prices, 1825–1866." *Review of Economic Statistics* 10 (August 1928): 117–39.

Coleman, Peter J. *Debtors and Creditors in America: Insolvency, Imprisonment for Debt, and Bankruptcy, 1607–1900.* Madison: The State Historical Society of Wisconsin, 1974.

———. *The Transformation of Rhode Island, 1790–1860.* Providence, Rhode Island: Brown University Press, 1963.

Coles, Harry L. *The War of 1812.* Chicago: University of Chicago Press, 1965.

Coll, Blanche D. "The Baltimore Society for the Prevention of Pauperism, 1820–1822." *American Historical Review* 61 (October 1955): 77–87.

Collins, Winfield Hazlitt. *The Domestic Slave Trade of the Southern States.* New York: Broadway Publishing Co., 1904.

Combs, Jerald A. *The Jay Treaty: Political Battleground of the Founding Fathers.* Berkeley and Los Angeles: University of California Press, 1970.

Commons, John R. et al. *History of Labour in the United States.* 4 vols. New York: Macmillan Co., 1918–35.

Copeland, Melvin Thomas. *The Cotton Manufacturing Industry of the United States.* Cambridge, Massachusetts: Harvard University Press, 1912.

Cordell, Eugene Fauntleroy. *Historical Sketch of the University of Maryland School for Medicine—1807–1890.* Baltimore: Isaac Friedenwald, 1891.

Coyle, Wilbur F. *The Mayors of Baltimore.* Baltimore: n.p., 1919.

Cranwell, John Phillips, and Crane, William Bowers. *Men of Marque: A History of Private Armed Vessels Out of Baltimore During the War of 1812.* New York: W. W. Norton & Co., 1940.

Bibliography

Craven, Avery O. "The Agricultural Reformers of the Ante-Bellum South." *American Historical Review* 33 (January 1928): 302–14.

———. *Soil Exhaustion as a Factor in the Agricultural History of Virginia and Maryland, 1606–1860.* Urbana: University of Illinois Press, 1926.

Crosby, Alfred W., Jr. *America, Russia, Hemp, and Napoleon: American Trade with Russia and the Baltic, 1783–1812.* Columbus: Ohio State University Press, 1965.

Crowl, Philip A. *Maryland During and After the Revolution: A Political and Economic Study.* Baltimore: Johns Hopkins University Press, 1943.

Dakin, Douglas. *British and American Philhellenes During the War of Greek Independence, 1821–1833.* Thessalonike, Greece: Nicolaides Press, 1955.

Dangerfield, George. *The Awakening of American Nationalism, 1815–1828.* New York: Harper & Row, 1965.

———. *The Era of Good Feelings.* New York: Harcourt, Brace & World, 1952.

Danhof, Clarence H. "Farm Making Costs and the Safety Valve, 1850–1860." *Journal of Political Economy* 49 (June 1941): 317–39.

Daniel, Hawthorne. *The Clipper Ship.* New York: Dodd, Mead, 1928.

Daniels, George W. "American Cotton Trade with Liverpool under the Embargo and Non-Intercourse Acts." *American Historical Review* 21 (January 1916): 276–87.

Davidson, Robert A. *Isaac Hicks: New York Merchant and Quaker, 1767–1820.* Cambridge, Massachusetts: Harvard University Press, 1964.

Davis, Joseph Stancliffe. *Essays in the Earlier History of American Corporations.* 2 vols. Cambridge, Massachusetts: Harvard University Press, 1917.

Davis, L. E., and Hughes, J. R. T. "A Dollar Sterling Exchange, 1803–1895." *Economic History Review* 13 (1960): 52–78.

Day, Clive. "The Early Development of the American Cotton Manufacture." *Quarterly Journal of Economics* 39 (May 1925): 450–68.

Della, M. Ray, Jr. "The Problems of Negro Labor in the 1850s." *Maryland Historical Magazine* 66 (spring 1971): 14–32.

Demos, John and Virginia. "Adolescence in Historical Perspective." *Journal of Marriage and the Family* 31 (November 1969): 632–38.

Dewey, Davis Richard. *Financial History of the United States.* 9th edition. New York: Longmans, Green & Co., 1924.

Dickson, P.G.M. *The Financial Revolution in England: A Study in the Development of Public Credit, 1688–1796.* New York: St. Martin's Press, 1967.

Didier, Eugene L. "The Social Athens of America." *Harper's New Monthly Magazine* 65 (June 1882): 20–36.

Dillon, Merton L. *Benjamin Lundy and the Struggle for Negro Freedom.* Urbana: University of Illinois Press, 1966.

Dodd, Edwin M. *American Business Corporations Until 1860.* Cambridge, Massachusetts: Harvard University Press, 1954.

Dorfman, Joseph. "Anglo-American Finance." *Journal of Economic History* 11 (spring 1951): 140–47.

Bibliography

Dorsey, Dorothy Baker. "The Panic of 1819 in Missouri." *Missouri Historical Review* 29 (January 1935): 79–91.

Dorsey, Rhoda M. "Comment." In *The Growth of the Seaport Cities, 1790–1825*, edited by David T. Gilchrist, pp. 66–69. Charlottesville: University Press of Virginia, 1968.

———. "The Pattern of Baltimore Commerce During the Confederation Period." *Maryland Historical Magazine* 62 (June 1967): 119–33.

Dowd, Mary Jane. "The State in the Maryland Economy, 1776–1807." *Maryland Historical Magazine* 57 (June 1962): 90–132; 57 (September 1962): 229–58.

Dulles, Foster Rhea. *The Old China Trade*. Boston: Houghton Mifflin Co., 1930.

Dunbar, Charles F. *Laws of the United States Relating to Currency, Finance, and Banking from 1789 to 1891*. Boston: Ginn & Co., 1893.

———. *Theory and History of Banking*. New York: G. P. Putnam's Sons, 1922.

Durrenburger, Joseph Austin. *Turnpikes: A Study of the Toll Road Movement in the Middle Atlantic States and Maryland*. Cos Cob, Connecticut: J. E. Edwards, 1968 [1931].

East, Robert A. *Business Enterprise in the American Revolutionary Era*. New York: Columbia University Press, 1938.

———. "The Business Entrepreneur in a Changing Colonial Economy, 1763–1795." *Journal of Economic History* 6 (supplement, 1946): 16–27.

Eaton, Clement. *The Growth of Southern Civilization, 1780–1860*. New York: Harper & Row, 1961.

Eaton, Leonard K. "Medicine in Philadelphia and Boston, 1805–1830." *Pennsylvania Magazine of History and Biography* 85 (January 1951): 66–75.

Eliason, Adolph Oscar. *The Rise of Commercial Banking Institutions in the United States*. New York: B. Franklin, 1970 [Minneapolis, 1901].

Ely, Roland T. "The Old Cuba Trade: Highlights and Case Studies of Cuban-American Independence During the Nineteenth Century." *Business History Review* 38 (winter 1964): 456–78.

Emmons, George Foster. *The Navy of the United States, from the Commencement, 1775 to 1853*. Washington, D.C.: Gideon & Co., 1853.

Ernst, Joseph Albert. *Money and Politics in America, 1755–1775: A Study in the Currency Act of 1764 and the Political Economy of Revolution*. Chapel Hill: University of North Carolina Press, 1973.

Evans, G. Herberton, Jr., and Kanwisher, Walter C., Jr. "Business Organizations in Baltimore, 1859." *Journal of Political Economy* 62 (February 1954): 63–67.

Evitts, William J. *A Matter of Allegiances: Maryland from 1850 to 1861*. Baltimore: Johns Hopkins University Press, 1974.

Ezell, John Samuel. *Fortune's Merry Wheel: The Lottery in America*. Cambridge, Massachusetts: Harvard University Press, 1960.

Farnum, Henry W. *Chapters in the History of Social Legislation in the United States to 1860*. Washington, D.C.: Carnegie Institution, 1938.

Bibliography

Fenstermaker, J. Van. *The Development of American Commercial Banking, 1782–1837.* Kent, Ohio: Bureau of Economic and Business Research, Kent State University, 1965.

Ferguson, E. James. "Speculation in the Revolutionary Debt: The Ownership of Public Securities in Maryland, 1790." *Journal of Economic History* 14 (winter 1954): 35–45.

Ferry, John William. *A History of the Department Store.* New York: Macmillan Co., 1960.

Fischer, David Hackett. *The Revolution of American Conservatism: The Federalist Party in the Era of Jeffersonian Democracy.* New York: Harper & Row, 1965.

Fishwick, Marshall W. "*The Portico* and Literary Nationalism After the War of 1812." *William and Mary Quarterly,* 3rd Series, 8 (April 1951): 238–45.

Folz, William W. "The Financial Crisis of 1819: A Study in Post War Economic Readjustment." Ph.D. dissertation, University of Illinois, 1935.

Foner, Philip Sheldon. *Business and Slavery: The New York Merchants and the Irrepressible Conflict.* Chapel Hill: University of North Carolina Press, 1941.

Forbush, Bliss. *Moses Sheppard: Quaker Philanthropist of Baltimore.* Philadelphia: J. B. Lippincott, 1968.

Foster, Charles I. *An Errand of Mercy: The Evangelical United Front, 1790–1837.* Chapel Hill: University of North Carolina Press, 1960.

———. "The Urban Missionary Movement, 1814–1837." *Pennsylvania Magazine of History and Biography* 85 (January 1951): 47–63.

Foulke, Roy Anderson. *The Sinews of American Commerce.* New York: Dun & Bradstreet, Inc., 1941.

Frasure, Carl M. "Union Sentiment in Maryland, 1859–1861." *Maryland Historical Magazine* 24 (September 1929): 210–24.

Friedman, Lee M. "The Drummer in Early American Merchandise Distribution." *Bulletin of the Business Historical Society* 21 (April 1947): 39–49.

Galpin, William Freeman. "The American Grain Trade Under the Embargo of 1808." *Journal of Economic and Business History* 2 (November 1929): 71–100.

———. *The Grain Supply of England During the Napoleonic Period.* New York: Macmillan Co., 1925.

Garitee, Jerome R. *The Republic's Private Navy: The American Privateering Business as Practiced by Baltimore During the War of 1812.* Middletown, Connecticut: Wesleyan University Press, 1977.

Garrett, Jane N. "Philadelphia and Baltimore, 1790–1840: A Study of Intra-Regional Unity." *Maryland Historical Magazine* 55 (March 1960): 1–13.

Gatell, Frank Otto. "Secretary Taney and the Baltimore Pets: A Study in Banking and Politics." *Business History Review* 39 (summer 1965): 205–27.

———. "Spoils of the Bank War: Political Bias in the Selection of Pet Banks." *American Historical Review* 70 (October 1965): 35–58.

Bibliography

Genovese, Eugene. *The Political Economy of Slavery, and Society of the Slave South*. New York: Vintage Books, 1967.

Gibbons, James Sloan. *The Bank of New York, Their Dealers, the Clearing House, and the Panic of 1857, with a Financial Chart*. New York: Greenwood Press, 1968 [1858].

Giddens, Paul H. "Trade and Industry in Colonial Maryland, 1753–1769." *Journal of Economic and Business History* 4 (May 1932): 512–39.

Gilbert, Arlan K. "Gunpowder Production in Post-Revolutionary Maryland." *Maryland Historical Magazine* 52 (September 1957): 187–201.

Gilchrist, David T., ed. *The Growth of the Seaport Cities, 1790–1825*. Charlottesville: University Press of Virginia, 1968.

Goebel, Dorothy Burne. "British-American Rivalry in the Chilean Trade, 1817–1820." *Journal of Economic History* 2 (November 1942): 190–202.

———. "British Trade to the Spanish Colonies, 1796–1823." *American History Review* 43 (January 1938): 288–320.

Goldin, Claudia Dale. *Urban Slavery in the American South, 1820–1860: A Quantitative History*. Chicago: University of Chicago Press, 1976.

Goldscheider, Calvin. *Population, Modernization, and Social Structure*. Boston: Little, Brown & Co., 1971.

Goodrich, Carter. *Government Promotion of American Canals and Railroads, 1800–1890*. New York: Columbia University Press, 1960.

———. "Recent Contributions to Economic History: The United States, 1789–1860." *Journal of Economic History* 19 (March 1959): 25–43.

———. "The Revulsion Against Internal Improvements." *Journal of Economic History* 10 (November 1950): 145–69.

———, ed. *Canals and American Economic Development*. New York: Columbia University Press, 1960.

Goodrich, Carter, and Segal, Harvey H. "Baltimore's Aid to Railroads: A Study in the Municipal Planning of Internal Improvements." *Journal of Economic History* 13 (winter 1953): 2–35.

Gordon, Scott. "The London *Economist* and the High Tide of Laissez–Faire." *Journal of Political Economy* 63 (December 1955): 461–88.

Goss, John Dean. *The History of the Tariff Administration in the United States*. New York: Studies in History and Economics, and Public Law of Columbia College, vol. 1, no. 2, 1891.

Gould, Clarence P. "The Economic Causes of the Rise of Baltimore." In *Essays in Colonial History Presented to Charles McLean Andrews by His Students*, pp. 225–51. New Haven: Yale University Press, 1931.

———. *The Land System of Maryland, 1720–1765*. Baltimore: Johns Hopkins University Press, 1913.

———. *Money and Transportation in Maryland, 1720–1765*. Baltimore: Johns Hopkins University Press, 1915.

Govan, Thomas Payne. *Nicholas Biddle: Nationalist and Public Banker, 1786–1844*. Chicago: University of Chicago Press, 1959.

Bibliography

Gray, Lewis C. *History of Agriculture in the Southern United States to 1860.* 2 vols. Washington, D.C.: Carnegie Institution, 1833.

Gray, Ralph D. "Early History of the Chesapeake and Delaware Canal." *Delaware History* 8 (March 1959): 207–64.

Greene, Evarts B., and Harrington, Virginia D. *American Population Before the Federal Census of 1790.* Gloucester, Mass.: Peter Smith, 1966.

Greer, Thomas H. "Economic and Social Effects of the Depression of 1819 in the Old Northwest." *Indiana Magazine of History* 44 (September 1948): 227–43.

Griffin, Charles S. "The Taxation of Sugar in the United States, 1789–1861." *Quarterly Journal of Economics* 11 (1896/97): 296–309.

Griffin, Richard W. "An Origin of the Industrial Revolution in Maryland: I. The Textile Industry, 1789–1826." *Maryland Historical Magazine* 61 (March 1966): 24–36.

Griffith, Thomas Waters. *Annals of Baltimore.* Baltimore: William Woody, 1834 [misprinted 1824].

Gunderson, Robert Gray. "The Great Baltimore Whig Convention of 1840." *Maryland Historical Magazine* 47 (March 1952): 11–18.

Hagensick, A. Clarke. "Revolution or Reform in 1836: Maryland's Preface to the Dorr Rebellion." *Maryland Historical Magazine* 57 (December 1962): 346–66.

Hales, Charles A. *The Baltimore Clearing House.* Baltimore: Johns Hopkins University Press, 1940.

Hall, Clayton Colman, ed. *Baltimore: Its History and Its People.* 3 vols. New York: Lewis Historical Publishing Co., 1912.

Haller, Mark H. "The Rise of the Jackson Party in Maryland, 1820–1829." *Journal of Southern History* 28 (August 1962): 307–26.

Hammond, Bray. *Banks and Politics in America from the Revolution to the Civil War.* Princeton: Princeton University Press, 1957.

Hammond, Matthew B. *The Cotton Industry: An Essay in American Economic History.* New York: Macmillan Co., 1897.

Handlin, Oscar, and Burchard, John, eds. *The Historian and the City.* Cambridge, Massachusetts: M.I.T. Press and Harvard University Press, 1963.

Handlin, Oscar, and Handlin, Mary Flug. *Commonwealth: A Study of the Role of Government in the American Economy: Massachusetts, 1774–1861.* Revised edition. Cambridge, Mass.: Belknap Press of Harvard University Press, 1969.

Haney, Lewis H. *A Congressional History of Railways in the United States, 1850–1887.* 2 vols. in 1. New York: Augustus M. Kelley, 1968 [1910].

Hanna, Hugh Sisson. *A Financial History of Maryland, 1789–1848.* Baltimore: Johns Hopkins University Press, 1907.

Hanna, Mary A. *The Trade of the Delaware District Before the Revolution.* Smith College Studies in History, vol. 2. Northampton, Massachusetts, 1917.

Harlow, Alvin Fay. *Old Towpaths, the Story of the American Canal Era.* Port Washington, New York: Kennikat Press, 1964 [1926].

Bibliography

Haskell, Louisa P. *Langdon Cheves and the United States Bank: A Study from Neglected Sources.* Washington, D.C.: American Historical Association, 1897.

Hazard, Blanche E. *The Organization of the Boot and Shoe Industry in Massachusetts Before 1875.* Cambridge, Massachusetts: Harvard University Press, 1921.

Heaton, Herbert. "Non-Importation, 1806–1812." *Journal of Economic History* 1 (November 1941): 178–98.

Hedges, Joseph Edward. *Commercial Banking and the Stock Market Before 1860.* Baltimore: Johns Hopkins University Press, 1938.

Hemphill, John, II. "Annapolis: Colonial Metropolis and State Capitol." In *The Old Line State: A History of Maryland*, edited by Morris Leon Radoff, vol. 1, pp. 3–28. 2 vols. Hopkinsville, Kentucky: Historical Records Association, 1956.

Hepburn, A. Barton. *A History of Currency in the United States.* New York: Macmillan Co., 1915.

Hidy, Muriel Emmie. "George Peabody, Merchant and Financier, 1839–1854." Ph.D. dissertation, Radcliff College, 1939.

Hidy, Ralph W. *The House of Baring in American Trade and Finance: English Merchant Bankers at Work, 1763–1861.* Cambridge, Massachusetts: Harvard University Press, 1949.

———. "House of Baring and the Second Bank of the United States, 1826–1836." *Pennsylvania Magazine of History and Biography* 68 (July 1944): 269–85.

———. "Organization and Function of Anglo-American Merchant Bankers, 1815–1860." *Journal of Economic History* 1 (supplement, 1941): 53–66.

Hobsbawm, E. J. *The Age of Revolution, 1789–1848.* London: Weidenfeld & Nicolson, 1962.

Hoffman, Ronald. "Economics, Politics, and the Revolution in Maryland." Ph.D. dissertation, University of Wisconsin, 1969.

———. *A Spirit of Dissension: Economics, Politics, and the Revolution in Maryland.* Baltimore: Johns Hopkins University Press, 1973.

Holdsworth, John Thom, and Dewey, Davis Rich. *The First and Second Banks of the United States.* Washington, D.C.: Government Printing Office, 1910.

Hollander, J. H. *The Financial History of Baltimore.* Baltimore: Johns Hopkins University Press, 1899.

Hollander, Stanley C. "Nineteenth-Century Anti-Drummer Legislation in the United States." *Business History Review* 38 (winter 1964): 479–500.

Holt, Michael Fitzgibbon. *Forging a Majority: The Formation of the Republican Party in Pittsburgh, 1848–1860.* New Haven: Yale University Press, 1969.

Horsman, Reginald. *The War of 1812.* New York: Alfred A. Knopf, 1969.

Hoselitz, Bert F., and Moore, Wilbert E., eds. *Industrialization and Society.* The Hague: UNESCO, 1963.

Howard, George W. *The Monumental City: Its Past History and Present Resources.* Baltimore: n.p., 1873.

Howard, William Travis, Jr. *Public Health Administration and the Natural*

Bibliography

History of Disease in Baltimore, Maryland, 1797–1920. Washington, D.C.: Carnegie Institution, 1924.

Hoyt, William D., Jr. "Land for a Cathedral: Baltimore, 1806–1817." *Catholic Historical Review* 36 (January 1950): 441–45.

———, ed. "Civilian Defense in Baltimore, 1814–1815." *Maryland Historical Magazine* 39 (September 1944): 199–224; 39 (December 1944): 293–309; 40 (March 1945): 7–23; 40 (June 1945): 137–232.

Hughes, J.R.T., and Rosenberg, Nathan. "The United States Business Cycle Before 1860: Some Problems of Interpretation." *Economic History Review* 15 (April 1963): 476–93.

Hugins, Walter. *Jacksonian Democracy and the Working Class: A Study of the New York Workingmen's Movement, 1829–1837.* Stanford: Stanford University Press, 1960.

Hulbert, Archer B. "Western Ship-Building." *American Historical Review* 21 (July 1916): 720–33.

Hungerford, Edward. *The Story of the Baltimore & Ohio Railroad, 1827–1927.* 2 vols. New York: G. P. Putnam's Sons, 1928.

Hutchins, John Greenwood Brown. *The American Maritime Industries and Public Policy, 1789–1914: An Economic History.* Cambridge, Massachusetts: Harvard University Press, 1941.

Ingersoll, Charles Jared. *History of the Second War Between the United States of America and Great Britain, Declared by Act of Congress, the 18th of June, 1812, and Concluded by Peace, the 15th of February, 1815.* 2 vols. Philadelphia: Lippincott, Grambo & Co., 1852.

Jacobs, Jane. *The Economy of Cities.* New York: Random House, 1969.

Jacobstein, Meyer. *The Tobacco Industry in the United States.* New York: Columbia University Press, 1907.

James, Alfred R. "Sidelights on the Founding of the Baltimore and Ohio Railroad." *Maryland Historical Magazine* 48 (December 1953): 267–309.

James, C.L.R. *The Black Jacobins: Toussaint L'Ouverture and the San Domingo Revolution.* New York: Vintage Books, 1963.

Jenks, Leland Hamilton. *The Migration of British Capital to 1875.* New York: Alfred A. Knopf, 1927.

Jennings, Walter Wilson. *The American Embargo, 1807–1809, with Particular Reference to Its Effect on Industry.* Iowa City: University of Iowa Press, 1921.

Jensen, Frederick G. *Capital Growth in Early America.* New York: Vantage Press, 1965.

Johnson, Emory Richard et al. *History of Domestic and Foreign Commerce of the United States.* 2 vols. in 1. Washington, D.C.: Carnegie Institution, 1915.

Johnson, Keach. "The Baltimore Company Seeks English Markets: A Study of the Anglo-American Iron Trade, 1731–1755." *William and Mary Quarterly* 16 (January 1959): 37–60.

Johnson, Laurence A. *Over the Counter and on the Shelf: Country Storekeeping in America, 1620–1920.* Rutland, Vermont: Charles E. Tuttle Co., 1961.

Jones, Fred M. *Middlemen in the Domestic Trade of the United States, 1800–1860.* Urbana: University of Illinois Press, 1937.

Josephson, Hanna. *The Golden Threads: New England's Mill Girls and Magnates.* New York: Duell, Sloan & Pearce, 1949.

Kammen, Michael. *Empire and Interest: The American Colonies and the Politics of Mercantilism.* Philadelphia: J. B. Lippincott, 1970.

Kearny, John Watts. *Sketch of American Finances: 1789–1835.* Westport, Connecticut: Greenwood Press, 1968 [1887].

Keith, Alice B. "Relaxations in the British Restrictions on the American Trade with the British West Indies, 1783–1802." *Journal of Modern History* 20 (March 1948): 1–18.

Keller, David R. "Nativism or Sectionalism: A History of the Know-Nothing Party in Lancaster County, Pennsylvania." *Journal of the Lancaster County Historical Society* 75 (Easter 1971): 41–100.

Kent, Frank R. *The Story of Alexander Brown & Sons.* Baltimore: Alexander Brown & Sons, 1950.

Kent, James. *Commentaries on American Law.* Edited by George F. Comstock. 4 vols. 11th edition. Boston: Little, Brown & Co., 1866.

Kett, Joseph F. *The Formation of the American Medical Profession: The Role of Institutions, 1780–1860.* New Haven: Yale University Press, 1968.

Keyes, Emerson W. *A History of Savings Banks in the United States.* New York: Bradford Rhodes, 1876.

Keifer, Sister Monica, O.P. "Early American Childhood in the Middle Atlantic Area." *Pennsylvania Magazine of History and Biography* 68 (January 1944): 3–27.

King, Thomas. *Consolidated of Baltimore, 1816–1950: A History of Consolidated Gas, Electric Light and Power Company of Baltimore.* Baltimore: n.p., 1950.

Kinley, David. *The History, Organization and Influence of the Independent Treasury of the United States.* New York: T. Y. Crowell & Co., 1893.

———. *The Independent Treasury of the United States and Its Relation to the Banks of the Country.* New York: Augustus M. Kelley, 1970.

Klingaman, David. "The Significance of Grain in the Development of the Tobacco Colonies." *Journal of Economic History* 29 (June 1969): 268–78.

Kouwenhoven, John A. *Partners in Banking: An Historical Portrait of a Great Private Bank, Brown Brothers, Harriman & Co., 1818–1968.* Garden City, New York: Doubleday & Co., 1968.

Kuhlmann, Charles Byron. *The Development of the Flour-Milling Industry in the United States, with Special Reference to the Industry in Minneapolis.* Boston: Houghton Mifflin Co., 1929.

Land, Aubrey C. "Economic Base and Social Structure: The Northern Chesapeake in the Eighteenth Century." *Journal of Economic History* 25 (December 1965): 639–54.

———. "Economic Behavior in a Planting Society: The Eighteenth-Century Chesapeake." *Journal of Southern History* 33 (November 1967): 469–85.

Bibliography

———. "A Land Speculator in the Opening of Western Maryland." *Maryland Historical Magazine* 48 (September 1953): 191–203.

Lander, Ernst M., Jr. "Charleston: Manufacturing Center in the Old South." *Journal of Southern History* 26 (August 1960): 330–51.

Larson, Henrietta M. "S. & M. Allen, Lottery, Exchange, and Stock Brokerage." *Journal of Business History* 3 (May 1931): 424–45.

Latrobe, Ferdinand C. *Iron Men and Their Dogs.* Baltimore: Ivan R. Drechsler, 1941.

Leander, Bishop J. *A History of American Manufacturers from 1608 to 1860.* 2 vols. New York: Augustus M. Kelley, 1966 [1868, 3rd edition].

Leipheimer, Robert Eugene. "Maryland Political Leadership, 1789–1860." Master's thesis, University of Maryland, 1969.

Lemon, James T. "Urbanization and the Development of Eighteenth-Century Southeastern Pennsylvania and Adjacent Delaware." *William and Mary Quarterly* 24 (October 1967): 501–42.

Lewin, H. G. *The Railway Mania and Its Aftermath, 1845–1852.* New York: Augustus M. Kelley, 1968.

Lewis, Walker. *Without Fear or Favor: A Biography of Chief Justice Roger Brooke Taney.* Boston: Houghton Mifflin Co., 1965.

Leyburn, James G. *The Scotch-Irish: A Social History.* Chapel Hill: University of North Carolina Press, 1962.

Livermore, Seward W. "Early Commercial and Consular Relations with the East Indies." *Pacific Historical Review* 15 (March 1946): 31–58.

Livermore, Shaw. "Unlimited Liability in Early American Corporations." *Journal of Political Economy* 43 (October 1935): 674–87.

Livermore, Shaw, Jr. *The Twilight of Federalism: The Disintegration of The Federalist Party, 1815–1830.* Princeton: Princeton University Press, 1962.

Livingood, James Weston. *The Philadelphia-Baltimore Trade Rivalry, 1780–1860.* Harrisburg: Pennsylvania Historical and Museum Commission, 1947.

Lokke, Carl Ludwig. "Jefferson and the Leclerc Expedition." *American Historical Review* 33 (January 1928): 322–28.

Luthin, Reinhard H. "A Discordant Chapter in Lincoln's Administration: The Davis-Blair Controversy." *Maryland Historical Magazine* 39 (March 1944): 25–48.

———. "Organizing the Republican Party in the 'Border-Slave' Regions: Edward Bates's Presidential Candidacy in 1860." *Missouri Historical Review* 38 (January 1944): 138–61.

Macesich, George. "Monetary Disturbances in the United States, 1834–1845." Ph.D. dissertation, University of Chicago, 1958.

———. "Sources of Monetary Disturbances in the United States, 1834–1845." *Journal of Economic History* 20 (September 1960): 407–34.

Maclay, Edgar Stanton. *A History of American Privateers.* New York: D. Appleton & Co., 1899.

Madeleine, M. Grace. *Monetary and Banking Theories of Jacksonian Democracy.* Philadelphia: Joeblen Press, 1943.

Bibliography

Magazin, Louis. "Economic Depression in Maryland and Virginia, 1783–1787." Ph.D. dissertation, Georgetown University, 1967.

Main, Jackson T. "Political Parties in Revolutionary Maryland, 1780–1787." *Maryland Historical Magazine* 62 (March 1967): 1–27.

Manchester, Alan Krebs. *British Preeminence in Brazil, Its Rise and Decline: A Study in European Expansion.* Chapel Hill: University of North Carolina Press, 1933.

Marburg, Theodore F. "Manufacturer's Drummer, 1832." *Bulletin of the Business Historical Society* 22 (April 1948): 40–56.

———. "Manufacturer's Drummer, 1852, with Comments on Western and Southern Markets." *Bulletin of the Business Historical Society* 22 (June 1948): 106–14.

Marine, William M. *The British Invasion of Maryland, 1812–1815.* Baltimore: Society of the War of 1812 in Maryland, 1913.

Martin, Edgar W. *The Standard of Living in 1860: American Consumption Levels on the Eve of the Civil War.* Chicago: University of Chicago Press, 1942.

Martin, Thomas P. "Some International Aspects of the Anti-Slavery Movement, 1818–1823." *Journal of Economic and Business History* 1 (November 1928): 137–48.

Matthews, R.C.O. *A Study in Trade Cycle History: Economic Fluctuations in Britain, 1833–1842.* Cambridge: Cambridge University Press, 1954.

Matthews, Sidney T. "Control of the Baltimore Press During the Civil War." *Maryland Historical Magazine* 36 (June 1941): 150–70.

McConville, Sister Mary St. Patrick. *Political Nativism in the State of Maryland.* Washington, D.C.: Catholic University of America, 1928.

McCormac, Eugene Irving. *White Servitude in Maryland, 1634–1820.* Baltimore: Johns Hopkins University Press, 1904.

McCormick, Richard P. *The Second Party System.* Chapel Hill: University of North Carolina Press, 1966.

McDonald, Forrest; Decker, Leslie E.; and Goven, Thomas P. *The Last Best Hope: A History of the United States. Part 2: 1815–1898.* Reading, Massachusetts: Addison-Wesley, 1972.

McFaul, John Michael. *The Politics of Jacksonian Finance.* Ithaca: Cornell University Press, 1972.

McGouldrick, Paul F. *New England Textiles in the Nineteenth Century: Profits and Investment.* Cambridge, Massachusetts: Harvard University Press, 1968.

McGrain, John W. "Englehart Cruse and Baltimore's First Steam Mill." *Maryland Historical Magazine* 71 (spring 1976): 65–79.

McGrane, Reginald C. *Foreign Bondholders and American State Debts.* New York: Macmillan Co., 1935.

———. *The Panic of 1837: Some Financial Problems of the Jacksonian Era.* Chicago: University of Chicago Press, 1924.

Meerman, Jacob P. "The Climax of the Bank War: Biddle's Contraction, 1833–34." *Journal of Political Economy* 71 (August 1963): 378–88.

Bibliography

Merrill, Walter M. *Against Wind and Tide: A Biography of Wm. Lloyd Garrison.* Cambridge, Massachusetts: Harvard University Press, 1963.

Meyer, Balthasar Henry et al. *History of Transportation in the United States Before 1860.* Washington, D.C.: Carnegie Institution, 1917.

Middleton, Arthur Pierce. *Tobacco Coast: A Maritime History of Chesapeake Bay in the Colonial Era.* Edited by George Carrington Mason. Newport News, Virginia: Mariners' Museum, 1953.

Miller, Harry E. *Banking Theories in the United States Before 1860.* Cambridge, Massachusetts: Harvard University Press, 1927.

Miller, Stuart C. "The American Trader's Image of China, 1785–1840." *Pacific Historical Review* 36 (November 1967): 375–95.

Mitchell, Broadus. *The Rise of Cotton Mills in the South.* Baltimore: Johns Hopkins University Press, 1921.

Mitchell, Harry A. "The Development of New Orleans as a Wholesale Trading Center." *Louisiana Historical Quarterly* 27 (October 1944): 933–63.

Mohl, Raymond A. *Poverty in New York, 1783–1825.* New York: Oxford University Press, 1971.

Mohl, Raymond A., and Betten, Neil, eds. *Urban America in Historical Perspective.* New York: Weybright & Talley, 1970.

Montgomery, David. "The Working Classes of the Pre-Industrial American City, 1780–1830." *Labor History* 9 (winter 1968): 3–22.

Morris, Richard B. "Labor Controls in Maryland in the Nineteenth Century." *Journal of Southern History* 14 (August 1948): 385–400.

————. "The Measure of Bondage in the Slave States." *Mississippi Valley Historical Review* 41 (September 1954): 219–40.

Morriss, Margaret S. *Colonial Trade of Maryland, 1689–1715.* Baltimore: Johns Hopkins University Press, 1914.

Mott, Frank Luther. *A History of American Magazines, 1741–1850.* Cambridge, Massachusetts: The Belknap Press of Harvard University Press, 1930.

Mullaly, Franklin R. "Fort McHenry: 1814: Part I, The Battle of Baltimore." *Maryland Historical Magazine* 54 (March 1959): 61–103.

Muller, Charles G. *The Darkest Day: 1814, the Washington-Baltimore Campaign.* Philadelphia: J. B. Lippincott, 1963.

Myers, Margaret C. *The New York Money Market.* 4 vols. New York: Columbia University Press, 1932.

Nettels, Curtis P. *The Emergence of a National Economy, 1775–1815.* New York: Holt, Rinehart & Winston, 1962.

Newman, James Wilson. *Dun & Bradstreet, Established in 1841 for the Promotion and Protection of Trade.* New York: Newcomen Society in North America, 1956.

Nichol, A. J. *The Oyster-Packing Industry of Baltimore: Its History and Current Problems.* College Park, Maryland: University of Maryland Press, 1937.

Nichols, Roy F. "Trade Relations and the Establishment of the United States Consulates in Spanish America, 1779–1809." *Hispanic American Historical Review* 13 (August 1933): 289–313.

Bibliography

Norris, James D. "One-Price Policy Among Antebellum Country Stores." *Business History Review* 36 (winter 1962): 455–58.

North, Douglass C. *The Economic Growth of the United States, 1790–1860.* New York: W. W. Norton & Co., 1966.

O'Leary, Paul M. "The Coinage Legislation of 1834." *Journal of Political Economy* 45 (February 1937): 80–94.

Overdyke, William Darrell. *The Know-Nothing Party in the South.* Baton Rouge: Louisiana State University Press, 1950.

Owens, Hamilton. *Baltimore on the Chesapeake.* Garden City, New York: Doubleday, Doran & Co., 1941.

Pancake, John S. "Baltimore and the Embargo, 1807–1809." *Maryland Historical Magazine* 47 (September 1952): 173–87.

————. "The General from Baltimore: A Biography of Samuel Smith." Ph.D. dissertation, University of Virginia, 1949.

————. "The Invisibles: A Chapter in the Opposition to President Madison." *Journal of Southern History* 21 (February 1955): 17–37.

————. *Samuel Smith and the Politics of Business, 1752–1839.* University: University of Alabama Press, 1972.

Papenfuse, Edward C. *In Pursuit of Profit: The Annapolis Merchants in the Era of the American Revolution, 1763–1805.* Baltimore: Johns Hopkins University Press, 1975.

Pares, Richard. *War and Trade in the West Indies, 1739–1763.* Oxford: Oxford University Press, 1936.

Parker, Franklin. "George Peabody, Founder of Modern Philanthropy." Ph.D. dissertation, Peabody College, 1956.

Parkinson, Cyril Northcote. *Trade in the Eastern Seas, 1793–1813.* Cambridge: Cambridge University Press, 1937.

————, ed. *Trade Winds: A Study of British Overseas Trade During the French Wars, 1793–1815.* London: Allen & Unwin, 1948.

Parks, Joseph H. "Felix Grundy and the Depression of 1819 in Tennessee." *Publications of the East Tennessee Historical Society* 10 (1938): 19–43.

Payne, Peter Lester, and Davis, Lance Edwin. *The Savings Bank of Baltimore, 1818–1866: A Historical and Analytical Study.* Baltimore: Johns Hopkins University Press, 1956.

Perkins, Bradford. *Castlereagh and Adams: England and the United States, 1812–1823.* Berkeley and Los Angeles: University of California Press, 1964.

Perkins, Edwin J. "Financing Antebellum Importers: The Role of Brown Bros. & Co. in Baltimore." *Business History Review* 45 (winter 1971): 421–51.

Pessen, Edward. *Jacksonian America: Society, Personality, and Politics.* Homewood, Illinois: Dorsey Press, 1969.

————. "Should Labor Have Supported Jackson? or Questions the Quantitative Studies Do Not Answer." *Labor History* 13 (summer 1972): 427–37.

Phillips, Ulrich B. *A History of Transportation in the Eastern Cotton Belt to 1860.* New York: Columbia University Press, 1908.

Bibliography

Pinkett, Harold T. "The American Farmer: A Pioneer Agricultural Journal, 1819–1834." *Agricultural History* 24 (July 1950): 146–50.

Pitkin, Timothy. *A Statistical View of the Commerce of the United States of America*. New York: Johnson Reprint Corporation, 1967 [1835].

Pitman, Frank W. *The Development of the British West Indies, 1700–1763*. New Haven: Yale University Press, 1917.

Pole, J. R. "Constitutional Reform and Election Statistics in Maryland, 1790–1812." *Maryland Historical Magazine* 55 (December 1960): 275–92.

Poor, Henry Varnum. *History of the Railroads and Canals of the United States of America*. New York: Augustus M. Kelley, 1970.

Poore, Benjamin Perley. "Biographical Sketch of John Stuart Skinner." *The Plough, the Loom and the Anvil* 3 (June 1851): 12–36.

Porter, Frank W. III. "From Backcountry to County: The Delayed Settlement of Western Maryland." *Maryland Historical Magazine* 70 (winter 1975): 324–49.

Porter, Kenneth Wiggins. *The Jacksons and the Lees, Two Generations of Massachusetts Merchants, 1765–1844*. Cambridge, Massachusetts: Harvard University Press, 1937.

Pratt, Edwin J. "Anglo-American Commercial and Political Rivalry on the Plata, 1820–30." *Hispanic American Historical Review* 11 (August 1931): 302–35.

Pred, Allan R. *The Spatial Dynamics of the U.S. Urban-Industrial Growth, 1800–1914: Interpretive and Theoretical Essays*. Cambridge, Massachusetts: M.I.T. Press, 1966.

Radoff, Morris Leon, ed. *The Old Line State: A History of Maryland*. 5 vols. Hopkinsville, Kentucky: Historical Records Association, 1956.

Ragatz, Lowell Joseph. *The Fall of the Planter Class in the British Caribbean, 1763–1833: A Study in Social and Economic History*. New York: Century Co., 1928.

Randall, Edwin T. "Improvement for Debt in America: Fact and Fiction." *Mississippi Valley Historical Review* 39 (June 1952): 89–102.

Ransom, Roger L. "Interregional Canals and Economic Specialization in the Antebellum United States." *Explorations in Entrepreneurial History* 5 (fall 1967): 12–35.

Redlich, Fritz. *The Molding of American Banking: Men and Ideas, Part I: 1781–1840. Part II: 1840–1910*. New York: Hafner Publishing Co., 1947.

———. "Payments between Nations in the Eighteenth and Early Nineteenth Centuries." *Quarterly Journal of Economics* 50 (August 1936): 694–705.

Reiser, Catherine Elizabeth. *Pittsburgh's Commercial Development, 1800–1850*. Harrisburg: Pennsylvania Historical and Museum Commission, 1951.

Reizenstein, Milton. *The Economic History of the Baltimore and Ohio Railroad, 1827–1853*. Baltimore: Johns Hopkins University Press, 1897.

Remington, Jesse A., Jr. "States' Rights in Maryland, 1787–1832." Ph.D. dissertation, University of Maryland, 1940.

Remini, Robert Vincent. *Andrew Jackson and the Bank War: A Study in the*

Bibliography

Growth of Presidential Power. New York: W. W. Norton & Co., 1967.
Renzulli, Libero Marx. "Maryland Federalism, 1787–1819." Ph.D. dissertation, University of Virginia, 1962.
Rezneck, Samuel. "The Depression of 1819–1822: A Social History." *American Historical Review* 39 (October 1933): 28–47.
————. "The Influence of Depression upon American Opinion, 1857–1859." *Journal of Economic History* 2 (May 1942): 1–23.
————. "The Rise of Industrial Consciousness in the United States, 1760–1830." *Journal of Economic and Business History* 4 (August 1932): 784–811.
————. "The Social History of an American Depression, 1837–1843." *American Historical Review* 40 (July 1935): 662–87.
Rice, Edwin Wilbur. *The Sunday School Movement, 1780–1917, and the American Sunday School Union, 1817–1917.* Philadelphia: American Sunday School Union, 1917.
Richardson, Harry W. *The Economics of Urban Size.* Lexington, Massachusetts: Lexington Books, 1973.
————. *Urban Economics.* New York: Penguin Books, 1971.
Ridgway, Whitman Hawley. "A Social Analysis of Maryland Community Elites, 1827–1836: A Study of the Distribution of Power in Baltimore City, Frederick County, and Talbot County." Ph.D. dissertation, University of Pennsylvania, 1973.
Ridgway, Whitman H. "Community Leadership: Baltimore During the First and Second Party Systems." *Maryland Historical Magazine* 71 (fall 1976): 334–48.
————. "McCulloch vs. the Jacksonians: Patronage and Politics in Maryland." *Maryland Historical Magazine* 70 (winter 1975): 350–62.
Rippy, James Fred. *British Investments in Latin America, 1822–1949: A Case Study in the Operations of Private Enterprise in Retarded Regions.* Minneapolis: University of Minnesota Press, 1959.
————. *Rivalry of the United States and Great Britain over Latin America (1808–1830).* New York: Octagon Books, 1972.
Risch, Erna. "Immigrant Aid Societies Before 1820." *Pennsylvania Magazine of History and Biography* 60 (January 1936): 15–33.
Risjord, Norman K. "1812: Conservatives, War Hawks, and the Nation's Honor." *William and Mary Quarterly* 18 (April 1961): 196–210.
Robert, Joseph Clarke. *The Tobacco Kingdom: Plantation, Market, and Factory in Virginia and North Carolina, 1800–1860.* Durham, North Carolina: Duke University Press, 1938.
Rohrbough, Malcolm J. *The Land Office Business: The Settlement and Administration of American Public Lands, 1789–1837.* New York: Oxford University Press, 1968.
Rose, J. Holland. "British West Indian Commerce as a Factor in the Napoleonic War." *Cambridge Historical Journal* 3 (1929): 34–46.
Roseboom, Eugene H. "Baltimore as a National Nominating Convention City." *Maryland Historical Magazine* 67 (fall 1972): 215–24.
Rosenberg, Carroll Smith. *Religion and the Rise of the American City: The New*

Bibliography

York City Mission Movement, 1812–1870. Ithaca: Cornell University Press, 1971.

Rosenberg, Charles E. *The Cholera Years: The United States in 1832, 1849, and 1866.* Chicago: University of Chicago Press, 1962.

Rosenblatt, Samuel N. "The Significance of Credit in the Tobacco Consignment Trade: A Study of John Norton & Sons, 1768–1775." *William and Mary Quarterly* 19 (July 1962): 383–99.

Rothbard, Murray N. *The Panic of 1819, Reactions and Policies.* New York: Columbia University Press, 1962.

Rubin, Julius. "Canal or Railroad? Imitation and Innovation in the Response to the Erie Canal in Philadelphia, Baltimore and Boston." *Transactions of the American Philosophical Society* 51 (1961): 1–105.

Russel, Robert Royal. *Economic Aspects of Southern Sectionalism, 1840–1861.* Urbana: University of Illinois Press, 1924.

Rutter, Frank R. *South American Trade of Baltimore.* Baltimore: Johns Hopkins University Press, 1897.

Sanderlin, Walter S. *The Great National Project; A History of the Chesapeake and Ohio Canal.* Baltimore: Johns Hopkins University Press, 1946.

Sapio, Victor. "Maryland's Federalist Revival, 1808–1812." *Maryland Historical Magazine* 64 (spring 1969): 1–17.

Sawyer, John E. "The Social Basis of the American System of Manufacturing." *Journal of Economic History* 14 (1954): 361–79.

Scharf, John Thomas. *The Chronicles of Baltimore: Being a Complete History of "Baltimore Town" and Baltimore City.* Baltimore: Turnbull Brothers, 1874.

———. *History of Baltimore City and County.* Philadelphia: Lewis H. Everts, 1881.

———. *History of Maryland, from the Earliest Period to the Present Day.* 3 vols. Baltimore: J. B. Piet, 1879.

Scheiber, Harry N. "The Pet Banks in Jacksonian Politics and Finance, 1833–1841." *Journal of Economic History* 23 (June 1963): 196–214.

Schlesinger, Arthur M., Jr. *The Age of Jackson.* Boston: Little, Brown and Co., 1945.

Schmeckebier, Laurence Frederick. *History of the Know Nothing Party in Maryland.* Baltimore: Johns Hopkins University Press, 1899.

Schmidt, Louis B. "Internal Commerce and the Development of a National Economy Before 1860." *Journal of Political Economy* 47 (December 1939): 798–822.

Schouler, James. *History of the United States of America, Under the Constitution.* 7 vols. New York: Dodd, Mead & Co., 1894–1913.

Schultz, Charles R. "The Last Great Conclave of the Whigs." *Maryland Historical Magazine* 63 (December 1968): 379–400.

Schur, Leon M. "The Second Bank of the United States and the Inflation After the War of 1812." *Journal of Political Economy* 68 (April 1960): 118–34.

Schwartz, Anna Jacobson. "An Attempt at Synthesis in American Banking History." *Journal of Economic History* 7 (November 1947): 208–17.

Bibliography

Scisco, Louis Dow. *Political Nativism in New York State*. New York: Columbia University Press, 1901.

Scott, William A. *The Repudiation of State Debts*. New York: Greenwood Press, 1969.

Seaburg, Carl, and Paterson, Stanley. *Merchant Prince of Boston: Colonel T. H. Perkins, 1764–1854*. Cambridge, Massachusetts: Harvard University Press, 1971.

Sears, Louis Martin. "British Industry and the American Embargo." *Quarterly Journal of Economics* 34 (November 1919): 88–113.

———. "The Middle States and the Embargo of 1808." *South Atlantic Quarterly* 21 (April 1922): 152–69.

Setser, Vernon G. *The Commercial Reciprocity Policy of the United States, 1774–1829*. Philadelphia: University of Pennsylvania Press, 1937.

Shackelford, George Green, ed. "To Practice Law: Aspects of the Era of Good Feelings Reflected in the Short-Ridgely Correspondence, 1816–1821." *Maryland Historical Magazine* 64 (winter 1969): 342–95.

Sharrer, G. Terry. "Patents by Marylanders, 1790–1830." *Maryland Historical Magazine* 71 (spring 1976): 50–59.

Shepherd, James F., and Walton, Gary M. *Shipping, Maritime Trade, and the Economic Development of Colonial North America*. Cambridge: Cambridge University Press, 1972.

Shryock, Richard Harrison. *Medicine in America: Historical Essays*. Baltimore: Johns Hopkins University Press, 1966.

Sioussat, Annie Leakin. *Old Baltimore*. New York: Macmillan Co., 1931.

Sioussat, St. George L. *Economics and Politics in Maryland, 1720–1750, and the Public Services of Daniel Dulany, the Elder*. Baltimore: Johns Hopkins University Press, 1903.

Sitterson, J. Carlyle. "Financing and Marketing the Sugar Crop of the Old South." *Journal of Southern History* 10 (May 1944): 188–99.

Slagle, L. W. "Ross Winans." *The Railway and Locomotive Society Bulletin* 70 (1947): 7–21.

Smelser, Neil J. *Social Change in the Industrial Revolution: An Application of Theory to the British Cotton Industry*. Chicago: University of Chicago Press, 1959.

———. *The Sociology of Economic Life*. Englewood Cliffs, New Jersey: Prentice-Hall, 1963.

Smith, C. W. *Roger B. Taney, Jacksonian Jurist*. Chapel Hill: University of North Carolina Press, 1936.

Smith, Robert Sidney. "Shipping in the Port of Veracruz, 1790–1821." *Hispanic American Historical Review* 23 (February 1943): 5–20.

Smith, Walter B. "Wholesale Commodity Prices in the United States, 1795–1824." *Review of Economic Statistics* 9 (October 1927): 171–83.

Smith, Walter Buckingham. *Economic Aspects of the Second Bank of the United States*. Cambridge, Massachusetts: Harvard University Press, 1953.

Smith, Wilbur Wayne. "The Whig Party in Maryland, 1826–1856." Ph.D. dissertation, University of Maryland, 1967.

Smith, W. Wayne. "Jacksonian Democracy on the Chesapeake: The Political Institutions." *Maryland Historical Magazine* 62 (December 1967): 381–94; 63 (March 1968): 55–67.

Soulé, Leon Cyprian. *The Know Nothing Party in New Orleans: A Reappraisal.* Baton Rouge: Louisiana Historical Association, 1961.

Sprague, Oliver Mitchell Wentworth. *History of Crises Under the National Banking System.* Washington, D.C.: Government Printing Office, 1910.

Stanwood, Edward. *American Tariff Controversies in the Nineteenth Century.* 2 vols. New York: Houghton Mifflin and Co., 1903.

Stark, Francis Raymond. *The Abolition of Privateering and the Declaration of Paris.* Columbia University Studies in History, Economics and Public Law, vol. 8. New York: Columbia University Press, 1897.

Starobin, Robert S. *Industrial Slavery in the Old South.* New York: Oxford University Press, 1970.

Statham, E. P. *Privateers and Privateering.* New York: J. Pott & Co., 1910.

Statistical History of the United States from Colonial Times to the Present. Stamford, Connecticut: Fairfield Publishers, 1965.

Staudenraus, P. J. *The African Colonization Movement, 1816–1865.* New York: Columbia University Press, 1961.

Steiner, Bernard Christian. *Life of Henry Winter Davis.* Baltimore: John Murphy Co., 1916.

———. *Life of Reverdy Johnson.* Baltimore: Norman Remington Co., 1914.

———. "Maryland's Adoption of the Federal Constitution." *American Historical Review* 1 (October 1899): 22–44; 2 (January 1900): 207–24.

———. "Maryland Privateers in the Revolution." *Maryland Historical Magazine* 3 (June 1908): 99–103.

Stephenson, George M. *The Political History of the Public Lands from 1840 to 1862.* Boston: G. Badger, 1917.

Sterns, Worthy Putnam. "The Foreign Trade of the United States from 1820 to 1840." *Journal of Political Economy* 8 (December 1899): 34–57; 9 (September 1900): 452–97.

Stockett, Maria Letitia. *Baltimore: A Not Too Serious History.* Baltimore: Norman Remington Co., 1928.

Stone, Alfred H. "Cotton Factorage System of the Southern States." *American Historical Review* 20 (April 1915): 557–65.

Sullivan, David K. "William Lloyd Garrison in Baltimore, 1829–1830." *Maryland Historical Magazine* 68 (spring 1973): 64–79.

Sumner, William Graham. *Andrew Jackson.* Boston: Houghton Mifflin and Co., 1910.

———. *A History of American Currency: With Chapters on the English Bank Restriction and Austrian Paper Money.* New York: H. Holt and Co., 1884.

———. *Lectures on the History of Protection in the United States.* New York: G. P. Putnam's Sons, 1877.

Supple, B. E. "Currency and Commerce in the Early Seventeenth Century." *Economic History Review* 10 (December 1957): 239–55.

Bibliography

Swisher, Carl Brent. *Roger B. Taney.* New York: Macmillan Co., 1935.

Tansill, Charles Callan. *The United States and Santo Domingo, 1798–1873: A Chapter in Caribbean Diplomacy.* Baltimore: Johns Hopkins University Press, 1938.

Taus, Ester Rogoff. *Central Banking Functions of the United States Treasury, 1789–1941.* New York: Columbia University Press, 1943.

Taussig, Frank W. *The Tariff History of the United States.* New York: Johnson Reprint Corporation, 1966 [1892].

Taylor, George Rogers. "American Economic Growth Before 1840: An Exploratory Essay." *Journal of Economic History* 24 (December 1964): 427–44.

———. "American Urban Growth Preceding the Railway Age." *Journal of Economic History* 27 (September 1967): 309–39.

———. *The Transportation Revolution, 1815–1860.* New York: Harper & Row, 1951.

Temin, Peter. *Iron and Steel in Nineteenth-Century America: An Economic Inquiry.* Cambridge, Massachusetts: M.I.T. Press, 1964.

———. *The Jacksonian Economy.* New York: W. W. Norton & Co., 1969.

Thernstrom, Stephen. *Poverty and Progress: Social Mobility in a Nineteenth-Century City.* New York: Atheneum Press, 1970.

Thomas, Brinley. *Migration and Economic Growth: A Study of Great Britain and the Atlantic Economy.* Cambridge: Cambridge University Press, 1954.

Thomas, John L. *The Liberator, William Lloyd Garrison: A Biography.* Boston: Little, Brown and Co., 1963.

Thomas, Thaddeus P. *The City Government of Baltimore.* Baltimore: Johns Hopkins University Press, 1896.

Thomas, Wilbur R. *A Preface to Urban Economics.* Baltimore: Johns Hopkins University Press, 1965.

———. "Urban Economic Growth and Development in a National System of Cities." In *The Study of Urbanization*, edited by Philip M. Hauser and Leo F. Schnore, pp. 43–62. New York: Wiley, 1965.

Thompson, Robert Luther. *Wiring a Continent: The History of the Telegraph Industry in the United States, 1832–1866.* Princeton: Princeton University Press, 1947.

Thon, Robert William. *Mutual Savings Banks in Baltimore.* Baltimore: Johns Hopkins Univerity Press, 1935.

Thorp, Willard Long. *Business Annals.* New York: National Bureau of Economic Research, 1926.

Timberlake, Richard II., Jr. "The Specie Circular and the Distribution of Surplus." *Journal of Political Economy* 68 (April 1960): 109–17.

———. "The Specie Standard and Central Banking in the United States Before 1860." *Journal of Economic History* 21 (September 1961): 318–41.

Treat, Payson Jackson. *The National Land System, 1785–1820.* New York: E. B. Treat & Co., 1910.

Trends in the American Economy in the Nineteenth Century. Studies in Income and Wealth, vol. 24. Princeton: Princeton University Press, 1960.

Trescott, Paul B. "Federal-State Financial Relations, 1790–1860." *Journal of Economic History* 15 (September 1955): 227–45.

———. *Financing American Enterprise: The Story of Commercial Banking*. New York: Harper & Row, 1963.

Treudley, Mary. "The United States and Santo Domingo, 1789–1866." *Journal of Race Development* 7 (1916): 83–145.

Tryon, Rolla Milton. *Household Manufacturers in the United States, 1640–1860*. Chicago: University of Illinois Press, 1917.

Tucker, Rufus S. "Statistics of Gold and Prices, 1791–1932." *Review of Economic Statistics* 16 (January 1934): 8–16, 25–27.

Turner, Frederick Jackson. *The Rise of the West, 1819–1829*. New York: Collier Books, 1962.

Tuska, Benjamin. "Know Nothingism in Baltimore, 1854–1860." *Catholic Historical Review* 5 (July 1925): 217–51.

Tyler, Samuel. *Memoir of Roger Brooke Taney, LL.D.* Baltimore: John Murphy & Co., 1872.

Van Vleck, George W. *The Panic of 1857: An Analytical Study*. New York: Columbia University Press, 1943.

Van Wagenen, Jared, Jr. *The Golden Age of Homespun*. Ithaca: Cornell University Press, 1953.

Venit, Abraham H. "Isaac Bronson: His Banking Theory and the Financial Controversies of the Jacksonian Period." *Journal of Economic History* 5 (November 1945): 201–14.

Wade, Richard C. *Slavery in the Cities: The South, 1820–1860*. New York: Oxford University Press, 1964.

———. *The Urban Frontier: Pioneer Life in Early Pittsburgh, Cincinnati, Lexington, Louisville, and St. Louis*. Chicago: University of Chicago Press, 1971.

Walters, Raymond, Jr. "The Origins of the Second Bank of the United States." *Journal of Political Economy* 53 (June 1945): 115–31.

Warburton, Clark. "Variations in Economic Growth and Banking Developments in the United States from 1835 to 1885." *Journal of Economic History* 18 (summer 1958): 283–97.

Ward, David. *Cities and Immigrants: A Geography of Change in Nineteenth-Century America*. New York: Oxford University Press, 1971.

Ward, George Washington. *Early Development of the Chesapeake and Ohio Canal Project*. Baltimore: Johns Hopkins University Press, 1899.

Ware, Louise. *George Foster Peabody, Banker, Philanthropist, Publicist*. Athens: University of Georgia Press, 1951.

Warner, Sam Bass, Jr. *The Private City: Philadelphia in Three Periods of Its Growth*. Philadelphia: University of Pennsylvania Press, 1968.

Warren, Charles. *Bankruptcy in United States History*. Cambridge, Massachusetts: Harvard University Press, 1935.

Weedon, William B. *Economic and Social History of New England, 1620–1789*. 2 vols. New York: Hillary House Publishers, 1963.

Bibliography

Westerfield, Ray Bert. "Early History of American Auctions—A Chapter in Commercial History." *Transactions of the Connecticut Academy of Arts and Sciences* 23 (May 1920): 159–310.

Wettereau, James O. "The Branches of the First Bank of the United States." *Journal of Economic History, Supplement: The Tasks of Economic History* 2 (December 1942): 66–100.

———. "New Light on the First Bank of the United States." *Pennsylvania Magazine of History and Biography* 61 (July 1937): 263–85.

Whedbee, T. Courtenay J. *The Port of Baltimore in the Making, 1828 to 1878.* Baltimore: F. Bowie Smith & Son, 1953.

Wheeler, William Bruce. "The Baltimore Jeffersonians, 1788–1800: A Profile of Intra-Factional Conflict." *Maryland Historical Magazine* 66 (summer 1971): 153–68.

Whitaker, Arthur P. *The United States and the Independence of Latin America, 1800–1830.* Baltimore: Johns Hopkins University Press, 1941.

Willett, Thomas D. "International Specie Flows and American Monetary Stability, 1834–1860." *Journal of Economic History* 23 (March 1968): 28–50.

Williams, Basil. *The Whig Supremacy, 1714–1760.* Oxford: Oxford University Press, 1939.

Williamson, Harold F., ed. *The Growth of the American Economy.* Revised edition. New York: Prentice Hall, 1951.

Williamson, Jeffrey G. *American Economic Growth and the Balance of Payments, 1820–1913; A Study of the Long Swing.* Chapel Hill: University of North Carolina Press, 1964.

———. "International Trade and United States Economic Development: 1827–1843." *Journal of Economic History* 21 (September 1961): 372–83.

Wiser, Vivian. "Improving Maryland's Agriculture, 1840–1860." *Maryland Historical Magazine* 64 (summer 1969): 105–32.

Wishy, Bernard. *The Child and the Republic: The Dawn of Modern American Child Nurture.* Philadelphia: University of Pennsylvania Press, 1968.

Woodham-Smith, Cecil. *The Great Hunger: Ireland, 1845–1849.* New York: Harper & Row, 1962.

Woodman, Harold D. *King Cotton & His Retainers: Financing and Marketing the Cotton Crop of the South, 1800–1925.* Lexington: University Press of Kentucky, 1968.

Wright, Carroll D., and Hunt, William C. *The History and Growth of the U. S. Census, Prepared for the Senate Committee on the Census.* Washington, D.C.: Government Printing Office, 1900.

Wright, Chester W. *Wool Growing and the Tariff: A Study in the Economic History of the United States.* New York: Russell & Russell, 1968 [Boston, 1910].

Wright, James M. *The Free Negro in Maryland, 1634–1860.* New York: Columbia University Press, 1921.

Wright, Richardson. *Hawkers and Walkers in Early America: Strolling Peddlers,*

Bibliography

Preachers, Lawyers, Doctors, Players, and Others, From the Beginning to
the Civil War. Philadelphia: J. B. Lippincott, 1927.
Wyckoff, Vertrees Judson. Tobacco Regulation in Colonial Maryland. Baltimore:
Johns Hopkins University Press, 1936.
Young, G. M. Early Victorian England, 1830–1865. 2 vols. London: Oxford
University Press, 1934.

INDEX

A

Abbott, Horace, 142, 146, 182
Abolitionism, 101
Adams, John Quincy, 76
Albert, Jacob, 94
Almshouse. *See* Baltimore: poor relief
American Bank, 168
American Exchange Bank, 171
American Republican & Baltimore Clipper, 204
American Republican party, 204–5
American Revolution, 5, 8–12, 219
American Society for the Promotion of National Industry, 87
Anglicans, 5
Annapolis, 4–5, 8, 11–12, 37, 101, 106, 141, 165
Annapolis & Elk Ridge Railroad, 141, 165
Anti-Jacksonians, 152–53. *See also* Whigs
Antislavery, 100–101
Apprentice's Library, 102
Associational activities, 19–25, 36
Association for the Benefit of the Poor, 171
Association for the Improvement of the Condition of the Poor, 214
"Association of Relief," 31
Astor, John Jacob, 74
Athenian Society of Baltimore, 55
Australia, 229

B

Baltimore: population, 3, 5, 8, 10–12, 64, 87, 91, 145, 187, 190–91, 201; class structure, 10–11, 23–24, 32–

33, 43–45, 80–82, 86–104, 178–83, 203–4, 208–9, 213, 216–17, 223–24, 229, 231–33; and Boston, 21; and New York, 21, 83, 115; and Philadelphia, 21; municipal courts, 37, 104–5, 157, 210; municipal government, 37–40, 42–50, 104–10, 156–58, 212–13, 219; municipal politics, 40–46, 101–13, 149–58, 196–215, 224–25, 233–36; police, 43, 48, 104–5, 156, 199–200, 202–3, 210; harbor maintenance, 43, 49, 157; public health, 43, 49, 104, 121, 157, 198–200; street lighting, 43, 48–49, 104; municipal finance, 46–47, 65, 112–13, 147–55, 198–202, 210–12, 219; municipal regulation of trade, 46–50, 219; taxation policies, 46–47, 105–6, 110, 112–13, 148–55, 202, 212; fire protection, 48, 104, 156–57, 198–99, 210–11; gas street lighting, 48–49, 91, 104; streets and roads, 48, 104, 155–56, 200, 211–12; water, 48, 104, 157, 199–200, 210; poor relief, 49, 105, 157, 199; and the trans-Allegheny West, 83, 165, 169, 222–23, 228–29 (*see also* Western trade); boundary expansion, 105; and Liverpool, 115; land use, 145–47, 197; residential development, 145–46, 187, 190, 199, 201–2, 205, 211; municipal markets, 157; transportation, 197–99, 205, 211, 213; parks and squares, 199, 211–12; city planning, 211

Index

Baltimore & Ohio Railroad, 84, 94, 112, 127, 134, 141–42, 146–47, 152, 154, 165, 170–71, 174, 184, 190, 201, 223, 229, 232
Baltimore & Port Deposit Railroad, 141, 146
Baltimore & Susquehanna Railroad, 83–84, 146, 152, 164, 184
Baltimore & Washington Railroad, 83, 165
Baltimore & Westminster Railroad, 84
Baltimore Association of Firemen, 1831, 156
Baltimore City Cotton Factory, 86, 146
Baltimore City Court, 104
Baltimore City Jail, 101, 210
Baltimore City Passenger Railway Company, 213
Baltimore Clearing House, 168
Baltimore Clipper, The, 204
Baltimore County, 37, 49, 77, 105
Baltimore County Court, 37, 62
Baltimore Gas Light Company, 91, 104
Baltimore Mechanical Society, 56
Baltimore Orphans' Court, 100
Baltimore Steam Works Factory, 86–87
Baltimore United Fire Department, 1834, 156
Baltimore Water Company, 48, 157, 201–2, 218
Bank of Baltimore, 31, 56
Bank of Commerce, 168
Bank of England, 30, 119, 130
Bank of England Act, 1844, 163
Bank of Louisiana, 123
Bank of Maryland, 24, 31, 56, 122–24
Bank of North America, 24
Bank of the United States, 31, 53–54, 73–81, 119–25, 128, 220, 222, 225
Banking, 21–25, 31–32, 71–79, 119–34, 166–69, 222, 230

Bankruptcy Act, 1841, 166
Bankruptcy procedures, 76–77, 222
Baptists, 3, 41, 102, 194
Baring Brothers, 23
Barker, John, 86
Beatty family, 146
Benton, Thomas Hart, 126
Biays, James, 112
Biddle, Nicholas, 78, 121, 222
Bigelow, Elisha, 86
Bills of exchange, 9, 12, 22–23, 30, 53–54
Blacks. *See* Free blacks; Slaveowners; Slaves
Bland, Theodorick, 62
Board of Fire Commissioners, 211
Board of Health. *See* Baltimore: public health
Board of Trade, 180
Boggs, Harmanus, 143
Boston, 3, 101, 148, 217
Boyle, Hugh, 80
Brazil, 163
Bridge companies, 20
Bridgetown, New Jersey, 63
Brown, Alexander, 92, 94, 143
Brown, George, 143
Brown, George William, 214
Brown, William, 92
Brown and Sons, Alex, 123, 131
Brune family, 80, 95
Buchanan, James A., 74–75, 80, 143
Buchanan, Robert, 146
Buchanan family, 12, 41, 95, 146
Business revolution, 17–25, 32–33, 51–52, 218–19

C

Calhoun, James, 44, 80
Calhoun family, 12, 41, 95
California, 166, 229
Campbell, Archibald, 31
Campbell, James, 143
Canals, 83–84, 107, 110
Canton Company, 145–46, 211, 226
Carroll, Charles Ridgely, 95

Carroll County, Maryland, 84
Carroll family, 12, 95
Castleton, Maryland, 84
Charities, 97–98, 102, 214
Charleston, South Carolina, 3
Chase, Samuel, 12–13
Chase-Ridgely faction, 12–13, 104
Chemical industry, 86, 135
Chesapeake and Leopard Affair, 27
Chesapeake and Ohio Canal, 84, 110, 127, 141, 165, 171, 174
Chesapeake Bank, 128
Cheves, Langdon, 75, 78
Chew, Henry B., 86
China, 163–64, 170, 172
Church, William, 86
Churches, 194, 232
Cincinnati, Ohio, 124
Citizens Bank, 128
City Bank, 75–77
City charter, 1796: provisions, 37–40
City Council. *See* Baltimore: municipal government
City finances. *See* Baltimore: municipal finance
City planning. *See* Baltimore: city planning
"City Reform Association," 213–14, 235
City Water Board, 202
Class structure. *See* Baltimore: class structure
"Club" of speculators, 74–75
Coinage Act of 1834, 116, 126–27
Colonization, 101
Colt, Roswell Lyman, 95
Comegye family, 56
"Commercial revolution" of 1830s, 162, 225
Committee of Correspondence and Observation, Maryland, 41
Committee of Safety, Baltimore, 41
Conowingo, Maryland, 84
Continental Congress, Second, 41
Cooper, Hugh A., 142

Cooper, Peter, 146
Copper factories, 86
Corn and Flour Exchange, 180
Corporations, 101–2, 142, 179–80
Court of Common Pleas, 210
Courts. *See*Baltimore: municipal courts
Credit, 21–25
Creditor-debtor relations, 32–33
Crime, 104, 157, 202–3
Crimean War, 172
Criminal Court, 210
Crook, Charles, Jr., 86
Cultural institutions, 102
Cumberland, Maryland, 152, 201
Curson family, 12
Curtis, Junia, 86

D
Dallas, Alexander James, 74
D'Arcy, John, 80
Davies, Jacob G., 199
Debtor-creditor relations. *See* Creditor-debtor relations
Deflation, 130–38, 144, 153, 164, 168–69, 227
Democratic party, 107, 185–86, 197–215, 234–36. *Also see* Republican party, Jacksonian party
Democratization, 32–33, 43–46, 97–99, 114, 158, 226–27
Depersonalization, 19–21, 32–33, 136–38, 161, 183
Depression of 1798–1803, 30–31
Depression of 1837–43, 130–39, 155, 212, 225–26
Depression of 1857–60, 213
Deshon, Christopher, 80
Didier, Henry, 80
District of Columbia, 32, 83, 101, 141
Donnell, John, 42, 80
Donnell family, 95
Dorsey, John, 12
Dorsey family, 12
Druid Hill Park, 211, 214

Index

E
Eastern Shore, 4–5, 37, 101, 165, 206
Edmondson, Thomas, 143
Education, 97, 102, 194, 232–33
Eichelberger, Martin, 143
Election procedures. *See* Baltimore: municipal government
Elections. *See* Baltimore: municipal politics
Elkton, Maryland, 124
Ellicott, Benjamin, 143
Ellicott, Evan J., 86
Ellicott, George, 86, 143
Ellicott, Thomas, 123–25
Ellicott, William, 143
Ellicott, William Miller, 123
Ellicott family, 12, 56
Embargo Proclamation, 52–53, 64
Epidemics. *See* Baltimore: public health
Episcopalians, 37, 102, 194, 206
Erie Canal, 83–84, 110, 222
Erskine, James, 143
Ethnic groups. *See* Germans; Irish
Eutaw Square, 211
Exchange, 91; rates, 81
Exchange Bank, 168
Exports. *See* Trade, export

F
Farmers and Planters Bank, 129
Federal Hill, 211
Federalist party, 40–45, 64, 105–6
Fell's Point, 4, 107, 199, 224
Fell's Point Savings Institution, 167
Female Penitent's Refuge, 102
Finances, municipal. *See* Baltimore: municipal finance
Financial revolution, 19–25, 126–27, 147–48, 216–18
Fire insurance companies, 20
Fire protection. *See* Baltimore: fire protection
Forman, William L., 42

Franco-American Alliance, 1778, 26
Franklin Bank, 56
Franklin Square, 211
Frederick, Maryland, 5, 84
Frederick County, Maryland, 84
Free blacks, 58–59, 97–100, 102, 190–92, 232
Freeman, E. V., 86
Friends of Ireland Society, 88

G
Gambrill, Horatio N., 142
Garrett, John Work, 142, 170
Garrett, Robert, 142
Garrison, William Lloyd, 100–101
Gary, James S., 142
General Workingmen's Sick Relief Union, 193
Generalist-manufacturers, 55–56
Genius of Universal Emancipation, 100–101
Georgia, 126
Germans, 3, 103, 145, 179, 191, 205, 224, 232
German Society, 88
Gibbes, Robert Morgan, 95
Gilmor, Robert, 23
Gilmor, Robert, Jr., 95
Gilmor family, 12, 80, 95, 146
Gittings, Richard, 143
"Golden Age" of Baltimore, 95, 140
Goldsborough, Robert, 41
Goodwin, Lyde, 143
Green, Duff, 75
Ground rents, 95
Grundy, George, 80
Guano, 163
Guild system, 62–63
Gwinn, Charles, 55, 64, 143

H
Hamilton Bank, 128
Harden, Samuel, 143
Harford County, 106
Harper, Charles Carroll, 95, 101

Index

Harpers Ferry, Virginia, 152
Harrisburg, Pennsylvania, 164
Harrison, Hall, 143
Havre de Grace, Maryland, 84, 164
Hayward brothers, 142
Hermange, Anthony, 86
Hibernian Society, 88
Higginbotham, Ralph, 75, 95
Hinesly, John, 210
Hinks, Samuel, 209–11
Hoffman, Peter, Jr., 143
Hoffman family, 12, 80, 95
Hollingsworth, Samuel, 28, 143
Hollingsworth, Thomas, 28
Hollingsworth family, 12, 41, 56
Hollins, John, 42, 80
Hollins family, 95
Hong, 119
Hope and Company, 23
Hopkins, Johns, 142
House of Correction, 199
House of Refuge, 157
Housing, 58, 145–46, 187, 190, 199
Howard, Benjamin Chew, 95
Howard, Charles, 95
Howard, John Eager, 42, 146
Howard family, 12, 95
"Howard Park," 146
Howard Street Savings Institution, 167–68
Howland and Woollens, 146
Hunt, Jesse, 104, 148, 155

I
Immigrant aid societies, 88
Immigration, 3, 5, 12, 41, 64, 88, 91, 97–98, 139, 145, 187, 190–92, 232, 234
Importers, 81, 119
Imports. See Trade, import
Independent Methodists, 102
Independent Treasury Act, 1846, 166–67, 229
Indigent Sick Society, 102
Industrial innovations, 86

Industrialization, 51–65, 85–89, 139, 161–87, 190–91, 217, 220, 223, 230, 232
Industrial revolution, 32–33, 51–65, 139–40, 142–48, 161–95, 217, 221, 223, 226, 228–33
Inflation, 116–18, 129, 169, 200–201
Institutionalization, 9, 17–20, 29, 35–37, 51–52, 92, 101–2, 161, 193–95, 216–17, 231–33
Internal improvements, 127, 130–31, 152–53, 164–65, 173, 198, 200–201
International trade, 4–5, 8–12, 25–29, 51–54, 72, 125–26, 162–64, 173
Irish, 103, 145, 179, 191, 200, 205–6, 224, 232, 234
Iron industry, 86, 135

J
Jackson, Andrew, 119–27, 225
Jacksonian party, 103, 111–13, 118–27, 146–58, 165–67, 186, 224–26, 229
Jay's Treaty, 26
Jeffersonians. See Republican party
Jerome, John H. T., 200, 202–3
Jewish synagogues, 194, 232
Johnson, Edward, 44, 103–4, 106–7, 110
Joint Committee Report on the Almshouse, 1845, 203
Joint stock companies, 20, 101–2, 218–20
Jones, Talbot, 143
Jones, William, 74–75
Jones's Falls, 4, 107, 205, 210, 232
Justices of the peace. See Baltimore: municipal government
Justices of the Peace of the State of Maryland in and for the City of Baltimore, 104–5
Juvenile delinquency, 157, 199

K

Karrick, Joseph, 80
Kearney bill, 206–7, 234
Kendall, Amos, 119–20
Kennedy, John, 62
Kennedy, John Pendleton, 96
Key family, 12, 95
Kirwan, John, and Sons, 23
Know-Nothing party, 186, 196–215, 233–36

L

Land use. *See* Baltimore, land use
Lawyers, 40
Levering, Aaron, 80
Levering, Jesse, 143
Levering, John, 80
Levering, Nathan, 55
Levy, Erasmus ("Ras"), 210
Libertytown, Maryland, 84
Lincoln, Abraham, 214
Little Rock, Arkansas, 124
Liverpool, 83, 85, 115, 222
Lloyd family, 12
Lorman, William, 94
Lorman family, 56
Louisville, Kentucky, 124
Lundy, Benjamin, 100–101
Lutherans, 3, 102, 194, 224

M

McBlair, Michael, 80, 95
McCormick's reaper, 165
McCulloch v. *Maryland*, 74–75
McCulloh, James William, 74–75
MacDonald, Alexander, 143
McElderry, Hugh, 112
McHenry, James, 41–42
McHenry, James Howard, 95–96
McHenry family, 12, 42, 95
McIlvaine, William, 121
McKim, Alexander, 86–87, 143
McKim, Isaac, 143
McKim, Robert, 86
McKim, Samuel, 143

McKim, William D., 143
McKim family, 41, 56, 64
McLane, Louis, 121
Madison Square, 211
Managers of the Poor, 105
Manufacturers, 11, 81, 87–88, 97–98
Manufacturing: in town, 10–11, 57–58, 86–89, 134–36; out of town, 55, 80–81, 134–36
Marine Hospital, 200
Marine insurance companies, 20
Marshall, John, 74–75
Maryland, 23–24, 27, 37, 50, 141–42
Maryland Association for the Encouragement of American Manufacturing and Domestic Economy, 87
Maryland Institute for the Promotion of the Mechanic Arts, 102
Maryland Insurance Company, 44
Maryland Savings Institution, 122
Maryland Society for Promoting the Abolition of Slavery, 100
Massachusetts, 75, 142, 182
Matthews, Leonard, 80
Mayor's office. *See* Baltimore: municipal government
Maysville Road Veto, 1830, 127
Mearis, Malcolm, 210
Mechanics, 34, 43, 56
Mechanics' Bank, 56
Merchant-millers, 55–56, 64
Merchants, 8–9, 23–24, 40–43, 80–81, 98, 142–43, 178–81
Merchants Bank, 128, 133
Merchants' Bank of New York, 31
Metals industry, 86, 135
Methodist-Episcopals, 209
Methodists, 3, 109, 194, 209
Metropolitanism, 82–85, 94, 140–42, 164, 169–70
Mint Act of 1792, 126
Modernization, 139, 224–25
Monetization, 8–10, 20–25, 36, 77–80, 219–21

Monocacy River Valley, Maryland, 4
Montgomery, John, 103, 105–7, 110–11
Moore, Philip, 143
Moreau, Thomas, 80
Mount Clare Station, 147, 190, 232
Mount Vernon Square, 146
Multiple elites, 96
Municipal finance. *See* Baltimore: municipal finance
Municipal government. *See* Baltimore: municipal government
Municipalization of public services, 233–34
Municipal regulation of trade. *See* Baltimore: municipal regulation of trade
Municipal politics. *See* Baltimore: municipal politics
Municipal services. *See* Baltimore: fire protection, police, water

N
National Road, 84
Nativism. *See* Know-Nothing party
Neighborhoods, 205
Newburyport, Massachusetts, 3
New Hampshire, 142
New Orleans, 93, 116, 123–24, 126, 141, 169
Newport, Rhode Island, 3
New York, 3, 10, 21, 31, 72, 78–79, 82–85, 111, 115–16, 119, 124–26, 131, 133, 141–42, 148, 154, 165, 169–72, 182, 221, 225, 227–29
Nonintercourse Act, 53
Norfolk, Virginia, 3, 85, 141
Norris, William, 143
North Carolina, 126
Northwestern Railroad, 201

O
Oblate Sisters of Providence, 102
Odd Fellows, 102
O'Donnell, Columbus, 145

Ohio Life and Trust Company, 171
Ohio-Mississippi Valley, 162, 165
"Old Line Whigs," 207
Old Town, 224
Old Town Savings Institution, 167
Oliver, John, 23, 53, 95
Oliver, Robert, 23, 53, 95, 143
Oliver family, 80
Opposition to Baltimore: from Maryland's rural gentry, 37–39, 50
Order of United American Mechanics (OUAM), 186, 207
Orphan's Court, Baltimore, 43

P
Panic of 1798–99, 17, 29–31
Panic of 1819, 74–77, 80, 94–95, 103, 106, 114, 132, 153, 222–23
Panic of 1825, 111
Panic of 1834, 122–25, 132
Panic of 1837, 118, 127–36, 142–43, 153, 167, 212
Panic of 1839, 118, 130–34, 143, 153, 167
Panic of 1842, 133–34, 143, 167
Panic of 1857, 171–72, 197, 229
Panic of 1860, 214
Parkersburg, Virginia, 201
Patapsco River, 3
Patterson, William, 42, 95–96, 143
Patterson family, 12, 80, 95
Patterson Park, 211
Pennsylvania, 3–4, 11, 41, 56, 83–84, 106, 135, 141–42, 164, 170, 174, 230
Pennsylvania Railroad, 190
People's Bank, 168
Philadelphia, 3, 10–12, 31, 63, 72–75, 78, 82–83, 85–86, 88, 111, 116, 125, 133, 141, 148, 164–65, 170–72, 186, 199, 207, 222, 227
Philadelphia Bank, 31
Philadelphia-Wilmington-Baltimore Railroad, 164
Pittsburgh, Pennsylvania, 201

Pittsburgh & Connellsville Railroad, 201
Pocock, John, 62
Point-of-Rocks, Maryland, 141
Police. *See* Baltimore: police
Politics. *See* Baltimore: municipal politics
Poor relief. *See* Baltimore: poor relief
Population. *See* Baltimore: population
Port Deposit, Maryland, 84, 141
Potomac Bank of Virginia, 31
Potomac Canal, 127
Potomac River, 141, 152
Poultney, Ellicott and Company, 123
Poultney, Evan, 123–25
Poultney, Sarah, 123
Poultney and Company, Evan, 123–24
Poverty. *See* Baltimore: poor relief
Powhatan Cotton Mills, 55
Pratt, Enoch, 142
Presbyterians, 3, 37, 41, 56, 102–3, 106, 194
Prices, 28
Primary system, 204
Princeton, 41
Pringle family, 12
Private society, 8, 19–20, 35–36, 47–48, 102–3, 113, 139–40, 147, 158, 161, 178, 193–97, 217
Privateering, 9–10, 51–65, 93
Property qualifications: for holding municipal office, 37–40, 42–50, 104–10, 156–58, 212–13, 219; for voting, 37–40, 42–50, 104–10, 156–58, 212–13, 219
Protestants. *See* Baptists; Episcopalians; Lutherans; Methodists; Presbyterians
Providence, Rhode Island, 3
Public debt, 94–95
Public health. *See* Baltimore: public health
Public Park Commission, 211
Public Park Stock, 211
Public schools. *See* Education
Public society, 93, 101–4, 113, 139–40, 147, 158, 161, 177–78, 195–97, 205, 226–28, 233–34
"Puff," 125
Purviance family, 41

Q
Quakers, 11, 28, 41, 56, 100, 102–3

R
Railroads, 83–84. *See also* railroads by name
Raymond, Daniel, 100–101
Reeder, Charles, 142
Reeder, Charles, Jr., 182
Reisterstown, Maryland, 84
Rentiers, 94–95, 143–44, 147–48, 216, 227
Republican party, 31–32, 43–45, 64–65, 105–6, 225
Residential development. *See* Baltimore: residential development
Rhode Island, 3, 75
Ridgely, Charles, 12
Ridgely family, 12, 56, 95
Riots, 199, 203, 213, 220
Rivers and Harbors Improvements Bill, 1848, 166
Roman Catholics, 3–5, 37, 56, 103, 111, 191, 194, 200, 205–7, 209, 224, 232, 234
"Row house," 190

S
St. Andrew's Society, 88
St. David's Society, 88
St. George's Society, 88
Salem, Massachusetts, 3
Sanitation. *See* Baltimore: public health
Savage, Maryland, 141
Savage Railroad Company, 141
Savings Bank of Baltimore, 102
Schools. *See* Education

Scotch-Irish, 41, 56, 106
"Second War for American Independence," 220
Seven Years' War, 8–10, 12
Sheppard, Thomas, 80
Shippers, 81
Shipping, 25–29, 53–54, 70–71, 116–18, 125–26, 225–26
Shoemaker, Samuel, 142
Slaveowners: male, 43–44, 192; female, 192
Slaves, 57–58, 190, 192, 232
Small, Jacob, 103, 107, 110–12, 148
Smallpox Hospital, 200
Smith, Dennis A., 75
Smith, John, 41–42
Smith, John Donnell, 96
Smith, John Spear, 96
Smith, Robert, 41–42
Smith, Samuel, 41–42, 74–76, 80, 95, 106, 143
Smith, Thorowgood, 44
Smith, William, 41
Smith faction, 41–42, 103–11
Smith family, 12, 146
Social structure, 8, 10–12, 17–18, 32–36, 51–65, 80–81, 86–104, 142–48, 178–93, 203, 216–17, 220–23, 231–34
Spear, John, 42
Spear, Joseph, 42
Spear family, 12, 41
Spedden, Edward, 112
Stamp Act of 1765, 9
Star-Spangled Banner, 65, 220
Steamboats, 141
Steam-engine factories, 86
Sterett, James, 75
Sterett, John, 12
Sterett, Joseph, 12
Sterett, Samuel, 12
Sterett family, 12, 41, 95
Steuart, George Hume, 96
Steuart, William R., 103, 112, 148
Steuart family, 95

Stewart family, 12
Stiles, George, 103–5
"Stock orders," 154
Story, Benjamin, 123
Streets and roads. *See* Baltimore: streets and roads
Street lighting. *See* Baltimore: gas street lighting, street lighting
Strikes, 184–86, 204, 207–8, 234
Stump, Henry, 210
Suburban developments, 205
Superior Court, 210
Supreme Order of the Star-Spangled Banner (SSSB), 207
Susquehanna and Tidewater Canal, 164–65
Susquehanna Canal Company, 153
Susquehanna Railroad, 201
Susquehanna River, 83, 107, 110, 141, 164
Susquehanna Valley, 83–85, 141, 164
Swann, Thomas, 209, 210–13
Swann family, 146

T
Taney, Roger Brooke, 119–20, 123–26
Tariff of 1828, 118
Tariff of 1832, 117, 225
Tariff of 1833, 116
Tariff of 1842, 173, 230
Tariff of 1846, 166–67, 173–74, 229–30
Taylor, Asa, 143
Taylor, Lemuel, 75, 80
Taylor family, 12
Technological change, 10–11, 51–89, 134–36, 142, 164–65, 169–70, 172–75, 216–17, 223, 228
Thompson, Henry, 143
Tiernan, Luke, 143
Tilghman family, 12
Townshend Duties, 9
Trade: export, 3, 11, 25–30, 53, 116–17, 125–26, 162–64, 168–71; be-

tween Baltimore and the West In-
dies, 5, 8–12, 25–30, 82, 117,
162–63, 170; coastal, 11, 132, 141,
169–71; between Baltimore and
Europe, 11, 25–30, 53, 162–63,
170; import, 25–30, 53, 116–17,
125–26, 162–64, 168–71; between
Baltimore and South America, 93,
163, 170
Trade unionism, 196
Transportation. *See* Baltimore, trans-
portation
"Transportation revolution," 142
Treaty of Morfontaine, 26
Trustees for the Poor of Baltimore
City and County, 105
Turnpikes, 20, 83–84
Tyson, Isaac, 86
Tyson, Philip T., 143
Tyson family, 56

U
Unemployment, 198–200, 214
Union Bank of Maryland, 31, 56, 75–
77, 122–25
Union Manufacturing Company, 55
Union Square, 211
Unions. *See* Trade unionism
Unitarians, 102
United Sons of America (USA), 205
United States Insurance Company, 122

V
Valck, Adrian, 23
Virginia, 141, 201, 214
Virginia Pilot Boat, 27
Voting. *See* Baltimore: municipal gov-
ernment, municipal politics

W
Wage rates, 63, 98
Walker, Robert James, 165–66, 229
Walker's Report on the Treasury,
1845, 166
Walters, William T., 142

Warehousing Act of 1842, 166–67,
229
War of 1812, 37, 43, 49, 51–65, 95,
125, 133, 218, 220
Washington, D.C. *See* District of Co-
lumbia
Washington, George, 41
Washington Cotton Manufacturing
Company, 55
Washington County, Maryland, 84
Washington Monument, 146
Water. *See* Baltimore: water; Water
Company
Water Company, 20, 157, 218
Wells and Pocock v. *Kennedy*, 62
Wells, David, 62
Western Bank, 129, 133
Western Shore, 37
Western trade, 71–72, 82–85, 107,
110, 127–28, 133, 140–42, 147,
152, 164–66, 171, 180–81, 222–
23
Westminster, Maryland, 84
Wheeling, Virginia, 152, 165, 201
Whetstone Point, 4, 107
Whigs, 154–57, 186, 198, 205–8,
213–14, 234–35
White, John, 121
Whitney, Reuben, 126
William IV, of Great Britain, 118
Williams, Amos A., 75
Williams, Cumberland Dugan, 75,
143
Williams, George, 75
Williams, Nathaniel, 75
Williams, Otho Holland, 41–42
Williams family, of Baltimore, 42, 80,
95
Williams family, of Frederick County,
95
Willinks, Jan, 23
Willinks, Wilhelm, 23
Wilson family, 12, 80
Winans, Ross, 142
Winchester, George, 143

Woodyear, Edward G., 143
Workingmen, 91, 96–98
Wrightsville, Pennsylvania, 165

Y
Yeaman, Royal, 86
York, Pennsylvania, 153, 164, 201